D0462554

cosmic presence

a dynamic vision of life

Roger J.A. Lebeuf

cosmic presence

a dynamic vision of life

LES ÉDITIONS BELLARMIN
8100, boulevard Saint-Laurent, Montréal
1980

Dépôt légal — 4e trimestre 1980 — Bibliothèque nationale du Québec

ISBN 2-89007-295-9

In which is established the nature of Existence, of the Existential-Atom and, by derivation, of the Self; in which also a Unified Cosmic Vision is set forth.

cosmic presence
is dedicated to
the memory of my
father and to Gladys

To Raymond, my father, a sincere, understanding Christian, for whom only one "sin" was unforgivable: the lie — even the inoffensive inventions of a child —. I am profoundly indebted for having, through precept and example, indelibly etched in my mind the sacredness of Truth. Without a doubt, the dividends of this heritage, nurtured in the soil of hard work and in a profound respect for God and his neighbor, were a priceless asset as I wrestled to establish the dominion of the Real and Truth over "the rabble of the senses".

To Gladys McElroy Lembicz, my loyal and devoted friend, I owe a special tribute for her perseverance, interest and generosity, over the past twelve years. Her patience of endless re-typing the chapters of this work over this period, as well as the encouragement and moral inspiration she imparted, have been responsible for the completion of this first volume.

A note of appreciation is also extended to many friends, including Réal Gaudet, Curtis Wilson, Mr. and Mrs. A. Trépanier, Donald Gillespie and Venant Cauchy, whose counsel greatly assisted in preparing the manuscript for publication. Finally, there are many colleagues and associates who must remain anonymous. Nevertheless, I am obliged to acknowledge their advice and suggestions which, although intended to show me the error of my way, greatly contributed to a general clarification of ideas.

Roger Lebeuf

contents

PART II
Power

Pages

PART III
Cosmic Presence and Relationality

PART IV
Death, Entropy and a Theory of Cosmic Peace

PART V
Love and the Splendor of Cosmic-Man

introduction

THE two subjects dealt with in *Cosmic Presence*, generally considered unrelated, are the primary particle of matter and the basics of human psychology. It is therefore proper that the nature and consequences of this duality be explained at the beginning.

The work's overall objective being the discovery of the primary particle, the original Democritan atom, the bulk of the text falls within the purview of the cosmophysicist and the philosopher of the real. Any person concerned with the Self, and who is not ?, should find profit in the second topic. In Parts IV and V, the insights gained into the structure of the primary atom are used to decode the basic behavior patterns of the human atom. These insights which constitute an X-ray into the psychology, motivation and responses common to all Beings, animate as well as inanimate, can be of help in meeting ones daily challenges. Specifically, they can foster a realistic and optimistic, indeed a loving approach to life.

Within the context of a split-level, Aristotelian universe, the proposed conflating of the world of "matter" with that of the "spirit" [1], is clearly not permissible. Actually it is impossible. This, however, is the crux of the question; the theory of a two level universe does not withstand a scientific analysis. By the closing chapter, it is hoped that the inadequacies of a "matter-spirit" universe will be demonstrated conclusively. For the present, here is the key observation of fact which calls for a unitary approach to all processes, those of the mind, with those of the particle. A systematic dissection of the Cosmos into its elements reveals that you, the reader, are one of the primary particles of the universe, on an equal footing with an electron, a fir tree, and an uranium atom. In a word, the Cosmos is made up of a common stuff or, as the philosopher would have it, of a universal species — a *genus generalissimum*. This "primordial stuff" is cut-up and possessed in permanence by each atom. Each differs from its neighbor quality-wise only. Hence, once the laws which govern the behavior of the universal species are determined, the human atom appears as the logical specimen to be studied in detail, since it is the one examplar of the species with which we are most conversant.

At this point the reader will surmize, rightly, that he is being invited to peruse a highly unified view of life. The vision of the Universe — henceforth referred to as Dynamic Vision — which he will contemplate, eliminates all dichotomy between "matter and spirit", between electric and intellect-power. It is the universe which Plotinus, Aquinas, Comte and Marx, among others, also sought. To this vision, this statement, by A.N. Whitehead, of his own position, applies without reservation:

> For us the red glow of the sunset should be as much part of nature as are the molecules and electric waves by which men of science would explain the phenomenon. It is for natural philosophy to analyse how these various elements of nature are connected... What I am essentially protesting against is the bifurcation of nature into two systems of reality, ... One reality would be the entities such as electrons which are the study of speculative physics. This would be the reality

1. Quotation marks on words in common usage in the English language indicate that in such instances the meaning and/or relevance is being questioned. A prime example is that of "matter" the heuristic content of which is viewed as nil. Such terms are, as a rule, juxtaposed with their replacement within Dynamic Vision, and are intended to provide a measure of concordance. On the other hand, the capitalization of some common words is used to emphasize their importance within the overall scheme of Existential Atomism.

> which is there for knowledge; although on this theory it is never known. For what is known is the other sort of reality, which is the byplay of the mind. Thus there would be two natures, one is the conjecture and the other is the dream.[2]

Thereafter, Existence or Beingness can be dealt with empirically, on exactly the same basis as any "material object".

Premise number one, which should be kept constantly in mind, is that one is venturing into a one-dimension universe: that of the sum of the Facts-which-are. In it, each true Being, monkey or iron atom, possesses a parcel of the cosmic energy and communes physically with and through every other, beyond time and space. Each is a Cosmic-Presence. This is not to say that agreement is expected, initially or ever, with what follows, rather only that one should, for the time being, accept to situate each position adopted outside of conventional time-space. Failing this the pivotal theories, for example that of ones maximization, would remain practically unintelligible, for the whole stands or falls as a unit. An introduction to the more unusual principles and axioms to be entertained is provided in the coming paragraphs.

The work is divided into five Parts.

The first deals with the phenomenon of individuation, the particle, and quantization in general. It also sets out the basic epistemological principles which guide the research. These are contained embryonically in the Principle of Absolutes which states that "the modality of the Universe and its processes is one of absolute to absolute". An unexpected implication is that intellect-power (thought) is quantized exactly as are computer bits. The Principle of Absolutes has an impact far beyond epistemology. It provides the setting — one of absoluteneity or of absolute-speed — and the climate — one of sheer quality — in which life unfurls. The chapters which establish that such a principle governs all processes and thus rates as the Prime Universal Principle, may appear laborious. Yet, effort devoted to master them will be well repaid.

In Part I the primary particle is discovered and a preliminary sketch of its attributes is provided. Described as an Existential-

2. Laurence BRIGHT, *WHITEHEAD'S Philosophy of Physics*, New York, Sheed and Ward, 1958, p. 31.

Atom, a term which blends the insights of cosmophysics and ontology, the primary particle is a strict entity — a true Outsider. This observation in turn leads to the formulation of the Cosmic Equation, which reads: U = X(E : A), where U stands for the Universe, X stands for a myriadic, yet fixed number, and E : A for the primary particle or Existential-Atom. Two of the merits of a Cosmic Equation is that through it, objectivity and truth are set upon an unshakeable foundation and, the conservation of all Energy is guaranteed.

Part II, concerning Power or Energy, breaks new ground in many areas and may present the greatest challenges. In respect to Power as such, two points will be advantageously noted. One, the terms Power and Energy are held synonymous and are given the broadest interpretation. Two, either term is defined as the synact of Existence. The word synact, a neologism, implies that Power or Energy is a factor without which an Existent or Atom cannot be. Conversely, Energy resides only in real individuals. Since each Atom is a strict unit or fact, Energy is quantized and non-transferable. A consequence of the acquisition by the Existential-Atom of its quota of Power, is its first metamorphosis — from Existential-Atom to Dynamic-Fact. Effectively this makes of every Atom, man and muon, an adimensional motor whose impact is cosmic. The novelty, here, is that Power becomes a fact. To this day Power, viewed as an agent of Becoming, remains the Great Unknown of science — for the obvious reason that "that" or "It" which is in "real movement" or "changes" can never be studied objectively. Power as fact reveals itself as an agent of intensity and of quality, and the fit subject of analysis — as any raw material.

Also investigated are speed and the structure of a universe bathed in the Absolute. The speed of a strict, adimensional unit, one discovers, is absolute. The rationale is that an "It", without extent other than that of the Fact-of-to-be, is a Presence everywhere and moves nowhere. The work's title, *Cosmic Presence*, derives from this observation. A corollary of absolute-speed, existential maximization, reveals that everyone, in-fact, rests in his maximal or optimum state. An outline of this seemingly outrageous theory is provided. A last but controversial doctrine, is that mind or intellect-power is,

A. physical and of the same order as the Power generated by the so-called inanimates, the electron for example and,

B. quantized, as are the bits in a computer.

A final comment on Part II. The theory of Power which it sets forth is developed without much regard to other systems. The physicist may especially be tempted to raise a number of technical objections. Generally, it may be argued that the proposed concept of Power ignores the distinction between energy as a kinetic or mechanical force and the so-called metaphysical power of the mind. The relevance of such a departure from tradition is clearly appreciated. However, the issue is faced with equanimity, for it is quite simply one of disciplines. In a universe of existential univocity, cosmology embraces every science, even theology. Within that context Dynamic Vision broadens the spectrum of powers to take into account human and tree-power, etc. The conservation of energy or cosmic bookkeeping predicates as much. But the secondary disciplines are not thereby threatened. Nuclear physics, for example, remains unscathed, since its preoccupation is exclusively with the dynamics, or more specifically with the perceived relationships of a single subspecies of the universal species, that of the "particles".

The quarrel is actually with the Aristotelians, acknowledged or not, who subscribe to the concept of a split-level universe. That they should reject the theory that the intellectual power generated by man interacts with power generated by an electron or flea is to be expected. This squarely contradicts their own theory of a "bifurcation of nature into two systems of reality which, insofar as they are real, are real in different senses". They may be right. Teilhard and Whitehead, among others, unhappy with the resulting dichotomy, suggested alternative schemes. If for purposes of academic interest, the advocates of a "matter and spirit" universe, including a number of physicists, should proceed on the premise that thought-power is physical, they may be pleasantly surprised. For instance, they will discover that a seamless universe solves the paradox of the discontinuous in the continuous and of the finite situated in the infinite. Also the spectre raised by the Heisenberg Uncertainty Principle is laid to rest.

Part II presents a difficulty of an other order. It may appear repetitive and the temptation to give it short shrift may be strong. This would be unfortunate. As indicated, the realization that Power is factual, quantized and owned in perpetuity, clears up many an intractable paradox. For example, in these chapters the quantization of Power is established. The arguments developed in Part I are indeed repeated, but in respect to a different subject. Since it is argued that Power is the synact of Existence, it is necessary to establish that the criteria applicable to the atomizing agent apply equally to the dynamic factor.

Relationships or alternately relationality are dealt with for the first time in Part III. As such, these, it is suggested, are the proper subject of an independent discipline, tentatively named "relationy". In a one-dimension universe, inhabited by a fixed number of Dynamic-Facts, the apparent incompatibility of a transcendent subject bathed in a medium of immanence, vanishes, there being but a single contact between each entity, and all relationships being cosmic. Hence the notion of cosmic presentiality. To cope with the limitations of human perception, this universal mode of presentiality is broken down into three primary modes; those of foundationship, mediumship and coagentship. While the latter are developed in some detail, their very basicness eliminates the need for protracted analysis and the bulk of this Part deals with the last of three experiments, that which demonstrates that each of us is a dimensionless motor which aggressively imposes itself upon every Being which, "was, is and will be".

In respect to this third experiment, two observations seem appropriate. The first concerns the nature of experiments and applies equally to the two conducted in Part I upon a synthetic atom or IT and upon a model universe of 1,000,000, similarly synthetic units. The second has to do with the legitimacy and relevance of the evidence drawn from physics and biochemistry, etc., used to support the theory that the primary particle of "matter" has no extent.

It is a commonly held view that experiments cannot be performed with pen and paper, but rather only upon "external and physical objects" and with the aid of a more or less complex apparatus, with crucibles and microscopes, for instance. The summary character of the two experiments completed on Part I, especially that upon a model universe, would seem open to such criticism. The merit of the third experiment, which closes Part III, should be to show that the first two were genuine experiments and that indeed all experiments, in any field, are conducted, not with test tubes or what have you, not even upon paper, but exclusively within the researcher and with the use of thought-power. The sole experimental agent is the mindscope. Dimensioned entities such as pen or bubble-chamber are but its tools. In a word "the method transforms its object", or as Eddington would have it, "through science, man only discovers his footprints".

Throughout the text, but notably for the purpose of experiment number three, data from physics, biology and other disciplines, provide supporting evidence. Generally, this takes the form of extensive quotations, some drawn from trade journals. In respect to this method the reader may note the following. Since *Cosmic Presence* sets out the broad outline of a unitary world, logically its basic principles should link the secondary sciences. On the other hand no claim is intended to an in-depth knowledge of the sciences called upon. Two reasons explain this. Firstly, to acquire an expertise in any discipline is a lifelong project. Secondly, most of the basic theories upon which the applied sciences presently rest are subject to heated debate and undergo constant revision. A case in point is the existence or nonexistence of the neutrino. At least as late as 1975, qualified physicists were found to defend both positions. It would therefore be ill-advised to stake the coherence of a cosmic scheme upon limited and debated evidence. Specifically, when biochemistry serves to demonstrate that bodies, human or other, are but intense foci of relationality, which an Existential-Atom entertains in its otherwise cosmic relationships, only its common sense principles are relied upon. After all, a doctorate in biochemistry is not required to understand that the specificity of an enzyme differs from that of an iron atom or a human. Further, to guard against quoting out of context, the citations are comprehensive.

Another feature of the text deserves mention, namely its lack of intricate and, to the layman, esoteric equations of the type which usually accompany technical works, in particular, those which deal with particle physics or formal logic. When the subject is the primary components of the universe, a general simplicity of presentation and the use of nothing but basic equations follows. Once it is established that the primary particles belong to a single species, the Universal Equation avers itself elementary. The same economy is in order when dealing with the relationship of identical entities or the basic qualities of the primary unit. In both instances calculus and similar methods are clearly out of place. Again it is a matter of disciplines. The chemist, logician and physicist rightly tailor their sciences to their raw material. So must the cosmologist. His raw material, as Democritus had anticipated, is univocally shared by strict entities. In accord with the Principle of the Proportionality of Extremes, his findings must be couched in terms fundamental as his raw material.

Part IV should present no new difficulty. Its main feature is Cosmic Peace. A corollary of absolute-speed, the theory of Cosmic Peace affirms that each Existential-Atom constitutes an immobile motor or inversely, that the true state of the Universe is one of tension and maximization. Such a view falls into the category of the *honest-fact*. That is to say, an honest accounting of the energy in the Universe imposes this view as an ethical imperative. The theory is further supported by evidence of a quasi universal intuition, experienced throughout the ages, that man's ultimate state is one of peace, enjoyed in a happy hunting ground, heaven or nirvana, etc. The latter is presented as purely circumstantial. Its rejection would not weaken the statistical and physical proof adduced in the preceding sections. The theory is important because it links the Order or Universe of the Real with those of the Now or Perceived. The latter are referred to in plural because each atom creates its own universe, tailored to its personal dynamism. As a by-product, the theory of a Cosmic Peace sheds new light upon the riddle of physical entropy. A brief outline of this is included for perusal.

Maximization in a state of tension (not necessarily of happiness), is not easily visualized. Many, perhaps, may be sorely tempted to reject it outright. Before doing so there would be advantage in reconsidering chapters III and V of Part II which deal with stationary-points and speed. Initially the content of both may appear highly technical. However, a second reading should reveal that these chapters explain the physical process whereby maximization is achieved and entropy is rationalized.

Part V introduces in its second chapter the Cosmic Code. The Code, whose two principles and five laws cover less than a page, governs every mode of behavior and embraces all other statutes as particular cases. Through it, a common denominator binds the various disciplines into a harmonious whole. A practical demonstration is provided when, in chapter one, the guidelines established in the four preceding Parts, in conjunction with the Code, yield a cameo of pyschological man. The closing chapter concludes upon an unexpected theme. In it, one observes that in a universe of strict atoms, each a Cosmic-Presence, love is the law of the land. Logically, It which fills the Universe is, in the physical sense of the word, flesh of the Universe. And only the masochist does not love his own flesh.

The phrase "flesh of the Universe" raises an important issue. Few will care, at least initially, to interpret it literally. Ones flesh ends with the body, does it not? Such is indeed the prevailing view. Yet it is accurate only for the merchant of dimensioned pieces of meat — the neighborhood butcher, for instance. Each of us, being without extent and thus present in and to every Existent in the Cosmos, is flesh of the other — physically. That raw affirmation distills the spirit of this book and explains the fact that both its opening paragraphs and closing chapters are devoted to this theme.

A further observation is in order. It applies to isolated statements throughout and concerns specifically the opening pages of Part I, the chapters in Part IV which deal with Cosmic Peace and all of Part V. Therein man, the center of attention, is frequently the subject of lyrical remarks. For the layman, such passages will create no problem. Instinctively, one feels oneself to be, at the very least, the equal of any non-descript molecule. Many students of the physical sciences are apt, however, to see things otherwise.

The rationale for dealing evenhandedly with the inanimate particle and the animate specificity was stated from the beginning. Briefly, any living atom is fully as primary as a proton or charmed particle. The unwary may deem such a proposition innocuous. On the contrary, it speaks of a novel universe — democratic and honest — in which all entities are accounted for. And it is this accountability and relatedness which characterize

Dynamic Vision. Should one refuse to entertain the premise that the human or feline atom is as strict and permanent an entity as an iron atom, there is little purpose in going beyond this point.

Now to close on a reassuring note. Without a doubt the universe of the Cosmic-Presence is a radical universe. Bereft of any dimension other than that of the Fact-of-to-be, it is the ultimate universe. Yet it does not, for all that, break the continuity of the scientific tradition. Rather, by a return to the source of all Existentialisms, that of the "Being which is", as intuited by Parmenides, it draws and binds into a harmonious whole the accumulated insights of the intervening centuries. As even the briefest overview of speculative thought reveals, the feeling of cosmic presentiality accommodates the essential Plato as well as the essential Teilhard and Planck.

Unquestionably, the world of the person who, as a Cosmic Presence, feels a fleshy contact with every Being, animated and inanimated, which ever was or will be, is altogether as different from that of time and space, birth and death, which 20th century man sees himself as inhabiting, as this latter was from the universe of pre-Copernican man, who as Augustine, debated the pros and cons of the antipode and the probabilities of men walking underneath a flat earth with their heads pointing downwards. It now seems established that the cosmology of Augustine and his peers did not correspond to Reality. It could be that a universe of « matter and spirit », situated in a true time-space, yet bound by infinity, which most men now imagine as being their home, is the Real Universe. However, this contemporary concept could be as inadequate as its predecessor.

The gist of my book is that the present time-space and movement cosmos is only less confining than that of Ptolemy. It invites the reader to enter the boundless and timeless dimension of the Fact-of-to-be. As in any novel situation, one can expect to encounter upon ones journey into this unknown, features which may disturb or even shock. Indeed, some of its vistas do exceed the boldest scenarios of science fiction. Nonetheless, as indicated, no break with tradition is involved. Only one item was missing to solve the ontological puzzle; the dimensionless and dynamic prime particle, whose speed is absolute. This acquired, everything falls into place. Philosophy's most contradictory theses are reconciled and some of the perplexing paradoxes of applied science lose much of their sting. Parmenides' inspired, yet long neglected, affirmation:

> One way only is left to be spoken, that it is; and on this way are full many signs that what is is uncreated and imperishable, for it is entire, immovable and without end. It was not in the past, nor shall it be, since it is now, all at once, one continuous...[3]

is vindicated. Added to the Parmenidean view is the multitude. Whereas, for the Eleat Being was unique, in Dynamic Vision the number of Beings or Atoms is a myriadic myriad. Yet each being, even the most famished and dejected louse, rests "entire, immovable and without end". The same applies to Democritus. The Existential-Atom or ontological-quantum was embryonic in his primordial atom, as also in the Leibnizian monad. To rationalize such concepts it was necessary to establish precisely the key criterion which any genuine physical entity must satisfy, namely that of being a fact, of being one-in-truth. This, in turn, implies avoiding like the plague any trace of Becomingism, of "sedimentation". The situation is clearly stated when, to the following quote from Whitehead's *Process and Reality*:

> This is a theory of monads; but it differs from Leibniz's in that his monads change. In the organic theory, they merely *become*.[4]

one adds that the Universe of the Cosmic-Presence is equally one of monad-like Existential-Atoms, save that these neither change nor become. All simply *are*.

As to the strictly dynamic and qualitative characteristics of a true physical entity, these also were intuited respectively by Plato, for whom Power was of the essence of being, and by Aristotle, whose physics stresses quality. One had but to return to the source, to Democritus, and vest power and quality in each Atom. Conjugated with Buridan's thesis that motion (movere) is an inherent attribute of the mobile, this reveals the inalienability of Energy. Each Atom or Being then avers itself an independent motor, in absolute possession of its quota of cosmic energy, each

3. "Presocratic Philosophy, The Eleatics, (trans. by G. S. Kirk and S. E. Raven), in *Greek Philosophy: Thales to Aristotle* (ed. Reginald E. Allen), New York, The Free Press, 1966, p. 45.
4. Alfred NORTH WHITEHEAD, *Process and Reality*, New York, The Free Press, 1969, p. 97.

limited by its qualities. At the epistemological level, the Principle of Absolutes and the quantization of intellect-power, which together explain the mind's mechanism, come to rationalize the Idealism of Berkeley and others, as well as the strict nominalism of Ockham for whom: "everything that can be predicated of many things, is by its nature in the mind either psychologically or logically". The same holds in respect to the paradoxes which bedevil contemporary physics. Whether it is a question of the Gouiran particle which "has an extent", but "no clear edges", and which "in reality covers the entire universe"; or of Einsteinian Relativity or still of the Feinberg tachyon whose "speed is infinite", to these and such other hypotheses as speak of relativism or relativity, only the energy and quality-packed quantum whose impact is cosmic, misses. At least so it seems. Of this the reader may judge.

Part I

The Primary Particle, an Existential-Atom?

chapter I

Existence, Sole Dimension of the Cosmos

A philosopher is not a philosopher if he is not a metaphysician. And it is the intuition of being — even when distorted by the errors of a system as in Plato or Spinoza — that makes the metaphysician.

J. MARITAIN
Existence and the Existent, p. 29

1. What Can the Reader Expect in Return For His Investment?

WHAT can the reader expect in return for his investment in the pages that follow? Due to the complex and interdisciplinary character of *Cosmic Presence*, this is the first question in need of an answer. Two categories of benefits offer themselves: the technical and the personal. I begin with the personal, for it can be summed up in a brief message. "You are flesh of the flesh of the Universe." Such, in a nutshell, is the message of *Cosmic Presence* to man, the person. Passport to the ultimate universe, it is a message which, when thoroughly understood and taken to heart, transmutes the common variety of *Homo-sapiens* into *Homo-cosmicus* — Man, the Cosmic Presence.

Several years ago, a cold dissection of the dynamics of the Universe had caused me to write down the phrase: Flesh of the flesh of the Universe. Initially, the words had remained naked, as symbols in a chemist's equation. The code was deciphered — but I did not feel. Gradually, however, it did acquire an intimate content, it did become a something lived, an added dimension to the Self, as witness the closing chapter. By then my personal universe was transformed. This fleshy feeling had revealed itself as the-feeling, the-sense in which all subsumes, and thus containing the message which should be conveyed in the opening pages, if the work was to be introduced in a human and complete manner. Otherwise, the layman might set it aside as a semi-metaphysical and technical work of research into the structure of "matter" and its components; the atoms and particles.

So I say, "You who now read these pages, when you are through and finished, if you do not feel in your heart, in your deepest Self, that you are flesh of the Universe and that the Universe, in its far-out reaches, is you; if you have not evolved from the stodginess of a space-bound *Homo-sapiens* to the glory and freedom of *Homo-cosmicus*, then you hardly understand what life is about. Certainly, you do not know what this book is about. *Let these words be interpreted literally, physically. Ones flesh does not end with the body. The universe of Beings beyond time and space, they are our flesh — to ignore, to hate or to love.* »

These quasi-esoteric opening paragraphs, as well as the closing chapters which deal with death, peace and the basics of human psychology, may appear as out of place in a work dedicated to research into the Real, whose aim is to discover the primary particle of matter and — should this ambitious quest succeed — to disrobe and dismantle the particle's mechanism. Briefly, the reasons which justify this approach are the following. As implied, the universe of *Cosmic Presence* is, in the full sense of the words, a new universe. Its sole dimension is Existence or the Fact-of-to-be, and the modality of its processes is of absolute to absolute. As a consequence all sciences are affected, psychology and ethics inclusively. Upon reflection it becomes clear that while the discovery of the primary particle is relevant, nonetheless the vision of the Self which a new universe offers is more so, since even one whose interest in the primary particle is technical, is fully as concerned with his personal development, as the layman.

A reader searching primarily for the answer to the questions "what am I" and "what is my role in the Cosmos", can therefore take a short-cut, and still look forward to a rewarding experience. A short-cut might consist in concentrating upon Parts IV and V, both relatively short and quite accessible, in which cosmic presentiality, as it applies to man, is developed. Granted such a course will deny him an in-depth understanding of the rationale and experiments which establish each human as, simultaneously, a prime unit or particle of the Universe, and flesh of the flesh of this Universe. Yet, even the intuition of being a Cosmic-Presence will more than repay any investment, for such a revelation can have a wholesome impact upon ones outlook on life, its cruelties and presumed absurdities. He who feels a fleshy communion with his brother squirrel and sister rose is a man different from a Sartre or a Bunuel, for whom life is an exercise in sadomasochism, a "hell"; and the Outside, even ones mother, is "the enemy".

Upon transcending into the dimensionless universe of the As-is, the traditional earthbound person, bursting out of his strait jacket of Aristotelian "dimensioned matter" will, in the physical sense of the phrase, obtain his citizenship and passport to the ultimate universe; will enter into a new world to become brother and lover of all Outsiders, of his enemy also.

Regardless of the course adopted, there is one essential point to bear in mind, for failing this a reader, especially one who may skim over certain chapters, will waste his time. All terms and affirmations, specifically those of "beyond time and space" and "flesh of the Universe", are to be interpreted at face value. These and other unexpected discoveries, such as that of the absolute speed of relationships, are not metaphors nor lapses into poetry. Each is systematically demonstrated. Integral to a tightly knit whole, together they reveal the basic structure of the Cosmos. Conversely, the concepts of time, space, speed, process, and their corollaries must be reinterpreted. While retaining their usual meaning within the context of secondary sciences like history or chemistry, each from the point of view of man as a total person, must be situated in a medium of cosmicity and absolute-speed. In a word, the psychological jump required parallels that performed by 15th century man when he broke out of the narrow Ptolemean universe into the "spatial infinity" of the Copernican. If anything the leap is more radical, for in the Absolute one moves neither in time nor space; one is neither born nor does one grow. *One merely is and discovers.*

From the philosopher or physicist's point of view, there are advantages to being aware initially that the research and experiments in which he is invited to participate open upon an earthy and yet inspiring vision of the Self and the Cosmos. To begin with, he also is a mortal and as such has personal values. From a technician's point of view, the realization that a rigorous analysis of the structure of the Real or "matter" yields the answer, not only to many enigmas which bedevil contemporary physics, but also offers the psychiatrist and moralist help, should reassure him as to the validity of the said experiments. The observation that the lay reader must interpret physically key terms such as ultimate universe, flesh of the Universe, physical discovery, experiment, maximization, absolute-speed, etc., applies more strictly to the physicist and philosopher. However, it should be noted that a willingness on their part to at least consider the possibility of a break with some of the sacred dogmas of our era, for example, to entertain the instantaneity of all processes, including that of thought, does not imply a blind acceptance, only openmindedness — a prerequisite for an honest assessment of any coherent unit. If by the end, the evidence remains unconvincing, then it will be time to reject the whole, because Dynamic Vision stands or falls as a unit. Its Parmenidean universe-of-facts, bathed in the Absolute (every other being universes of Becoming) is either the true universe or it is not. Let the reader be the judge, but a judge who passes verdict when all the evidence has been presented.

Since with the best of goodwill it is difficult to entertain novel viewpoints, it seems advantageous to preface the text with a brief explanation of the paradox of a continued use of conventional terms such as process, conflict, etc., within a universe-of-facts, in which time and space are reduced to real-illusions. This offers the added advantage of providing a synopsis of the basic supporting arguments. Such a step, fatal to a mystery novel, recommends itself in a scientific treatise which purports to propound a clear answer.

Actually the apparent contradiction involved in a continued use of the notion of process and conflict in a universe from which movement, evolution and change are removed, dispels itself when these and related concepts are situated in a medium of cosmicity and absolute-speed. Then, both a process and conflict take on a new meaning. Since in the Absolute one moves neither in time nor space, these dimensions and the sensation of a sequence which accompanies them are induced in the subject by the quality of his intellect. Here the word "quality" is the key. Because each Existent is a Cosmic-Presence, its feeling of the Outside (as distinct from consciousness) is a function of the quality and/or intensity of its thought-power: that of a cat and a zinc atom being different from man's quality-wise only. At absolute-speed, sequence and process are real, are still facts-of-life. *The difference is that a process performed between strict entities, at absolute-speed, by the appositing of aggression-laden thought-quanta ceases to be causal, deterministic and evolutionary, to become one of self-realization through corresponsibility.* It is also the only type of process which allows for the conservation of all energy — beyond time and space.

Emphasis on the above is warranted because, on the one hand everything hinges upon it and on the other, the chapters devoted to demonstrating that processes in general and thought in particular operate instantaneously, in a medium of quality and tension, are lengthy and run the risk of being glossed over. The same remark applies to Power and its corollaries, efficiency and maximization, for the simple reason that without Power or Energy there is no prime particle or Existential-Atom. In other words, due to the complementarity or synactivity of Existence and Power, Part II which deals with Power analyzed as a fact, required a restatement of the fundamentals established in Part I. The reader in a hurry may see in a reconsideration of identical principles an unnecessary repetition and be tempted to by-pass it. Such an approach while not necessarily fatal, would render further progress arduous. This would apply especially if the theory of maximization was given short shrift. A basic grasp of this unexpected, and admittedly difficult to visualize state, is essential to a deciphering of the mechanism of the Cosmos, and particularly to a resolution of the issues of cosmic peace and entropy, both dealt with in Part IV.

The theory that the maximal speed of the Universe is not that of light, but absolute-speed, aside from dispelling the paradox of processes in a world-of-facts, also solves two major difficulties referred to earlier, namely the need to interpret literally the twin affirmation that he who masters *Cosmic Presence* will discover a cosmos hitherto unknown, a cosmos richer in every sense, than the new world discovered by Christopher Columbus, and will capture the prime particle of matter now furiously chased in betatrons and similarly exotic machines. The detail of this demonstration can only be provided in the text proper. Yet its key, and simultaneously the key to an understanding of the learning process, experimentation and the nature of science, is contained in the simple percept that each Atom is of one "substance" and a radical Outsider. Neither a composite of "matter and spirit" nor a conglomerate of electrically joined chemicals, each of us, the reader, neutron-X and Napoleon's white horse, is a dimensionless motor, a quantum of non-transferable energy or Dynamic-Fact, in cosmic relationship with every Atom

(Being) in the Universe, beyond time-space. We make each other. Hence the affirmation that we are flesh of the flesh of the other.

Together, the notions just advanced, have farreaching consequences. To begin with, the most nefarious intellectual perversion ever to afflict Western thought : the Aristotelian-Cartesian theory of a split-level universe of "matter-spirit", ceases. Also, the idea of finitude and infinity being eliminated, the theory of learning or language and specifically of scientific research, is affected profoundly. In particular, the theory that scientific experiments can only be conducted upon pieces of "matter", live or inanimate, and with the aid of "material" instruments, such as test tubes or microscopes, avers itself incorrect. Once each Atom possesses its quota of the cosmic power in perpetuity, the fact that all scientific instruments, paper and pen inclusively, are but secondary tools, the mindscope being the sole agent with which in final analysis an experiment is made, follows. Simultaneously, the physicality and specificity of thought-power solves several frustrating problems, including that presented by the Heisenberg Uncertainty Principle and explains the affirmation that the experiments conducted herein lead to the discovery of the primary particle.

Let us consider more closely the situation in respect to the discovery of the ultimate universe which, as stated, constitutes an event more physical than the discovery of America in 1492. This was perhaps interpreted as a figure of speech. Such a view is at once right and wrong. One would err if, in using the phrase "figure of speech", one succumbs to the hypothesis that the intellect is some ethereal or spiritual gew-gaw which operates mysteriously, outside or at least independently of "finite matter". This hypothesis is contradicted directly by a scientific analysis of the structure of the Universe, and indirectly by the latest findings of subnuclear physics. These show that even the insignificant, subatomic photon, "in reality covers the entire universe"; that, in a word, the Universe is of one piece. On the other hand, the phrase "a figure of speech" or the expression "an intellectual exercise" accurately describes Reality when the concept of an intellect or language refers to a quality of a non-transferable power quota. Stated inversely, *human-power, of which thought is but one feature, differs from electron-power by its quality only. Thought, physically and objectively, fills the Universe and through it we aggress and impose our Self upon every particle in the*

Cosmos. The remainder follows. Since each is a Cosmic-Presence, all-in-all, each has, physically, present in and before him, the entire Universe. Each, even if ever so faintly, *feels and knows* the faintest death tremor of every mosquito, also every radio-wave which was, is and will be. Specifically this cosmic-feeling, albeit in great part buried in the subconscious, is at this moment experienced by the reader. In that sense nothing is ever discovered, if discovery means that one, in time, comes into spatial contact with someone or thing which was not there before; that, for instance one will cuddle, ten years hence, a *then newly born* grandson or embrace a *yet unknown* lover or generally *become aware in time* either through touch, sight, smell or other localized sense, of an event which would ooze out of a Hegelian nothingness. Reality is a physical and cosmic presence. Even the most famished louse is a permanent dynamic fixture in the Cosmic Equation — hence the marginal validity of astrology and the scientific tenor of the parapsychological sciences. Consequently, a discovery results from the exercise of a power (primarily but not entirely intellectual) to presentialize oneself before the Outsiders which, with the reader and myself constitute the concept defined as universe. In summary, *every discovery is an operation of consciousness and all experiments are conducted within the Self.* Every instrument of research, be it ball pen or bacteria culture, merely extends the mindscope. This vindicates Berkeley's basic intuition by drawing the distinction between an objective presence before all Atoms and a subjective grasping of them through a more or less successful exercise of thought-power.

That which applies to a lost set of keys applies to the concept of a universe. The Universe's true dimension is discovered not by moving about in it, but by becoming aware of its ultimate dimension: the Fact-of-to-be. He for whom every particle is present physically beyond time-space, for whom Sirius and the Andromeda nebula are apartments lived in, indeed lives in a universe more different from the contemporary than the latter was from that designed by Ptolemy and his peers. Citizen of everywhere and resident in everyone he can go no further. *The sole remaining frontier to discover and explore is that of his feeling.* With the introduction of the concept of a generic feeling, of which secondary senses are only facets, the phrase "flesh of the flesh of the Universe" bares its splendor and warmth. *To be is to feel. And the quintessential feeling is love* — the deliberate drawing unto the Self of the universe of Outsiders, for they are ones flesh.

The same logic applies to the claim of a discovery of the prime particle of matter through experiments conducted entirely with mind-power. However, due to its importance, psychological, political and other, it also warrants separate consideration. At first hearing, the bald affirmation that the elementary particle of matter was discovered by conducting three experiments within the covers of a book will seem difficult to accept, especially when it is added that the same results can be achieved by anyone — if sufficient power is invested in the project. Most skeptical, and with reason, will be the subnuclear physicist. "How", he will ask, "can laymen discover, with mere intellect-power, a primary particle, when we, who dispose of cyclotrons and betatrons which generate billions of volts, are unable to do so?" The frustration of microphysics in its quest for the element of matter, easily explained, will persist for as long as the present angle of attack is maintained. It is premised upon two fundamental misconceptions. Firstly, the wrong item is being sought and secondly, all seek for their unknown prey in the wrong locale. Clearly, either error is fatal. Given both, a more hopeless quest is hard to imagine. Mistake number one assumes that the ultimate particle has an extent, albeit infinitesimal, whereas, an analysis of the structure of Reality demonstrates that each genuine primary particle must be an adimensional motor or Dynamic-Fact. The second flaw, (a corollary of the first), is that microphysics, intuiting the need for adimensionality, refuses to bow to the evidence, and concentrates its efforts upon the most unlikely candidate: the barren subatomic entity. Aborting the intuition of adimensionality as a prerequisite of primariness, it chooses instead to chase after the closest imaginable thing to an adimensional, the invisible, massless neutrino and other likewise furtive quarkian creatures.

These observations are not an attack upon the legitimacy of particle physics. They only underscore a case of mistaken identity. The object of particle research is not the primary particle *per se*, but rather the structure and kinetism of the weakest primary entities as yet observed. Such an endeavor is legitimate because, it provides useful knowledge of the behavior of an entire tribe of Existential-Atoms, as witness the harnessing of the atom for commercial purposes. In short, to be "weak", barren or generally small, as the leptons, hardly entitles one to claim the title of primary. Only in the topsy-turvy world of Becomingism and abiogenesis can such a view be entertained. The second prerequisite to the discovery of a primary particle is a proper understanding of the nature of intellect-power. He who seeks to capture an outside entity must be a true Outsider to the intended victim, be the latter an escaping budgy bird, a hypnotist's subject or omega-minus No. 13424699. Hence, it is essential to realize: one, that thought-power is possessed in permanence by the Existent which generates it; two, that it is specific, that each species of Atom generates its own brand, and three, that it is physical, exactly as electricity — that it moves things, is kinetic. In a word, man is a cosmic motor, one of whose prominent qualities is the intellectual.

The above explains the failure of contemporary physics to seize the primary element with sophisticated instruments. Since each particle fills the Universe, (a point upon which many physicists agree), logic predicates that none can be grasped with dimensioned tweezers, even tweezers as exquisitely miniaturized as an electron-scanner or bubble-chamber. Indeed the higher the miniaturization and precision in time-space, the weaker the grasp upon a prospective prey. A finger applied at the base of Mount Everest can never compass it. How much more impossible, the task of the physicist who centers his attention upon an infinitesimal space-point such as that attributed to a proton, when the said proton's field of action and presence is not merely that of Everest, but cosmic. The only modality or guise under which a prime particle of the Real can be captured is that of an Obscure-Absolute, e.g. as an intuited fact, obscurely grasped. And an Obscure-Absolute, as any fact, can be compassed only with an instrument which operates at absolute-speed, namely the intellect, of which the eye, the hand, the pen, the microscope and the cyclotron are extensions, each not one wit different from those mechanical hands used to manipulate the rods, etc., in the fueling machine of a nuclear reactor.[1] This aspect of scientific research is

1. An Obscure-Absolute is an entity such as an iron atom, Pope Paul VI or a willow tree whose individuality and dynamism is observed as a fact, but

noted in answer to the anticipated objection that the first and second experiments conducted in chapter IX, Part I upon a synthetic Atom or IT and upon a model universe of 1,000,000 ITs, respectively, and the third upon the "bodies" of a human and an orangutan in chapter I, Part III are not experiments in the accepted sense.

At this point the rationale of a theory of adimensionality and its unconscionable corrollaries, absolute-speed and the coexistence of Nero, the reader, Adam and Eve, and of all Beings which were, are and will be, may be questioned. Existential adimensionality rests upon the inoffensive observation that "a fact, is a fact, is a fact," which is to say, upon a literal interpretation of the notion of facticity and upon the intellectual honesty which this exacts. The five word phrase "a fact is a fact" or its briefer *alter ego* "What-is, is", may appear trite. Nonetheless nothing more than, but also nothing short of, an honest interpretation of either is required to decipher the code of the Self and earn ones citizenship in the ultimate universe.

The question of facticity under its ontological, dynamic and epistemological aspects, dealt with in Parts I and II, is singled out for special notice here for two reasons. The first and general, just outlined, is to emphasize the binding obligation which the scientist, regardless of discipline, has to respect the What-is or to state the case colloquially, the need to "face facts"; to "not play around with facts" — a temptation to which the philosophical fraternity yields too often for its own good. The second motive for anticipatory remarks upon facticity and absoluteneity and their mates, the absolute and absolute-speed, is that absoluteneity is the trademark of Dynamic Vision and that a preliminary introduction to its basics may facilitate the understanding of the detail. The apparently inoffensive triad of facticity, absoluteneity and absolute-speed and the Principle of Absolutes which it begets, turns all previous universes inside out. Yet, even a cursory evaluation of the following observations reveals that the absoluteneity of relationships and processes is deducible from an elementary logical analysis of the real world.

---

remains obscure — literally in a cosmic fog before any observer whose perception is not absolute, (see Pt. I chap., VI, sec. 3, B4).

Briefly, the terms fact, oneness, one, unit, discrete-entity, bit, monad, digit, atom and absolute, all synonymous, simply *are*, and whether existential or epistemological, whether motor or thought-quantum neither begin nor change. Further, each as a oneness or absolute can only relate absolutely. The subject is analyzed extensively in chapters VI, VII and VIII of Part I and chapter V of Part II. The latter deals with absolute-speed and its seeming contradiction. Presently it suffices to reiterate that absoluteneity permits the continued usage of conventional criteria such as process, life, etc. (not, however, Becoming or evolution), but gives these a new meaning. A process which occurs at absolute-speed, between two strict units, differs radically from one which dawdles along in time-space, such as that of a racing gazelle or photon. Whereas the time-space or evolutionary process assumedly involves a transfer of energy through which the generation of the conqueror is achieved at the cost of the degeneration of the conquered — literally he who grows must eat and nihilate his brother-victim — the absolute-speed process reveals each to be the maker of the universe of his brother. The absolute-speed process conserves all Energy. No one digests and makes his the flesh of his neighbor. Rather there is relationship and communion. Each communes with the other, each is flesh of the other, all the while remaining a true Self, a true Outsider.

This opening section closes with a note of advice and of welcome. From here on, dear reader and pilgrim, you are on your own. The ultimate universe is yours to conquer and inhabit. But its conquest you alone can achieve, because every conquest, every voyage is a solitary voyage — the voyage of an Outsider. Welcome. Over the years I have done my best to cut a straight path through the sense jungle. Such an enterprise always remains a personal enterprise, subject to improvement. At the best sign posts are set up. In your universe some features of the landscape may loom larger than in mine. The Absolute, boundless, offers no end of marvels, for the like of we humans, to explore and revel in. Welcome. And let your sign posts add to humanity's science and wisdom.

As you proceed, you as I, here and there, will find the going rough. When you do, the best advice is the following. As you hack your way through the carnal jungle, remember that the only reliable guide is the rational sense or feeling. Beware of the tactile and visual senses. Both sight and touch deceive. Reason alone can be trusted. First and foremost place your faith in that cosmic feeling sung long ago, by Francis of Assisi in his canticle of love to "Brother Wolf and Sister Sun". Remember, the person does not begin and end with its "body"; the "body" is only a fortress behind which one retires to conduct the cosmic war called life. Remember, resident of the broad Universe; you are one in all and all are one; you are indeed flesh of the flesh of the Universe and the maker and brother of all Existents — God, man, photon and flea.

2. Basic Premise: Existence, Fact and Raw Material

The premise which contains embryonically the data required to decode the Real and specifically to discover the primary particle is that the sum or mass of the That-which-is, otherwise known as Existence, Reality, Universe or "matter", etc., constitutes the prime conglomerative fact, pregnant with all secondary facts, ontological and epistemological. It follows that *the cosmic existential fact is the raw material of those sciences, such as philosophy and cosmophysics, which deal with the Universe and is, like any raw material, a fit subject for experimentation.*

This diagnosis, it will be noted, endorses the traditional Existentialist's stand, yet flaunts his most sacred tenets. Making Existence the first and encompassing fact, it simultaneously affirms that the ontological question — *what is, what-is*? can be resolved experimentally. Actually, the claim is not that one can rend the Marcellian veil of mystery which conceals, from layman and professional alike, the inneity of any It-which-is. Mystery shrouds even the Self from itself, and will continue to do so — certainly for as long as the human mind operates in its present state. The affirmation is that Existence is not an "unthinkable". As ground of objectivity, it is subject to conceptualization and experimentation. Indeed, provided the proper procedures are utilized, the Being or Atom can be isolated and its mechanism blueprinted.

Such an Existentialism makes possible the dismantling of the Real or "matter" into its primary components because it is not man-centered as, for instance, the Kierkegaardian or Sartrian, but rather cosmic and scientific, which is to say factual, democratic and empirical. Closely related to that of the original Existentialist, Parmenides, in it the Fact-of-to-be reigns over the act and process. By replacing these nearsighted concepts with those of facticity and absolute, the researcher acquires the key to the decoding of Reality, namely the Existential-Atom, an absolute and its modality, absoluteneity.

3. Introductory Observations

The following introductory observations are offered as indicators. They fall under four headings, the propositional, ontological, epistemological and structural.

The propositional, contained in a brief paragraph, adopts the full Parmenidean position. It rests upon the premise *What-Is, Is*, a seminal intuition whose first revelation is:

Existence is a fact — not an act nor in act.

From here on, under no circumstances, will evidence, sensual or logical, be allowed to jeopardize, to wound this facticity of the Real.

Ontologically, the positing of a harmless "f" before the commonplace concept of "act", turns the contemporary universe inside-out. Among other equally iconoclastic corollaries, it predicates the elimination of all quantitative norms, time-space inclusively. Notions such as spirit and idea are relegated to secondary and analytical roles or, as in the case of "matter", void and infinity, are cast into science's dustbin for sterile, noxious concepts. A further casualty is causality. Reduced to a subjective Now phenomenon, this is, in the Order of the Real, replaced by cosmic relationality and corresponsibility. A merit of the Principle of Cosmic Relationality is that by substituting for the snail-paced speed of light, the speed of the Real : absolute-speed, it provides for the ultimate formulation of the Principle of General Relativity.

Only the existential one or absolute remains unscathed. *Existence, individuated, dynamic, tensorial, qualitative and univocal, yet equivocally shared by each Existent, reveals itself as the sole dimension of the Universe — a universe inhabited by a fixed number of cœval Existential-Atoms.*

The epistemological upheaval attendant to the upgrading of Existence to the status of an unchanging fact is equally severe. Since epistemic modalities are dealt with at length in chapters VI to IX of Part I, only a statement of basic principles is called for:

A. Thought-power, integral to the Existent, is physical, tensorial, qualitative and aggressive. Its fruit, truth and knowledge, partake of the dynamic, exactly, for instance, as electron-power.

B. Each Existent, being a fact and an absolute, the modality of learning is one of absolute to absolute or, for short, of absoluteneity, for firstly, only absolutes can reside in an absolute, and secondly, absolutes regardless of order, can only relate absolutely, as quantum (strict unit) to quantum. As a consequence thought is quantized i.e., consists of quanta, and operates instantaneously.

C. Further, the mood or quality of the Perceived or Now being one of aggression, each thought represents one of two aggressors in an intellectual skirmish (each pitted against another), both being superseded by a third. This sequence of minor skirmishes terminates when the thinker spends his last quantum.

Since learning structures or the hierarchy of the sciences will not be again directly investigated, the remarks on the subject are more extensive, but nonetheless concern primarily the perennial debate on the relationship of philosophy, ontology, metaphysics, physics and cosmophysics to each other — a restriction justified by the fact that the field of Cosmic Presence is the universal.

The controversy over the standing, and indeed frequently over the nature of the disciplines, has through the centuries stirred up heated debate. The problem is nowhere as formidable as usually reckoned, providing one goes to the heart of the matter to there discover in Reality or Existence a univocal fact in which each Existent shares on an equal footing. Then the master science — its name being irrelevant — becomes that which has as raw material this univocal sum of the That-which-is. The issue of paramountcy being thereby settled, the way is paved for the taylorization of scientific categories. Once each real individual has vested in it its inalienable share of the cosmic mass, each unit becomes a quality factor and simultaneously the proper matrix for a subdiscipline.

On the proviso that the name of the paramount science is optional, and that any substantive agreed upon as to content is acceptable, the terms philosophy or cosmontology henceforth describe the first science — that which has Existence or "matter" as raw material. The term cosmontology, a neologism, has the same merit as that of Existential-Atom, namely to marry the concept philosophy or ontology with cosmophysics. The rationale will reveal itself shortly. Next in line of succession, all three being of equal standing, come ontology, physics and the science of cosmic relationality herein named relationy. Thereafter each category of non-universal phenomena or qualities provides the basis of a subdiscipline.

Such a schema offers the double advantage of simplicity and conformity with the Real. Specifically it puts an end to the guerilla warfare waged between schools, witness Positivism, Materialism, Idealism and Existentialism, etc. Their feuding is seen to arise from the overemphasizing of secondary facets of Reality to the detriment of the whole. *Grosso modo,* their respective insights are valid and, save for those such as Becomingism which involve intellectual perversions, and must be rejected outright, their reconciliation is a simple matter. Each has its legitimate territory, and as long as it stays within this, conflict ceases. For instance, Pragmatism and Positivism, are fruitful, as are Empiricism and Idealism. As example, thought-power can be held responsible for the self-realization of an Existent such as man — provided self-realization is not equated with the Berkeleian *esse est percipi*, but rather describes the intellectual facet of ones presence to the Universe.

A brief foray into the question of the content of philosophy or cosmontology and of its relationship to the natural sciences confirms the soundness of this approach. In our era it is axiomatic that philosophy differs radically from natural or physical science. An insuperable barrier supposedly divides philosophy from cosmophysics. By and large, the subject of the former is purported to be the intangible, ideas, principles and metaphysical issues, whereas cosmophysics is held to deal with "matter", with the physical, and the sensual generally. The outcome is costly in terms of human happiness. In a dichotomous Universe, if coherence is maintained, double standards must be established. Many, unhappy with such an alternative, react by cavalierly dismissing the metaphysical and spiritual as irrelevant or even as a myth. The price tag for such an amputation is high. The amputator ends up sadly impoverished. Imprisoned in the strait jacket of an unfeeling, evanescent "matter"; his vision confined to the closet-like horizon of his senses, the more faithful he is to "materialism" the colder, more inhuman he becomes. Also, as the flesh degenerates and the libido flags, and his dreams of glory, of lust, of power fade into the dark night of time, a heavy weariness, a "Nausée", invades him — despair, also, often.

If possible, the fate of those who attempt to conciliate both spheres is worse. Moral schizophrenics, they go through life torn between "the noble aspirations of the spirit and the crass cravings of the world of matter and the flesh". Brute, aspiring to angelhood, doomed to a quixotic struggle against imaginary enemies, they live an unrelenting anguish — a torment of self-inflicted guilt and shame.

The minutiae of this ancient, but still burning controversy which affects profoundly the well-being of individual and civilization alike, falls beyond the purview of this book. Its relevance to the basics of the present issue is however critical. The philosopher or cosmophysicist who subscribes to the hellenic theory of a dichotomous Universe, and sees his science as cosmic, yet as wholly divorceable from that of the other, might advantageously consider the inconsistency of such a view. Since each claims the Universe for his subject, the fact that each has a different concept of the nature of an identical entity, should cause both to question their outlooks. Both cannot be right, if indeed either is. Granted, since the aims differ, the data generated can be expected to differ. Yet, with the universal as their common concern, the entire Universe must fall under their respective scrutiny. It is, for example, no more justifiable for the philosopher when preoccupied with the inneity of Existence, to ignore the nuclear, electrical or gravitational forces and fields, than for a physicist when searching for a Unified Field Theory, to leave out of his calculations thought-power, and the fields, sexual, economic and national which this engenders. The Universe and its processes reveal no such dichotomy — neither between the seen and the unseen, nor between the so-called "spiritual and material".

In accord with the same logic, philosophy is sadly underrated when demoted to the status of "the science of word juggling, of semantics". To affirm, as did Wittgenstein that "Philosophy is a battle against the bewitchment of our intelligence by means of language",[2] is to mistake the shadow for the bone. Certainly, a philosophy of language is essential to a proper deciphering of Reality. The fact remains that the raw material of philosophy is "matter", or more accurately the Fact-of-to-be, of which words are but a pale reflection. As to logic, formal or otherwise, its role in philosophy is no greater than in any other science. On the issue, Kant's statement that

> ..., logic is properly only a propaedeutic — forms, as it were, the vestibule of the sciences; and while it is necessary to enable us to form a correct judgement with regard to the various branches of knowledge, still the acquisition of real, substantive knowledge is to be sought only in the sciences properly so called, that is, in the objective sciences.[3]

is valid. The same comment applies to those who, relying upon etymology, reduce philosophy to a love for wisdom. Whether the wisdom sought be universal or not, is beside the point. Wisdom, intimately related to ethics, as semantics, rates only the status of a subdiscipline. Nor does the theory of philosophy as the science of first principles make more sense. Principles are not of the realm of fact. Whether prime or secondary, all partake of the process or hermeneutic. Principles are a by-product, not the subject.

For their part, the cosmophysicists might note that their quest for a unified field is doomed to failure as long as they leave out of the Cosmic Equation, with a pretext to realism, the slightest of dynamic factors, for example the vital dynamism of a single lazy, three fingered sloth, let alone the intellect-power of a man. Of a different order, but directly related, is the duty of the cosmophysicist to exceed sense perception and in particular, any radical kinetism or quantization. Power — a fact — partakes of the Absolute. All secondary dimensions, time, space, mass and

2. L. Wittgenstein, *Philosophical Investigations*, 1953, p. 47.
3. I. Kant, *The Critique of Pure Reason*, (trans. J.M.D. Meiklejohn) 1934, p. 9, London, J.M. Dent.

quantity inclusively, are the fruit of anthropocization — are mind-creatures. While these are proper tools of applied physics when this addresses itself to specific situations, cosmophysics must, if its equations are to be sound, situate itself in the Absolute.

It may be argued that in the light of the above propositions philosophy becomes "the science", and the other disciplines subsciences. Within this framework, ontology would remain linked to philosophy — its handmaid, so to speak — while cosmophysics (natural philosophy) becomes a second generation, wholly dependent discipline. This categorization, paralleling closely that of the pre-Cartesian era, would be as unsatisfactory as that which divides the epistemic into airtight compartments, the metaphysical (speculative) and the experimental (empirical).

Instead, a third classification seems preferable. This cuts philosophy's career short, but has the merit of leaving it with a clearly delineated territory. Philosophy would be restricted to the study and dissection of the cosmic mass, while its heirs, ontology and cosmophysics, would divide its kingdom into two distinct yet coextensive satrapies. Then ontology has, as its preserve, the study of existential individuation, and cosmophysics enjoys its exclusive domain, Power or Energy, both being reunited through the agency of quality and an independant science of relationships (relationy).

In summary, since the Universe, a conceptual-conglomerate, is subdivisible into Dynamic-Facts, each possessor in fee simple of its quota of Existence and Power, it is logical to see in philosophy the study of the cosmic mass, and in ontology and cosmophysics, two equally universal sciences dedicated to the twin and synactive facets of this mass : Existence and Power, with relationy correlating the whole.

The advantages are considerable. It suffices to cite two. One, the sciences are unified. Two, empiricism is introduced to ontology — with a concomitant exorcism of a metaphysics. The metaphysical then becomes a proper subject of scientific inquiry, albeit one reaching into the furthest frontiers of perception. While the metaphysical and/or spiritual may lie beyond the grasp of many, it does so not because of an insuperable ontological barrier, but solely of a qualitative handicap. The situation parallels that of an Australian aborigine or average Canadian housewife, when either faces the mysteries of aeronautics. If either has the opportunity and the desire to master the principles involved, both can. The same applies to metaphysical and spiritual knowledge. Neither exceeds the normal range of the human intellect. Rather, quality only is at play. Some lack the power or will to become proficient in either field.

The fact that the synactive, Existence-Power theory promotes a coherent hierarchization of the sciences is discerned the moment one considers that while ontology and cosmophysics are duty bound to retain their independence, still, if their legitimate roles are to be fulfilled, each must come to an accurate view firstly, of its subject: Existence and Power respectively, and secondly, of the intimate bond which unites these. Coequal and complementary, either can achieve its goal only when its findings can be integrated with those of the other. The second, and in a sense the more important benefit — the introduction of empiricism into ontology — while not due solely to a restructuring of categories, owes much to this. Once ontology's raw material becomes the cosmic mass, factual and concrete and a fit subject of experimentation, it follows that ontology, from a metaphysical game, becomes the first empirical science, a logical development, since the deciphering of the inneity of the existential unit must precede research into its secondary qualities. For instance, before the workings of the human mind or blood system can be fathomed, an understanding of the basic structure of the human atom is essential.

While from the point of view of epistemic efficiency, there is merit in this tripartite classification, the whole of *Cosmic Presence* can be seen as a philosophical treatise. Nomenclature is not after all so critical. However, many of its chapters are devoted to Power, mechanical, kinetic, intellectual and other. These are conventionally considered beyond the pale of philosophy, and the preserve either of physics or psychology. In practice both are so dependent upon their parent philosophy and so inextricably interwoven, that a clear-cut delineation of jurisdiction is nigh unfeasible. The essential is to recognize as prime science that which deals with the cosmic fact. Next, it must be remembered that progress from that first step can be fruitful only if research is conducted simultaneously on two fronts: the ontological and the physical. Since this is the categorization adopted herein — it will prove advantageous to keep the following in mind. The jurisdiction of cosmontology terminates with this first chapter, wherein the cosmic mass is circumscribed and analyzed in its role of universal raw material and of prime conglomerative fact. Ontology takes up the remainder of Part I. In this, the qualities and prerequisites of existential individuation are established. This leads to the discovery of the Existential-Atom, and to the formulation of the Cosmic Equation. So conceived ontology deals only with the Atom, grasped as a fact immune to change.

Cosmophysics, studied in its cosmic range, ends with Part II. To define it as the science of all types of Power, might appear as a deviation from tradition. Closer scrutiny reveals no departure, but rather a broadening of its province and an in-depth exploration of its subject : Power. Presently, cosmophysics is viewed as the science which deals with visible or tangible Energy, kinetic and otherwise, observed at both the micro and macro-levels, excluding, however, all animal or vital dynamism. To make a bad situation worse, Energy is equated with a potency or agent of Becoming. Inevitably, since that or It which becomes is not there, Power once conceived as potential, assumes the status of a mystery. Herein cosmophysics remains in full ownership of its recognized territories and extends these to incorporate all dynamisms, the vital and spiritual inclusively, as well as all fields — not only the magnetic, electrical and gravitational but the national and emotional in general. This respects the Principle of the Conservation of Energy.

4. **Relationy, the Science of Relationships**

The above would seem to present a dilemma. The sciences defined as cosmic have had alloted to them their entire patrimony. Still unaccounted for is relationality, a factor equally universal. Since relationality partakes of the individual and the dynamic, two factors unambiguously allocated to ontology and cosmophysics, should not each be granted their share of the relational ; or still should the relational be included entirely within the province of either ?

Custom haphazardly apportions relationality between the disciplines, with as a result acrimonious debate. Some hold relationships to be internal, others external, while others see them as assuming either characteristic. Some schools even see in the issue a question of linguistics! The problem is easily resolved. Cosmic relationality is a subject sufficiently broad and well defined as to rate as an independent science, a convenient name for which would be relationy. The term relationality could also be marshalled for the task. This could, however, lead to ambiguities since, among other factors its connotation is very general. On the other hand, the concise neologism, relationy, clearly establishes the field of relationships as a discipline in its own right.

An autonomous science of relationships is the reward for solving the paradox of the incompatibility of the transcendent with the immanent or alternately of the continuous with the discontinuous. By reuniting through synactivity, two disciplines considered as vaguely, if at all related, a first step is taken. Next by making of ontology the science of existential individuation, the problem of transcendence is tackled "head-on", but is never divorced from that presented by the equally wholesale immanence of all in all. The thesis here is that in a general way, the dynamic factor accounts for immanence, and existential individuation for transcendence. To some, this may appear as an unwonted tampering with scientific realities, since in their view cosmophysics has no interest whatsoever in Existence. Such a theory ignores the fact that man's age-old quest for "the elementary particle", one of cosmophysic's prime objectives, constitutes an uninhibited foray into the thicket of existential individuation — a foray which ends with the discovery of the Existential-Atom, dimensionless and qualitative. In a word, while the qualitative is eminently ontological, and the processional eminently physical, yet, due to the synactivity of both and, it follows, of both sciences, each partakes invincibly of the other. The process is in the unique, and the unique is the process, and yet the process is on its own.

Since the ground of relationships partakes of two factors only, individuation and power, it is logical, firstly, to establish a hermeneutic dichotomy between the existential and the dynamic, and secondly, to investigate independently the modalities through which the immanent and transcendent are made one. The corpus of this third category of investigation, the strictly relational aspect of Reality constitutes relationy. Only its principles are discussed in this work. The detail of the laws which govern relationships at the cosmic plane are dealt with in the second tome of the trilogy, *Cosmic Jurisprudence.*

5. Of "What" Does Existence Consist?

What is encompassed within the boundaries of Existence, or of what does Existence consist? The question, crucial, is complex and the source of deeply felt dogmatisms. Hence, this initial statement of position, will involve only basics and two brief explanatory remarks.

Firstly, *Existence will be dealt with empirically, exactly as any natural science would deal with its subject.* This is proper, since Existence is a raw material. At this stage semantics are of no concern, only the massive Fact-of-to-be, grasped empirically in its most concrete and all encompassing is-ness. In many respects such a starting point parallels Parmenides'.[4] However, it will lead far beyond the monistic vision of *The Way of Truth* — to a universe of many Beings. The second remark, which concerns the relevance of the word Existence, is a corollary of the realism implicit in the first. No special significance attaches to the preeminence given here and throughout, to the term Existence and its derivatives or alternates such as Existent, Beingness, Being, etc. When used generically, it is synonymous and interchangeable with "matter", "substance" (the Aquinian)[5], the As-is, the Real, Being, the cosmic mass, etc.

As with any empirical project, the initial statement of position describes. Existence as the cosmic raw material encompasses the

4. The above interpretation of the Parmenidean premise, squarely contradicts the usual which, far from seeing in Parmenides an Empiricist, holds him to be the inventor of the principle of contradiction and of dialectics. An analysis of his text does not justify such a view. The negation and rationalization are with Parmenides posterior and incidental to his prehension that: "Being (or it) is". By all criteria, he should be considered as the original Existentialist and the father of Empiricism.

5. Aquinian substance is a concept defined by P.B. Grenet as: "ce qui est, au sens vrai, complet et fort. Socrate est dans Athènes, il est grand et il est vertueux: mais ni sa vertu, ni sa présence dans Athènes ne sont rien, sans lui, ou en dehors de lui... Il ne sont qu'en lui, par lui. Lui n'est en rien d'autre". P.B. GRENET, *Ontologie*, Paris, Beauchesne et ses Fils, 1959, p. 101.

Objective. This is to say that it includes all of the That-which-is, the sum of realities, all that which can be kicked about, or is beyond the senses but nonetheless real — every cat, every component of every galaxy, every tree, positron and angel, every clam, iron atom and woman. To speak legalese, as raw material, Existence includes all realities without limiting the generality thereof. Further, this catalogue encompasses all the Real:

A. whether known to man or not, and

B. time and space notwithstanding.

General agreement with the fact that *Reality extends beyond the known, beyond immediate human perception*, can be safely assumed. Only a radical Idealist could object. Willingness to transcend anthropocentricity does, after all, constitute the minimal criterion of scientific objectivity. Man does not know, and still less, can he see or touch "everything". If the obligation to account for a broader gamut of Reality than registers upon the feeble barometer of human sensuality is a premise widely accepted, the same does not apply to the second: namely, that *the Real extends and persists beyond time.* Indeed, there is reason to believe that this will be received with skepticism. A demonstration of how and upon what basis all Beings integrate into a single universe-of-immediacy, must be deferred to later chapters. At this stage, it is enough to note that failure to consider as real and in-fact present the so-called future and past, entails leaving out of ones equations, real entities; be these Cleopatra, a kaon, a rose or Christ, and that such omissions vitiate the Cosmic Equation. The issue is the nexus around which revolves the secondary, yet critical issues of causality, determinism and the nature of time-space, and consequently any cosmontology which does not solve it is defective.

Technically the task of circumscribing our raw material is completed. Nonetheless to avoid all trace of ambiguity at this crucial phase, attention is drawn to a feature which, even though already specified, might pass unrecognized: the facticity of Existence. When earlier it was affirmed that *Existence, sum of the Real and raw material of the Universe, constitutes the prime conglomerative fact, pregnant of all minor facts, processes and relationships, this was to be read literally, as in the Way of Truth:*

> One way only is left to be spoken of, that it (Being) is; and on this way are full many signs that what is is uncreated and imperishable, for it is entire, immovable and without end. It was not in the past, nor shall it (Being) be, since it is now, all at once, one, continuous; ...[6]

One final precision, related to epistemology and specifically to intellection, imposes itself. While both are covered by an all-inclusive cataloguing of the manifestations of Existence, these are mentioned independently, to make clear a dissociation from the broadly held theory that "the intellect or mind" resides unsullied by crass "materialistic" goings-on, in a sphere of its own. Dynamic Vision eschews all dichotomies, and specifically the mind-body dichotomy. In its one piece universe, the raw material is at once univocal and equivocal. Univocal, here means that Existence is a universal genus, a *genus generalissimum*. Equivocal implies that the quality of the parcel of the Real possessed by a given Existent differs from that of every other. Intellect-power is qualitatively different from, but otherwise identical and hence miscible with all types of power. Thus, the phrase "all of the manifestations of the Real", embraces all manner of thoughts, the reader's inclusively; not inasmuch as those thoughts are philosophical, but rather in that they are a quality and manifestation of his power, and as such, are through him integral to the

---

6. PARMENIDES, *The Way of Truth*, (trans. Reginald E. Allen) in *Greek Philosophy: Thales to Aristotle*, London, Collier-Macmillan, 1966, p. 46. Anticipating Parmenides by several millennia one of the authors of the *Bhagavad Gita* in the "Song Celestial" advanced views similar to the Eleat's, albeit in a language more lyrical still. The words, attributed to Krishna, address Arjuna, the Terror of Foes.

> "I will not war!" he said to the Lord of Herds, and so made an end of speaking. And as he sat despairing the High-Haired Lord with seeming smile spoke.
>
> "You grieve over those for whom grief is unmeet. The instructed grieve not at all either for those whose lives are fled or for those who live.
>
> Never have I not existed. Never have you nor these princely men not existed. Never shall the time come when we do not exist.
>
> As the body's tenant (the soul) goes through childhood, manhood and old age in his body, so does it pass to other bodies.
>
> It is (only) the stirring of the instruments of the senses that begets cold ant heat, pleasure and pain. It is they that come and go and do not stay. Bear with them, son of Pritha!

Would that Plato, Aristotle and their heirs had paid more heed to the wisdom of their predecessors.

cosmic economy. In summary, Existence, a univocal fact and a raw material, comprehensively subsumes beyond subjectivity, the Real and, it follows, all phenomena, past, present and future.

6. Existence, a Fact and an Absolute

Some may still think that I exaggerate the difference between the present and other systems. While possibly allowing that its approach is down to earth and objective they may opine that the divergences, be they what they may, remain a question of vocabulary and emphasis; that, when all is said and done, this is no more than one system among many. Such an assessment, to be expected, is to a degree valid. It is to be expected because until a work is demonstrated to contain more than speculation, it properly fits in the catchall category of philosophy. It is valid to a degree because labor, invested for the purpose of decoding the mechanism of the Real, must technically be defined as a system, and for the same reason an automobile or a human body also fall in the category of systems. The reservation implicit in "to a degree" arises from motives simultaneously academic and physical. Academically, a system can rightly be considered as in a class of its own if, by incorporating one or several radical tenets, it offers more than a variation upon a theme. This criterion Dynamic Vision fulfills, for it incorporates several insights, each of which sets it on an independent course. Physically, an intellectual exercise becomes more than speculation, if its product operates — if it works. Again the parallel with the automobile applies. Anybody, even an imaginative child, can fool around with a stack of precisely machined pieces of metal and gears but, as a rule, the practical value of the conglomerate remains nil — just another collage. The effort acquires a new status if the pieces of metal and the pieces of thought, by being assembled according to a blueprint which conforms to the laws of physics, yields an efficient transportation or behavioral motor. Such a product, intellectual or mechanical, becomes a useful component of the cosmic economy. Whether or not this last criterion is satisfied can only be determined when all research is completed. The first, which requires solely that one or more radical tenets be incorporated, can be established at this stage.

Presently, only one such proposition, already touched upon, need be considered, for being a corollary of the principle What-is, is, it contains, embryonically, every other. This is the theory of the facticity of Existence, namely that Existence, as a sum and in its units, partakes neither of an act nor a passage, but is a fact and hence an absolute. That the individual Being constitutes a fact — in the strict sense — is a view apparently never endorsed. Parmenides in the dim past, Scotus in the 13th century, and Leibniz in our era, did take stands akin to this. However, of the Parmenidean doctrine too little has survived to permit a valid assessment. Scotus, for his part, while advancing a measure of univocity, remained committed to potency, a thesis which no amount of finessing can conciliate with Truth, let alone with an existential fact. As for Leibniz, his monad ambiguously depends upon a "material substance" of sorts, in which several "degrees of materiality" are to be distinguished. Also, time-space led him to entertain the notion of divisibility *ad infinitum*. Because of this subservience to dimensioned, divisible "matter", the monad notwithstanding, the Leibnizian universe is dichotomous. Aside from the above, and a handful of less well known authorities, in the opinion of most, the person remains some sort of active receptacle or pipeline — a "ground of Becoming", a vague "something which draws its substance from the other". *Generatio unius est corruptio alterius*, "the generation of the one is the corruption of the other" — the Aristotelians have affirmed for millennia, and to this day the immense majority concurs.

On this issue Dynamic Vision hews a virgin path. Without hedging, it deals with Existence as a fact, as an absolute, subject to no dimensions and quantities save that of the Fact-of-to-be and impervious to substantial change or evolution. To make a rash position rasher, it extends the same status to the Existent. Each of us becomes an independent motor and an Outsider in the full sense of the word. Power, as synact of Existence, is equally dealt with in its status of fact. The result is a clear break with tradition and a novel universe.

7. Rationale Upon Which Facticity of Existence Rests

Next in order is an exposé of the rationale upon which the facticity of Existence rests. The issue presents itself under two headings: the ontological and epistemological. Since basic premises are being established, in respect to ontological facticity the key factors only need be outlined. The same applies to the propositions of an epistemological character. Except for a statement of general principles, these are deferred to chapter VII of this Part in which absoluteneity (absolute-speed) and the quantization of thought-power are analyzed.

The position-argument in behalf of the facticity of the Real will no doubt appeal to the Positivist, but will certainly fail to convince a Radical Skeptic. This boils down to the bald statement that ontological facts and truths are never proven, only observed and/or accepted. They either *are*, or they *are not*. The problem ends there. Their existence and facticity or objectivity do not depend upon the knowledge of limited intellects. Further, they are immune to logic. Granted ontological facts can be doubted, but doubt, in their case, is not resolved by sophisticated syllogisms or dialectics, only by more accurate observations and/or a consensus freely given. The use of logicisms to prove an existential fact puts the cart before the horse, an error brilliantly expounded by Descartes, who failed to perceive that he had to be before he could cogitate, and that his cogitations proved nothing except that he could cogitate. In sum, the Fact-of-to-be precedes all else.

To those who agree with Kant that:

> ... it still remains a scandal to philosophy and to human reason in general that the existence of things outside of us... must be accepted merely on faith and that if anyone thinks good to doubt their existence, we are unable to counter his doubts with any satisfactory proof...[7]

---

7. I. Kant, *The Critique of Pure Reason*, Bk. IX (trans., Kemp Smith) Macmillan, 1953.

such a solution to the sceptic's challenge may appear simplistic and unworthy of the human intellect. Yet, as an objective assessment of the following three factors reveals, the "a fact is a fact" approach, when Existence or an Existent is being debated, far from being facile and a "cop-out" is the only coherent one.

A. every Existent, animate and inanimate, in its role of fact residing outside of time-space, in the As-is is at once transcendent and immanent; is at once an Outsider and a Cosmic-Presence.

B. each, as radical Outsider, enjoys an unqualified freedom, and

C. intellect-power, limited in scope, establishes aggressive, self-centered relationships with a perpetual Outside.

Even a cursory evaluation of the above, reveals that only one modality of proof is available to one intent upon proving the existence of a third entity and that this, while theoretically effective, exceeds the reach of man. An ontological process, it would involve the physical appropriation, by the individual towards whom the proof is directed, of the inneity or "substance" of the entity which the prover would attempt to prove as existing. Could such an operation be effected, that or It which was proved to exist, and the target of the proof, would become one. Under those conditions, proof could not be resisted, because the object of the demonstration would then rest in and flow from "within" the receptor. The catch? The operation required to achieve physical possession is inoperable. In return for their invincible outsideness, and consequent inviolable freedom, all Beings are restricted to a diet of relationships. *While we own our Selves in perpetuity, with the Other we can but relate.*

Next, if firstly, the relational character of any commerce with Outsiders, and secondly, the fact that reason is but one of the agents utilized by man to establish a self-centered relationship, are taken into account, the why of Existence resting beyond rational proof is revealed. A logical proof equals a relationship of reason, and rational relationships do not in one whit differ from any other. Relationships, no matter how persuasive or dominating, never breach the inneity and will of an Outsider. While the As-is of each Existent, i.e. its truthfulness, is always available to the Outside, these are not necessarily grasped by the percipient.[8] Biological and psychological factors enter into the picture, and are responsible for two types of circumstances, either of which wound and often nullify, the presentiality of all to all. Hence our inability, deplored by Kant, "to counter a sceptic's doubt with satisfactory proof". These circumstances are:

A. the intellectual limitations of the prehensor and
B. the obduracy and/or selfishness of the person to which the intended proof is addressed.

The sole exception to "A" is The Absolute whose power is absolute. Before Him, Outsiders stand naked, in utter subjection — their presence transparent and unquestionably proven. For the remainder of the community of the Existents nothing is automatically proven. Indeed the non-provability or negative zones, in every instance, greatly exceed the positive. A radical exemplar of non-provability, which the Cartesian hypothesis ignores, is that which afflicts an Existent lacking all power of perception — if such exist. To these, a lead atom or a proton, for example, nothing could be proven. They must be content with being and to blindly suffer the attacks, intellectual, chemical or other of the Outside.[9] The status of the sentient and intelligent is

8. On this point, Scientific Existentialism parallels closely the Critical Realism of Andrew Seth for whom "the conscious being cannot in the nature of things overleap and transcend itself; what we are directly aware of must be in our mind." Also, Locke's option of representative perception is in no manner allied to our common stand. Knowledge is not of ideas, but through ideas. Ideas are of the Self, and constitute a dynamic and qualitative possession of each Self which, to use Seth's words, "is a unique existence, which is perfectly impervious, if I may so speak, to other selves... The very characteristic of a self is this exclusiveness... I have a centre of my own, a will of my own, which no one shares with me or can share — a centre which I maintain even in my dealings with God Himself."
J. PASSMORE, *A Hundred Years of Philosophy*, Harmondsworth, Penguin Books, 1970, p. 279 and 73.
Such a transcendence in a Cosmos of immanence is made possible by the miscibility of Power and the concomitant relation of medium which each entertains with the Outside. Cf., sec. 4, chap. I, Pt. III.

9. The reservation, "if such Existents exist", is called for, for the scientist, regardless of discipline, has no right to dogmatize upon the inneal quality, the what-goes-on-within of Outsiders from other orders with which he has not learned or quite possibly not even tried to communicate. For instance, it is now documented that the emotional and the intellectual quality, extends to the vegetable realm as well as to animal cells or organelles. Also, the crystallization feat performed by the metalloids — by zincs or calcites — speaks of an

in this respect only relatively superior. These, witness a cow or ones teen-age son cannot understand arguments aimed at their blind spots, be the latter due to congenital deficiencies or to an emotional perturbation such as anger. To the blind one cannot prove redness, nor to the deaf the sound of a high "C". Non-provability zones run the gamut of phenomena and relationships. Even a Presence as overwhelming as God remains unprovable to otherwise well endowed individuals. Regardless of its relevance or visibility, in situations of deficiency, the fact of the ungrasped person or phenomenon or relationship, while present, continues unknown or unacknowledged. Even time-space impediments, in particular phenomena referred to as historical, differ only in quality. Because Tamerlane, who died in 1405, is not present to our Nows, today in 1979, the Calgary student or Northern Alberta fur trapper must accept the great Mongol either upon blind faith or circumstantial evidence. Granted, Kant's scandal is rarely seen as encompassing historical events, and is rather understood as arising from an inability to prove, through a debate or rationalization, to a recalcitrant hearer or unfriendly witness the "existence of things" within visual or tactile range. Again, closer scrutiny reveals the difference to be strictly qualitative. In the first instance, the blind lacks the power to accept proof, while in the scandal causing situation, the incredulous refuses proof. If a student's rejection of Tamerlane, or a Holstein cow's refusal to accept proof of the hypothesis of evolution causes no scandal, it is because our feelings are not thereby hurt. We understand why the Holstein does not respond, and are not inclined to make much of an issue of Tamerlane, being in his case ourselves restricted to circumstantial evidence.

Actually, this complex issue yields to the simple expedient of transcending time-space. Then the reason why the intellect is rape-proof becomes clear. *The rationalization (rationalizing relationship) has no hold upon Existence. The portion of the existential or cosmic mass possessed by an individual rests beyond the*

---

organizational technique which clearly rivals that of the anthill or the human city. At the very least, when placed before a phenomenon such as crystallization, the objective researcher must reserve judgement as to the extent of the thought of the Atoms responsible for it. Stated otherwise, we humans have no right, if we wish to maintain scientific objectivity, to categorically affirm that "Zincs do not think."

intellectual assaults of any aggressor. Each Existent, even the puniest, remains forever an Outsider, forever free. Each is, period. For a proof to "enter" it, it must "open itself from the inside", it must welcome or at least be willing. That unbelief should result either from blindness or mongolism, or from pride, anger or self-interest matters little. Objectively the outcome is identical. When the latter are at play, the individual wills to be blind or deaf and thereby renders a proferred proof, no matter how overwhelming, as ineffective as would be an attempt to convince a pet calf or stone Buddha of the desirability of sexual continence.

To sum up, non-provability, to this day, scandalizes philosophers, because the whole man is not considered. To prove is to aggress, to seek to penetrate the Other. Due to the facticity and concomitant inviolability of each Existent, no one possesses the power to so penetrate. Thus, to be unable to convince should offend only the proud who will not reconcile himself to the innate freedom of the next man. *To the inviolably free, nothing is proven. Rather, by it certain evidence is, for egocentric reasons, willingly accepted. This explains why the best method of proving things is an appeal to self-interest.* The introduction of self-interest releases a swarm of ethical issues. Some are dealt with further on. Most fall in the province of other disciplines.[10]

---

10. The radical freedom of the Atom, as Outsider, and its consequent imperviousness to intellectual assaults, is described in terms which require little comment, in these passages from *The Great Roman-Jewish War: A.D. 66–70 (De Bello Judaico)*, trans. William Wiston, New York, Harper & Brothers, 1960, p. 271-3. This Masada drama is quoted at length, since in it each of the points argued in this section, in respect to outsideness, is tragically documented. Note in particular the emphasis upon freedom to die and the alternative chosen by "an ancient woman, and another who was kin to Eleazar", who lived to tell the story.

> (383) We revolted from the Romans with great pretensions to courage, and when, at the very last, they invited us to preserve ourselves, we would not comply with them. (384) Who will not, therefore, believe that they will certainly be in a rage at us, in case they can take us alive? (386) But while our hands are still at liberty, and have a sword in them, let them then be subservient to us in our glorious design: let us die before we become slaves under our enemies, and let us go out of the world, together with our children, and our wives, in a state of freedom...
>
> (389) Now as Eleazar was proceeding on this exhortation, they all cut him off short, and made haste to do the work, as full of an unconquerable ardour of mind... Miserable men indeed were they! whose distress forced them to slay their own wives and children with

Returning to the facticity of the Universe, one finds that if ontological facticity, when entertained as a general principle, is barely debatable, so is the fact of the Universe, when defined as the sum of the That-which-is. Even the rankest Solipist is hard put to disagree. While doubt is rightfully entertained about an isolated fact, the Cosmos, observed in a massive, undifferentiated embrace, rests beyond doubt. The particular can be questioned. One may for instance, challenge the existence of Nero and chairman Mao, of Martians and angels, and maintain sanity. One can even doubt that ones father ever lived, and of ones own existence, in which case, mind you, sanity becomes suspect. However, to question the facticity of the cosmic mass implies irrationality. Presently only the fact of the Universe in its status of an undefined object is being posited. Processes and value judgements are left entirely out of the picture. At this point, some will retort that they also look upon the Universe as a fact. Certainly — the "fact of a universe" is accepted. And, to that extent, positions coincide. Nevertheless, such a community of views is superficial. Specifically, divergence arises when the time comes to investigate processes. Whereas the factual is allowed by just about everyone to dissolve, to melt into a sea of potency and of nihilating processes, *in Dynamic Vision the ontological fact actualizes itself in an absolute-speed process.* In it, the notion of facticity offers the point of reference from which all radiates and by which all is gauged.

---

their own hands, as the lightest of those evils that were before them. (395) They then chose ten men by lot out of them, to slay all the rest: everyone of which laid himself down by his wife and children on the ground, and threw his arms about them, and they offered their necks to the stroke of those who by lot executed that melancoly office... (397) so, for a conclusion, the nine offered their necks to the executioner, and he who was the last of all took a view of all the other bodies, ... when he perceived that they were all slain, he set fire to the palace, and with the great force of his hand ran his sword entirely through himself and fell down dead near to his own relations. (398) So these people died with this intention, that they would leave not so much as one soul among them all alive to be subject to the Romans. (399) Yet was there an ancient woman and another who was of kin to Eleazar, and superior to most women in prudence and learning, with five children who had concealed themselves in the underground conduits... (400) Those others were nine hundred and sixty in number, the women and children being withal included in that computation. (401) This tragedy took place on the fifteenth day of the month Xanthicus (Nisan) (May 2, 72).

8. Facticity Introduces Absolutes Into the Universe of the Real and of the Mind

Having asserted that existential facts are not amenable to proof, it would be ill-advised to thereupon set out to demonstrate as much. That would be to fall into the same trap as the Becomingist who spares no effort to establish as a truth or dogma that there is no truth, no dogma in his evolving world. After all a modicum of coherency must be maintained. The non-provability of facts does not, however, condemn the researcher to impotency. To the contrary, as Parmenides long ago intuited, the bedrock of ontological facticity is the researcher's safeguard or metaphorically, his best friend. Once facticity as this resides in the observation: *What-Is, Is*, is realistically and humbly accepted, then much can be learned through an analysis of its implications and operation — in particular, how it dominates epistemology. To note that facts and facticity dominate epistemology is an understatement. In the first instance, a factual universe, by providing philosophy with a delineated raw material, makes possible an empirical approach to ontology. Next, the introducing of the absolute and its modality: absoluteneity to science scuttles all traditional academic norms. This revolution is wrought through the Principle of Absolutes which reads:

> *The modality of the Universe and of its processes is one of absolute to absolute.*

Due to its importance, Absolutes, first principle of the Universe, is the subject of a substantial chapter — VII of Part I. It here suffices to note that absoluteneity and its principle are key factors in the cosmic process and that together they encapsulate the spirit of Dynamic Vision.

chapter II

Facticity and Absolutes, Answer to Many a Philosophical Controversy

Either it is or is not — (Fr. 8–16) What is (exists) remains the same, — held fast in the bonds of limit by the power of Necessity.

PARMENIDES, Fr. 8–29

1. Philosophy Provided With a Precisely Delineated Subject of Study

To state that a factual approach to the cosmic mass supplies the researcher with an accurately delineated working material, does not imply that the philosopher or, for that matter any scientist, can start off with a full grasp of his subject. Rather, it is to affirm that the proper scientific attitude presupposes a determination to respect the integrity of ones subject — in particular, this precludes any arbitrary addition or substraction to or from the working material initially chosen. Examples of unwarranted tampering would be respectively, the birth *ex nihilo* of an elephant and the vanishing into an imaginary void, of ones mother-in-law — at her death. Evidently, this lack of integrity is intellectual rather than moral. The guilty subscribe, in good faith, to an error which vitiates all their findings, namely Becomingism or the theory that Reality is a process. Under the concept of a processional Reality, shelter hypotheses as varied as an infinite regression, Aquinian potency, Whiteheadian actuality, evolution, Teilhardian or other, Hegelian dialectics and the derivatives thereof, as well as nihilistic Existentialisms such as Sartre's. Further, the condemnation extends to any cosmogonic hypothesis which rests upon premises drawn from the above, witness Hoyle's "big bang" theory. Regardless of the finessing in which the ontologist or cosmophysicist indulges, the error implicit in "substantial change" or Becoming, inexorably leads either to view Existence and hence the Universe, as an indeterminate. This view adopted, existential objectivity fades irretrievably, and the theorist is reduced to a diet of speculation, the skein of which lends itself to infinite unravelling, and a consequent evaporation of both thinker and cosmos, into that fool's paradise, the void.

Rightly therefore, the members of other disciplines who utilize as starting point a well-defined subject (be this the absolutized notion of Aztec ruins or of human eyesight), and thereby arrive at positive conclusions, are reluctant to admit to the scientific inner sanctum, philosophers whose entire output consists of verbalizations born in the nowhere from nothingness, and doomed to evaporate — nothingness in the nowhere. He who looks upon the mass of existence as constituting the Fact-of-the-Universe, finds himself in a different relationship both to Reality and the scientific community. *Located in the As-is, his reach extends neither into a dead past, nor a hypothetical future, but rather into the fibre of a vibrant Reality, cosmically present beyond time-space. Custodian of every particle and interpreter of the cosmic code of relationality, the cosmophysical philosopher takes on the role of banker to the scientific community.* His is the science from which other sciences, hat in hand, borrow their working capital — the one borrowing the firmament and its stars, and the other the human nervous system, etc. To one who languishes in the prison of time-space, sandwiched in the exiguities of an ever evanescing present, the affirmation that a fact, even universal and existential, is delineated and limited by its as-isness, may sound droll. The difficulty is real, and many pages will be devoted to elucidate the paradox of cosmic as-isness. However, one can presently profer the one observation which contains embryonically all nuances. This is: *any fact, entity, absolute or whole is pregnant of its full self, and, it follows, of the relationships and processes which fall under its aegis. This applies equally, to Existence as fact, or to a fact by definition, i.e. to a concept*, and is most true of the cosmic fact. As defined, Existence when dumped upon the cosmontologist's workbench, places before him the fullness of the That-which-is, including all of men's concepts, those related to dimensions, quantities and the temporo-spatial inclusively.

2. Modality of Absolutes, Transcending the Existential, Rules the Epistemological

The same remark applies to this section as to the previous. It is introductory. Not only does it concern the complex subject of learning, but it also introduces the principle of absoluteneity to the thought process. This, upon first encounter, may appear outrageous. Since a detailed demonstration is provided in coming chapters, judgement, it is suggested, would be best reserved until then.

Both the question and its answer are contained in the axiom "the speed of thought is absolute-speed". While such a proposition releases a swarm of controversies, for instance innate ideas versus coeval ideas, induction versus deduction, etc., consideration of these is deferred, to instead concentrate upon those aspects of absoluteneity and facticity which contrast an objective and absolutist epistemology with the conventional Aristotelian approach in which, logic and analysis are given precedence over Parmenidean empiricism.[1]

The axiom "the speed of thought is absolute-speed" is an inescapable corollary of the facticity of Reality. Existence, being a massive fact, constitutes a closed circuit or absolute, and an absolute's primary mode of relationship has to be that of absolute to absolute. The same logic holds for its constituents: the Existential-Atoms. Each, if it is to be It-which-it-is, must also be factual, i.e. an absolute, with the consequence that at the plane of the Real all relationships involve absolutes. Further, since consciousness and intellection manifest a quality possessed by certain Atoms, the thought process is equally dominated by absolutes. Hence the principle:

The modality of absolutes transcends the existential and rules the epistemological.

These two observations in turn predicate that:

the general precedes and embraces the detail.

On the surface this may seem an inoffensive reiteration of an argument often bandied about in the controversy over the sequence of the learning process. Reiteration yes, but inoffensive it ceases to be when interpreted existentially and physically.

When earlier it was emphasized that the Fact-of-Existence encompasses the Real beyond time-space, the existential detail,

1. Cf. Chap. VI.

dead or alive, was effectively embraced in the general. This same cosmic facticity, when introduced to intellection, reveals that the Universe *in toto* is present in the primordial intuition of to-be, which an Existent endowed of consciousness has — even though to the knower such knowledge may appear either as a deduction or as "part of the experience". The affirmation that each has, in-fact, his full universe present before him from the instant he is conscious, seems hard to credit. The mechanism responsible for this state of affairs will be dismantled and explained. However, even now its rationale is available. The moment one notes firstly, that thought is physical and secondly, that its range is cosmic, each of us, our thought-power inclusively becomes flesh of the flesh of the Universe. It follows that, due, not to an imperative of logic, but rather to the laws of physics, ones awareness of the Outside and the subsequent graspings of consciousness have, as initial reference, an absolute: the Cosmos, and the particulars and the constructive process generally are ontologically coeval; all are embryonic in an initial openness to the Real, no matter how faint, how blurred, as in, for example, the eyes of the foetus.[2] Thereby, even the highly controversed concept of innate ideas is exceeded. Ideas, it turns out, are, not only innate but coeval: firstly within the Existent and secondly as between all beyond time-space.

Such a thesis might prove acceptable provided it be restricted to the Order of the Real. This cannot be granted. While enemies, such as viruses and inner lassitude due to the degeneration of his bodily equipment, combine to give man a feeling of progression, of time and sequence; nonetheless, even in the Now of daily life, these sequences, this construction process, predicates a prior knowledge of the whole. *Knowledge never results from deductions which follow analysis. Rather, the Whole, the That-which-is, frequently imagined as discovered through a series of analytical moves, is present to the mind, albeit most vaguely, before the hunt ever begins. The fragments of knowledge captured, only come to render more vivid the embryonic, innate and immanent.*

The above challenges two quasi universally accepted dogmas: evolution and the primacy of induction; the first supposedly

---

2. Documentation of this thesis in the form of an analysis of the discovery or growth of the notion of intensity and maximization is found in sec. 3, chap. V, Pt. II.

accounting for ontological processes and by devolution the genesis of thought, and the latter for specifically epistemological operations. Evolution, whether ontological or intellectual is of no concern here. To a limited extent it is dealt with in Part IV, in the context of the broader issue of birth-death and cosmic peace. While a detailed refutation of the theory of the primacy of induction in the intellectual process also must be deferred, a brief encounter with it is warranted.

Of Aristotelian vintage, this theory achieved the status of a sacrosanct dogma when it received official sanction from Thomas Aquinas who stated it succinctly in the opening paragraph of *De Ente et Essentia*:

> Because indeed we must receive knowledge of the simple from the composite and arrive at what is prior from what is posterior, in order that beginning with the less difficult instruction may be made more suitably...[3]

To detect the error in the thesis that one proceeds intellectually from the "composite" to the "simple", from the pieces to the whole, one has only to consider commonplace events such as the building of a house or sexual urges and experiences. Sex and housebuilding, it hardly needs mentioning, belong to two distinct categories of phenomena. Together, they cover the entire learning spectrum, namely that of the so-called instinct and that of intelligence.

The coevality of sex knowledge requires no protracted, Freudian-like analysis of the sex appetite and relationship. This is acknowledged by everyone, most emphatically by the Aristotelians, who lay great store upon the theory of "instincts". Sex does not require teaching. It wells from the innermost fibre of the person. Indeed the innate and intimate character of the reproduction urge is such that it is commonly referred to as an instinct. Generally those who speak in terms of instinct versus intelligence, wrongly see the dichotomy as radical. For the present purpose it suffices to note firstly, that the sex instinct can be improved upon as, through experience acquired theoretically or first hand, new techniques and pleasures are discovered, and secondly, that

---

3. Thomas AQUINAS, *De Ente et Essentia*, trans. George G. Leckie, New York, Appleton-Century-Crofts, Inc., 1937, p. 4.

whether instinctual or pedagogic, an increased sexuality results not from external stimuli but rather from an inner, dormant pulsion which Outsiders only awaken, trigger and intensify. While the fact that the general precedes the particular is glaring where sex is concerned, a systematic and unbiased study of any psychological response confirms an identical sequence.

The lesson to be drawn from housebuilding, a more social and technical phenomenon, is the same. Assuming a dozen men of average I.Q., perfectly normal in all respect save one — they have no concept whatsoever of a house and of its usefulness — then, were the twelve provided with the materials necessary to construct a home, they could play with these till doomsday, yet never would there arise a kitchen to eat in nor a bedroom to sleep in. Going a step further and granting the unlikely, the same result obtains. Should the twelve, through a process similar to that often attributed to a hypothetical chimpanzee, who by a chance picking of the keys of a typewriter recreates the Odyssey, also end-up building a fine home, they, as the chimpanzee, would ignore their achievement. As for the chimpanzee the Odyssey would remain a non-event; so would the house built by chance stand unutilized and insofar as the lucky artisans are concerned, non-existent. Houses and all existential conglomerates achieve a meaning only if prior "residents" of a mind. All must include in their starting point the whole of the project at stake. The philosopher setting-out to investigate Reality is no exception. He also must encompass the sum of That-which-is before preoccupying himself with the detail, with parts and minutiae. Only thus can he be assured of not emulating the blind man in the fable who, taking the elephant's trunk for a snake, pronounced thereupon elephant to be snake. Consider now the reverse. Should a researcher into the Universe begin by saying with Descartes, "I think"; with Sartre, "I make myself"; with both, "the Universe is my construct"; with Einstein, "I am in curved space"; and with Spinoza, "I am a coordinate of the Supreme-Intellect", and was he not satisfied with this, but chose to indulge in biological, astronomical and geometric speculation lasting from now till judgement day, would he be better informed? Rather, would not his conception of the Universe, as more and more uncoordinated detail was piled-on, become fuzzier and the margin for error increase in direct ratio with the detail? Would he not indeed risk losing sight entirely of his objective?

That which applies to the mass of Existence, applies to an individual, if such an entity can be discovered, for presently only the mass has been identified. Assuming, subject to verification, that there are discrete Existents, then, until the sign of a particular Existent is authenticated, added particularities only create a wall of incomprehension between those attempting to communicate. The whole is not grasped anymore, only detail. For example, to affirm "Henry is", infers the fullness of Henry's presence, whereas to begin by describing Henry's nose, the cut of his clothes, his temper or height, enlightens no one. Granted, in the case of an individual the order or genus must be proclaimed. However, this, far from invalidating the proposition that knowledge results from a gradual disrobing of an innately sensed universal, actually strengthens it. In the case of a hypothetical Henry knowledge acquired of his manness, implies prior knowledge of an arche-type human unit or universal.

This precedence of the general over the detail holds even when acts are involved. To yell into the public address system at Calgary's Mac Mahon stadium: "a murder is being committed", will cause fears in the thousands present, more universal and deeper than: "Henry Smith of Balzac is being murdered". In the first case, everyone in the stadium would worry personally. Anyone's friend, mother or son could be murdered, whereas Henry Smith would probably be a stranger to most present.

To sum up, the philosopher, to proceed scientifically, must take a leaf from the geochemist's book. Just as a geochemist does not start by pontificating that the ore laid before him is solid platinum, and then proceed as an afterthought to assay, to end-up denying that platinum ever existed because he cannot discover any, so must the philsopher not pontificate or, worse, arbitrarily restrict his inquiry to such subjects as appeal to him. Scientific research thrives only in an atmosphere of open-mindness. This, when the universal mass is under scrutiny, implies a willingness to encompass, with utter objectivity, the sum of the Real. The whole must firstly be posited, for it, whether that of Existence or of a house, initiates all relationships. Predicates come second. All are instruments which the grasper uses to presentialize for himself the Cosmic-fact-of-to-be and/or such parts as he singles out as a focus for more intense involvement.

3. **The void and Negatives Ignored**

A first reward of such an approach — henceforth defined as Objectivism — is to assure the researcher of excluding initially no factor whatsoever. *An unpredicated whole being his subject, all avenues remain forever open.* An ancillary benefit offers itself. The void and its brood of empty-headed negatives, such as infinity, can safely be relegated to their legitimate as well as "logical location" : the nothingness of the nowhere. In other words, the scientist, by disregarding ontological negatives, is freed to deal with the positive. Negations are restricted to their proper status, that of logical or literary tools. Even the principle of exclusivity, foundation of Aristotelian logic, and the most useful of such, can be ignored.

The sacrifice is painless, indeed pleasurable, for nothing is lost by dispensing with the syllogistic approach to Reality — to replace it with an As-is or positive stance. To begin with, since an objective prehension of Reality places the Whole on the researcher's dissection table, any necessity to prove by negating vanishes. One need only proceed from one observation onto the next, unravelling the chain of relationships, much as an efficiently wound ball of yarn. Further, an open-minded attitude excludes nothing *a priori* and welcomes the unknown. This feature of Dynamic Vision is revealed evermore clearly, as one observation of fact constantly leads to another, the entire structure remaining receptive to all valid insights. In summary the cosmic empiricism embryonic in the Parmenidean position comes into its own.

4. **Some Objections Answered**

The inferences from the above put to rest the more salient objections raised against Existentialism. Nonetheless, two of the latter warrant mention, because each attacks Existence at its root and thus concerns this phase of the research. Also, the marshalling of counter-arguments throws an oblique light on the subject, while providing the landmarks whereby a Scientific Existentialism is distinguished from that of Descartes, Sartre, Heidegger or

Marcel. Kierkegaard is left out, because with the Dane there is no quarrel upon basics, and for as far as he went, namely to the boundary of the psychology of Existence as revealed by and in the human consciousness. So far so good; but the Universe exceeds the man-dimension. Indeed, no accurate understanding of man is possible save when he is perceived as integral, beyond time-space, to the Cosmos and therein as subject to Cosmic Law.

First in importance is the objection that to speak of Existence is to preoccupy oneself with naught, since Being represents an empty conceptualization. Some, arguing in the same vein, assert that we owe the "concept of existing" entirely to the intellectual process involved in banning the void from one's mind! The second, repeating somewhat the same charge, but zeroing in on a specific point, would forbid the "metaphysician" from seeing Being as susceptible to univocity and/or to equivocity. According to this school, Existence constitutes merely "an implicitly multiple object of thought", analogically attributable even to a negation!

A. *Existence is an Empty or at Best Metaphysical Concept*

The theory that to discuss Existence or Being is an exercise in futility, is valid; only, however, when either is viewed as an act and in particular, as understood by Heidegger or Sartre. Indeed, to apply unpredicated terms to acts or processes, even to a man surging out of the void, is meaningless. To say "walking", for instance, unless a predicate follows, is a waste of breath. The same applies to dying, eating, etc. The hearer can rightly affirm that, until advised as to who is dying or eating and as to how or where each act occurs, he is not interested. He who views "being" and by implication Existence, as a process, as a happening or worse, as a "something" issuing out of a void to re-enter a Sartrian nothingness (Thomistic animals other than man in this respect suffer the fate of Sartrian man), is justified in taking the same attitude as when confronted by any other gerund.

Revealing also, is the fact that Existence, even as a noun, retains its ephemeral character when considered an act. Semanticists and those who define philosophy as the science of language, might ponder this prime example of the vacuity of words and their helplessness to mold the Existential. Here one word leads a double life, humbly accommodating itself to the philosophy of the utterer. Of itself, the verb is impotent. The concept, the in-the-mindness rules. Those who would reduce Existence to an intellectual process, whereby one sets out to "exclude nothingness from about oneself", err. *Existence does not depend upon concepts such as "matter", time, space or primary building blocks composed of some exotic substance.* All such merely embellish upon the raw materials imagined by earlier philosophers, Aryan, Greek, or Hindu, in whose opinion water, fire, etc., were the primordial elements which Existence and, specifically life equated with Existence, came to inhabit. Rather, the Fact-of-to-be precedes all else. It embraces both the doer and the deed. *Existence is complete in itself.*

B. *Existential Univocity: the Worst Metaphysical Error*

The second objection apt to be leveled, albeit for different reasons, against Existence as described, relates to the first. It differs mainly in that it specifically attacks the key premise which must be posited once Existence becomes a raw material: namely, that Existence is an univocal fact, a something shared indiscriminately by all Existents. An accurate statement of the argument against the univocity and, by implication, the facticity of Existence, is contained in this passage from Maritain's *Existence and the Existent*:

> The worst metaphysical heresy is that which regards Being as the *genus generalissimum* and makes of it at one and the same time a univocal thing and a pure essence. Being is not a universal; its infinite amplitude; its *super-universality* if the reader prefers, is that of *an implicitly multiple object of thought* which, analogically, permeates all things... And when it (philosophy) treats of existence (it always treats of it, at least in some fashion) the concept of which it makes use does not display to it an essence but, as Etienne Gilson puts it, that which has for its essence not to be an essence.[4]

The above faithfully tows the Thomistic line, analogy *et al.* Some may counter that semantics only separate both positions and

4. J. Maritain, *Existence and the Existent*, trans. Lewin Galantiere and Gerald B. Phelan, New York, Doubleday, Image D 45, 1960, p. 42.

that, if "prime matter" or some similar concept was interposed between, Existence as analogical rather than univocal the disagreement would vanish. Not so. Generally, the argument against univocity can be traced to a desire, either to escape Monism or to reduce Existence to some sort of cosmic concept, which can account for and describe both the Real and the Perceived. In Maritain's case both motives undoubtedly operate. Monism can be ignored since not the slightest trace of it taints Dynamic Vision. On that score the ground is the same.

However, the gulf which separates Scientific Existentialism from the idea of Existence being a cosmic conceptual blanket, a notion clearly enunciated in Maritain's "Existence is... an implicitly multiple object of thought which, ... permeates all things...", is unbridgeable. If the proponents of this thesis were satisfied with the theory of "an implicitly multiple object of thought", the harm would not be irreparable. To add, however, "which, analogically, permeates all things...", makes a shambles of the philosophical science and, by filiation, of all disciplines. From then on the line which divides ontology from epistemology is systematically blurred, for the concept of analogy conceals a subterranean Idealism. Analogy, when extended into the Real is the supreme intellectual lie and the source of unexpungeable confusion. The Real, the "material", becomes inextricably confused with the concept. One, for example, is treated to such affirmations as, at the beginning of Aquinas' *de Ente et Essentia*, ... "being by itself is said to be taken in two modes... by virtue of this mode (the second) privations and negations are called beings..." Lest the reader think that 20th century Aristotelians and their kin have progressed beyond such confusion, the following quote from *Connaissance de l'Être*, shows existential analogy to be alive and well:

> Let us now consider a judgement of the Order of the ideal: (a + bi) (a − bi) = a2 + b2. Here it would seem there can be no question of concrete existence... We are indeed presently in the domain of the *being of reason*, ... Further we note two things; the *being of reason* is conceived within a mental schema which differs in nothing from that through which we conceive the real being...[5]

---

5. Jos. De Finance, *Connaissance de l'Être*, Paris — Bruges, Desclée de Brouwer, 1966, p. 38. (Translation provided by the author).

Having denied to Existence its sole, but paramount, role — that of cosmic raw material or primal fact, of which thought is but one quality, all Materialists must search for an ingredient, unambiguously concrete, which will share facticity with Existence. A hopeless quest. In any situation, there can be but one top man. The candidate for primacy in the Universe would have to supplant Existence. Was the usurpation total the problem would disappear. One could forget about Existence and concentrate upon its replacement; be this matter, thought, fire, water, or what have you. The out-and-out Materialists, in particular, the Marxists, come close to adopting such a stand and, were it not for other errors inherent to their systems, might have provided mankind with a workable cosmontology. Actually, Maritain and his allies rightly affirm that Existence is not a "thing". The victory, however, is Pyrrhic. Talk of a "thing" implies a hazy philosophical vocabulary — the connotation of "thing" being so general as to prove meaningless. Indeed, further analysis of the word shows it to be the quintessence of analogy, since "a thing" can be said of a house, star or mouse and, even of a concept, and simultaneously confirms that analogical semantics contributes nothing precise, nothing upon which to establish a fact scientifically. If this is true of words, how fatal must analogy be when its shaft is shot at Reality itself!

In sum, the argument against the univocity-equivocity team and in favor of existential analogy, stems from a misplaced sense of the Real. The case rests upon a scaffolding of logicisms, semantics and sophistry. Try as one might, with or without syllogisms, it remains impossible to vest Existence in a concept. The proper approach sees in Existence a *genus generalissimum* or universal raw material — that of the ontologist and cosmophysicist, exactly as copper ore is that of the geochemist — of which all Existents are univocally made or composed.

At this juncture, some perhaps will raise the spectre of Monism. Those that do can relax. While subscribing to the notion of a universal species; while also accommodating the idea of a "univocal thing", the line is drawn at a "pure essence", if "pure essence" implies an indivisible essence. *The uniform is divisible*. Herein the term *genus generalissimum*, means that an identical ingredient is responsible for the fact that a cat, lead atom, angel, martian or woman *are*. This does not endorse the concept of Existence as a monistic "something", subject to an endless recycling through internal transmutation or evolution *à la* Huxley. Quite the contrary. *Existence is cut-up into as many units as there are Existents, and each possesses in total equivocity, its share of the mass. Existence is at once univocal and equivocal.*

5. Origin of the Universe Not My Concern. Rather, Its Mechanism

Through the ages the question of origins, that of the Universe and of living creatures, has rated high priority. As examples, one can mention such landmarks of cosmogonic speculation as the Enuma Elish (the Babylonian Genesis), the Hebrew Genesis, the Hegelian scheme and in our day, the theories of Lemaître, Hoyle and others. In a break with tradition, only three brief paragraphs are devoted to the subject, their sole purpose being to make clear beyond questioning a total lack of interest in origins. What-Is, Is, and from a scientific point of view this suffices.

The rationale here is simple. Our raw material is the sum of That-which-is, or for short, the cosmic fact. Now, elementary logic has it that facts, ontological or epistemological, neither begin, change, nor end. Facts are, period. Of no other is this as true as of the Fact-of-to-be. Leaving therefore to others the legitimate but herculean and it seems hopeless task of discovering how it all began, I concentrate entirely upon the decoding of the mechanism of the Universe observed as a fact — the primal fact pregnant of all facts, that of the reader and my own.

In summary, while there are few authors with whom I disagree as fundamentally as with Lucretius and by filiation with Epicurus, where beginnings and the attainment of knowledge are concerned, I, in a general manner, endorse his sentiments as voiced in this excerpt from *De Rerum Natura.*

> This dread and darkness of the mind cannot be dispelled by the sunbeams, the shining shafts of day, but only by an understanding of the outward form and inner workings of nature. In tackling this theme, our starting-point will be this principle: Nothing can ever be created by divine power out of nothing...

> Accordingly, when we have seen that nothing can be created out of nothing, we shall then have a clearer picture of the push ahead, the problem of how things are...[6]

To this one might add: nor can anything be created in time or space; less still by the appositing of the Hegelian opposites known as "Being and Nothing which together constitute becoming". Each simply *is.*

Needless to say, the last statement stands in direct contradiction to the theory of natural and random evolution upon which rests the Lucretian cosmogony. The orderliness and optimism of the "universe which-is", is as sublime, as is stark and dismal that of the melancholic Roman Evolutionist, in whose opinion:

> The old order changes, yielding place to new;
> No man goes down to Hell or loathsome Tartarus.
> There must be matter that new things may grow.
> These, too, will follow you when they have lived their life
> Just as the things before you died, so die will they.
> Life's law still holds that thing must grow from thing
> And life is something we can rent, not own.[7]

The point of convergence is a common Objectivism, and insistence upon dealing with facts, even though the concept of "a fact", in both views, diverge radically. A factual approach to the Cosmos has the merit of introducing the scientific outlook and method to philosophy and/or cosmontology. The Evolutionist's "kitten chasing its tail" syndrome makes place for a systematic dissection of the Atom.

---

6. LUCRETIUS, *The Nature of the Universe*, trans. R.E. Latham, Penguin Books, 1951, pp. 31-32.
7. LUCRETIUS, *De Rerum Natura*, ed. Smith and Leonard, Wisconsin 1942, 3, 995, in Alan D. WINSPEAR, *Lucretius and Scientific Thought*, Harvest House, Montreal, 1963, p. 46.

chapter III

Monism or Atomism?

They (atoms) move in the void and catching each other up jostle together, and some recoil in any direction that may chance, and others become entangled with one another in various degrees according to the symmetry of their shapes and sizes and positions and order, and they remain together and thus the coming into being of composite things is effected.

SIMPLICIUS, *De Caelo*, 242, 15.
(Quoted by Cyril Bailey: *The Greek Atomists and Epicurus).*

1. Individuation: Is There One or Many Existents or Beings?

BEFORE us now spreads in utter profusion Existence: the concrete Fact-of-to-be. It lays in bulk. As yet nothing specific is known about it, nor has anything been posited. The only license taken was to define it as the Universe. The term universe adds or takes nothing away from the existential mass. It only simplifies the task when referring to it as a whole. We have, in other words, identified our raw material, in the process ascertaining its nature and circumscribing it as to extent. This may seem a minor achievement. A closer look reveals the opposite. *The Universe so circumscribed, provides the scientist with an objective starting-off base, pregnant of all truths and antropocities (subjectivities).* Furthermore, this avoids all dogmatism; such a universe remaining open-ended and receptive to any manner of facts and phenomena of which man, or any intelligent Being, may "in time" become aware.

At this point the next problem in order of priorities, is that of the one or the many. The definitive answer must be provided to the question: is Existence a monistic mass, or is there more than one existential fact, the sum of which composes the Universe? because the solution given to the issue of Atomism versus Monism will affect critically all subsequent findings.

The issue being determined, it is necessary to decide upon the method with which it will be examined. Due to its long range objective (the discovery of a physical particle) and to its complexity, it is proper to deal with it empirically. Whereas the debate between Monism and Atomism involves an either-or, Atomism itself presents the beholder with an intricate skein of suboptions, which concern the modality through which individuation is achieved. Presently these are left in abeyance, the logic being that initially the problem is not so much with the "how" or "what", as with whether or not individuation of any kind is detected within the Cosmos. Upon the question so restricted, the consensus is unanimous. At the level of daily life, everyone from ditch-digger to nuclear physicist behaves as though the Universe is not one entity, but is made up of many.

Ignorant or proudly disdainful of metaphysical niceties, Mr. Average Man thinks and acts as a genuine Self. He has not, in most instances the faintest notion as to why he so knows, still less as to what constitutes Atomism — the fact-of-being-an-individual; yet, intuition convinces him that, at the very least, he is an individual, an Outsider. Even philosophers, whose theories when followed to their conclusions, impose Monism upon their devotees, ignore the precepts of their systems. Pragmatic, they refuse to jump-off the logical cliff. Common sense dictates that they themselves are for real, and so is the cow in yonder field, and neither Plato nor Spinoza, or their own logic, will convince them to behave otherwise. For example, Santayana who saw fit to describe man's condition in the following gossamer-like and dismal imagery:

> I believe there is nothing immortal... no doubt the spirit and energy of the world is what is acting in us, as the sea is what rises in every little wave; but it passes through us; and, cry as we may, it will move on. Our privilege is to have perceived it as it moved.[1]

nonetheless was a dedicated champion of the individual and his rights. Even the Marx-Engels pair recognized a measure of biological-atomism. In sum, with the possible exception of the rare Solipsist, everyone subscribes, at least pragmatically, to some mode of individuation or atomism.

2. Individuation: What Does It Cut-up? Existence Into Existential-Atoms

An assessment of progress in the search for the primary building block of "matter" or ontological unit, reveals only two

1. George SANTAYANA, *Winds of Doctrine*, New York, 1913, p. 199, in Will Durant, *The Story of Philosophy*, New York, Washington Square Press, 1970, p. 494.

completed steps. The first consisted in defining the Universe's raw material; the second in joining the unanimous consensus that individuation of some sort is a fact. However, to agree that individuation is fact, without agreeing as to what is being cut-up, is a waste of breath. Just about every "Joe", philosopher and physicist, holds differing views on the question. Nor is the disagreement limited to incidentals. The divergences invariably center on fundamentals, with as result, a dividing of mankind into inimical camps, each determined to impose upon the other its vision of the human entity and destiny.

An analysis of basics traces this lack of understanding to the fact that ontological individuation has not been approached scientifically, but, rather with logic or intuition. While everyone rightly accepts individuation as a fact of life, many jump directly from that raw intuition to the assumption that they "know what it is to be one". Those who attempted a systematic investigation were as a rule satisfied with a logical demonstration, and have usually compounded the initial error by attempting to fit their assumed individual in a time-defined process known as life. Effectively, process is privileged over fact, and, it follows, no genuine individual human or other, is ever grasped — only a fleeting shadow. The outcome is disaster, for even the slightest margin of error injected into the heart of Reality breeds confusion and leads the coherent into the Realm of the Absurd.

The steps and experiments undertaken, in this and the chapters immediately following, are intended to correct the errors of method which continue to mar research into individuation. Two main features distinguish the present attack from the previous. The first, is a determination to go to the core of the matter and discover what primary individuation does cut-up. The second implies adapting the methodology of the natural scientist to the existential raw material, namely, to proceed empirically upon the basis of an assumption which subsequent findings may or may not confirm. *This assumption is that, if Reality does host real individuals, each real individual possesses his private parcel of the Real, in the radical sense of possession.* The terms Existential Atomism and Existential-Atom seem appropriate to describe the resulting new species of atomism and atom respectively.

Existential Atomism is primary. No modality of individuation can ever prove feasible beyond it. It comes to stake a claim to the as yet unoccupied extreme line on the atomistic end of the existential spectrum, the outright Monists having long ago occupied theirs. Its rationale, in a nutshell, is as follows. The Fact-of-to be, observed in a massive and unspecific manner, constitutes the raw material of primary science. This mass, for reasons of semantic economy, can be defined as the Universe. Preliminary observations reveal within it two main phenomena, one of movement and one of individuation. The latter manifests itself in many modalities, as witness a man, carbon molecule, river, nation or monkey. Individuation, however, does not mean the same thing to everyone. To some it partakes of the intellectual process. In the opinion of others, the discrete resides in as yet unidentified material building blocks, generally assumed or suspected of being uniform and energetic or energized. This last hypothesis has of late gained ground, due to the confirmation of it which many read into the twin discovery of the subnuclear particles and quantum physics. For complex reasons, the theories advanced to this day as to primary individuation are untenable. While admittedly treading different paths, all end up sponsoring an individual bereft of any "matter", "substance" or Existence to which it can lay *unquestioned* claim.

The Existential-Atom, whose presence has still to be confirmed, differs from atoms of other species in that it reaches into the very flesh of the Universe, there to cut-up on an As-is basis, the cosmic mass into a finite number of physical entities.

Since the Existential-Atom is physical, proof of its presence predicates that it be grasped physically. This in turn presupposes physical contact and experimentation. Before proceeding with experiments, additional data seems required. While the nature of the object sought is established, namely that of a primary physical unit, the requisites or criteria of individuation or atomicity *per se* are not yet clearly set-out. Indeed it would appear that the inability of science to grasp primary units is due to a failure to systematically establish these criteria. In short, one must know what one is looking for.

3. Individuation, a Key Problem, Coherence, Honesty and Daring Required

Since upon the problem of individuation depends the course of science, one must, as one focuses upon it, adhere to the strictest code of mental honesty. The precautionary measures necessary in any experiment to keep out foreign elements — to prevent contamination — must be redoubled. Verbal double-talk, even the slightest inclination to use logic as a wrench with which to bend Reality to fit a myopic anthropocentricity is to be eschewed. In particular, that logical, purely intellectual "What is, is", of which Bertrand Russell says that it is "impossible to doubt", must be made to correspond faithfully to the existential What-Is, Is. The moment conflict arises, the error must be assumed to originate in a faulty logic, or inaccurate data, and the existential granted precedence. *The philosopher is not called upon to build systems of logic for the mind to admire. Rather, his duty is to conduct experiments into the Real or Physical.* That insidious enemy of truth, intellectual pride, must be curbed and facts faced squarely. Time honored concepts and conventions, regardless of how sacred and commonsensical, if found empty of existential correspondence, must be unceremoniously garbaged. If, as an example, a reevaluation of time-space is required, let us dare to venture into whatever dimensions offer themselves. The loss can hardly be so damaging. After all, time as conceived by 20th century man, is a strictly helio-centered convention. New norms could possibly herald an era of undreamed progress. The same goes for the concept of "matter". If upon being subjected to the clinical scrutiny of the mindscope, this reveals itself useless, why be burdened with it? The It-which-is, and not time or space nor any intellectualization, such as "matter", constitutes the groundswell of Reality.

4. Individuation *per se*, What Does It Involve?

To the unwary, individuation presents little difficulty. That the reader *is*; that I *am*, and that the others which *are*, are distinct entities, appears a clear-cut matter, easily stated and as easily understood. Certainly, he would hardly expect to find it the most troublesome of philosophical issues: that of continuity versus discontinuity. Yet, it is also true that its mysteries are so glaring that every first year philosophy student spends many a heated hour debating them.

Close scrutiny soon explains this intractability. The Principle of the Proportionality of Extremes is at work. As ever, the simple is pregnant with complexities proportional to its apparent simplicity. In this instance the unique avers itself hopelessly entangled in an endless skein of limits, indeterminates and interrelationships. The more one struggles to disentangle oneself, the deeper the mystery. Then one realizes that, while it is easy to say, "I am an individual, a Being", it is proportionately as difficult to clearly delineate the "limits" of this entity or, to speak Aristotelese, to "locate its essence". That which at first hearing seems a cut and dried affair, soon disillusions the seeker. Whereas certain categories of units, the mathematical for example, are readily identified, and so remain, others are evanescent. Particularly elusive is the one type whose identification matters: the human. Human beings have an amazing capacity to overlap in time and space with other entities which reside in "their bodies", such as cells, viruses, metaloids, etc. Even as between men, due to the unstableness vested in "matter" and a factor commonly referred to as "spirit", the physiological and ethical boundaries are hopelessly blurred. For instance, the debate over the status of the foetus and its abortion (murder).

The first impression is the more accurate. In itself, individuation is clear-cut. It does not offer even the either — or options available when one must decide whether the Universe is a solid mass or a sum of entities. No in-between position offers itself. When individuation, conceptual or existential, lacks, there are no entities. There the tale ends. "I am not" or "it is not" are not alternatives to "I am" or "it is". It-which-is-not, is not a contrary but rather a naught. Concern, otherwise than for literary purposes, with any modality of no-it-ness, is a plunge in the nonsensical, and a sheer waste of energy. Hegel notwithstanding, individuation owes nothing to negation. To the philosopher, who under any pretext, seeks to integrate no-thingness, let alone a void, into his vision of Reality, the admonition of Parmenides still applies.

> For it is possible for Being, but not for nothing, to be; that is what I bid thee ponder. This is the first way of inquiry from which I hold

> thee back,...(Fr 6) For never shall this be proved that, things that are not, are. (Fr 6)[2]

At the Order of the Real, the individual or It-which-is constitutes the ground of Reality. Epistemologically the unit acts as fountainhead of truth and knowledge.

Actually, most do respect the facticity (immutability) inherent in abstract units such as numerals or logical propositions. However, when Existence, "matter", time, space, mind and the plethora of relationships which these create, enter into an existential equation, many get fouled-up. In an attempt at explaining away the overlapping of entity upon entity, embarrassing factors are arbitrarily excised from, and others whose sole redeeming feature is their cosmetic, face saving value are sneaked, more or less surreptitiously, into it which is either in-fact or, by definition, one. The mental honesty and accuracy exacted from a biologist are sacrified.

That individuation is a clear-cut matter, is confirmed by the generally accepted definition: "individuation involves the act or fact of making or being single or one". Since the above can hardly be improved, it is adopted, with one reservation, the inclusion of the term "act". *An act cannot be individuated. Its individuation occurs solely in a mind, and therein ceases to be an act, since it:*

A. *becomes an absolute, and*

B. *is subject to the speed of absolutes, namely absolute-speed.*

Provided this is kept in mind, the notion that "individuation involves the act or fact of making or being one" holds. Such a quasi-axiomatic character actually increases its pedagogic usefulness, since such nakedness renders more stringent the demands upon the intellect and imagination. The idea of "unit" fences the researcher within a corral of permanence, beyond which he is forbidden to stray. An existential or epistemological unit remains forever one. This noted, in respect to generic individuation, all is said. Here a logical question arises. Why over millennia has so simple a problem not been solved? Since, to all intent and purpose, this book is dedicated to the question, only an outline of

---

2. Parmenides, *Greek Philosophy, Thales to Aristotle*, (trans. Reginald E. Allen), Toronto, Collier — Macmillan, 1967, p. 45.

major factors need be considered. It would seem that those who have wrestled with the issue failed to master it for two reasons mainly.

In the first instance even that most primal requisite, a clear concept of the existential or physical "thing", It or oneness being sought, was, as a rule, wanting. Since metaphysicians and physicists, have quite invariably, operated behind a screen of evolving, swirling "matter", it could hardly be otherwise. Through this material mist none but the most blinding aspects of Reality ever pierce. The second, while bound with the first, is primarily psychological. Philosophers in general — and in their wake the cosmophysicists — lacked either the mental quality or the daring to break into new frontiers. Many, being congenital logicians, were prevented by that quality from penetrating beneath the surface of issues, as witness Bertrand Russell. As to a lack of daring, it has meant that those whose natural bent might have inclined them to experiment, to apply the scientific method to Existence until the inneity of the cosmic building block was firmly grasped, have, practically to a man, felt bound by the parameters of their predecessors. Particularly, the taboo against going beyond the secondary sense of sight was scrupulously respected. Such pusillanimity surprises. Philosophers and cosmontologists will allow, indeed expect, engineers and astronomers to dream far-out visions — to innovate outrageously. For their own account, mesmerized still by Aristotle's dogma that knowledge comes through the senses, they refuse to look beyond their noses. Content with logical deductions upon that which they see and feel in the four dimensioned time-space continuum, those concerned with individuation, many were not, as a consequence offered mankind only superficial observation based upon Now phenomena — an approach which culminated in the contemporary craze with Phenomenology or worse, with Phenomenalism. The sole exceptions are the Scholasticists, as and when preoccupied with the human soul. Then, a genuine existential entity was posited. An eternal soul, however, does not fit coherently in their system. Incorporated to satisfy the exigencies of Revelation, this *Deus ex machina* at the heart of Scholasticism largely accounts for the latter's wholesale rejection by the present generation, and for, in many instances, a concomitant loss of the Christian faith — due to a mistaken assumption that the

Christian world view is tied to a given philosophy. The above, let it be understood, does not belittle the efforts of those thousands who, toiling unselfishly and in sincerity, contributed to humanity's intellectul patrimony. Rather, it highlights the fact that without a solution to the problem of existential individuation, any world theory falls flat on its intellectual face.

5. Modalities of Individuation

If individuation and the concept of atomicity are so simple an affair, why then this on-going failure to discover the primary atom? Intellectual daring, a willingness to venture into the unexplored cosmic dimension of the existential absolute, has already been singled out as a precondition to success. A second closely related factor is a shunning of word solutions, of Idealism and the discovery of a new physical atom: the Existential-Atom, of which all other modalities of individuation are but secondary manifestations.

There has been a tendency on the part of philosophers to intellectualize the Real, to lapse into Idealism and Subjectivism, as distinct from getting lost in the process and evolution, and to thus vitiate all knowledge of the Real. The prime culprit responsible for the perpetuation of Idealisms of varying hues, is, it would seem, the Aristotelian dogma, subsequently refined by the Thomists, that Existence is not a fact but rather a general principle subject to attribution, by analogy, to concepts, to negations even. This excerpt from Aquinas' *De ente et essentia* sets out the error clearly:

> Therefore one should know, as the Philosopher says in the fifth of the Metaphysics,[1] that being by itself (*ens per se*) is said to be taken in two modes: in the one mode, that it is divided into ten genera; in the other, that it signifies the truth of propositions. Moreover the difference between these is that in the second mode everything can be called being concerning which an affirmative proposition can be formed, even if it posits nothing in the thing (*in re*); by virtue of this mode privations and negations are likewise called beings, for we say that affirmation is the opposite of negation, and that blindness is in the eye.[3]

3. Thomas AQUINAS, *De Ente et Essentia*, (trans. George C. Leckie), New York, Appleton — Century — Crofts, 1937, p. 4.

Once trammeled in those quicksands the battle is lost. One can, to extricate oneself from the initial ambiguities, talk of essence, signated matter, form, and potency, etc., until blue in the face; more pernicious still, one can plead and finesse analogy; forever the distinction between the Real and the conceptual will remain blurred. A worse case of the intellectualizing is Hegel's statement that: "pure Being and Nothing are the same".[4]

The issue is complex, and a host of contributing factors could be identified. However, the above exemplifies the type of intellectualization to avoid if the Real is to be decoded, and simultaneously contrasts the status of Existence within Dynamic Vision, wherein the word-concept: Existence, plays but one role, namely to picture a fact grasped intuitively and independent of all outside and/or secondary factors. Existence is an ingredient, a "substance" immune to the aggression of any Outsider. The preservationist would say that it has no known enemy, except the human mind.

With regards to the new category of atoms to be added to the list of atomicities, a brief survey of modern thought on atomism has some point and profit. In the first place, a survey of this kind can allay the skepticism of those familiar with subnuclear physics who may inquire how one can recede beyond the twilight zone haunted by the massless, chargeless neutrino, or that of his more elusive cousins, the quarks. Secondly, a listing of the major

---

4. The theory of dimensioned or signated matter and its corollary finiteness is explicitly expounded in this text of Thomas Aquinas, chap. II of *De Ente et Essentia*, (trans. George E. Leckie), New York, Appleton-Century Crofts, 1937, p. 9:

> "One should therefore understand that matter in any mode whatsoever is not taken to be the principle of individuation, but only signated matter (materia signata). And I call signated matter that which is considered as under determinate dimensions."

The discoveries of subnuclear physics, and in particular the convertibility of "matter" into Energy, should lay to rest the notion of finiteness (and infiniteness). Yet, "matter" bolstered by the "commonsensical evidence of the senses", still claims the allegiance of many philosophers and cosmophysicists, for the quest for the ultimate dimensioned building block of the Universe only serves to reduce in size, but not to eliminate, the massily dimensioned "material" unit.

modalities uncovered to date, will indirectly reveal the structure of the missing atomicity.

Lancelot Law Whyte's *Essay on Atomism* is admirably suited for the purpose, requiring but one precision. While generally our subject is described as that of individuation, and *Essay on Atomism* speaks of atomism, the difference is strictly semantical.

> In the broadest sense, atomism means the reduction of complex phenomena to fixed unit factors. This includes *epistemological* atomism, or the doctrine of units of perception; *linguistic* atomism, the use of an alphabet; *logical* atomism, the postulation of unit propositions; *biological* atomism, the assumption of discrete cells, genes, etc.; and various kind of social, *economic*, and *psychological*, as well as *physical* atomism, which is our concern here.[5]

Whyte's list is tolerably comprehensive. The qualification "tolerably", is used, for while his list does encompass all known units, it fails to include the prime unit: The Existential-Atom. Although one might assume that physical and biological individuation or atomism collectively encompass all of the Real, Whyte's text dispells such an assumption. Throughout, there is no hint of the univocity and discreteness of Existence, and where these lack, the Existential-Atom is absent. The physical and biological atomicities referred to, cover clearly restricted areas — namely, the "material" and animate realms. This is particularly true of the physically dimensioned atom, Whyte's main concern, which is conceived in terms of the physicist's ultimate and uniform particle, albeit not necessarily a "material" unit.

It may be argued that Whyte, possibly for technical reasons, ignores one or more atomicities. The point would be well taken, if *Essay on Atomism* was presented as a personal thesis. This is not the case. Granted, the author advances several truly perceptive personal insights, but the bulk of his work in consecrated to a chronological table of philosophers and scientists who from Pythagoras through Boscovich, to Heisenberg contributed to the development of atomic theory. In the author's own words:

> All that I have attempted here is to present for busy teachers, research workers, and students a brief introduction to the idea of

---

5. Lancelot LAW WHYTE, *Essay on Atomism*, New York & Evanton, Harper & Row, 1963, p. 12.

> atomism and its history, including a Chronological Table, and stressing the variety of the basic conceptions and their gradual transformation.[6]

The thoroughness of his research seems confirmed by the fact that the missing category is not found in other works on the subject. At best, the missing is vaguely entertained by some, only to be rejected for a multitude of reasons, all directly traceable to a refusal to abandon time-space — a barrier which even the Theory of Relativity balks at crossing.

Further, and it would seem conclusive confirmation that science still gropes in the dark after the primary particle can be read in this commentary, made in 1960 by a member of the Lawrence Radiation Laboratory of the University of California, at the time of the discovery of the omega minus:

> for a fleeting instant, one positive and one negative pion cling to the uncharged pion, forming a single unit. That unit lives for only 10 one billion billionth of a second. It travels only one 10 billionth of a centimeter before it disintegrates. But in the precise world of physics, this short life is enough to get a particle classed as "actual matter"... (shades of Whitehead's "actual entity") some physicists are playing with the idea that new found particles, such as an omega, may have complex structures of their own. Some experts suspect that there may never be an end of this process of peeling onion like skins from the mystery of matter...

As anyone conversant with the latest developments in subnuclear physics knows, 15 years later, the situation has, if anything, degenerated. Particles such as the muon or omega minus, being rejected as "complex rather than elementary", the chase is now after, "simpler things", "quarks" for instance. These, and here the quote is from a contribution to Scientific American (10-1975), by Sheldon Lee Glashow,

> may be truly elementary. Their "colors" explain why they cannot be isolated; their "flavors" distinguish four basic kinds, including one that has the property called charm... A solitary quark has never been observed, in spite of many attempts to isolate one. Nonetheless, there are excellent grounds for believing they do exist. More important, quarks may be the last in the long series of progressively finer structures. They seem to be truly elementary...

---

6. *Ibid*, p. 11.

6. The Existential-Atom or Primary Particle is Discovered

Coming immediately after two quotes which illustrate the fantastic complexities of the machine-instruments which have failed to isolate the elementary particle, the title of this subsection may perhaps strike as presumptuous.

Actually, the key to the discovery of the primary particle or Existential-Atom is deceptively simple. Success is predicated, firstly upon knowing exactly what is the object of the hunt and, secondly upon searching for it in the correct place. Contemporary physics and philosophies satisfy neither condition. All propound some measure of Becomingism, and no strict entity can susbist in a processional world. That the physicists for their part, ignore the very structure of the primary unit which they seek is explicited by repeated affirmations to the effect that their finds "seem to be truly primary" — the specifications of "primariness" being never provided, or at best, stated in problematical terms. The hopelessness of the task compounds when, next the search is conducted in the wrong locale: time-space. It then becomes a foregone conclusion that they will not, even by chance, locate their prey. Clearly, he who knows not what he is searching for and is in any case not searching in the right place, wastes his energy.

In a nutshell, the solution requires that instead of trying to fit the primary unit to the process, the Existent to the relationship, the process should be tailored to the unit. This implies:

A. discerning its nature of fact, of radical entity, and
B. decoding the inner structure, the radicals or yet the univerqualities which satisfy the criteria of existential or physical discreteness.

Only thereafter can the concern be with whether or not the primary particle is electrical, spiritual, blue, intelligent, massive or logical; whether it is endowed with "flavor" or "charm" or whether still its life span is 10 one billion of a billionth of a second or some 400 odd years, as the Galapagos sea turtle. The idea that the primary particle i.e. the Self of a human or uranium atom can be seized with microscopic tweezer in a cyclotron or in a Whiteheadian-like "actuality net", has to be abandoned. It is necessary to adapt, to the ontological science, the methodology of the applied scientist. Since, a primary particle and the reader, to be their selves, must both be facts and not processes or acts, it is essential to proceed from the assumption that this is the case.

Such an assumption can rightly be challenged, in isolated situations, but is not open to question when the sum of putative facts equal the cosmic fact. In the first instance, the facticity of the whole rests beyond doubt. In the second, while the researcher may not have the exact number of the units in the conglomerate at his finger tip, yet the "x" in the Cosmic Equation stands for a real number — if of course the Universe is atomistic. Stated otherwise, *once Existence reveals itself as a massive fact, it follows that if individuation is grounded in Reality and upon fact, then any real individual must own factually, i.e. permanently, a share of the conglomerate — a share, no matter how minute, of the Real. It is each such real-individual, which is categorized as an Existential-Atom.*

Since the concept of Existential-Atom is difficult to entertain, some elaboration seems in order. The first observation which made the discovery of the Existential-Atom possible was a mental compassing of the mass of the Real; the observing of Existence, all about, around and in the Self. Clearly one does not know, see or touch all of this mass. On the contrary, experience reveals that by exercising certain powers — to propel oneself outward, to travel or to draw others inward, as with a telescope — it is possible to alter its size, without foreseeable end. This for the humble creates no difficulty. Intellectual honesty leaves no alternative but to look upon the Cosmos — both the portion known, and that which-is, but lies beyond the reach of the secondary senses, as the ground of objectivity.[7] If next one is faced with real individuals interspersed throughout his raw material as raisins in bread; Presences foreign to the Self;

7. While on the issue of the dimension: "size of space" the dynamic way differs from the Einsteinian, it would seem that both end up at the same spot: at the start-off point. The similarity however ends there. For where the one speaks of relativity, the other speaks of presentiality. Such universes differ in that where the first is, even though unbounded, finite, the latter knows neither finiteness nor infinity. Rather its universe, a concept, describes a sum of dimensionless Dynamic-Facts, and hence has no more substance than the number 12 has in reference to a dozen eggs. Presentiality or Fact-of-being-present is the sole

Outsiders which cannot be possessed, then such individuation, if anchored in the Real, must by any standards, those of logic even, cut-up the cosmic mass among whichever Presences as do in-fact partake of the Real, the term "Presence" being synonymous with those of prime particle or Existential-Atom.

Any objection at this point has no rational basis, for the clause: "whichever Presences as do in-fact partake of the Real", leaves all doors wide open, save the one which leads to bare, raw existential individuation. The atomicities catalogued by Law Whyte, and such others as might be uncovered, are unaffected. To sum up, to the recognized list of atoms must be added one which encompasses all others: the Existential-Atom.

Such a step provides the common ground to be occupied by philosopher and cosmophysicist — their objective, the study of the Cosmos, being identical — for the Existential-Atom in its pristine state lends itself to having discovered in it any property which either discipline might uncover. Each, an entire Self, constitutes a blank, admirably malleable matrix. Due furthermore to its univocity (its communally shared identical "substance"), the Atom can be integrated into any existential equation, thereby making feasible the cross-breeding of disciplines, even those held to be invincibly separated by a metaphysical fence. This feature will become evident in Part II, once the miscibility of the synact of Existence, Power, is revealed, and with this, the immanence of each Atom to every other.

Finally the Existential-Atom pulls the last peg out from under conventional philosophy. Once the Universe's building block is identified, and found to be qualitative and univocal, philosophy loses its status of a metaphysics. Further, subdisciplines such as ontology, ethics, physics and sociology, all participate in the dismemberment — each walking away with its particularized fief,

---

dimension, and the ground of presentiality is owned power. Consciousness is but a quality, and the sense of direction or space but a secondary modality of exercised consciousness. This is readily ascertained even in everyday life. Through a telescope or field-glass it is possible to visit with neighbors, be these a hunter across the Blaeberry River valley in British Columbia or Orion in the far reaches of space. In either case increased eye power does the trick. Where the body is involved the same situation prevails. The body is not man any more than are the light-photons through which eyesight is exercised; rather it constitutes a focus of intense relationships.

its herd of tailor-made pseudo existents, its private brand of Antropocities, the one with its *être-de-raison*, the other with its *être-de-mathématique*, etc., all down the length of the analogical highway. It was this observation which prompted the statement in the first chapter that philosophy, or still cosmontology, closes its books with the formulation in chapter IV, of the Universal Equation. Setting aside this controversial thesis, it remains that a common denominator such as the Existential-Atom provides all disciplines with an identical raw material, and yet permits each to retain full sovereignty. This of itself constitutes a breakthrough on the road towards a unified world view.

Having remarked upon the similarity between the Existential-Atom and the "primary building blocks of the Universe", it is essential to indicate the radical manner in which they differ. Granted, both share the property of primary units. Yet, the difference between them exceeds that between night and day — being not one of degree, of darkness but of fact versus process. The mythical Democritan-like building block is seen as empty of quality, as a sterile matrix, and yet enabled to produce all qualities — somewhat as out of a cosmic magician's hat, simply through a haphazard combination and agglomeration, two roles evidently incompatible. One cannot be at once barren and fertile. The Atom, on the other hand, is well equipped for the task. Initially endowed with the fulness of its Self, self-sufficient and an absolute, in that nothing can be added to it, it concretizes, in the literal sense, the Parmenidean It-which-is. Two entities more different, cannot be conceived.

7. **Summary**

Subject to elaboration, one can sum up as follows. *There are but two generic modalities of individuation: the existential and the conceptual.* Every other, as witness the biological (man) and the chemical (iron atom), represent qualitative distinctions within either — in the above cases within the existential. This latter encompasses all Atoms — any It truthfully one. An Existential need not be animated, but its oneness can be neither of its own making, nor that of an outside agent. Its status is that of a fact — one of a multitude which together constitute the massive fact known as the Universe. Relevant also, is its objectivity. The

Existence vested in an inanimate, as in some lonely iron atom lost in the heart of the Andromeda nebula, which is unaware of itself, and of whom all other Atoms would be equally unaware, is real. Thus, its exceeding value. Each, even the puniest, is ground of Reality and a possessor and conveyor of Truth. Also, each becomes an integral and critical factor in the cosmic economy.

The existential having staked-out so comprehensive a jurisdiction, the conceptual is relegated to the relational and/or qualitative, and denied the right to reification. For, *while a concept can "materialize", as in an automobile or a rock, its unity resides solely in someones mind. A rock is not a Being (Atom) but rather, a subjectively dimensioned absolute (Antropocity).* Such Antropocities, defined generically as existential-conceptual-absolutes [8], forever remain a mere intellectual factor in the cosmic process. The same applies to value concepts such as proletariat, liberty, evil, one thousand or nation. In their case, greater care must be taken, firstly not to adulterate the original definition, and secondly to avoid reification. No concept should ever be transmuted into "things" — as is too often done in our ideology-oriented society where liberty, for example, a subjective and normative appetite, rates the status of a god. The danger in the reification of conceptuals, be these nation, church, proletariat or revolution, is that the reified inevitably becomes identified with the reifier. The worst dictatorships are imposed in the name of such man-made gods. Two tragic examples are the Hitler tyranny justified in the name of racism, and the Stalin abomination wrought in that of class warfare.

With respect to the structure of either mode, nothing of consequence need, at this point, be added. Individuation as noted, is simplicity itself. Whether fact or phenomenon the same criteria apply, namely, those of unicity: indivisibility and integrity.

8. The Existent and Its Metamorphoses: The First Into an Existential-Atom

A passing reference was made to the metamorphoses which the Existent would undergo. The notion of an existential metamorphosis was perhaps the cause of some perplexity. The first

8. Cf. secs. 3 and 5, chap. VI, Pt. I.

being completed, elucidation will therefore be welcomed. The term, herein, assumes a more literal connotation than one would surmise. A closer look at the progress to date confirms this.

In most cosmologies the Existent, specifically man, makes its entry upon the scene fully matured. Generally, save for speculation upon the operation of the intellect, little effort is devoted to understanding its inneity or mechanism. The procedure herein opted for is well-nigh the antithesis of this. To begin with, Existence is seen as a raw material, homogeneous or univocal. The applying of the term Existent to any portion of this mass, could only yield an embryonic entity. So it did. The type of Being which initially offered itself was nondescript, its identity couched in terms so general that it could be equated with an Aristotelian, Leibnizian, Santayanan or Whiteheadian Being.

This philosophical ecumenism was however rudely brought to an end, when both Existence and the Existent averred themselves facts. Whereas an act or process, cannot be anatomized — acts and processes merely describe relationships, and are not amenable to scientific analysis — facts invite dissection. Thus one could expect, as one ventured into the Existential-Atom's entrails, to find that it, which was shrouded in mystery, would reveal hitherto obscure facets of itself. This happened. As the dissection proceeded, the Atom underwent transformations profound enough to typicalize it or, to use a biological term, to operate a full-fledged metamorphosis.

By the end of the experimentation, the Existent will undergo three such metamorphoses. Since each successive revelation is more striking than that evidenced by the jump from a nondescript, ecumenic Existent to a factual Existential-Atom, the aptness of the idea of metamorphosis, as applied to an original Existent, seems acquired. Certainly, each transformation is as radical as that operated upon a caterpillar when the latter passes from the state of pupae into that of a winged butterfly or moth. Here are, briefly outlined, these existential metamorphoses. The original Existent, whether animate or inanimate — lead or orange tree, man or muon — having progressed beyond its first metamorphosis, that of an Existential-Atom, finds itself transformed into a Dynamic-Fact. Beneath the grey garb of the Dynamic-Fact, lurks a more complex beast. Depending upon the Order in which it is situated, the Existent appears as either a One-Intense (Order of the Real) or a Free-Efficient (Order of the Perceived). Respectively, these correspond to a maximized act and an aggression-prone, efficiency-minded individual. Its ultimate state, relatively uncomplicated, is that of a Presence in the fullest sense — an immanent Cosmic-Presence.

chapter IV

The Universal or Cosmic Equation

Are not two sparrows sold for a penny? And not one of them falleth to the ground without your Father. But as for you, the very hair of your head are all numbered.

St. Matthew, 10: 29-30

THE UNIVERSAL OR COSMIC EQUATION

After a few brief chapters, it may be thought presumptuous to present the equation of as comprehensive and intricate a structure as the Universe or Cosmos. Actually, when reduced to its basics, the subject is not as complex as normally assumed. Presently we are concerned solely with Existence, the raw material of the Universe, and with the problem of its individuation. Clearly, if this is to prove genuinely divided, individuation must physically cut it up into a fixed number of individuals. Any structure falling short of this, would not individualize existentially. When approached thus, the problem becomes of disarming simplicity. Having a mass of Existence upon which to experiment, and having chosen to see this as individuated, there is no alternative but to find that each individualizing factor, each Existential-Atom, in-fact, owns its portion of the mass. Once the above data is available, a single step establishes the equation accounting for the cosmic mass. With U standing for the Universe, E : A for the Existential-Atom and X for an unknown but finite number, this reads:

$$U = X\,(E : A)$$

In view of the novelty of a Cosmic Equation, several remarks in respect to its import and handling seem in order. Should it remain restricted to the realm of pure theory or speculation, at that level it would provide revolutionary insights into the basic structure of Reality. As its practical applications gain broader acceptance, its impact on the applied sciences should prove farreaching. Because it includes an unknown "X" factor, some may question its usefulness. Such fears are groundless. The fault lies not with the Equation. The human intellect and its limitations is the culprit. The exact number is there. It is man who is unable to compass it. Granted, the myriadic complexities which man's analytic mind discovers in an otherwise unitary Cosmos, precludes forever the elimination of X. Yet, reduced to its minimal level, this unexpugnable indeterminacy is no more fatal to equations of a social, ideological or economic character, than the same factor is to the equations of the nuclear physicist. Equally groundless are objections of those who pose a universe founded upon the Democritan theory, with its cosmos cut-up into dimensioned atoms, each neatly localized in space and strung out as some monster latice in time. Adimensionality and its unnerving corollaries apply even to the photon. In this instance, however, intellectual limitations are not to blame. Rather, the dimensionless nature of each Existent and its total interpenetration by every other (two aspects of the Atom yet to be investigated), are responsible for the fact that the Equation only operates beyond man-devised dimensions, and in an atmosphere of quality-intensity.

These handicaps notwithstanding, the Universal Equation is called upon to exert beneficial effects in many ways. To begin with, it delineates the Universe, uplifting it from the status of a will-o'-the wisp-like concept to that of the all-encompassing object. This insight, in particular, should work to imbue the philosophical fraternity with an increased sense of accountability. As indicated, philosophers have rarely respected the duty which all scientists have of accounting for the ingredients which they juggle. Unable to free themselves from the spidery web of "change", most are content to embroider the existential cloth with a multihued thread called logic, embellishing their masterpieces with the odd gem of poetized imagination. The product may be dazzling when the content of fantasy, as in Teilhard or Hegel for instance, ends up out-shining, quite possibly intentionally, an otherwise wobbly infra-structure. As was to be expected, the concrete results have been meagre. Thus, a Universe composed of a fixed number of Atoms and its Equation should prove a boon for those philosophers whose natural inclination would lead them to respect accuracy, but who, being denied the mooring upon which to tie their ship, bob about on the waves of movement, potency and act.[1]

The benefits of ontological facticity, as enshrined in the Universal Equation, are not restricted to ontology. Psychiatry, sociology and ethics, stand to achieve a more balanced perspective of the Cosmos and of man's role in it, once these are provided a firm foundation upon which to build, and are freed from the influence of a dichotomous, "spirit-matter" vision of the world.

The same remarks hold in respect to ontology's twin, cosmos-physics, subnucleonic as well as astral. By and large, the accusation of tampering with facts levelled against philosophers does not apply to the physicists, who always insist upon the conservation of matter or alternately, upon the conservation of energy. Witness the statement of W. Heisenberg:

> Then I noticed that there was no guarantee that the new mathematical scheme — (quantum mechanics) — could be put into operation without contradictions. In particular, it was completely uncertain whether the principle of the conservation of energy would still apply, and I knew only too well that my scheme stood or fell by that principle.[2]

While therefore, physicists may find the stress upon accountability "old hat" and congenial, it seems that nonetheless the Equation can serve them well. Their ultimate objective, a unified world view, is brought closer once the dichotomy between "spirit" and "matter" is exorcised by a Cosmic Equation whose every unit possesses an identical structure — quality and intensity alone serving to distinguish the humanoid from the neutron, the metalloid from the Absolute-Atom, God. Instead of having to cope with relativating fields they are introduced to a stable, yet

---

1. A Cosmic Equation and the moral obligation which the scientist, ontological or otherwise, has to keep an honest set of books, are both implicit in this affirmation of Jesus Christ:

> Are not two sparrows sold for a penny? And not one of them falleth to the ground without your Father. But as for you, the very hair of your head are all numbered.
>
> St. MATTHEW, 10, 29-30

2. Werner Heisenberg, Physics & Beyond (trans. Arnold J. Pomerans), New York, Harper & Row, 1971 p. 61.

dynamic Cosmos, wherein each type of phenomenon harmonizes with every other, and where each Atom retains its unity, quality and integrity.

Finally, the validity of an assumption in respect to the Existential-Atom and of the Equation which it makes possible, must be established. This is disposed of by stating that it will be, and that the Equation, by itself sterile, will be cured of this defect once a code of Cosmic Laws becomes available. The Equation is still in its most rudimentary formulation. This could not be otherwise since, as yet, nothing is known about the Real save that its individuation seems a reasonable assumption and, if there is individuation, each unit constitutes an absolute. As one penetrates into the core of the Atom, witnessing with each step a metamorphosis, it will become feasible to reformulate it to take into account each new factor.

chapter V

A Question of Orders; that of the Real and that of the Perceived

The rose that with your earthly eyes you see, has flowered in God from all eternity.

Angelus SILESIUS

My religion consists of a humble admiration for the illimitable superior spirit who reveals himself in the slight details we are able to perceive with our frail and feeble minds. That deeply emotional conviction of the presence of a superior power, which is revealed in the incomprehensible universe, forms my idea of God.

A. EINSTEIN

1. Ontological Orders, General Remarks

SINCE every major scientific issue is linked to the question of the demarcation line between the Orders of the Real and that of the Perceived or Now, or alternately between the Order of Truth and that of Knowledge, the present investigation is restricted to basics.[1]

Because there is only one Reality, there is only one "real" Order: that of the Real and talk of two or more orders involves exactly that: talk and nothing else. This admonition is necessary to prevent any statement which follows from being interpreted as an endorsement of any form whatsoever of existential dichotomy, specifically that implicit in a Cartesian split-level world of "mind" and "matter". Each Atom shares univocally in a common raw material, and each is integral to the skein of cosmic relationality. Discernability being a function of quality-intensity, each whether man, flea or iron, differs from the other in quality only. Presently, the concern is therefore with quality and specifically with that known as intellect-power or for short, intelligence.[2] Because man's intelligence is not absolute, but can nonetheless conceive of the Absolute and is equipped to deal with absolutes, his knowledge of the Absolute corresponds to the Order of the Real, (identical for everyone), while through his play with

1. The terms: Order of the Now and its abbreviated form the Now are occasionally substituted for Order of the Perceived and the Perceived. Each member of both pairs is interchangeable. To the extent that a distinction is to be made, *Perceived* pertains primarily to the epistemological and *the Now* to the relational and lived.
2. Re: quality, cf. chap. VI, Pt. II; re: intensity and Power, cf. chaps. I, II, and III of Pt. II.

conceptual-absolutes (Antropocities) each human creates his personal Order of the Perceived or Now.

2. The Order of the Real: Order of the What-Is or of Truth

If the impossible were to occur and the Order of the Real should become personified it would no doubt describe itself as That-which-is; declare its name to be Objectivity, and claim as aliases Reality and Truth. Such an event will never happen. The Order of the Real is only a concept and concepts never speak, fight or breed. They merely reside in thinking Atoms, of which they constitute an integrant. Effectively, the concept of an Order of the Real, speaks of an abstraction which encompasses the sum of the Existential-Atoms resting beyond all time-space dimensions. Its role is that of epistemological substitute for the vaguer term of Universe.

The initial reaction to the above, may perhaps be to situate the universe of Dynamic Vision in the category of mind-dependence universes. *Grosso modo*, such an assumption is correct. Yet, Dynamic Vision differs from such on several substantive points. It does, for example, have a close affinity to that of A. S. Eddington for whom "Events do not happen; they are just there, and we come across them"; or to that of H. Weyl for whom: "the objective world simply is, it does not happen". It also shares many characteristics with A. N. Whitehead's *Process Universe*, of which the author affirms:

> But no two actualities can be torn apart: each is all in all. Thus each temporal occasion embodies God, and is embodied in God.[3]

These and others of the same lineage, in particular the Leibnizian, have much to commend them, for each in its way testifies to a sense of ontological honesty. None, however, accounts faithfully for all of the Real, for the simple reason that their authors lacked a clear understanding of what a Fact-of-to-be consists of. Indeed, except for Leibniz, none evidenced a profound awareness of the crucial importance of the ontological particle to the developing of a sound cosmontology.

---

3. Alfred NORTH WHITEHEAD, *Process and Reality*, New York, The Free Press, 1969, p. 410.

The vision which unfolds in the coming chapters, being free from evolutionary Becomingism as well as of Determinism, simultaneously balances the cosmic ledger and unifies the disciplines through a common code.[4] As noted previously, two simple discoveries, make this possible: That of the Existential-Atom and that of the Principle of Absolutes with its corollary of absolute-speed. The contribution of Absolutes to epistemology is all-embracing. It at once provides an understanding of the modality of the Real and the insights needed to decipher the mechanism of the Perceived. One could say that it manufactures and molds the raw material of the Perceived — to the extent that thought-quanta can be referred to as a raw material. In view of Absolutes' relevance, the remaining paragraphs of this overview can be advantageously devoted to a brief exposé of its rationale and operation.

The Existential-Atom, we have seen, is a discrete unit, an absolute in perpetual possession of its private parcel of the Cosmos. The latter, being the conglomerate which encompasses the sum of these discrete, adimensional motors is therefore one-dimensioned and bathed in absoluteneity. It, whose every unit is an absolute, itself constitutes an absolute, and since absolutes can only relate absolutely, the modality of both the units and the conglomerate becomes one of absolute to absolute. Hence, Absolutes, Prime Principle of the Universe:

The modality of the Universe and of its processes is one of absolute to absolute.[5]

Mindful of its paramountcy, the Principle of Absolutes extends its sway to rule over Energy. Reformulated, Absolutes then reads:

The state of the Universe is one of maximum tension.

At this point the synactivity of absoluteneity with maximization appears, and the deeply qualitative character of Existence is bared. For, the germ of quality, detected implicitly in unicity or absoluteneity, is explicitly affirmed in maximization, this being

4. For the text of the Cosmic Code's two Principles and five laws refer to chap. II, Pt. V.

5. The phrase Prime Universal Principle, subject of the next chapter, for reasons of semantic economy, is frequently abbreviated to Absolutes.

synonymous with the ultimate in qualitativity. The maximized of necessity manifests the ultimate degree of every facet of its Self. The relevance to cosmontology of absoluteneity-maximization is primordial. Aside from resolving a host of secondary issues, we are indebted to it for a definite understanding of the relationship of the Real to the Perceived, or alternately of Truth to Knowledge. Of the secondary issues which it solves, two, causality and the paradox presented by immanence in transcendence, have a direct bearing upon our topic.[6]

Absoluteneity-maximization readily exorcises the problem of causality and its spectre, determinism. In an absolute-speed universe, whose state is one of maximization, causality in the conventional sense, has no meaning. No one is before-and-after the other. All simply are, each being a Cosmic-Presence. Thus, real-relationships involve not causality but corresponsibility. In a medium of absoluteneity, each self-contained Atom is a free agent whose responses to the pressures of the Outsiders contribute to their mutual self-realization. A clear appreciation of the latter allows one to view causes and effects and the scandalous situations which these often precipitate, in their correct perspective. Both involve only special Now situations — each constituting an Antropocity; which is to say, an absolutized knot of relationships, subjectively assessed.

The absoluteneity-maximization team resolves with equal ease one of the Materialist's bedeviling paradoxes: the incompatibility of immanence with transcendence, or conversely of the discontinuous in the continuous. In a conglomerative Universe of univocal Atoms whose common characteristic is quality-power, the conciliation of transcendence with immanence poses no problem, for, in such, power and quality mix and blend indiscriminately. Concepts such as nothingness, infinity, space, time, negation, etc., become either meaningless or at best, subjective — with a meaning only in the perceiver's private universe. In the Real, all of us, man, mandrake and muon, simply *are* in-fact a Cosmic-Presence, each to everyone.

Summing up, the Order of the Real reveals to the beholder a one dimension universe: that of Existence or the Fact-of-to-be.

---

6. Re: Maximization, cf. secs. 2, 3 and 8 of chap. V, Pt. II.

In it, all relationships are cosmic. Subject to the rule of Absolutes, its real speed is that of an absolute, i.e. absolute; and its modality, one of maximized presentiality. One could say that each Atom in-fact bathes in every other, and is a Presence in the fulness of itself — beyond time-space. Such are the realities, rules and vision of the Order of the Real.

3. Order of the Perceived-Now or Alternately of Knowledge

If one could with conviction affirm that the Order of the Real would never speak, the proposition is by no means as clear where the Perceived is concerned. Indeed, an excellent case can be made that the Perceived is perceived only when it does speak, when it does signify itself. For the Perceived or Now governs the subjective. Hence, it can rightly be argued that firstly, there are as many such orders as there are perceptive Atoms, human and other, and that secondly, each takes on a meaning only to the degree that it is signified by its creator. Signification in this context is not restricted to the spoken word. It encompasses all modalities of assertion or witness, and always carries an element of aggressivity. Further, perception is a two-way street. *There is not a perceiver and a perceived, but rather two or more perceptants who self-realize by mutual presentialization.* In summary, each creates and owns his personal order — a private preserve which he shares completely only with The Absolute for whom all is present.

Those who are familiar with mind-dependence theories will observe that to the Perceived so defined, the same general comments apply as did to the Real, when the latter was situated within the category of mind-dependence theories. Subject to the reservations called for by the reference to "continuous(ly) changes in time", the following paragraph by H. Weyl, the first sentence of which was quoted in section 1, is accurate.

> The objective world simply is, it does not happen. Only to the gaze of my consciousness, crawling upward along the life-line of my body, does a section of this world come to life as a fleeting image in space which continuously changes in time.[7]

---

7. H. Weyl, Philosophy of Mathematics and Natural Science, Princeton, 1949, p. 116.

The subject is complex, and since it is dealt with in the two coming chapters, the present outline is limited to an enumeration of the key factors which together provide an understanding of the mechanism of perception, and simultaneously place in relief the divergences between conventional mind-dependence and Dynamic Vision.

The key to the deciphering of any code, be it that of the Universe, of the KGB or of perceptivity, is the discovery of the entity involved in its operation. Where perceptivity is concerned, the unit happens to be the thought-quantum. *A concept*, in other words, *is composed of a fixed number of quanta or bits, similar to those used in a computer.* The nature and operation of thought-quanta is readily established with the aid of the Existential-Atom and the Principle of Absolutes. The role of Absolutes where perception is concerned, is the following. Because of Absolutes' sovereignty over the Real, when the Perceived comes to claim a raw material of its own, it must settle for one upon which the stamp of Absolutes is indelibly imprinted ; namely the absolutized percept or thought-quantum. Each of these can be compared to the frames in a motion picture.

The role of quality is equally easy to discern. Quality, the factor through which analytical concepts are reunited or synthetized, must in the Perceived be investigated at two levels : the general and the particular. The spirit or quality of the Now is an aggression-oriented efficiency, and, it follows, its Prime Principle is one of Clash. This reads :

> *The modality of all processes, at the Order of the Now, is one of aggression.*

The relevance of the Principle of Clash to the human destiny is crucial. For, while Clash remains subordinated to Absolutes, it nonetheless reigns supreme throughout the Now, imparting an aggressive spirit to Now relationships.

At the level of the individual, quality is multihued, each Existent being a discernible and endowed with a unique personality. Thus, the universe of an Existent will be a function of the quality of its perception. Presently, one quality only concerns us, that of thought in man. Of the primary characteristics of thought there is one of immediate interest, discontinuity. The confluence of Absolutes and Clash results in cutting-up man's thought quota into quanta, each a battle in which the stronger conquers. The scope and/or variety of the quanta created by a given Atom is a correlate of its indiviqualities, e.g. its catness, angelity, humanity, etc. Hence the term Antropocity coined to describe quanta of human mindfacture — while those of the reader's cat could be felineities and those of his guardian angel angeleneities. Restricted to men, this means that depending upon the use to which he puts his quota of thought-power, a man throughout his life becomes aware of an indeterminate but fixed number of absolutized perceptions, of so many miles, trees, stones, orgasms, winters, etc., and it is the sum of such which constitutes his universe.

The issue of Antropocities will resurface throughout these pages. It therefore suffices to bring to the attention two seminal observations. One. It is through the discontinuity of thought that division and its corollary, quantity, is introduced into our private worlds. Conversely, all dimensions other than that of *to be* are subjective percepts. Two. The number of Antropocities is fixed (as is that of the Atoms). Hence, the level of conflict in the Universe decreases with the death of each Antropocity. "Death of an Antropocity", means the expenditure of a thought-quantum. It follows that the real state of the Universe is one of peace. Such a view, as unconscionable as it might appear upon first reading, is being physically confirmed by the phenomenon of entropy.[8]

Such are the two Orders into which fall all facts and phenomena. The first, that of the Real is the realm of the Obscure-Absolute and of Truth. The second, that of the Perceived or Now is that of the Antropocity and of Knowledge.

---

8. For more detail re death and its relationship to entropy and cosmic peace, cf. chaps. I to V of Pt. IV.

chapter VI

The Principle of Absolutes — Prime Cosmic Principle

It is some untold mystery of unity in me, that has the simplicity of the infinite and reduces the immense mass of multitude to a single point.

This One in me knows the universe of the many. But, in whatever it knows, it knows the One in different aspects. It knows this room only because this room is One to it, in spite of the seeming contradiction of the endless facts contained in the single fact of the room... Therefore it is said in the Upanishads that the advaitam is anantam, — "the One is Infinite"; that the advaitam is anandam, — "the One is Love".

Rabindranath TAGORE

1. First Universal Principle: Modality of the Universe and of Its Processes. One of Absolute to Absolute

UP to this point, the structure of the Universe has been the primary concern. This has yielded the Existential-Atom. Before passing on to the next logical assignment — the inner nature of this Atom, analyzed in its role of individual — it seems that the general principles which govern the universal structure should be determined. Since, as yet, the data obtained is of a universal character, one can expect that any principles and laws uncovered will prove equally universal.

When dealing with the Fact-of-to-Be the starting point was the Whole, encompassed intellectually. This led to individuation, to the fact of being an absolute. The analysis of the structure of the Atom, reveals that absoluteness also characterizes both the sum of Existential-Atoms and the inner mechanism of each. Due to the complexity of the issue of absolutes and their Principle, a synopsis of the observation-positions, upon which the Principle rests, is called for. This will provide at the onset a panoramic view of an intricate subject.

A retrospective glance upon the road covered bares between Existence and its components, the Atoms, a common feature, facticity and the latter's synact, absoluteneity. This statement rests upon three suppositions: firstly, when factually encompassed, the Universe constitutes the ultimate absolute: secondly, each Atom in turn is by nature the embodiment of an absolute: thirdly, since the Atoms compose the Universe, the universal mechanism of processes and relationships, must operate according to the modality of an absolute, there being no other manner whereby an absolute can relate, save as absolute to absolute.

Passing from ontology to epistemology, the general observations made re the former, apply to the latter. Inferences drawn as to the operation of the mind, may seem premature at this early phase. Actually, these, when limited to the general, prove legitimate, since the mind, integral to any intellectual Atom, automatically partakes of whatever traits the whole exhibits. Indeed, the essence of the epistemological science was defined when Truth was tentatively listed as synact of Reality and Existence — an affirmation to be explained in detail in the next two chapters. Presently, it suffices to indicate that this means that Truth, Existence and Reality can subsist only if their integrity is preserved. Each must prevail against all comers; each must be one, indivisible and permanent. Stated otherwise, when Existence is under consideration, each Existent must remain It-which-It-is and, when Reality or Truth are involved, either must remain forever what it has been defined or represents. By that very fact, any entity which fulfills these requisites qualifies for the title of absolute — at both Orders. Once all Existential-Atoms and all Truths are found to represent absolutes, the fact that the universal modality is one of absolute to absolute is well on its way to being established. The only factors in the cosmic scenario to be accounted for, are relationships and sense percepts or knowledge. These, as will be shown, are equally subject to the rule of Absolutes.

Once relationships and sense percepts join the throng of the absolutes, no fact, phenomenon or process remains unaccounted for throughout the Cosmos, and the Principle of Absolutes imposes itself. This in its more comprehensive form reads:

> The structure and the modality of the Universe and that of all its processes, conceptual as well as existential, involve a relationship between absolutes.

A more concise formulation — which will be the most frequently utilized — is:

> The modality of the Universe and of its processes is one of absolute to absolute.

The Principle of Absolutes, whose centrality to science is second only to existential atomism, would have found little favor in philosophical circles, regardless of the era. Certainly, it will prove generally unacceptable in ours, whose trade-mark is Relativism served in as many sauces as there are disciplines and schools — an age wherein the word absolute itself is taboo. Having stressed that one can expect violent opposition on the part of die-hard Relativists to the universalizing of absolutes, it must, in fairness, be noted that in a mitigated form, witness numerals, absolutes are accepted by the majority. Also if the scope of Absolutes was restricted to inter Existent relationships it would prove acceptable to most, with the exception of radical Relativists. By extending it to encompass concepts, wholesale doubt as to its validity has probably been raised. Yet, this is the stand adopted.[1]

In summary, what will be demonstrated in the coming pages is that Existents constitute absolutes, and that all relationships and processes involve absolutes.

2. Terms Defined

Before proceeding to anatomize absolutes, two technical factors require clarification. The first concerns term-words — our tools. As always, maximal precision is required if scientific accuracy is to be achieved. The second is the categorization of the types of absolutes. This will, if nothing else, be of use to many disciplines which, as yet, lack a comprehensive list of the discrete units encountered in the cosmic fibre, in particular the psychological sciences. The main reason for providing this list, however, is the nature of the Principle of Absolutes. If this is to embrace all

1. That absoluteness constitutes the ground and a *sine qua non* of the synactive trio Existence-Truth-Reality, was intuited by Parmenides when, in fr. 7 of *The Way of Truth*, he affirmed: "Thus it (Being) must either completely (absolutely) be or be not". Unhappily for mankind this key insight was left fallow. Rather, due to the combination of human conceit with a justifiable concern with absoluteneity's apparent Nemesis, the "feeling" of change, of evolution, the notion itself of absoluteneity has become abhorrent to huge segments of humanity. In its stead, relativity reigns unchallenged and undermines the concept of Truth with all of the nefarious consequences which institutionalized untruth is bound to have upon socio-economic relationships.

relationships, all modalities of discretenesses should be inventorized, and then tested to ascertain whether or not all qualify.

Since, except for that of absolute, the key terms used in setting out both versions of the Prime Principle have been defined, item number one consists of a definition of the word absolute. Because the term is a multipurpose one, assuming different meanings according to context, and furthermore because it holds in the minds of many, specific ideological connotations, it will be useful to outline the reasons which led to its adoption in preference to other word-possibilities.

Traditionally mankind, accustomed to wrapping its thinking within a strait jacket of divisible, quantized "matter" made finite by space and time, has reserved the notion of absolute for the exclusive use of the Absolute-Atom, or for tyrants and, somewhat incongruously, notions such as absolute time and space. Unquestionably, there can be but one Absolute-Atom in the sense that God, Manitou, Allah, call It what you wish, alone possesses existential and dynamic absoluteness. However, absoluteness validly applies to other entities, for, upon closer scrutiny, one finds that absolute, generically, implies nothing more than a closed-circuit, entity or exhaustive concept, free or independent of anything foreign, or still circumscribed. So viewed, every Atom qualifies eminently for the appellation of absolute. The same applies to a concept and thought. Hence, save when otherwise stated, absolute throughout is used in this broad sense.

Controversy over the suitability of absolute could be avoided, by opting for one of its alternates, such as atom, unit, oneness and entity, as well as several others. Yet each would also raise ideological problems. Further, since none are fully synonymous, each has to be evaluated upon its merits. Such an evaluation reveals absolute to be the more promising candidate. Firstly, better than any alternative, it conveys the categorical. This is more in keeping with the positive character of both Dynamic Vision and the Universe. To refer, for instance, to something as an entity or unit leaves numberless doors open. An absolute, on the other hand, shuts out effectively all foreign interference. A second factor militates in favor of absolute. Even as a noun, absolute retains an adjectival connotation. This is important since the Principle of Absolutes encompasses the relational. Further, it conveys not only exclusivity, but also a sense of reaching-out beyond all limits, all dimensions, to encompass whatever falls within its jurisdiction.

In light of the above, the word absolute has been alloted the yeoman's work within the compass of the Prime Principle. Therein it performs a double duty. The first is to act as a stand-in for the conceptualized particular or unit. Then, absolute responds to the succinct definition:

It which is defined.

While applicable to both the existential and conceptual, when Atoms are at stake, the definition:

It which is unique,

can be advantageously substituted. Absolute's second duty is technical. For reasons of semantic economy, henceforth, the capitalized and plural form : Absolutes, will be synonymous with the phrase, the Principle of Absolutes.

3. Categories of Absolutes

Before demonstrating the validity of the Prime Universal Principle, there remains one major task ; namely, to identify the various categories of absolutes, then to put each individually to the test. Only once it is established that each satisfies the criteria of absoluteness and that together they account for the sum of the facts, phenomena and relationships throughout the Cosmos, can Absolutes be proclaimed an universal principle. With regards to the number of categories, the answer is two. The first encompasses the existential, and is subdivisible into two. The second embraces concepts. Of these there are four species.

A. *Existential-Absolutes*

As implied, category "A" encompasses the universe of the Atoms. A general remark applies to existential-absolutes : *they are perceived as Presences ; are not in themselves proper objects of reflection, and knowledge of them is not gained through analysis. Each is grasped as a fact, or not at all. Their perception provides the ground of consciousness — all other epistemological progress involving a secondary process of subjective quantification and aggression.* (This explains why Radical Scepticism is a spurious issue.) Finally the existential-absolutes are responsible for the Principle of the same name and for the absoluteneity of the cosmic process.

1. *Absolute-Existent or Atom*

Stranded by Its lonely Self in the first subdivision of category "A" is the Absolute-Atom otherwise known as Allah, Yahweh, Manitou, etc. The appellation is irrelevant. The distinction between the Absolute-Atom and other Existents is strictly qualitative. Existentially-speaking, there is no serious objection to Its inclusion with the less powerful. This would make category one unitary. However, according to all standards of differentiation, the abyss which separates the commoner, the reader and me and any nondescript flea, from The Absolute, justifies It being dealt with separately.

2. *Existential-Atoms (excluding only The Absolute)*

Subcategory two, while encompassing myriads of myriads, nonetheless consists of a single species, that of the Being or Existential-Atom. Is an Existential-Atom any It (not a that), which is individuated because it possesses, inalienably, as its very own, a particle of the mass of Existence or "matter". Each is dynamic and dimensionless. An alternate description, congenial to the physicist and natural scientist, would be:

> an adimensional and dynamic entity which generates an existential field, ideational, magnetic, emotional, electrical and gravitational, etc.

Such a field, being adimensional, operates "beyond infinity" and is tensorial and permanent.

B. *Conceptual-Absolutes*

All completed-thoughts fall into the category of conceptual-absolutes. *These, usually conceived of as abstract or metaphysical, are not. Nor are any neutral. All involve power and aggression.* A conceptual-absolute differs from an existential, in that it possesses nothing, but rather is integral to an Atom. Child of intellect-power, it resides solely in the mind that entertains it. Structure-wise the conceptual-absolute relates to the "universal" of Scholasticism, yet, this statement by Ockham applies to it.

> To conclude, I say that there is no such thing as a universal, intrinsically present in the things to which it is common. No universal, except that is such by voluntary agreement, is existent in any way outside of the soul, but everything that can be predicated of many things, is by its nature in the mind either psychologically or logically. (Sentences)

To this view, accurate as far as it goes, one must add that each is physical, constitutes a quantum and is aggression-oriented. *A motor within a motor*, peculiar to intellectual-existents, it is generated through a grasping of quality and relationality, in the form of concepts such as civilization, thirteen, color, chair, universe, race. Intimately linked with freedom-of-will, to the point of synactivity, thoughts simultaneously grasp the Outsider, and affirm the thinker's Presence. *All thoughts encompass a whole and constitute absolutes.* Animals, angels, bacteria, plants and spirits also possibly entertain conceptual entities. This, however, is of no concern at this time. The important point is that the sole reality in a concept is the Power expended upon it by the Atom which owns it.

Finally, conceptual-absolutes differ in the order of their greater or lesser dynamical involvement. Starting from the point of lesser involvement and progressing to the extreme, one finds four subcategories or species.

1. *Conceptual-Measuring-Absolute*

All measurements and in particular numbers, when entertained independently, as concepts in themselves, fall into this group. It includes mathematical symbols, geometric structures, numerals and concepts such as a pound, an acre, etc. Generally, these absolutes are utilized to define and/or describe the counterpart of existential-absolutes. *Whereas the latter provide the ground for consciousness, abstract-measuring-absolutes, by providing knowledge of the unique as unique and, by extension, of the qualitatively defined unique, reside at the epistemological root of the Principle of Absolutes.* This honor devolves upon the subcategory, because it counts in its ranks the only pure conceptual-absolute: the cipher one, all other concepts being qualitative or rationalizing embroidery upon the percept of unicity. A last and significant aspect is their rational content. They are directly related to and responsible for the mind's grasping of the rational order and processes of logic. This explains the superior clarity of the disciplines devoted to them such as mathematics. By participating in the ground swell of consciousness, they rise above the subjectivity inherent in a relational or qualitative concept.

2. *Conceptual-Qualitative-Absolute*

Love, hate and sensual percepts such as pain, sex, etc., fall in this subcategory. The qualitative-absolute, an intellectualization of primary animal powers, accounts for the intimacy factor. It encompasses the efforts by an Existent endowed with senses to discover itself, in its play with other Existents. *Sensual, in this context, has its source, not in the percepts which flow from the senses of touch, sight and hearing but rather in the intellect-sense.* This primordial sense or feeling, Heisenberg and Hume notwithstanding, resides in the Atom, simultaneously with "any bundle or collection of different perceptions", and propels its owner beyond the status of a "Heisenbergian actor" unto that of a spectator-actor — a proud and eternally free Outsider.

The subject is immensely complex and connected to the psychological sciences, and remarks upon it are best limited to the following. Perceptions of pain, love or hate generally, as experienced, either intimately or as a grasping of the sensuality of an Outsider, are subject to the same absolutizing process as is any other intellectual unit. *Pain, sex, hate, etc. are cut-up and assessed "bit by bit" in and by the mind, exactly as are numerals.* The question is dealt with in the pages immediately following.

3. *Conceptual-Ideological-Absolute*

Speculative ideas which consist of graspings towards Reality-Truth, and involve ethics and ideology, regardless of their degree of exteriorization, fall into the third subcategory. Ideological-absolutes are related to and converge upon the universal relationships of foundation and medium, which each Existent entertains with the other, and to an eminent degree with The Absolute. Whereas subcategories one and two involved respectively, intellectual abstraction and self-analysis, ideological-absolutes are ethical and conquest-directed.

4. *Conceptual-Existential-Absolute:*

A. The Obscure-Absolute

B. The Antropocity

Conceptual-existential-absolutes are the conceptualization of an Outsider or a conglomerate of such, perceived as existential facts. The Aristotelian would speak of a grasping of "the essence of Beings". This species could be interposed midway between the Kantian "Noumena" and "Phenomena". *Through it, the Existent — "the-thing-in-itself" — is not fully grasped, yet more is grasped than a phenomenon, for when an Atom is perceived in its facticity, a rapport establishes between Presences. Reality, in the person of the intuited fact-of-the-Outsider, is grasped — the intensity, depth and clarity, being proportional to the intellect of the grasper.*

Proper scientific discernment of the entities in this subcategory requires that it be split into further subcategories: the Obscure-Absolute and the Antropocity. Both are essential to any philosophy or epistemology which wishes to go beyond generalities. As a rule the distinction between the two types is made in a slipshod manner. Recognition of the fundamental difference between an Obscure-Absolute and an Antropocity, will banish that Jack-of-all trades and master of none, "the thing", to the coffee house.

A. *The Obscure-Absolute*

A conceptualization of the facticity of an Existential-Atom, intuited and grasped more or less obscurely, the Obscure-Absolute provides man with his sole peephole into the Real. Its prime characteristic is to be intuited as a fact. It is not dimensionable. As it must be. Since each Atom fills the Universe, each forever remains only faintly perceived by a non-absolute Being. Its adimensionality follows, the temporo-spatial being a strictly human phenomenon which cuts the cosmic into manageable pieces. Since there will be occasion to elaborate upon the subject, it suffices to emphasize that an Obscure-Absolute always comprises a single Atom, conceptualized as Atom. The "essence" only is grasped. When dealing with the fulness of an Existent all doors must remain ajar, a fact implicit in the earlier observation that for Dynamic Vision all avenues of investigation are forever open. The physical Presence of a man, God, a lead (atom), a whale, a neutrino, a carrot (growing), constitute examplars of Obscure-Absolutes.

B. *The Antropocity*

The word Antropocity, a neologism, describes mentally dimensioned existential entities. An Antropocity is a physical unit mindfactured by men and others who need such a tool. This is achieved by focusing mind-power upon an intense and salient concentration of relationships. The Antropocity becomes an entity by having attributed to it, limits referred to as physical dimensions, i.e. one cubic foot of ice, one yard of cloth, and surprisingly a sixteen mile-an-hour wind. Any type of Atom can be involved and may contribute any percentage of the defined powers. The physicist would define the Antropocity as a quantized field, and would describe it most accurately. Not only are the dimensions attributed always arbitrary, but the combinations, both of types of power and limiting factors, are, from man's point of view, innumerable. This innumerability of combinations and dimensions is accounted for by the miscibility of power and the nature of absolutes. Thus an Antropocity can involve a single dimension as contained by intensity, e.g., ardent love, or three, as in a temporo-spatial cube of ice, or any combination whatever of calibrating devices the definer wishes to marshall.[2] A real pen, army or table, the English race (the sum of flesh and blood which one defines as Englishmen), all constitute Antropocities. If some of the Atoms included in a conglomerate possess intellect-power, the English nation for instance, then the concepts lodged in the mind of Englishmen become a part of it.

---

2. The claim made earlier, that Dynamic Vision has an unifying impact upon the sciences, is verified when one observes that one of its key concepts, the Antropocity, accommodates itself as readily with a one dimensional love field as with the six and ten dimension-plus fields used by Eddington when developing his theory of spherical space:

Because Antropocities are predicated upon the coordinated activity of Existents, their reality is fully as objective as that of an Existent, with the difference only that the Heisenberg Principle of Uncertainty applies to them just as to a subatomic particle. When an Antropocity is set apart from the remainder of the Cosmos, the intellect, human or otherwise, which defines and dimensions, cuts up the Universe into (hopefully) manageable units; thereby creating its personal universe.

It is here that subjectivity takes over entirely a stage, already to a great extent occupied. Due to the intellect's inability to grasp fully any Existent, even its ownself, the hapless human is reduced to chopping-up the Universe into more or less neat units — into billiard balls, ounces of scotch whiskey, nations, neutrons or planets — and to these he proceeds to ascribe causality, origin (birth and death) and processes (growth and degeneration). The subjectivity (relativity) of an Antropocity varies with the norms used to absolutize it into "existence". These may be the

---

"We are familiar with curvature of *surfaces*; it is a property which we can impart by bending and deforming a flat surface. If we imagine an analogous property to be imparted to *space* (three-dimensional) by bending and deforming it, we have to picture an extra dimension or direction in which the space is bent. There is, however, no suggestion that the extra dimension is anything but a fictitious construction, useful for representing the property pictorially, and thereby showing its mathematical analogy with the property found in surfaces. The relation of the picture to the reality may perhaps best be stated as follows...

...Thus if we are not content to accept curvature as a technical physical characteristic but ask for a picture giving fuller insight, we have to picture more than three dimensions. Indeed it is only in simple and symmetrical conditions that a fourth dimension suffices; and the general picture requires six dimensions (or, when we extend the same ideas from space to space-time, ten dimensions are needed). That is a severe stretch on our powers of conception. But I would say to the reader, do not trouble your head about this picture unduly; it is a stand-by for very occasional use. Normally, when reference is made to space-curvature, picture it as you picture a magnetic field. Probably you do *not* picture a magnetic field; it is something (recognizable by certain tests) which you use in your car or in your wireless apparatus, ..."

A.S. EDDINGTON, *The Expanding Universe*, Cambridge University Press, 1933, chap. II.

From the point of view of Dynamic Vision, all phenomena are dynamic, and the Power-Existence synact being univocal, all fields, magnetic, sensual, electric, intellectual, gravitational, etc., are identical in nature, all interrelated and coeval.

conceptor's own, those of a minority group, or those more or less universal of an entire species, as for instance, the felines or humanoids. Evidently, if the norms are those of the conceptor, the Antropocity will be, if not wholly, at least primarily subjective. To the extent that the cosmicity of its norms increases, its objectivity will increase, and may become total from the point of view of a given society.[3]

Since the subject of an Antropocity is a knot of intense relationships centered upon one or, in practically all instances, a multitude of Atoms, it might appear that — all relationships being cosmic — no Antropocity constitutes an independent unit, but must encompass the Cosmos. If one bears in mind that the true speed of the Universe is absolute, and that the Antropocity, being a concept, is an absolute *this apparent paradox vanishes, because there is no limit whatsoever to the number of absolutes which can be stacked one in and/or upon the other.* Additional light will be thrown on the question when the Antropocity is investigated in its role of object, and also when the instantaneity of the thought process is established.[4]

All entities, both within the Real and the Perceived, are now catalogued. The next task consists in checking whether all constitute genuine absolutes, and if so, whether each category on its own, and in combination maintains its status of absolute in every situation imaginable. Should the last not apply, it was a mistake to speak of Absolutes as Universal Principle. Should it apply Absolutes is universal, and a key insight is acquired which, with the Universal Code, will allow the setting-up of existential equations. For, once the modality of all processes becomes one of absolute to absolute, mathematics loses its monopoly over

---

3. The resolution of the multitude of questions to which causality and ethics give rise, is, once a clear demarcation line is drawn between the Obscure-Absolute and the mindfactured Antropocity, immensely simplified. Causality, in a universe of as-isness assumes the status of a localized phenomenon, evaluated subjectively. As to ethics, this falls under the aegis of the Law of Extremes — the criterion in all instances being efficiency measured according to the norms of The Absolute. Simultaneously all modalities of situation ethics, if viewed as normative, are discredited. The sole just end and true norms of human behavior are those which in-fact promote the commonweal.
4. Cf. secs. 1, 4 and 7 of chap. VII, Pt. I.

equational structures. Every discipline, in particular the sociological and ideological, finds itself equipped with the tools and units necessary to set up its own dynamic equations.

4. Absolutes and Category A: the Existent or Existential-Atom

Having posited that the modality of the Universe is one of absolutes, and all relationships occur between absolutes, and further that even thought processes as fluffy as those in a daydream also consist of series of absolutes, some vindication is in order. The issue is two-tiered, each tier corresponding roughly to the Order of the Real and that of the Perceived.

As to the modality of Existent to Existent relationship, this can be summarily disposed of. There is no conceivable manner in which a relationship can be established, save if there are two strict units, i.e. two absolutes, present one to the other. To state the case colloquially, before there can be a rubbing against, there has to be one entity to be rubbed and another to do the rubbing. Marxism notwithstanding, interrelationships do not, nor cannot, relate — not even for the glorious purpose of "creating historical categories" called men.[5] Hence existentially, at the Real, relationships occur only between two absolutes.

---

5. The bankruptcy, in matters existential, of Marxism and by extension of its parent Hegelianism is implicit in the following definition of a man, excerpted from page 20 of a Novosti Press publication entitled *The Individual and Communism*, which Moscow distributed at the Montreal World Exhibition of 1967.

> "An individual is the sum of definite social relations and so presents a historical category. That is why the all-round development of the individual must be treated as a historical process."

Two comments come to mind, the one technical, the other pragmatic. Technically one is entitled to ask of the Marxist how relationships, whether economic, sexual or other can relate, since elementary logic predicates that before a relationship, a rubbing together can take place, there must firstly exist two or more discrete entities? Pragmatically the Marxian concept of man suggests this somewhat irreverent advice. When the next occasion offers itself for the Marxist to enjoy his bed partner, let him think and act not in terms of Self — of flesh, blood and love — but rather of and as a historical category and process. If the praxis fits the theory, his and his partner's gratification ought to be exquisitely enhanced.

5. Category B : The Conceptual-Absolute or Intellectual-Quantum

A. *General Remarks*

Had the scope of Absolutes been limited to inter Atom relationships, most would undoubtedly agree that, if there are Atoms, then the modality of relationship which these entertain must be one of absolute to absolute. As much, by standards, rationalistic as well as empirical, is hardly open to question. Were it next observed that thought-power is integral to the Existent, and that consequently the intellectual process must submit to the modality of the whole, then, a majority would again acquiesce. However, that easy way out was closed by the affirmation that even concepts are absolutes, "within" the Existent, and obey the Principle of Absolutes, which is to say that intellect-power operates through instantaneous bursts, identical to the bits in a computer; that, for instance, a youth's castles in the sky consist of a series of flashes, bits or quanta — each a strict unit, each set up in radical opposition to an other. To insert absolutes so deeply into the texture of the Real, is to postulate a theory by no means self-evident. The demonstration of the quantum-like nature of thoughts, will therefore be more elaborate.

The issue hinges firstly, upon the nature of thought-power, and secondly, upon Clash, the second Prime Principle, and upon The Cosmic Laws of Clash, Extremes and Oneness. While the latter are not elaborated upon in this book, all three are outlined in chapter II of Part V. The data provided therein, together with the reader's intuitive knowledge of the factors for which each accounts within the cosmic economy, should suffice. The situation differs in respect to Power to which Part II, in its entirety, is devoted. Any difficulty with concepts relating to it could be disposed of by anticipating. This should not prove necessary, if one keeps in mind that thought-power is in every sense identical to any other, be this gravitational, electrical, etc. In other words, the fact that thought apparently exists only in animates does not alter its structure, nor cause it to obey laws different from those which govern other dynamic processes.

Next, thought is physical and possessed outright. It cannot be distilled, isolated, and set apart in an airtight container. Neither ideational in the metaphysical sense, nor infused (caused in the thinker by outside agents, such as chemicals) nor situated in the brain, its efficiency fluctuates with that of the whole Atom. Obviously the intensity of interaction (coagency factor) between the chemicals used in the construction and maintenance of a brain, exceeds beyond computation that entertained by its possessor with the chemical and other Existents which "reside in", for example, the Andromeda nebula.

The apposition of "other" beside chemical existent emphasizes a critical aspect of the issue. Thought, far from being a mere chemical reaction, is an inneal attribute simultaneously triggered and influenced by a multiplicity of factors viz. a philodendron, family quarrels, musical notes, the family cat, etc. Integral to the Existent, it suffers from or revels in the entire cosmic network of relationships entertained by its owner. Further, in accord with the Law of Similitudes, it is miscible, meaning that electrical, intellectual or fist-power additivates or blends indiscriminately with thought-power to thereby produce all combinations and effects imaginable. The following passage by A.N. Whitehead aptly describes both the nature and scope of its relationality:

> The concrete enduring entities are organisms, so that the plan of the whole influences the very characters of the various subordinate organisms which enter into it. In the case of an animal, the mental states enter into the plan of the total organism and thus modify the plans of the successive subordinate organisms until the ultimate smallest organisms, such as electrons, are reached. Thus an electron within a living body is different from an electron outside it, by reason of the plan of the body... The principle of modification is perfectly general throughout nature, and represents no property peculiar to living bodies.[6]

The discoveries of theoretical and applied physics have recently accentuated a trend toward a similar view among physicists. However, affinities notwithstanding, a physical chasm separates the cosmic and, hence intellectual presentiality which flows from the Principle of Absolutes and processional and/or relativistic cosmogonies *à la* Whitehead or Einstein. While

---

6. BRIGHT, Laurence, *Whitehead's Philosophy of Physics*, New York, Sheed and Ward, 1958, p. 74.

theoretically committed to the conservation of energy, the latter lack the mechanism: absolute-speed, whereby all energies can be conserved, a defect all the more damaging in that the sacrificed: the intellectual, is the most priceless of all forms of energy. To sum up, thought-power, an integrant of the Atom, constitutes only one of its more efficient tools.

At this point, one would seem justified in countering: How can it be maintained that thought-power is of the same nature as other energies and obeys Universal Law, then, presto, be affirmed that it creates absolutes of its own, and pits such absolutes one against the other? Was it not emphasized that a prime requisite of Existence and, it follows, of Existence's synact, Power is indivisibility? If, as now asserted, the mind creates absolutes each subject to clash, Power as synact of the Existent, is either divisible or independent of its author-owner, and, in effect, thoughts belongs to a new and somewhat ethereal category of atoms. The objection, a logical one, presents a two-fold problem. One, puts in question the indivisibility of Power. Two, begs demonstration that the mind and its processes are indeed linked to aggression.

B. *The Intellectual-Quantum, a Function of Quality*

Since Power is dealt with in Part II, its indivisibility being a major characteristic is dealt with there. Presently, it suffices to indicate that both its indivisibility and quantization are a function of quality. The key factors at play, as previously observed, are:

A: the synactivity, facticity and univocity of Existence and Power, and

B: the absolute to absolute modality of the Universe.

It follows, firstly that each Atom owes its discernibility to quality and, secondly that quality, being inneal, poses no barrier to quantization of the type involved in the "production" of thought-quanta. While it would not be accurate to see in qualitativity the sole factor responsible for existential differentiation (the individuation principle in Existence also qualifies), the qualifying role of the dynamic is primordial. *Due to the juxtaposition of its univocity and individualizing characteristic, structure-wise, Power vests in all Atoms, a restricted number of prime qualities (five) and certain secondary or personal qualities.*

These, analyzed in detail chapter VI, Part II, are henceforth defined respectively as univerqualities and indiviqualities. All Existents manifest the former. The latter vary with each species and, within these, each individual.

Next, if the fact that Existence is at once univocal and equivocal (communally shared), and that even indiviqualities presentialize each Atom in a manner identical for all (albeit more effectively in some cases) is taken into account, an understanding of thought-power is at hand. Just as an indiviquality, let us say the yellowness of sunflowers or the sex appeal of the young can vary in intensity, both within a given Existent and between Existents of a same species, so can presentiality. The difference is that presentiality, in its role of univerquality, resides and varies in intensity and efficiency in and between all Existents. Thus thought, one among a phethora of qualities, avers itself one of a thinker's move effective presentializing agents. Since presently it is generally assumed that all Existents do not necessarily think, the intellectual quality falls in the category of indiviqualities — that through which man and other thinking Atoms impress their special brand of presentiality (their sign) upon the Outside. The option that all Atoms think, it will be noted, remains open.

This leaves the question of the speed and/or location in time-space of each quantum, a question related to the paradox of the discontinuous in the continuous. The problem vanishes when, taking into consideration the qualitativity of thought, it is further observed that each thought constitutes a quantum or fact. Since this feature is investigated in the following chapter, only the fact that each thought-quantum is an absolute and as such obeys the Principle of Absolutes need be noted here. Each simply *is*. Each resides outside time-space and moves at absolute speed. For Absolutes, an absolute autocrat, never relaxes its dictatorship. It may condone a degradation of the Real, like that operated by dull-witted individuals such as men, fir trees and cats, but insists upon the degradation being conducted along absolutist lines. If man, to grasp at Reality and Truth, must do so "bit" by "bit", Absolutes will permit this, but only upon the condition that each quantum should conform to its modality.

In summary, an analysis of the qualitative characteristics of Energy holds the key to the deciphering of the mental process.

C. *Clash Enters Upon The Scene*

The issue of aggression goes to the heart of epistemology. Hence, it also is complex, and only its basic aspects can herein be dealt with. As with every philosophical difficulty, an understanding of aggression and clash and their relevance to thought, is predicated firstly upon making the necessary distinctions between the Real and the Perceived, and secondly upon a conciliation of the latter's seemingly divergent imperatives. The first requisite need only be summarized, since a preliminary investigation has just been concluded. In a nutshell, *this requires considering the fact that the Order of the Real contains all thoughts on an As-is basis, while, in the Perceived, thoughts take the form of quanta subjectively and sequentially prehended.* To posit that thought, even in a daydream, operates instantaneously, through the agency of computer-like bits perceived sequentially, seems to court the irrational. Next, to find in aggression one of the prime factors responsible for conciliating the two Orders, may appear unconscionable. Yet, so it is. Since the Prime Principle of the Now is that of Clash, any road which would lead to conciliation must take it into account. While Absolutes is the Universal Principle, and none can escape its domination, in some situations it waives its paramountcy in favor of the Now. This implies allowing Clash to take over, but to do so in sufferance and in time only — one might fittingly add, after a make believe fashion.

Given the above, an analysis which is to exceed the superficial, must simultaneously take into account the interplay between the two universal principles and clearly distinguish the role proper to each. The present objective being to demonstrate that, at the Order of the Now, thought operates through quanta, a first assumption must be that intellectual-power is subject to the imperatives of the Principle of Clash, and that it achieves its quantizing through the agency of one or more of these imperatives. A cursory analysis of the key tenets of Clash reveals this surmise justified. Clash reads:

> The modality of all processes at the Order of the Perceived, is one of aggression.

From this, flow the following premises:

A. Power is positive (outgoing);

B. Power is aggressive (it protects) and

C. in the free-will realm of Clash, a minimal exercise of Power is required to maintain ones presence before the remainder of the clashing-universe.

Translated into operational terms, this implies that since at the Perceived all relationships in final analysis involve clash, each, animate and inanimate, uses its power (consciously or not) to conquer — intuitively sensing that the "moment" it ceases to aggress effectively it will vacate the Now, suffering in the process the fate referred to as death.[7] Next, since thought-power is

---

7. The phenomenon which, when it affects animates, is defined as death, is one which no cosmontology can ignore. It is analyzed in Part IV. Here, the following particulars situate the issue within the context of the Conservation of Energy or alternately the As-is.
    1. Death is a subjective Now percept.
    2. All Atoms in the Now, even inanimates such as uraniums and neutrinos, die.
    3. Within the Real and for the dying it coincides with the breaching of a critical-point and signifies that the last of ones conflictive relationships has been accounted for.
    4. The state of the dead is one of experienced (sensed) maximization and of peace.

   Such parameters firstly, are in accord with the findings of astro and subnuclear physics which indicate that the inanimate, in particular the metalloids, are born and die in time exactly as do felines. Secondly, such a reading accounts for all Energy whereas any annihilation theory of death reduces the Universe to the status of a melting "cosmic snowball", which must someday disappear, regardless of the remoteness of the vanishing event. Simultaneously entropy is explained (cf. secs 3 and 4, chap. III, Pt. IV) and an actuarial basis upon which to establish the theory of the Conservation of Energy is provided. Such a development is timely, for the Theory presently remains a hypothesis, as witness:

   > The difficulty in proving a law of conservation is to isolate the system from all external influence. This is impossible, for on the one hand the system is connected to the observer because of the very measurements themselves, and on the other hand it cannot be separated from the universe and its expansion, which define its mass, its inertia and its time in accordance with the former principle of Mach. Since we have no idea of the unknown cosmic forces which play on us, we can thus only establish approximate laws, such as the conservation of energy.
   >
   > Robert Gouiran, *Particles and Accelerators*, New York, Mc Graw, 1967, p. 96.

   Further, the enigma of the elusive neutrino may be thereby solved. While some physicists of stature maintain that a few neutrinos have been isolated, many equally qualified researchers argue otherwise. Presently there seems to exist less concrete evidence of neutrino interaction with the Now, than there is of human spirit or ghost interaction, the neutrino's sole, unimpeachable

identical to all other types, its processes obey Similitudes, and any difference between it and other powers, is one of quality and efficiency — it provides its owner with an efficient weapon of conquest.

This superior efficiency involves a four step sequence:

A. an act of consciousness and awareness;

B. a measuring act;

C. a decision (a choice between options) and

D. an act of aggression.

While the first three steps do not create units, the distinction between each is radical enough to warrant their being dealt with individually. Furthermore, item D, the act of aggression, is of a different nature. Integral to C, the decision phase, its inclusion emphasizes the fact that the thought process, firmly grounded in the "nitty-gritty" of life, is intimately linked to the aggression of Outsiders. In other words, the line drawn between C and D, makes it clear that each thought represents, not only a defined absolute, but a minor battle waged for the purpose of self-assertion. This is an aspect of the intellectual process overlooked by many epistemologists. In summary, when thought-power "goes to work", it operates through the modality of Absolutes: through bursts. These occur outside of time-space and serve to apprehend, measure, and decide upon a strategy whereby the owner will, or at least hopes to conquer upon a restricted battlefield.

A more detailed investigation reveals the following. As indicated, the first step, not in the order of time but of the Real, involves becoming aware. Without awareness, there is no thought in the human sense. Awareness and consciousness differ in that the latter always involves calibration and decision, while awareness is passive and closely related to mediumship.[8] As an

---

claim to existence being that "it has to be, if all of the energy involved in beta-decay is to be accounted for". The issue is critical, since it is estimated that from 10 to 20% of the Power in the Cosmos in owned by neutrinos. Finally, and of immediate relevance to the complex of issues under consideration, together the four propositions listed above provide the grid needed to decipher the operation of thought. In a world of as-isness, each thought-quantum, while situated in the Now of the perceiver, impregnates the Universe of the Real and becomes a factor to be reckoned with.

8. Re: Instantaneity of awareness, cf. sec. 1, subsec. A, chap. VII, Pt. I.

awareness producing agent, the mind operates much as a highly sensitized camera. It places before man a picture of the Outside. Thought thus, firstly opens the Existent unto the Universe — to set before him a more or less restricted segment of the universe of his relationships, physically, upon a screen. The words "physically, upon a screen" place the screen squarely within the Atom. The Outsiders merely provide the foundation-medium upon and through which, the knower exerts his power.

In this regard, a general observation offers itself. Awareness, being of-and-in man, is existential to the nth degree — an intuition such as drove Sartre to proclaim that for practical purposes, existence results from awareness, an assessment wretchedly restrictive. Rather, consciousness opens the conscious to the entire Universe. Consciousness does not make or create its owner. A quality, its amplitude is proportional to the caliber of the intellect involved.

Before passing to the second stage, it should be noted that an Atom different from man could conceivably have awareness and still retain a platonic or Buddhistic attitude *vis-à-vis* its knowledge. Such an intellect could occupy either of the two extremes of involvement: that ascribed to God in the Thomistic system, or that of a placid, computer-like intellect. Either would be spared involvement in the next two phases of the human intellectual process.

Man, and with him the animates and inorganics, suffers a more violent destiny. The spirit and prime dimension of the Now is one of conflict, conquest and death. Aggression is its law, and conquer or be conquered its only options. Literally man swims in conflict. He either copes with it or drowns. Yet the Universe, however cruel, constitutes a rational whole. The doomed are equipped with the attributes necessary to cope *temporarily* with conflict.[9] Consciously at times, or through automatic reflexes, all Atoms residing in the clash-prone Now respond to aggression, each in a manner corresponding to its qualifications. In man's case this involves, among other factors, two additional steps. Having photographed his surroundings, he must also weigh the pros and cons facing him. Hence, the second stage, described as a

9. Re: Fathering of time-space by aggression, cf. sec. 6, chap. VII, Pt. I.

measuring or calibrating process. Naturally, the photographic and all subsequent stages are coeval to one another. With regards to stages three and four, it suffices to note that they:

A. involve the act of free-will,

B. provide the cut-off point, and

C. "make room" for the initiating of a completed-thought-unit.

At that stage absolutes ingress upon the scene. Whenever the process is completed, an absolute enters into play. The word completed is crucial: A completed-thought implies that the thinker withdraws within his Self, to photograph and to measure the factors at stake, and finally to decide.

D. *Every Thought, Every Intellectual-Bit or Quantum, Involves a Decision*

Here, a number of issues, some psychological, others epistemological or even ethical arise — free-will having been brought into the picture. These must be deferred as not being directly relevant to Absolutes except for one. This query concerns the hypothesis that thoughts involve decisions. Would, for instance, the conceptualizing of the numeral one in the mind of a five year old child not be exempt? Surprisingly, the answer is no. Even in such a situation, Absolutes operates. Firstly, the fullness of an Atom and its quota of power, is at play. Secondly, the moment ones attention transfers to a different object, a measurement is made and a decision taken. To conceive of the figure one and concentrate upon it to the exclusion of all else is to measure and set aside. As to the decision in such a "chain of events", it also takes place at some instant or other, if and when, for example, the five year old diverts his appetite to chocolate ice-cream. This ruptures his thought into bits, exactly as in a computer. Because of the child's preoccupation, regardless of how casual, firstly with the figure one, and secondly with an ice-cream cone, his relationship to the Universe is forever altered, and so is the Cosmic Equation. The universal economy will never be the same.

What is the universal economy? We saw earlier, that the Universe consists of the sum of the Atoms, each of which owns its quota of energy. "Economy", in such a context, assumes the same meaning as in business and imposes upon the philosopher the same restraints and duty as upon any other honest mortal. The philosopher must, exactly as must the chartered accountant or geochemist, account for all of his raw material — for all of the energy owned by the sum of the Atoms. This applies to the most insignificant event, to, for instance, the energy expended on October 15, 1962, by radio station CJAD Montreal, FM, to broadcast a single Elvis Presley note, as well as to that of a puny mosquito biting the hind-end of buffalo number 22^{425} in 5222 B.C. Both events are physical and register permanently upon the cosmic balance sheet.

To sum up, each thought, being discrete, fully delineated and defined, qualifies for the role of absolute and Quantum physics applies to the intellectual Atom, if anything, more radically than to any known as an elementary particle. The modality of absolute to absolute, which operates between Atoms, having now been detected within the Atom at the level of the thought process, can be declared a universal modality and principle.

chapter VII

The Thought-Quantum, or Thought is Quantized and Instantaneous

To conclude, I say that there is no such thing as a universal, intrinsically present in the things to which it is common. No universal, except that is such by voluntary agreement, is existent in any way outside of the soul, but every thing that can be predicated of many things, psychologically or logically.

Ockham, Sentences

1. Phenomenon of the Quantizing of Thought-Power Observed In More Detail: Its Instantaneity Demonstrated

UNQUESTIONABLY a break, hence a quantization of thought, more radical than that which occurs when an electron jumps from one orbit to the next within the hydrogen atom, is consummated when Mr. Professor of biochemistry shifts his attention from the molecular structure of D.N.A. to the blonde lass in his classroom.[1]

Perfunctorily observed such quantization appears harmless enough. The phenomenon, however, assumes disturbing proportions the moment its full implications are drawn. Absolutes can only relate instantaneously, and as a consequence outside of time-space. Furthermore, this applies within and without the Atom — a hard statement. After all one can hardly be expected, merely upon the strength of rationalizations, to pre-emptorily cast overboard two dimensions so deeply anchored in Reality. A four course dinner, for example, is not instantaneously enjoyed. Time, space, continuity and quantity — a table, a steak — are required. Does not sheer common sense indicate that no mind, at least human, can enjoy a meal instantaneously? True. Yet the fact remains that the secondary senses operate in isolation,

1. The theory being advanced is that the mechanism through which thought-quanta are produced corresponds to that which Bohr postulates in respect to the generation of the various levels or wavelengths of radiation. In either case the observed quantization is a mindfacture; is the product of a mind whose particular intellectual qualities allow it to sense and absolutize a given knot of otherwise cosmic relationships.

outside of Reality, in a world of their own. Therein only time-space become relevant: not to the point of making time-space real, but rather solely by vesting real-illusions in the prisoner of the senses. Man lives in his own creation, a make-believe, "Alice in Wonderland" world. Since two visions now confront us, one of "real time-space" and one of "time-space as a real-illusion", either of which seemingly negates the other, it seems advisable, in view of the values at stake, to explore further the key concept which divides the two, namely the quantizing of thought-power. While a detailed analysis of the factors at play exceeds the scope of this work, general observations upon the instantaneous character of the three synacts of thought: awareness, measurement and decision should provide the data required to clarify the issue.

A. *Absoluteneity and Instantaneity of Awareness*

Of the three, the instantaneity and quantization of awareness presents the most difficulty. Yet the problem is simpler than might be anticipated. The key is to situate it in its proper locale: cosmicity. Instead of seeing in awareness a human and intermittent power (enjoyed in a second-rate fashion by "lower" animals), one must appreciate its universal, photographic and relational dimension. Then, it reveals itself as shared, albeit in differing degrees, by all. To the extent that the Cosmos and in it the Atom, can be carved into sequences, awareness corresponds to the sensory state wherein relationality is passively recorded for "future" reference.

A comparison to photography, may seem allegoric. Not so. Awareness *is* photography and it is the Kodak print, the X-ray film and any "stabilizing" process such as magnetic tapes, mirrors, photographic plates, etc., which are analogical, or more accurately, which involve instruments of secondary recall. *Awareness is not a limited operation, conducted on an off-and-on basis by the senses of sight, etc. Rather the whole Atom senses throughout the most intimate fibre of its inneity.* Just as the facticity of each Atom suffuses and permeates that of every other to the point of immanence, so does individual awareness, a coordinate of cosmic immanence, permeate the Cosmos.

To encompass in awareness the fact of sensing or feeling the entire Commonwealth of the Atoms, may seem to destroy any correspondence of the noun with the factor which it describes. Within the narrow province of the Antropocities, the objection is valid. However, he who so limits his field of reference abdicates the title of philosopher or cosmophysicist for that of anthropologist. To explore the depths of Reality, the philosopher must take into account its adimensionality. The latter, when applied to a quality, in this instance to awareness, predicates a relationship of medium, namely mediumship, (one of three modalities of cosmic relationality), and through mediumship, each is made present and available to every other, and is repaid in kind. In a word, awareness is a facet of cosmic presentiality; of the fact that we are, each of us, a Cosmic-Presence.

A close reading of the following text from Sigmund Freud's *New Introductory Lectures in Psychoanalysis* (1932), establishes that Freud's basic thesis is founded upon an identical intuition:

> There is nothing in the Id that corresponds to the idea of time; there is no recognition of the passage of time, and — a thing that is most remarkable and awaits consideration in philosophical thought — no alteration in its mental processes produced by the passage of time. Wishful impulses which have never passed beyond the Id but impressions too, which have been sunk into the Id by repression are virtually immortal; after the passage of decades they behave as if they had just occurred.

Understandably, Freud whose concern was the human psyche, does not extend timeless awareness to fleas, irons and electrons. However, that he was open to such an extension of the realm of the immortal Ids, is indicated by his description of this as: "a thing that is most remarkable and awaits consideration in philosophical thought".

In summary, *instead of seeing in awareness a localized human attribute, encrusted in a cement of finite time-space, one must think in terms of* a cosmic feeling *experienced by all.* The fact that each is a Presence before every other, and is flesh of the other's flesh, means that regardless of how minimal our awareness, our feeling of some lonely iron in the inner core of Venus may be, we cannot escape involvement with this iron and his cosmic feeling.

1. *Absoluteneity of Awareness*

Once the cosmicity of awareness is noted, its absoluteneity is automatic, for that which partakes of the Cosmic partakes of the Absolute. Hence only a brief expatiation of its photographic nature is called for, the purpose being to situate the issue simultaneously within the Real and the Perceived, and thus place in relief the similarities and differences between the two modalities. The cosmic photography process, as noted, results from the impact of each Atom upon every other, as each rests in the As-is, beyond time-space — *nothing is lost*, the most insignificant of quivers, of radio wave even, being indeliby branded upon each of our Ids. That which varies in the micro-filming from one species to another, is the quality of awareness. An Absolute-Atom enjoys absolute awareness, whereas "lower grade" Atoms, as witness a copper, feel most faintly. In this quality-spectrum, man occupies an intermediate position. As the germanium atom, he remains unaware of much scar tissue, of the submerged portion of the Self — the psychologist's subconscious. Mechanical photography, for its part, represents an effort at extending the depth of the conscious. A father who photographs his two year old son with an "Instamatic" camera, attempts to freeze in the As-is, an incident in his otherwise cosmic relationship with the child. The process commits an Antropocity to paper. Concurrent with its transposing, the relationship, already indelibly etched in the father's subconscious, was integral to his inneity. The photograph provides immediacy of recall, and an increased efficiency in his relationship with his son. The awareness achieved through photography compares in all respects with that registered by and upon the presumed inanimates, the uraniums and lichens, etc. These are, as man, Cosmic-Presences subject to cosmic relationality, or to use a Whiteheadian term, to the "principle of modification", which, and I quote, "is perfectly general throughout nature and represents no property peculiar to living bodies", (see footnote 6, chap. VI, Pt. I). In all instances, only quality is involved, the differences corresponding in a general way to different types of plates — some registering X-rays, others normal light, etc. In summary, since all Atoms are aware, each according to its own norms, and since furthermore all, from the divine to the feline, the aureal to neutronic, reside in the

Absolute, it follows that awareness, first synact of thought, operates in the Absolute and obeys the Principle of Absolutes.

2. *Instantaneity of Awareness, or Leaves Do Not Fall In Autumn*

In respect to instantaneity the same remarks apply as to absoluteneity. A systematic demonstration of instantaneity being part of the broader problem of Power, discussion of the items involved are here best limited to a minimum. Actually, once the cosmicity of relationships is established, the instantaneity of awareness follows. It which entertains a cosmic relationship cannot operate physically in time-space, for these imply finiteness and limits, both incompatible with absoluteneity. Thus, to establish the instantaneity of awareness, one has only to separate from the As-is, the subjective factors responsible for the sensation of time — to isolate the Real from the Perceived.[2]

Briefly here are the processes at play. While we bathe in a cosmic medium, due to the limitations of our feeling, we are unable to encompass in one shot, the full panorama of Reality. Making the best out of an unsatisfactory situation, we focus upon those facets which are to us intimate, outstandingly intense and relevant. To such, we attribute sequence and extent. In fact, both dimensions reside in the mind, and owe whatever realism they evidence to the intensity of ones power. This qualitative nature of time-space is starkly revealed the moment an attempt is made to situate a given incident in time and, it follows, in space — either being a coordinate of the other. Then time is nowhere "then or there" to be prehended. Perceived-time, a subjective yardstick and the result of a focussing upon a restricted area of the landscape, can in no manner impinge upon Reality. Rather, he who tries to weave it into the universal fabric, ends up bewildered by the irrational cruelty of a temporalized existence. This evanescence of time, and the frustrations which fill one who preoccupies himself with it excessively, is aptly decried in these paragraphs of "*la Nausée*", wherein Sartre, whose philosophy lacks a sense of genuine atomicity, describes his bafflement and rage at the "passage of time and of existence itself":

---

2. Re Cosmicity of relationality, cf. sec. 2, chap. 1, Pt. III.

And following the swaying branches, to myself I said, these movements never fully exist, they are passages, mere intermediaries between two existences, weak moments. And I made ready to see them rise from the void. Finally I was going to witness existences being born. Three seconds sufficed to sweep away my hopes. Nowhere on these hesitant, blindly grasping branches, could I succeed in witnessing a passage into existence...

All was fulness, all in act, there was no weak moment, all, even the most imperceptible start, was made-up of existence. All these existents bustling about the tree, oozed from nowhere and disolved into the nowhere. Suddenly they existed, and then suddenly they did not exist: existence is without memory...

... Then there are the imbeciles who come to speak to you of "will to live", "of struggle for life". Had they never watched a beast or tree...

... Impossible to see things that way. Softnesses, weaknesses, yes. The trees were floating. A gushing out towards heaven? No! "*un affalement*", a foundering; at every instant I expected to see the trunks shrink as tired penes, shrivel and drop, black masses upon the soil and soft with folds. They had no desire to exist, only, they could not help themselves...[3]

It is to be expected, that due to his Monistic Nihilism, Sartre, a man of some intelligence, should feel cheated as he intuits "*tant d'existences manquées*" — so many miscarried existences — his own inclusively, flowing into nothingness. He, as all Becomingists, starts-off from nothing, from the *néant*, and from nothing, nothing only ever grows. Dynamic Vision effectively exorcises such traumas. Within its context each Existent *is* and communes with every other, and the feeling of becoming aware of sequential events amounts to exactly that, to a feeling and nothing more.

A brief analysis of ones awareness of the following hypothetical events bears this out. Event number one will be an orgasm which the reader can situate "wherever in time" he pleases. Number two will involve the interval which, come autumn, spans the fall of the first leaf to that of the last from

3. J. P. SARTRE, *La Nausée*, Paris, Gallimard, 1937, p. 187. The English translation is the author's and is as literal as was feasible, given the polished French of Sartre, which is only with difficulty translatable into another language.

some given tree, for this purpose from the fantastic weeping willow outside my study window.

If the reader ascribes four minutes to the orgasm, and I, five weeks from the fall of the first to that of the last willow leaf, and if we both attempt to situate our respective awarenesses precisely in time, this avers itself unfeasible on two counts. Firstly, in our minds and in that of two Outsiders brought in to match events with us, *the "outer limits" of the orgasm and the fall of willow leaves must be set arbitrarily. None of we four could agree exactly as to when* in-fact *(as distinct from by common agreement), both events "started and ended"*. Secondly, any period of time singled out for a precise analysis is constantly divisible. Ultimately, one is driven to speak of some unconscionably brief time, of which, if a modicum of sanity is maintained, it must be stated, to paraphrase Leibniz, that no shorter time can be thought of. This expedient applied to time, is as unsatisfactory as when applied by Leibniz to "matter" and space. All three concepts are products of the syndrome of anthropocentricity from which mortals suffer. He who would divide a four minute orgasm or the five week fall of a weeping willow's leaves into exact time intervals courts the irrational. This was the source of Sartre's bafflement, and also that which attends a mathematical equation in which infinite numbers are inserted.[4] No time interval can be existentially, which is to say, factually isolated. *Every event is cosmic, and*

---

4. As with most philosophical paradoxes the controversy over infinite and transfinite numbers can be traced to a futile attempt to reduce all phenomena to human dimensions. In the present instance, the error consists in trying to situate the number, a concept, in human-time and in a concomitant flouting of the Principle of Absolutes. While the stand adopted on the issue corresponds closely to that of the Intuitionists of the Brouwer school, the notion of an infinite concept, numeral or otherwise, is rejected upon dynamic rather than upon logical grounds. Numbers constitute a species of universals of which Ockham rightly observed: "no universal, except that is such by voluntary agreement, is existent in anyway outside of the soul." It follows that a series, no matter how drawn out, of "conceived units" terminates when either of two events occurs.

    A: the thinker transfers, for any reason whatsoever, his attention from one series to another, either more appealing or compelling.

    B: the thinker dies, i.e. evacuates the conflict-prone Now.

In a word, an infinite number or series forever remains lost in the hypothetical and merely bears witness to the quantizing impact of Absolutes upon a non-absolute Atom.

awareness of it extends to the farthest reaches of time-space. Granted, the aggressive designs of iridium atom 4687^{312}, resident of Sirius, upon plesiosaurus flea 9025^{541}, resident of unknown planet 746^{631}, register but faintly upon our somnolent psyche here, on planet earth. Yet, register they do. It is the intuition of this faint impact of all upon all which through the ages has provided the astrologer and his client with the minimum of plausibility necessary to sustain both in their faith, and to shuck off with equanimity the barbs of their more "rational" cohumans.

Clearly, awareness — the phenomenon which records upon the magnetic tape of each Atom all phases of its relationality-operates in the Absolute. That awareness *in se* operates instantaneously, is also beyond question. Yet, that for which logic and physics seem to vouchsafe, does appear squarely contradicted by a phenomenon equally beyond question: namely that awareness of events is broken into an unconscionable multitude of quanta or ideas. An example would be the "countless times" at which my perception of the falling leaves interrupts over the five weeks. Certainly, it would seem, hundreds of isolated events such as the fall of a single leaf, do not occur instantaneously. The answer may strike as lacking seriousness. Actually, not only does each fall occur instantaneously, but *in-fact leaves do not fall in autumn.* To some it will appear that, in lieu of Sartre's bafflement and rage at his inability to grasp "nascent existence" in his swaying tree, levity is being substituted, possibly even a touch of insanity. The issue is complex and, while part of the answer is provided in this chapter, its full rationale is revealed only by the end of Part II, when the mechanism of Power has been dismantled. Presently, the observation that *absolutes, any number of these, can fit and rest comfortably in an absolute*, sums it up.

B. *Absoluteneity and Instantaneity of Measurements*

Upon transfering from awareness to measurement, one passes from mediumship to coagentship whereat the link is made between the Real and the Perceived and the two Universal Principles, Absolutes and Clash, are joined. Due to this, and because measurement, the initial step in a division, is the fruit of sheer idealization, its absolute to absolute character is more easily grasped than that of awareness. That certain measured items are absolutes, is universally accepted. As first examples, mathematical units, viz the numeral 40, and most of the symbols of Euclidean geometry, come to mind. Also the singling out for purchase at a fruit counter of half a dozen of McIntosh apples and four bananas, absolutizes. However, it can be said somewhat facetiously that between a consensus on the absoluteness of certain categories of measurements and a consensus upon the instantaneity of all measurements, the gap is absolute. Actually, the record of published material seems to indicate that the question of the speed of thought, i.e. of the intellectual act, has by one and all been nimbly side-tracked.

If for enlightenment one turns to Bergson — in some respects still the authority on the question of duration and hence of speed — one encounters many oblique references to quasi-instantaneities, as witness that contained in this statement, central to his position:

> The systems marked off by science endure only because they are bound up inseparably with the rest of the universe. It is true that in the universe itself two opposite movements are to be distinguished, as we shall see later on, "descent" and "ascent". The first only unwinds a roll ready prepared. In principle, it might be accomplished almost instantaneously, like releasing a spring. But the ascending movement, which corresponds to an inner work of ripening or creating, endures essentially, and imposes its rhythm on the first, which is inseparable from it.[5]

As is implicit in this text and explicit in his detailed analysis in subsequent chapters, Bergson intuits instantaneity, but recoils from it as an unthinkable. Yet on the basis of experimentation and logic, the instantaneous character of thought is evident. One has but to draw the distinction between the act of "physically circumscribing an entity" and that of "intellectualization" which makes it a strict unit, to observe the dichotomy between the two. The physically encircled is never totally nor finally encompassed — the impediment to this being rooted simultaneously in the necessity of "moving gradually in time" to complete the encircling, and in the dynamism and unity of the Real. Thus it

---

5. Henri BERGSON, *Creative Evolution* (authorized trans. Arthur Mitchell, Ph. D.), London, Macmillan and Co., 1913, p. 11-12.

has correctly been assumed that neither absoluteness nor instantaneity are to be detected in "matter". What is overlooked is that the "act of picturing" an entity in the mind, cannot occur in time. Granted, one has the sensation of encompassing an acre of farmland or the 3,621,616 square miles of Canadian territory in so many micro-seconds, but closer scrutiny reveals that such an operation not only exceeds the speed of light, but occurs at absolute-speed. This becomes clear when the object is the Universe. Nor does one need to extend himself so far. The astronomer who, through the Mount Palomar telescope, communicates at "a given point in time" with Betelgeuse, and then "in the flick of a second", allows his thought to range back to his wife, and thence retransfers it in "less than seconds" unto Betelgeuse and beyond, has immeasurably exceeded the speed of light which takes eight minutes to travel from a next door neighbor, the sun. The real speed in the Universe is not once nor twice that of light — the latter being the speed at which some galaxies are hypothesized to recede from us. *Existentially there is no such "thing" as speed, save only if one considers absolute-speed as a rate of progression.* Rather, certain mind-defined entities, i.e. fists, bullets and stars, are observed as crashing through mind-objects (Antropocities), thereby altering, with greater or lesser ease (speed), the relationships postulated between these mind-objects. All speeds are qualitative mind-constructs, and the intellect which ranges from one object to another, travels instantaneously.

As much "was there" to be rationally deduced from "all time", by any mind willing to venture "so fast". Of late, advanced technology confirms it experimentally. The electron-microscope, for instance, irremediably shatters the concept of a dimensioned "matter" (materia signata), Aquinian or other. The ultimate blow was struck when Einstein established that "matter" is Power, in a dense (intense) state. Indeed, that a measurement is in-and-of the Existent, and is accurate solely in the mind, can be attested to by anyone conversant with primary physics. Every self-respecting high-school student knows that the measuring of a yard of cloth for sale to a housewife, or the flow of 10,000,000 cu.ft. of high-pressure gas through a pipeline, results from an instantaneous abstraction which cuts off either knot of relationships into arbitrary units. All physical examplars of measure — rulers, containers, calipers, etc. — are approximators. Even atomic-clocks remain subject to the instabilities or vibrations of the Atom. Granted, physical accuracy increases in a ratio equal to an increase of the capacity to delve into and control microscopies. However, that this margin should be reduced to the infinitesimal in no way alters the situation — total accuracy means total, 100% is 100%, and not 99.999,999%.[6] The implications are evident. In particular, the age-old search for that elusive "material" building block of the universe should by now be abandoned. Once the units of physical measurements are found to be individualized and measured only in the mind, the problem is solved, for then the "act" of measuring "produces" an absolute. *The mind abstracts and defines a portion of whatever it may be resting upon, each unit being truthful to the extent that it corresponds and continues to correspond to the definition which created it.*

C. *Instantaneity of Decision*

The role of decisions in the thought process is pivotal, for the act of choosing is simultaneously an essential element to man's integration into the Real and the first step in the coagentship

6. The cesium atom clock, presently science's most accurate calibrating instrument, seems to confirm the radical indeterminacy of physical norms — as opposed to conceptual norms established by absolutizing and accepted by consensus. As uniform as the vibrations of cesium may be, these nonetheless vary sufficiently to cause an inaccuracy of 3 to 5 millionths of a second yearly. Even by the standards of an astronaut on his way to Mars such accuracy is more than adequate. Yet it is not absolute and the discrepancy, while minute, demonstrates that perfect physical calibration is unachieved, and in our opinion unachievable. More disturbing from the point of view of those who see in time and space, real or physical dimensions, subject to accurate calibration, is the discovery in 1967 that a cesium clock, which was being moved from Washington D. C. to Cape Fear N. C., ticked slower the farther away it got from the capital. Compounding the puzzlement of its keepers, it was also found to "tick" slower with the sunrise. To this "sunrise error" was next added, a slighter, yet detectable, "moonrise factor", at which point the scientists involved are said to have refused to comment upon astrology. Undoubtedly it is evidence, such as the above, of The Absolute's power to regulate the Universe to so exquisite a degree of ethereality, which prompted Einstein to affirm his: "humble admiration for the illimitable superior spirit who reveals himself in the slight details we are able to perceive with our frail and feeble minds".

process. Through coagentship man centers his attention upon certain knots of relationships to which for some reason he attaches greater than average relevance, and mensuration cum decision reduces these knots to manageable "size". Decision thus links the Principle of Absolutes with that of Clash, by providing the unit-criteria chosen by the measurer in his attempt to cope effectively with the challenges of the Outside.

Decision, third synact of thought-power, catapults man directly into the Now. Whereas with measurement, one travelled from Absolutes to Clash, with decision, the direction reverses. Leading-off with the particular, with the man created object, one eventually re-enters the Order of the Maximized. This occurs once the sum of an individual's personal clashes is exhausted.[7] While absoluteneity and instantaneity were only with difficulty associated with awareness and measurement, decision, a strictly temporal act, bares its character of absolute, of finality, for all but the blind. Literally it cuts Reality into items, "chunks", battles or, to use a generic term, into intellectual-units. This restores to it, its ancient, quasi-obsolete meaning of "the detachment of a part". With this restoration, a decision is existentialized. By encompassing whatever measure of Existence the abstracting mind choses to unitize or isolate, it engenders a real or "active" specimen of the category of Antropocities. Finally, to be noted, is an aspect of decision-making generally discounted, namely the agression factor inherent in decisions. Even in the transfer of ones gaze from the down-stream flow of a river to the up-stream, or still, the choosing of a spoonfull of ones vegetable soup from the center of the plate rather than from the edge, aggression plays a role. While the finality in a decision is so readily grasped that no further elaboration should technically be required, to illustrate the broad gamut of decisions, three additional examples which encompass the ideal, the insignificant and the catastrophic are provided. An instance of the latter,

---

7. Once the Universe is found to consist of a fixed number of Existential-Atoms whose modality, both externally and internally, is perforce one of absolute to absolute, infinity, infinite divisibility and infinite numbers can be dispensed with. When an Atom's quota of thought-quanta, that for instance of Bertrand Russell, has been used up, the divisibility process automatically comes to a halt.

would be President H. S. Truman giving the order to drop atom bomb number one upon Hiroshima, August 6, 1945. The decision character of this act is clear, for in it high drama and will are involved. Decisions are taken, however, even in as instinctive an act as in the putting down, by President Truman, of his left rather that right foot, upon getting out of bed the day of the bombing. The consciousness factor in Truman's decision in favor of one foot was undoubtedly quasi nil; yet an alternative being present, a decision was made. The third example, involving thought-power mainly, is double-edged. It involves a math professor who, having commented upon the weather, proceeds to proclaim that 2x2=5. Regardless of his motives, he thereby made a two-fold decision, that of switching his attention from the weather to arithmetic, and that of affirming an error or falsehood.[8]

It is most significative of the nature of Reality, that upon emerging unto the scene of the actively perceived relationship, the instantaneous quality of thought foists itself upon us. Awareness was, due to its essentially spatial character, difficultly accepted as absolutized. Mensuration, through which consciousness focusses upon time-space and their coordinates, speed and movement, appeared to mock the instantaneous. Only a detailed analysis and evidence drawn from physics, revealed it to also resolve itself into absolutes. With decision the reverse applies. While a decision ca be drawn out indefinitely, as by the congenital procrastinator, still the procrastinating is distinct from the belated decision; indeed the two are antithetic. The Choice of an objective, no matter how and when arrived at, involves a break, and any break or rupture is final — each being responsible for a new beginning and a new unit. Thus, at the level of decisions the paradox of the discontinuous in the continuous reveals itself. On the one hand, a decision can seemingly only be

8. A weather judgement and a deliberate mathematical error are opposed to highlight the key role of free-will. Agreeing with Royce — against the traditional Empiricists, who hold that error results from having an idea which fails to agree with its object — I maintain that there is error only if a concept fails to correspond with the Antropocities with which it is meant to conform. Further error, in the true or existential sense of the word, involves a decision to twist facts for the purpose of furthering aggressive aims. Aggression and free will are thereby situated at the heart of the Perceived. The subject is discussed at length in *Cosmic Jurisprudence.*

made if and when actualized amidst "flowing realities"; yet, on the other hand, each decision has its origin outside of our world, and "there" remains.

That each decision and with each, every intellectual birth should occur outside time-space, of itself offers no insurmountable obstacle. That which does, within the context of a materialistic ontology, is the fact that each beginning can be cut-up into what must, by Materialists, be held as an infinite number of new decisions, each infinity being pregnant of a further infinity of infinities. Faced with this dilemma, Leibniz sought a way out by seeing the process as ending at "a point in time-space smaller than which none could be imagined". An intelligent man, Leibniz was honest enough to claim in self-defence, that irrational or not, the stratagem, "the useful fiction", worked.

2. **Paradox of Divisibility at Infinity Solved: The Absolute Takes Over**

At this point two courses of action offer themselves. Choosing to consider a modality of absolute to absolute as empirically observed throughout the operation of thought, one could elect to see the case in favor of the Principle of Absolutes as closed. Going to the other extreme, one could dwell upon the key factors of each synact and their relationship. This would entail a detailed investigation of aggression and, specifically, of the Principle of Clash. Such an endeavor would exceed this work. The dilemma will be best solved by providing, in lieu of either alternative, an outline of the role of conflict in the absolute to absolute modality of thoughts, this minimal exposure to the aggressive aspects of the mind being essential to an understanding of its operation.

The reflections which follow and the conclusions which they impose, are implicit in the term thought-power. To see the intellect as dynamic, is not the same as to conceive it as some nebulous phantom from another world. Still less does the concept of thought-power as factual and integral to the Atom, correspond to the *Tabula Rasa* of Locke and company. Whereas those who ignore the dynamic content of thought must be satisfied with observing it as a foreign phenomenon, he who gives it its dynamic dimension, and takes into account the impact of Clash can tear its mechanism apart. The benefits are considerable.

Of immediate interest, is the fact that once aggression is integrated with the data provided by the Law of Critical Point, and set in the Universal Equation, the mystery of the seeming infinite divisibility of units dissolves.

A brief exposé of the weaknesses in the traditional attack upon the paradox of the finite in the infinite will provide contrast to the alternative about to be offered. It seems that to tackle the infinite divisibility question with the conventional weapons is to court failure for the basic reason that these deny all possibility of coming to grips with the real issue. Of course, it will be argued that this riddle has over the centuries been attacked from a multitude of angles, and that a broadside condemnation is unwarranted. Hardly, for their many differences notwithstanding, all previous theories are afflicted with the same disease: Becomingism. Whether Aristotelian, Cartesian, Hegelian, Marxist or Existentialist, all subscribe in some degree to the Whiteheadian thesis:

> It is nonsense to conceive of nature as a static fact, even for an instant devoid of duration. There is no nature apart from transition, and there is no transition apart from temporal duration.[9]

Restricted to speculation upon concepts and relationships, all deal with a Whiteheadian-like transitional. Metaphorically speaking, they float anchorless in time-space. Nor could it be otherwise. Short of Existential Atomism, there is no exit from the fog of Idealism. The reasons are threefold. Firstly, to ignore the atomic structure of Existence and its synactivity with Power, is to reject the homogeneity of both, to end up lost in a dichotomous, semi "ideal", semi "material" Cosmos, wherein all is evaluated upon an anthropocentric scale. Secondly, without a strict object the researcher can never identify his target. And how can he who knows not the identity of his subject, arrive at worthwhile knowledge? Thirdly, he who views the Universe as an undefinable, in which each evolutive "specificity" or "form" draws its "essence" from the "substance" of its neighbors, flounders in the grip of a vicious maelstrom of evanescent "nothings", upon

9. A. North Whitehead, Lecture Eighth, *Nature Alive* in Morton White, Editor, *The Age of Analysis, 20th Century Philosophers*, A mentor Book, New American Library, 1963, p. 88.

which even concepts as vaporous as "the continuous and discontinuous", cannot rationally be pinned. Without the Principle of Clash, conjugated with the Laws of Clash and Critical Point, and jointly applied to the Universal Equation, the philosopher is impotent. No accounting of the number of existential and conceptual-absolutes in the Universe can be made, let alone attempted. It is not, here, claimed that the exact number of units will be discovered. This rests beyond the grasp of an intellect as limited as man's. What is implied, is that he who dogmatically excludes a strict, transcendent subject from his calculations, condemns himself to generalities about an ever receding network of vacuities, whose nakedness and shame, even Whiteheadian robes of "actual entities" or "occasions" cannot hide. The outcome was predictable: The era of the Absurd. The coherent thinker had and did come to look upon life as a comedy and himself as a tragic joke whose personal freedom a Michel Foucault advises him to secure in insanity.

Even a cursory survey reveals the superiority of the tools already fashioned, as compared with the standard relativistic or processional kit, whose every working unit, being lodged in movement or in some facsimile of Bergsonian duration, reduces epistemology to shadow boxing. Together, the Existential-Atoms, Absolutes and the Cosmic Equation provide the researcher with a uniform raw material consisting of Dynamic-Facts, each of which, due to its discreteness, admits physical experimentation. To complete his equipment, only two additional items are required. These are an understanding of:

A. the synactivity of Existence, Truth and Reality, and

B. the profoundly qualitative character of the Real.

Due to their relevance, both subjects are dealt with separately in ensuing chapters — the synactive in the following and quality in chapter VI of Part II. Hence presently, in respect to the synactivity of Existence, Truth and Reality, one observation, which simultaneously provides the key to the question itself, and that needed to introduce quality will suffice.

Effectively the triad elaborates upon Absolutes, the principle which rules over all facts and relationships. In a nutshell, the synactivity of Reality and Truth to Existence, predicates that the former are subject to the same criteria as Existence, i.e. Reality or

Truth is indivisible, adimensional, univocal and coextensive. As was the case with Existence, all four criteria, when applicable to Truth, and by extension to knowledge translate into absolutes or thought quanta.

3. Quality Enters Into the Picture: Accounts for Time and Space

Hemmed in so tight a corral, and subject to as strict a code of behavior, each Atom, it would seem, becomes identical to the other, and must be indiscernible. This does not follow. As noted, both synacts of the Atom are qualitative. Because of this, the Universe as a unit is qualitative, and quality assuming the same role of cosmic radical as did oneness, synthesizes or homogenizes Existence and Power, and thereby makes immanence possible. Further, as a cosmic radical, it imposes its own radicals upon the Atom, which are freedom and efficiency. Hence, these also are constitutive factors of Power and Existence.[10]

Quality and its radicals owe their key role to the fact that they at once individuate and limit each Existent, thus rendering the Outside discernible. Stated otherwise quality endows man, caesium atom and lobo wolf with individuality.[11] However, every favor rendered has its price. Quality exacts in return for being ground of individuation that any non-absolute Atom be constrained within the limits of its individuality. In man's case, his qualities imbue him, among other things, with sensations of space and time, movement and achievement. Jointly, the sensations which result from these "natural limitations" force man to create a world to his own image, also to his own liking.

A thorough analysis of mind-dependence universes would involve a study of the relativistic character of time-space, and a conciliation of this with maximization, which is to say with the factual state of Power and the consequent immovability of each Atom. Since both subjects are studied in coming chapters, only those observations required to render intelligible the mechanism whereby thought, even when operating in time-space, must do so

10. Re status of master radical of quality, cf. secs. 6 and 7, chap. VI, Pt. II.
11. Limit, in this context, does not refer to the arbitrary ideal dimensions which correspond to a given Antropocity resident of a mind, but rather to the inneity itself of the Atom which is specific and qualitative.

by bursts, by appositing absolute to absolute, will be dealt with here.

Beginning with the easier task of establishing the rationale behind the absolutist modality of thought-power, one finds this implicit in earlier findings. Man, while allowed to "create" a cosmos to his size and liking, is not released from obedience to the Principle of Absolutes. His mind can only operate according to the modality of the Real. His peripheral world depends upon his ability to intellectually embrace absolutes, the more far-reaching and incisive the absolute, the greater the truth-factor, and the deeper the communion with Reality. Thus Absolutes provide man with his only peephole into the realm of Truth and, through Truth, into Reality itself. An unbiased reading of natural phenomena confirms this.

Harkening back to the falling leaves of the neighbor's weeping willow, the conventional interpretation has it that each leaf falls one by one, over a protracted period, covering in the process a determinable distance. Each leaf is seen as an object, indeed by some, as an Existent, capable of free movement in Cartesian space. From the perspective of a landscape painter out to capture an autumn scene, or from that of a disgruntled home owner sizing up the mess of leaves which he soon must rake up, the sequential nature of each falling is valid. In-fact there is no falling. Rather, only a subjective assessment of more or less intense, cosmic relationships, grasped weakly by a weak intellect, and by this intellect cut into Antropocities, into so many frames — as in a motion picture projected too slowly upon its screen.

To intimate that physically leaves in autumn do not fall, and, compounding the outrage, to affirm that the witnessing of the five weeks long episode is the result of a series of instantaneous intellectual flashes, an accumulation of instantaneities, may arouse disbelief. Such an interpretation does appear outlandish. Yet, close scrutiny vindicates it. Presently, to limit anticipation, only a summary analysis of the interplay of the factors responsible for the out-of-space and out-of-time nature of thought will be considered. This will leave many questions unanswered, yet should, nonetheless, provide a working knowledge of the overall process. In effect, it will place us in the position of the housewife who knows how to press the starter on the family car, but who has no idea as to what a starter is. Still, her ignorance of advanced mechanics does not prevent her from going shopping. Similarly, the technicalities of quality are not essential to a basic understanding of the present problem.

Quality is the product or alternately the agent responsible for the synactivity of Existence with Power. To this synactivity Existence contributes mainly specificity, and Power the more-or-less or intensity factor. If one realizes that, due to maximization, the As-is is not placed in jeopardy by the greater or lesser efficiency of an Atom, a host of otherwise intractable problems are solved, not the least of which being the apparent incompatibility of the time-space syndrome and its product — the feeling of witnessing discontinuities. Truth, Reality and Existence, as noted, are synactive. To make Truth a synact of Reality and Existence, implies that as Truth is an absolutized intellectual grasping of Reality, Reality in turn has its foundation upon Existence. Reality, in effect, constitutes the communication, as a Truth, of the fulness of It which possesses Existence; of It which is grounded upon the concrete, upon that which can be touched, felt, etc. The "etc." in this context is relevant. It encompasses, in total objectivity, all that which, while real, evades the grasp of non-absolute Atoms. These three abbreviating letters hold the key to many unresolved issues. In particular, they dispose of the Phenomenologist's notion that Truth is Becoming; is the product of a "sedimentation". This error did not originate with Husserl and his colleagues. It is as old as philosophy. Men seem incapable or unwilling to draw the distinction between knowledge and Truth. Yet, until this is done, any hope of deciphering the epistemological code, is foredoomed. The answer lies in realizing that Bergson, Whitehead and company notwithstanding, Reality hovers above all process. Reality is grounded upon-and-in fact. While knowledge is correctly defined as a "sedimentation", or by any other metaphor, and while it occurs in the Now, Truth forever resides in the Real, outside time-space, securely anchored in absolutes. Implicit in the above, is the Obscure-Absolute, the epistemological counterpart of the Existential-Atom. Obscure-Absolutes constitute the sole existential truths within reach of man. The It alone is grasped as a truth, its qualities and relationality can only be the subject of knowledge. Stated otherwise, it is possible to grasp the truth, the fact that other Selves are present. However, one must speak of such truths as

Obscure-Absolutes because these, due to their cosmic immanence, are grasped but obscurely. Even when prehended sensually, as when two humans are engaged in a fist fight each, before his opponent, remains hidden in an impenetrable fog. Much as one knows that a ship in the night is at sea — a horn has bellowed faintly, and a light glimmered — yet one knows not what ship and to what purpose, so it is between Existents. *Each is not only an Outsider in invincible ownership of itself, but each remains obscure before every other, excepting The Absolute.*[12]

That the total grasp of an existential truth — this would imply a grasp of the full inneity of an Atom, — exceeds our reach is readily ascertainable. To appreciate our limitations where relationships are at play, one has only to consider the bankruptcy of his understanding of his mother or wife, or still to consider how little he knows about the feelings and state of health of any one of the two billion cells in his liver — yet such are a "part" of him. Unable to grasp the Universe in the plenitude of its Presences, an Atom, whose powers are non-absolute, settles for the next best bet. It "creates" its own universe. In man's case, this means that boundaries or peripheries such as time, space and the coordinates thereof (activity, speed, etc.), and appetites (sense data, ideas and dimensions), are established to place a portion of the Real within his field of awareness. All such actualities and sense-data are subjective phenomena. He who surveys the Universe, soon realizes that for all of its residents except the sentient Atoms, neither time nor space has meaning. The question of dimensions and in particular those of thought for the non-thinking is a non-problem. The same applies to God before whom the full inneity of Its Self and of the Cosmos, is present beyond time-space and any Eddingtonesque dimensions.[13]

4. Order of Research Inverted: From Reality Into Time-Space Rather Than Vice Versa

The next premise is embryonic in the previous observations. Since perception and its fruit, knowledge implant the thinker

12. One of many reasons for the relevance of the Obscure-Absolute is its intimate link with the resolution of Kant's "scandal of philosophy"; namely, man's inability to prove the existence of Existence.
13. Re Eddington and the nature of dimensions, cf. footnote 2, chap. VI, Pt. I.

aggressively into the flesh of Reality, knowledge — a degenerative modality of Truth — must be obtained through the same process as that through which Truth is extracted from Reality, namely by the appositing of absolute against absolute. If this can be established empirically, the promise held out earlier, that the paradox of the discontinuous in the continuous dissolved once Absolutes took over, will be fulfilled. Actually, the fulfilment is assured by the first step. To make of Existence a fact divided into an X-number of facts, simultaneously inverts the order of research precedences usually respected by ontologists, and pre-empts all further right to divisibility. Thus to situate the seat of atomism at the core of the existential and make each Atom in the equation U = X (E : A), dimensionless, disposes of the problem of the apparent divisibility of the Real. *Since Existential-Atoms are invincibly unique and dimensionless, each is physically indivisible, and divisibility when-and-where encountered is apparent or illusory.* In short, divisibility is pushed-off the stage of Reality unto that of the Perceived.

Some probably remain unconvinced. While seeing merit in the notion that thought operates outside time — agreeing, for instance, with Bergson who saw: "intelligence... take from far to far, quasi-instantaneous views, upon the undivided mobility of the real...", yet, they may be perturbed in face of the stubborn persistence of time and space, both of which invest us, from "all sides and through night and day". It is, after all, one thing to see Absolutes reigning throughout the Universe, and quite another, merely upon that basis, to cavalierly dismiss time-space. The remainder of this chapter seeks to demonstrate with the aid of actual-life situations that both dimensions are illusory; are real-illusions born and residing only in minds endowed with the power to process the Universe through such parameters.

Generally ontologists have researched the relationship of time-space to reality by initially situating both in an anthropocentric context. They hoped to be able, it seems, to worm their way from the particular to the general, from the inside to the outside, thence to grasp the whole. The approach herein is different. Up to this point, time-space has been purposely ignored. The result: a universe peopled solely with absolutes. The problem hence presents itself from a different angle. Whereas those who see time-space as causative of the Real find themselves fitting man in time-space, which is to say fitting the discontinuous into the continuous, *the problem is now inverted: time-space fits into absolutes.*

5. Time-Space-Speed: Real-Illusions, a Few Observations

The inversion suggested above goes a long way towards solving the dilemma which discrete units, situated in a continuous medium presents, since space and time wise, the inserting of any number of absolutes upon absolutes presents no difficulty. Absolutes, being dimensionless, can be "piled-up" one upon the other indefinitely without danger of overcrowding.[14] As implausible as such a solution may sound to the ear of a Materialist, it is the correct one. Physically, there exists no such "thing" as the continuous. *The Real consists solely of dimensionless intensities, either absolute or absolutized, either existential or ideal.* Time and space, together with their coordinates must be relegated to the status of real-illusions, or still, to that of qualitative norms.

The advocates of real time-space cannot be expected to take this sitting down. It will be argued that, while any number of absolutes or instantaneities can be stacked in time-space, nonetheless a series of instantaneities can never add up to dimensions, either temporal or spatial. Also the term real-illusion will probably be declared contradictory. Actually, closer scrutiny does not reveal contradiction so much as inadequacy of language — a defect which afflicts all human term-symbols to some extent. The term real-illusion is to be interpreted as follows. The adjective, real, speaks in behalf of man. The noun, illusion, testifying on behalf of Reality, seeks to keep the record straight. It could be said that their joint role is that of a courtjester, called to deflate our anthropocentric pretensions. If ever there was need for some intellectual chastising, it is in our space-travel era in which man, more desperately than ever, seeks to reduce the Universe to his puny dimensions; seeks among other things the "outer limit" of the Cosmos with radio-telescopes and similar dishes and utensils.

---

14. The above, it seems, disposes of the medieval quarrel, real or apocryphal, concerning the number of angels which can comfortably sit upon the head of a pin.

The real in real-illusion is said to speak for man, to emphasize that at the humdrum level of day-to-day living time and space are valid concepts and that, with appetites and sense perceptions both have a legitimate role to play in all disciplines, including ontology and ethics. Ontology-wise the temporo-spatial quality, and the bias which this gives to relationships, constantly impinge upon ones concept of the Real. Ethic-wise, the same applies. The efficiency of a given behavior pattern can only be gauged upon a scale of past, present and future. Further, the Principle of Clash is eminently tied to time-space. Similarly, the first three Universal Laws apply exclusively to the Perceived — only the Fourth, Similitudes, and the Fifth, Oneness, being relevant to both Orders. To demote time and space to the status of real-illusions, does not deny or reduce their role in the human drama. Rather it respects the objectivity of Existence, and places an unshakeable foundation under Truth. If time-space is not assessed as a relative factor in a maximized universe, the fact-of-truth loses all meaning. Existence must be intellectually persecuted into oblivion; with the Self itself being vaporized into the void, as witness Santayana's concept of man as "the last bubble in a long process of fermentation".[15] In summary, to remain in contact with Reality it is necessary to entertain towards both time and space an ambivalent attitude. At the Order of the Real, both rate as illusions, while at the Now both are real, but owe their realism to a quality factor. This last observation is highly relevant. Since the seminal factor responsible for the sequential flux of knowledge is a quality, namely the human specificity, one can with considerable accuracy affirm that quality mothers time-space. This in part, explains the role of cosmic radical alloted to it earlier.

---

15. The sorry plight devolved upon man by the advocates of Becomingism is illustrated by this quote from Bertrand Russell's *Why I Am Not a Christian*, New York, Simon and Shuster, 1957, p. 89.

> "The mental continuity of a person is a continuity of habit and memory: there was yesterday one person whose feelings I can remember, and that person I regard as myself of yesterday; but in fact myself of yesterday was only certain mental occurrences which are now remembered and are regarded as part of the person who now recollects them. All that constitutes a person is a series of experiences connected by memory and by certain similarities of the sort we call habit."

6. Aggression Fathers Time-Space

Next on the agenda is aggression, the despot of the Now, which dictates the mechanics of thought, and in so doing accounts for the real in the pair, real-illusion. Indeed the influence of aggression throughout the Perceived is so radical that it determines, one could even hazard the expression "fathers time-space". In view of this, it is surprising that aggression has, by and large, been ignored by ontologists and/or epistemologists. Maine de Biran and Bergson must be absolved to an extent, while Hegel and his disciples, notably the Marxists, can be cited as full exceptions to the rule. However, since Hegelianism lacks all ontological foundation, an analysis of conflict attempted within its framework leads to weird conclusions, as witness the notion that Truth is Becoming. In sum, he who fails to recognize that aggression and clash govern all relationships at the Perceived, can never join the ranks of the Realists. Nor will he penetrate the core of Reality, there to grasp its inner mechanism, for *aggression, progenitor of time-space, exceeds its offsprings in importance, and surfaces as the determining factor in all cosmic and social processes.* Cosmic and social processes are, however, not presently the concern — only aggression's relationship to time-space and thought. Therefore only two directly related factors will get our attention. These are:

A. the qualities particular to human thought, and

B. the impact of aggression upon the intellect.

The justification for "B" is clear. "A", it may be feared, will involve repetition. Actually, additional inquiry into thought-power is warranted, since the aspects to be dealt with, essential to an understanding of the interplay of thought and aggression, have not yet been discussed.

7. Intellectual-Power: The Human Brand, Dynamic and Qualitative, Hence Absolutist

Research into the intellect is generally restricted to man. This approach, provided that adequate safeguards are taken, is justified, for the human mind alone can be dealt with empirically. Men can intelligently discuss the motivation and content of their thoughts, and can extrapolate their findings to a neighbor, friend or enemy, but hardly to a Rhesus monkey, angel or martian. The danger inherent in a man-centered approach is that the researcher, fenced-in, will forget and at times systematically refuse, to situate the issue in its cosmic context — the only one in which it can be compassed scientifically. Once the intellect is perceived as a non-physical, dichotomizing factor, exclusive to man, the mind is dissected clinically, in isolation from the Atom of which it constitutes but one quality, that of a presentialization agent.

Since the concept of presentiality is unfamiliar, it seems advisable to begin this investigation of the relationship between thought, time-space and aggression with a brief look at the univerqualities of the Atom, in particular that responsible for making man and his intellect, different from other species, namely quality.

A. *Thought-Power Substantially identical to Fist or Magnetic Power*

The first point to consider is that since Existence and its synact, Power, are univocal, any radical of either, such as quality, must also prove univocal. In other words, all that which is attributable to Existence and Power, is equally attributable to the qualitative. Next, presentiality — the Fact-of-being-a-Presence — represents the quintessential quality. Stated differently, the Atom upon achieving its final metamorphosis, reveals itself a Presence. There are, however, no end of manners in which one can present ones self to the Outside. It follows that the presential contains all qualities, as it must in a universe composed of univocal, coeval and dimensionless Atoms. Thus, the range of Presences in the Universe is from absolute to negligible. Before The Absolute all stand naked, in utter immanence, while to the bat venturing on its nocturnal hunt, the world must appear as a bleak, personalized barrenness. But adimensionality and its corollaries, coevality and coextension are not without their reward. Since it suffices for a Presence *to-be* that an It should exist and be dynamic, each Atom, even the puniest, imposes its presence with greater or lesser efficiency. This varying efficiency, the key to the nature, as distinct from the operationality of thought, reveals the ambivalence of the Atoms. Each is at once identical to and different from the other. While all are equal in their presentiality, the presence of each, because of the basic qualitativity inherent in the Fact-of-to-be, varies in its intensity (richness or diversity). As a Presence an uranium atom exerts a more profound impact upon the Universe than does a hydrogen atom; a mosquito atom an impact greater still than that of an uranium atom — which the mosquito might incorporate. Yet, thought, a measure of which the mosquito possesses, does not radically differentiate its existence from that of the uranium. Only increased efficiency is involved. Further, even as between the individuals of a same species, thought-power is eminently graduable. In this respect, consider the differences of intelligence between a mongoloid and a Lenin. The similitude or univocity of thought-power to every other type of power, by itself, would guarantee its homogenizing with the remainder of the physical or "material" universe. When, at the time of its metamorphosis, the Fact-of-to-be transmutes into a Cosmic-Presence, the qualitative and miscibility characteristics of thought become glaring.

B. *Thought or Intellect-Power: Absolutist in Its Modality*

The second characteristic of thought presently of concern, its absolutist modality, is also a corollary of the univocity of the Atom. Thought-power, we saw, constitutes an efficient presentializing agent. Since Existence and Presence are the two faces of the same coin, any agent which augments Presence is, firstly existential, and secondly, because of the synactivity of Existence to Truth, a participant in Truth. Further, such a factor will be integral to an absolute, for, as is demonstrated in the chapter following, truthfulness presupposes absoluteness. Thus, thought being eminently presential partakes of the modality of Truth and resides in absolutes.

Few will question the view that thought-power, when unitized through the medium of truths, involves absolutes. The difficulty arises when the time comes to define a truth, for agreement upon this is anything but general, except for the case of mathematical truths, viz. one plus one equals two, upon which the consensus can be deemed unanimous. Luckily, for the present demonstration, there is no need for a consensus extending beyond mathematics — save to have it include the category of the Obscure-Absolutes. This should be readily granted, for an

Obscure-Absolute encompasses no relationships, but rather only localizes a bare Self, grasped in-fact or in imagination, in its status of differentiated unit. Only a believer in outright Monism would deny this request.

The province of Truth thus restricted, the remainder of the realm of thought falls under the wing of knowledge. Since knowledge encompasses the majority of "intellectual" situations, lived or speculative, the overall argument may thereby seem weakened. This does not follow. Presently, the purpose is not to distinguish between truth and error and/or knowledge. Only the operation of thought-power is being investigated and clearly, the acquiring or purveying of knowledge, be this truthful, partial or erroneous, necessitates an expenditure of energy. The differences among these three categories are merely ones of quality. Knowledge of any type implicates Truth, degenerated to the norm of the knower, and as such, it partakes of the dynamic and presential, as well as of the instantaneous or absolute. In summary, thought-power, being integral to the human atom, partakes of the latter's absolutist character and, being quantized, resides in the Absolute and Instantaneous; is outside of all dimensions. It follows that its speed is absolute-speed.

8. Physical-Time as Distinct from Intellectual-Time

Next comes the problem presented by physical time-space, such as that involved in the actual falling of leaves. Until this is disposed of, to inject absolutes and instantaneities into falling leaves is an exercise in futility. Due to the cosmicity of each Atom, the issue of real-time is, as were the previous, closely related to cosmic coagency, and can be dealt with in detail only when the latter has been analyzed. Fortunately, the basics of cosmic coagency being simple, these can now be outlined, and this should provide data sufficient to demonstrate the conformability of physical with intellectual-time. *Coagentship describes the relationship which results when an Atom intensifies and focusses its power upon a specific knot of its relationships, which knot it seeks to use, consciously or subconsciously, as a controlled-agent in its struggle for self-realization. When performed by man the process produces an Antropocity.*[16]

16. Re Coagentship, cf. sec. 6, chap. I, Pt III.

Coagentship coupled with the fact that an intellectual conquest (prehension) represents but one among the many elements in an act of aggression, accounts for the disparity of speed between the thought which one has of a falling leaf and its actual falling. When under attack, the Atom, in its rolė of Outsider, can offer little or no resistance to its being grasped by the highly penetrating intellect-power of an adversary. However, an intellectual conquest is a far cry from an existential conquest — the actual taking-possession of the conquered, by the conqueror. What occurs in intellect-power conflicts is that:

A. because of the inviolability of every Atom, and

B. because of the immanence of all to all,

every conquest involves only a measure of domination. The conquered, man, martian, muon or molybdenum, is never possessed by any one or combination of aggressors. Conquest, as distinct from a defeat induced by the breaching of a critical-point and a subsequent death, speaks of flux and of control.

Further, no one is ever alone in his resistance to aggression. Indeed, due to coextensivity, each receives aid from all in its endeavor to deny itself to any enemy or conglomerate of enemies. Every Atom, the Universe throughout, even the aggressor, contributes its greater or lesser quota of dead weight; serves to render the attacked more opaque, more distinct to It or those seeking to dominate it. Nor is any satisfied with an anonymous aid. Coagentship enters the picture. Each, in its fight for survival, strives to attach to itself, by the myriad, coagential allies from all species — cells, atoms, armor plate, stone walls, etc. The more intimate and intense the coagential relationship, the heavier the mass, the denser the opacity, which the beleagured can oppose to the enemy. In other words, the moving of knights on a chess board by Fischer in the Reykjavik 1972 world championship match, and the planning by Napoleon of grenadier charges on the plains of Austerlitz, did not involve thought-power alone. In either project, the intellectual prowess of the champion was but one factor, as every will involved aggressed and resisted the wills of Fischer and Napoleon.[17] The low density of thought-power, is

17. Every Dynamic-Fact possesses a will and freedom and the Outsider is reduced, when not cooperating, to oppress it. It follows that, ontologically, the notions of neutrality and passivity have no meaning. Either only describes

especially evident when, as in the above scenarios, the intellectual content of the will to conquer is maximal — a situation which raises the ratio of resistive time-space proportionally, for while thought is instantaneous, it nonetheless, as part and parcel of the Atom, must submit to the sum of obstacles which its owners encounter. Reality is not purely conceptual. Dynamic-wise, thought-power actually plays but a minor, albeit in many situations decisive, role. A qualitative factor, it suffers the fate of its master.

This companionship of thought with the other qualities of its owner, stands out in the case of bodily health. For instance, perception and mind concentration can be gradually improved by a well-balanced diet. Similarly, the opposite occurs in cases of over-indulgence. If the gluttony is radical, as in an excessive use of alcohol, the effects can be dramatic. The secondary senses, which are but an extension of the intellectual sense, become perverted or even destroyed. At the very least, both are temporarily distorted. That thought-power, as distinct from a thought *per se*, is a quality of the Atom, is in such situations clearly established, most unquestionably so in the case of drug-induced hallucinations. As the drugging agent loses its grip, the sufferer's thought-power returns more or less to its original level.

The above is further confirmed by the fact that time-space and their coordinate, speed, as well as the multitude of critical-points breached during the chess and military conflicts cited, assume different readings for each individual. For the flu bugs which attacked Fischer, the chess tournament was a non-event. Fischer and the fertile medium which he provided for the propagation of their species, was their sole concern. Similarly for Napoleon's horse, Austerlitz amounted to nothing more than a lost opportunity to enjoy a good rest in the pasture — the faithful mount being quite unconcerned with the balance of power in Europe. The difference between Existential-Atoms, regardless of species, is qualitative and efficiency-oriented. Due to the similitude of process throughout the Universe (Fourth Universal Law), thought submits to the same parameters as any other

---

a state of lesser aggressivity, for all Atoms, because dynamic, operate above 0% efficiency, and are subsumed in conflict. Thus 100% passivity exists nowhere in the Now, nor for that matter in the Real.

quality. If anything, it is the form of power subject, quality-wise, to the broadest spectrum of variations. A good example of inter-species variety is the game of wits which pits man and weasel. While no trapper has succeeded in seeing life "through the mind" of a weasel, it seems safe to assume that each lives and fights in a different world. Yet both remain bound by Universal Law and, in final analysis, quality-intensity alone decides of the outcome between trapper and trapped. In some instances the weasel wins — it gets away with the bait. In others the trapper wins — he gets the pelt.

Progressing from the beast-human duel to that which pits man against man, one finds that the quality-intensity of thought performs the same differentiation function. Over and above this, one can observe quality-intensity as a factor which, in certain situations, literally dissolves and evacuates time-space. To illustrate, let us look at chess, a game in which a winning strategy, which may require hundreds of plodding moves on the part of the slower-witted or inexperienced, is reduced to a single eagle-like sweep, by the talented and experienced. Then, intellectual-time as distinct from physical-time — that required to move the pieces and to wait upon the plodding opponent — is held in abeyance. A Robert Fischer for instance, in a match with myself, could survey the board in one swoop (awareness), instantly size it up (measurement), and just as quickly anticipate the winning moves (decision). Conceding this telescoping, some will argue that Fischer would nonetheless "spend some time" in making up his mind. Firstly, to "allot so much time" to his intellectual operation, is arbitrary, it being impossible to, in-fact, pinpoint the beginning and the end of the decision process. Secondly, should the above be granted *prima facie* validity, it remains that as between master and novice, a single decision substitutes for a number of inefficient decisions, each an absolute in its own right. Effectively, hundreds of absolutes ensconce themselves in a single. This same telescoping on a broader plane occurs when a general's initial orders are so encompassing as to guarantee him victory — in anticipation. Napoleon is credited by strategists with such foresight. Intuiting and anticipating his opponent's every move, he could often with inferior forces, as at Austerlitz, sweep the battlefield. Nor is this trait restricted to military leaders. One discovers it among politicians, businessmen and, possibly at its highest level, in intellectuals who devote their energies to theory. The rationale is simple. Each Atom, being adimensional, enjoys an universal relationship and it follows: *each has existentially but one embracing point-of-contact with every other. Each is a continuity, and isolated incidents are merely grasped intensities or Antropocities.* The phenomenon is aptly described by A. N. Whitehead's notion of "concrescences" or "actual entities"; with the difference that, in this instance, the "concrescence" or "actual entity" is not an Atom, but a high-point in observed relationships. Quality and aggression-wise, Fischer and Napoleon and each of us, must submit to the aggression of every will throughout the Cosmos — that of their prime opponents, Spassky and Weyrother in the case of Fischer and Napoleon, *but equally of such conglomerations of lesser opponents as manifest their presence weatherly, horsely, virusly, fatiguely and bulletly, etc. It is these myriads of more or less intense knots of resistance which temporalize and spatialize "events". Thought-power, blended with and oppressed by these is forced to compromise, to see more or less far or clearly, to feel more or less pleasantly*. Indeed it constantly goes out of commission, as when one is knocked out or sleeps at night. Reality persists unscathed. But time and space are no more.

In sum, thought-power, because it must blend with its allies such as electric and calcium-power to overcome common enemies, suffers from being obscured, densified, and massified, etc., and it is the sensations, the "illusions", with which this aggression fills the intellect which are equated with time-space.

9. Memory-Foresight Throw Additional Light Upon the Nature of Time-Space

The above may seem contradictory. Has it not on the one hand been declared that thought operates by bursts through a stop-and-go process, and on the other, assumed that due to immanence there are no discontinuities; that for example *leaves in autumn do not fall* from branch to ground, but are only perceived as doing so? "Certainly", it is objected, "leaves do fall; Fischer and Napoleon did move in time-space; in any case, fall or no fall, the continuous and discontinuous remain forever incompatible."

Empirically the case could rest upon the assertion that quality explains the paradox. However, the relevance of the issue warrants further investigation into two subqualities which jointly throw considerable light upon Zeno's paradoxical arrow, which like my leaf, does not move. These two newcomers in the stable of qualities (shared in varying degrees by all thinking Atoms) are memory and foresight. Due to the need of dealing with first things first, neither will be analyzed extensively in this context. Only their status within the Atom, and their role in the conciliation of the thought process with Reality and Truth will be investigated. This is on the understanding that by the time the Atom completes its metamorphoses, and stands fully fleshed, the data required to decipher both in more detail and deductively as well as empirically, will be provided.

Outlined in general terms, the contribution of memory-foresight to the overall life process is as follows. Whereas man depends upon his perception of discontinuities or quantizing absolutes to insert himself into the Perceived, memory-foresight, reversing the flux of grasped data, allows him to maintain a foothold in the As-is. Effectively, memory-foresight connects the two Orders by providing a measure of continuity, tailored to the intellectual qualities of the thinker, and extending into a subjective "past" and "future". Intimately linked to aggression, the pair makes it possible for man to simultaneously conquer his adversaries intelligently (constructively), and achieve some degree of mastery over his Self.[18] Figuratively it acts as the connecting rod or agent between the inner world of the Self and the Outside.

When introspective, memory-foresight enables the individual to experience the Self as a oneness and fact residing outside his narrow Now and independent of all exterior influences. Without these helpmates, man would be reduced to the incoherent state wished upon him by Hume:

---

18. While the overall efficiency of man's understanding of his Self depends upon the quality of his intellect, it is also governed by extraneous factors and specifically by the efficiency with which he coagentizes with the Atoms said to compose his body. The memory factor, for instance, can be diminished by an insignificant shortage of infinitesimal iodines. An iodine is not, as most would have it, "part of man" but solely one of the multitudinous Existents with which we must struggle or coagentize effectively to maintain a presence in the Now.

> A bundle or collection of different perceptions, which succeed each other with inconceivable rapidity, and are in perpetual flux and movement...

With their aid, either being more or less efficient, he takes Possession-of-the-Self.[19] While essential to an understanding of human behavior, the memory-foresight complex when aimed at the Self, is not as pertinent to the present problem as when directed outwards, for then both become aggressive and constructive. Aggressive and constructive means that when man directs his memory and foresight, plus his will towards Outsiders, all three become conquest-oriented, and it is through an analysis of the intellectual content of conquest, that the absolutism of concepts is fully revealed.

The key to an understanding of memory and foresight is the realization that both are qualities, neither of which bears witness to true dimensions. Subjective faculties, they operate solely in the Now. Every Existent being present to every other, beyond all dimensions, both are absent at the Real. Therein all simply reside in the As-is — ones minutest, most harmless relationship with the most insignificant flea being neither stored nor foreseen, but factually prehended and felt. *Memory, conceived as a storage bin, and foresight, envisioned as a psychic trip into an imagined future, are so only for man and such as are immersed in clash. In effect, both are coordinates of the encounter of the qualitative with aggression.*[20]

The qualitativity of awareness being already dealt with, the next question to consider is the behavior of the intellect in an aggression-oriented medium. Aggression enters the picture, when one or more Atoms, each free (in inalienable possession of itself), refuses to mediumize (denies itself to the other). Refusal, warranted or not, threatens the survival of the grasping entity,

19. Consciousness of the Self is a fact intuitively grasped through an internal effort which precedes ontologically all consciousness of the Outside. Further, under the right psychological conditions a deliberate and rewarding act of Taking-Possession-of-the-Self can be achieved more or less at will — all Outsiders having been expelled, the Ego, in exclusive contact with itself takes over, becoming a solitary Presence to itself. The phenomenon is described in a polygraphed work entitled: *Taking-Possession-of-the-Self.*
20. The above reveals that the subconscious, a factor baffling for Materialists, is a natural outgrowth of the process being investigated.

and is tantamount to a declaration of war, for, he who needs the help of an Outsider (or thinks he does), and is rebuffed, has no alternative but to aggress. Quality becomes a factor, when each responding to the challenge, fights with the weapons, intellectual and otherwise, at its disposal. Man, immersed in Reality and hence in Truth, but unable to encompass either, uses whenever he can, the vehicle of Truth, absolutes, to aggress and hopefully existentialize. "Whenever" here is called for, because the perception of clearly delineated discontinuities is limited. There are thresholds, at the micro and macro ends of the spectrum of scopies, beyond which man cannot differentiate units with accuracy. At these extremes Antropocities and Absolute-Obscures, friendly or antagonistic, elude him. Relationships become blurred. *The intellect enters a fog. To navigate in this, it creates relativistic concepts. Then, both change (the flowing or evolutionary) and the boundless (infinity), are born. The utter space, the uncompassable is pronounced infinite. The minute, and by man's standards insignificant — an example would be one cell in his lungs — he fuses with myriads of equally undiscernable lung cells into a uniform mass, and these and their relationships with him, he defines as lungs and lungness.*

In between the extremes of sloppy consciousness lies the realm of Antropocities, each an outright creation, a mindfacture or objectification.[21] The Antropocity is born from the convergence of relevance with intensity. Of the two, only relevance was discussed when absolutes were categorized. It is still the only aspect implicated.

In a nutshell, Antropocities, objects or "things" are created for egotistical reasons. He who antropocizes responds to a need or desire to improve his standing in the Cosmos. Even though in the vast majority of cases, the conquering urge is subconscious, aggression always operates. Innately aware of its immersion in a hostile medium, the individual proceeds in self-defense and/or

21. Once the Real is dismantled into its genuine components, the nouns object and/or things, the key terms in many philosophical theses, are revealed for what they are, namely colloquial and imprecise pseudonyms for the notion of Antropocity. Together the terms Antropocity and Obscure-Absolute unambiguously differentiate the conceptual entity from the existential. Thereafter, the mindfactured : the rake, the chair and the orange, is no longer confused with the Existent, man, uranium or tree.

for self-promotion, to absolutize knots of relationships to which, rightly or wrongly, he attaches importance, simultaneously incorporating each Antropocity into an aggression equation. Each equation:

A. is complex, containing subequations, as in algebra,

B. partakes of the Absolute and resides outside time-space.

Thus the intimacy between time-space and memory-foresight. All four are by-products of the confrontation of a qualitatively non-absolute Atom with the Outside. The notions of memory and foresight merely describe intellectual limitations. Both, as time and space, would vanish if man were powerful enough to absolutely vanquish his enemies, be these men, rocks or oceans, or closer to home, if man could absolutely master those with whom he coagentizes to conquer a body; if he could, for instance, keep track of his every lung cell — of its health, demise, whether cancerous or not, etc. — and control each to his entire satisfaction.

Summing up, memory and foresight play a dual role. Epistemologically, they permit in-depth awareness and mensuration. Existentially, they link both Orders and thereby make intelligent aggression (existentialization) possible.

10. **Role of Aggression in the Intellectual Process**

The final, and a key factor of the mechanism of the intellect yet to be investigated is aggression and its corollary, the Principle of Clash. Since this work is restricted to an analysis of the Real and its components, the prime particles, only the basic features of the aggression content of thought-power will be considered.

An accurate interpretation of the role of aggression within the mind process predicates a grasp of two elements. The first concerns the ethics of the Law of Clash, and the second the status of the Principle of Clash relative to that of Absolutes.

Within the context of the Law of Clash, aggression and its consequences — conflicts, conquests and defeats — are void of moral or ethical connotation. Transcending good or evil, Clash is utterly objective and amoral. *It merely affirms the cruel but inescapable fact that prior cooperation notwithstanding, in final analysis, an Atom's perceived relationships involve conflict and subsequent conquest or defeat. Clash's sole criterion is a cold efficiency, gauged, in every instance, according to subjective goals defined* a priori. Both the Principle and the Law of Clash operate on the same basis as do mathematics, wherein the units are determined and the answers become foregone conclusions — as in 8 minus 3 equals 5. Where Clash is concerned, the more powerful and the less powerful are determined on the basis of the criteria of the other four Cosmic Laws. It follows that the relevance of aggression to thought is purely structural.

The second notion essential to an accurate reading of the aggression-thought script — the status of Clash with respect to Absolutes — is that since both Principles are prime, each rules its respective bailiwick unchallengeably. Both must also be compatible or comformable. *While conformability is to be expected, since Absolutes encompasses the cosmos, primacy rests with it. Their relationship is that of a condominium, with the role of* primus inter pares *devolving to Absolutes. As a consequence, just as thought-power, being a manifestation of Reality, evidences the characteristics of an absolute; so must it, when under the sway of the Principle of Clash, conform to a spirit of aggressivity. In sum, a condominium exercised over the mind by Absolutes and Clash causes thoughts to be at once, absolutes and conquest-oriented.*

Going back to an earlier analysis, one does not have to search long before discovering the trail of aggression. Any completed-thought, it was then noted, if reduced to its components, involves three synactive steps; awareness, measurement and decision. Even a cursory evaluation of this triad bares at once the aggressive character of thought and its absolute to absolute modality. While the first, awareness could operate in a placid Buddha-like medium or be reduced to the neutral receptivity of a computer, both measurement and decision speak of exercised will-power. Granted, in a universe at peace, one can measure and decide without aggressing. Not, however, in our Now. Concentrating upon decision, for it encapsulates its partners, one observes that decisions cut up the life force into as many absolutes as there are decisions. Further, since to decide is to be for or against, each completed-thought, each decision becomes a battle engaged and terminated — even when the operation occurs entirely "within the mind". Not only is thought broken up into a fixed number of quanta or absolutes, but each is a microcosmic exemplar of the titanic struggle which subsumes the Cosmos. A summary analysis of two real-life events referred to earlier, namely the Reykjavik chess tournament and the battle of Austerlitz, confirms such a thesis.

It would be belaboring the obvious, to insist upon the fact that Napoleon and Fischer expended a percentage of their life-energy at Austerlitz and Reykjavik, and that both, as principals, were involved in conflict. In excess of 31 000 men died at Austerlitz, and the reverberations of the Fischer-Spassky contest were still being manifest in the actions of the Soviet government eight months later. Moscow, humiliated by the defeat of its standard bearer, under the pretext of raising the "moral caliber" of Soviet sportsmen, launched a campaign of vilification of Spassky — to eventually reduce him to a social pariah. Next, a closer look at both events confirms at once, the theory of thought unitization and its nature of conflict *cum* minor conflict within the greater, thus validating an earlier affirmation that, "any number of absolutes can fit and rest comfortably in an absolute without danger of overcrowding". This latter is of considerable relevance for it establishes experimentally the adimensionality of the Atom and the intensity characteristic of Power. That the champions of Austerlitz and Reykjavik did firstly form a global strategy, and secondly broke this up into subplans, as they transferred their aggressive impulses from enemy to enemy, thereby cutting up their intellect-power into quanta, is hardly open to doubt. For example, while no official record states that during either event Bonaparte and Fischer took time-off to satisfy the call of nature, its probability is such that a biologist would automatically insert it in his equations. Further, regardless of ones concentration upon a problem — even that of winning the battle of Austerlitz — it is physically impossible for a normal person to urinate and/or defecate without diverting, at least subliminally, his mind from his prime task. This being the case, upon either Bonaparte or Fischer having relieved himself, a break in the continuity of their main trend of thought occurred and their aggression was diverted from one set of enemies to another. Physically, a battle within a battle took place. The two requisites — a cutting-up of thought-power and an aggression-oriented behavior were thereby fulfilled. To ponder and decide whether or not to order ones reserve battalions to bolster the left wing rather than the right, is to concentrate upon an enemy different from those pressuring an overflowing bladder. In the one situation, other humans are the prime antagonists. In the other, waters and miscellaneous chemical agents attack and press with increasing urgency (intensity), in *a concerted effort* to escape from the domination of he who a few hours earlier, imposed his jaws, gullet and will upon them.

In summary, in these two, as in any situation real or imaginable, the three synacts of thought, namely a survey, an assessment of priorities and a choice-decision, are at some time or other triggered by different goals, and the mind fills with a series of thought-quanta. As a result, thought-power submits to the rule of the Principle of Absolutes, on the same basis as does the Atom as Atom.

The profound impact of a theory of aggressive-thought-quanta upon epistemology and the social and behavioral sciences in general, suggests a few preliminary reflexions. The theory, by imparting to Now situations an aggressivity which carries its own justification and makes of aggression the norm of life, widens further the breach between Dynamic Vision and other world views. Granted, other systems include aggression in their computations. However, such as do, do so either incidentally or subliminally, or, going to the other extreme, they inject it on so heroic a scale — the reference is to the Marxist hypothesis of Thesis, Antithesis and Synthesis — that aggression thus depicted, bears no relevance to day-to-day events, nor any whatsoever to Reality, and instead constitutes the basic dogma of a new religion. The theory's impact upon epistemology viewed as an independent discipline is equally salutary. Over the centuries epistemologists have dealt with concepts as with abstractions issued from and residing in another world — a view dramatically reinforced by the spread of Cartesianism. The ideational, while accepted as a fact-of-life, is simultaneously treated as independent of "matter"; as non-physical. Hence, the ambivalence. The ideal will be, by the same individual or school, at one time idolized and at another scorned. When thought is reduced to a fixed number of battles, not only is the usual "matter-spirit" dichotomy eliminated but, to all intents and purposes, the aggressive urge becomes the stuff of existence in the Now. Man loses any right to neutrality, pacifism and even peace, save that known as inner peace — a peace earned as reward for battles well fought. Thereafter, in truth, one can affirm that to conquer is to live. The implications of this proposition, especially where society is concerned, perhaps frightens. As the closing chapter will reveal, such a fear is not only unwarranted, but unless exorcised, is deadly to individual and civilization alike.

11. Conclusion

Since each Existential-Atom is transcendent and an absolute, and as such entertains a cosmic relationship with every other, existentially (at the Real) the modality of the Universe is one of absolute to absolute. Further, since thought operates through a three phase cycle of awareness, measurement and choice-decision, which produces, once completed, a conquest-oriented quantum, each of which aggresses against another quantum, the modality of the intellect also is one of absolute pitted against absolute. The existential and conceptual being both subject to a modality of absolutes, the Prime or First Principle of the Universe becomes :

The modality of the Universe and of its processes is one of absolute to absolute.

chapter VIII

Requisites of Existential Individuation Analyzed

Reality itself makes demands, and the method must follow; reality offers itself in different ways. An exclusive method applied to everything closes many ways of approach... In this respect a genuine pragmatism is much more realistic than a dogmatic empiricism.

Paul Tillich, "The Problems of Theological Method".

1. General Remarks

AN unflinching determination to ignore processes and to deal with facts until a thorough understanding of the mechanism of facticity had been gained, yielded two key insights into the cosmic structure: the Existential-Atom and the Principle of Absolutes. Added to this, preliminary investigations revealed that generically, individuation synacts with oneness and honesty. Oneness, it was also noted, applies to existential individuation, as it does to all modalities of individuation, whereas honesty translates into a *de facto* possession. Technically having discovered the primary particle or atom and established the requisites of individuation, one could cut short the investigation into unitization, and plunge directly into the sea of fascinating problems presented by movement and change. The temptation is powerful. Instinctively we assume that we unambiguously know what is a Self — what is involved in being unique. Considering the issue settled, we are inclined to proceed immediately to analyzing relationships — those, for example, of a star upon a planet, of male to female.

The fault with this approach is that lacking a clear concept of individuation, and having before ones eyes undeniable evidence of a melting, of a blending of units — some actually seem to vanish, or worse, seem to be transformed — the "substance" or the factual or more specifically the Existent, ends up being sacrificed upon the altar of the God: Becoming. Becoming however is an exacting deity. It is not to be placated with the initial intellectual sacrifice which it exacts from its devotees. Once enmeshed in its net, the coherent thinker finds unavoidable "progress" from a "changing entity" unto outright existential monism. Given broad enough a time perspective, the Believer is inexorably led to proclaim the individual a mere high-point in a flowing process, and must see, even in his own Self an evanescent, lying illusion. Not even the most convoluted foreplay with concepts such as "specificity", "actual entities" and "duration" can save the thinker from the contemplation of his gradual dissolution into the hungry maw of an insatiable void. These quotes from the opening pages of Bergson's *Creative Evolution* illustrate the process graphically. Beginning at page 11 by affirming:

> The universe *endures*. The more we study the nature of time, the more we shall comprehend that duration means invention, the creation of forms, the continual elaboration of the absolutely new.

Bergson adds on the following page:

> Suppress this action, and with it consequently those main directions which by perception are traced out for it in the entanglement of the real, and the individuality of the body is re-absorbed in the universal interaction which, without doubt, is reality itself.

Having already sadly reduced the status of the individual, the author being coherent, on page 13 draws the horrendous, but logical conclusion that:

> No doubt, it is hard to decide, even in the organized world, what is individual and what is not. The difficulty is great, even in the animal kingdom; with plants it is almost insurmountable. This difficulty is, moreover, due to profound causes, on which we shall dwell later. We shall see that individuality admits of any number of degrees, and that it is not fully realized anywhere, even in man.[1]

---

1. Henri BERGSON, *Creative Evolution*, London, MacMillan and Co. 1913, pp. 11, 12 and 13. The several symbiotic, concrescenting, etc., theories referred to, when applied within the context of a subdiscipline yield views such as those of Dr. Lewis Thomas M.D., president of New York's Memorial Sloan-Ketering Cancer Center. Thomas, dispensing with the usual philosopher's smoke-screen, "cheerfully offers to argue that — as a separate living entity — he Lewis Thomas does not exist". This closing paragraph of an article devoted to Thomas by Newsweek (24-6-74), effectively summarizes the complex of issues, viewed from an Evolutionist's point of view:

   > Although he is a physician, Thomas believes that recent breakthroughs in biology have philosophical implications that transcend whatever uses medicine can make of them. "Most people outside of science tend to think that the last meaningful piece of work was Darwin's", he told Newsweek's Judith Gingold. "But some of the new things coming out

In summary even Bergson himself is not a discrete individual.

While the preceding excerpts illustrate the nihilism inherent in any measure of Becomingism, they are more relevant still to the present point. Literally, Bergson, as so many before and since, gives up the battle without a fight. Admitting defeat from the beginning of his master thesis, he resigns himself to the fact that "individuality... is not fully realized anywhere, even in man". With such a premise he will never discover the prime particle, since he starts by dogmatizing that there are no enduring entities in his enduring universe. Here, the position adopted — the antithesis of the Becomingist's — is premised upon a firm determination to make of individuation the prime concern — not to be abandoned until a thorough understanding of its mechanism is obtained. The initial research has yielded considerable data. Nonetheless, even this is insufficient. Before launching into a study of relationality, it is essential to analyze in greater detail what the fact-of-being-existentially-unique implies. This will involve a methodical search for and an analysis of the requisites of any type of individuation, specifically, the conditions which must be fulfilled before that which appears to be an Existential-Atom, is found to be one. For the time being, the relationships between Atoms will be ignored. To use the mechanic's language, the Existent's motor will be torn into, in the hope of discovering what makes it a motor and fact. In short, the Real as it resides in each part, in total objectivity, on an As-is basis, will be dissected. Further, since the prerequisites already uncovered are highly disturbing — together they negate such familiar sense notions as time, space and quantity — the second portion of this assignment is devoted to finding out whether or not these seemingly unconscionable requisites can be conciliated with a world of birth and death. A final observation. The present search does not seek to demonstrate that any given entity is an Existent, i.e. to prove that a man, sponge, iron or omega-minus, is or is not an Atom.

---

of biology are going to prove irresistible to people who are interested in nature and man's place in it." To Thomas, perhaps the most irresistible conclusion he has drawn from his knowledge of mitochondria, blepharisma and other denizens of the biological deep, is this: "The whole dear notion of one's own Self — marvelous old free-willed, free-enterprising, autonomous, independent, isolated island of a Self — is a myth."

Rather, its purpose is restricted to the discovery of the generic criteria particular to an existential, as opposed to a conceptual-unit.

An initial survey revealed that in final analysis individuation predicates unicity and nothing more. When a distinction was drawn between generic individuation and that which would affect the Real, it was summarily noted that conceptual individuation presupposes oneness, facticity (honesty) and permanence, whereas existential individuation implies oneness and possession. The criteria which must therefore be investigated in more detail, are:

A. oneness as this affects the Atom, and

B. the factual, in its role of a possessed parcel of the Real.

Each will yield subcriteria to be studied individually. Of the two, possession is dealt with first, since it concerns a portion of our raw material.

2. **Existential Individuation Entails Possession**

He who preoccupies himself with existential individuation, in effect signifies his intention to "materialize" objectivity, or alternatively, to cut up the Objective into pieces. It will be observed that here, for two reasons, the What-is is equated with the Objective — and, because of synactivity, with Truth. Firstly, such an approach is scientific. Since no one has grasped the inneity of Existence, to vest objectivity in Existence and in nothing else, will prove more rewarding than to dogmatize about the primordial status of "matter", "substance" or any type of substratum. Secondly, objectivity is the one feature which all atomicities share. All must be what they are, and must remain so even against the onslaught of The Absolute. Even the God of Moses could not make any It-which-is, become a different It. On this point Parmenides had long ago rightly observed that:

> ... motionless within the limits of mighty bonds, it (Existence) is without beginning or end, since coming into being and perishing have been driven far away, cast out by true belief... For strong Necessity holds it firm within the bonds of the limit that keeps it back on every side.[2]

---

2. PARMENIDES, *The Way of Truth*, (trans. Reginald E. Allen in *Greek Philosophy: Thales to Aristotle*, London, Collier-Macmillan Limited, 1966, p. 46.

Having equated the sum of That-which-is with objectivity, or more accurately with a substantified objective, to atomize the cosmic mass or object, it is necessary to vest in each putative Existential-Atom a parcel of the whole. Between them, the sum of Atoms must add up volume, quantity and quality-wise, to the object cut up. Inversely, the sum of individuals will have to possess exactly as much volume, etc., as does the original conglomerate. The notion of possession, here for the first time officially injected into the universal economy, is intimately related to honesty and existential individuation. The term possession being overworked and controversial, its meaning in this context needs to be precisely defined, especially since it constitutes one of a handful of master ideas which can reveal facets of the cosmic economy hitherto ignored.

To most ears, the assertion that possession corresponds to honesty will ring preposterous and indeed sacrilegious. Marxists, Christians and the sundry Socialists, all of whom commonly equate ownership with greed and evil, will see, in this, a frontal attack upon the very foundations of their respective ideologies. Given the usual "material" meaning associated with the term, they would be justified. Possession, however, does not within Dynamic Vision convey the type of "materialistic grasping" currently associated with it. It implies far more than a degree of control, which modality, because relational and temporo-spatial, suggests that possession can eventually be lost. Rather the word assumes its radical sense of "to occupy or be occupied in person, to have as occupant or to be held". Such an interpretation was implicit in the definition of the Universe, and is explicit in the Universal Equation, U = X (E : A). Stated otherwise, possession herein signifies a state of factual occupancy which can, under no condition whatsoever, be lost by the owner and acquired by an aggressor, or even be sold, which is to say, willingly transferred. It-which-is can cooperate, submit or additivate, but can go no further. It must remain a perpetual Outsider.

The above may strike some as flying in the face of all tangible and visible evidence. Does not, for instance, the human body constantly either acquire or lose its "substance"? Granted. However, it is also fact that the senses do not bear full or even consistent witness. The Real, as sensed by a rational mind, alone bears reliable witness. *He who wishes to grasp Reality rather than the phenomenal and transitory, whenever conflict arises between the dictates of reason and the evidence of the secondary senses, must rely upon reason.* In this situation, the raw material being the mass of That-which-is, each ontological entity, no matter how puny, must be in-fact and on an As-is basis in full ownership of a portion of the whole ; must have as perpetual and unencumbered a title to its minute patrimony, as that enjoyed by the greatest of them all : God. Otherwise, its presence before the remainder of the commonwealth of Atoms, would aver itself false, both from a scientific and accounting point of view. The logic should be evident to one familiar with accounting and/or stocktaking practices. At inventory time, no merchant cares to enter non-existent items in his books, unless of course he is emulating Sol Estes.[3] The same accuracy is clearly called for when the Universe is inventorized. All must be accounted for — every louse and sand fly inclusively. It is in this meaning that possession is predicated the necessary endowment of a Self or Existential-Atom.

In summary, Existential-Atoms, as distinct from conceptual-entities, share and possess, in utter univocity, a common property : Existence. It is agreed that this statement rests upon an assumption which may have to be altered should it not be confirmed by subsequent experiments. Further, what Existence consists of still remains to be ascertained. Possession, then, is the first requisite of individuation. Applied to my Self, this means that *I, Roger Lebeuf, inalienably possess a "chunk" of the Universe on exactly the same basis as all other Existents, animate or inanimate, and that together, we who do in-fact possess some Existence, constitute the community of Beings called the Universe.*

3. Billie Sol Estes, Democrat from Texas, was a "wheeler-dealer" involved in monumental fraud during the Kennedy-Johnson administrations (late 1960's). He was implicated in storing non-existent government grain in his non-existent warehouses for fees, and in the sale of mortgages on equally non-existent fertilizer tanks to banking institutions, all of which netted a fortune until facts and the law caught up. Cruel as the parallel may be, the proponent of Becomingism is guilty of the same practices, albeit at the ontological level, when he chooses to add (create) and subtract (nihilate) Existents to and from the cosmic economy to satisfy the whims of his theories and system.

3. Existential Individuation Presupposes Indivisibility

Emphasis upon possession of a parcel of Existence, as the first condition for a genuine Atom to be present, stresses its existential content more than individuation. The precision that possession in the case of an Atom means *factual* and in *perpetuity* ownership, extends the investigation into the realm of unicity and honesty, for according to all norms, to be individuated predicates oneness and, by implication, honesty. In this context, honesty implies that when a unit has been defined and granted criteria — let us say appleness — thereafter the one hundred percentness of these must be respected. The slightest alteration, one even which would make the said apple only .0000001% less than the apple it was initially, would destroy the original unit, and entail dealing with a new one. This imperative, furthermore, holds whether the alteration, the wound is inflicted consciously or subconsciously, physically or conceptually. In a sense to vest in the Atom possession in perpetuity of a parcel of the Real does set out at one swoop the requisites of existential individuation. Was not the belief in a physis called "matter" so widespread, the case could rest. Since "matter" is uncritically assumed to represent "the primordial stuff of which the Universe is made", and since, through it, the dimensions of time, space, quantity, mass, divisibility and change are injected into the cosmic economy, one must now, to avoid ambiguities, investigate in detail, indivisibility, the safeguard of the integrity of the Atom.

When tackling the indivisibility of existential units, I am overcome by contradictory feelings of redundancy and bafflement, compounded by urgency. The task seems redundant, for it is senseless to devote energy to establish the fact that it which by definition is one, is indeed one. The urgency arises with the knowledge that on this issue there are presently theories being promoted throughout every continent which undermine Truth, and worse still, the person.[4] The quasi-universal acceptance of

4. While the "scientific-philosophers", the Whiteheads, Teilhards, etc., whose background is at once technological and ontological, strive manfully through verbal acrobatics to hide the nakedness of a strictly processional entity, concrescenting or otherwise, their counterparts among the biologists feel no such qualms, as witness Haldane, or Thomas quoted earlier or still Julian HUXLEY in the following from *Evolution in Action*, (N.Y., Mentor, 1957, p. 30):

these theories, all founded upon the hypothesis that "matter evolves", is the more baffling in that on the subject of the indivisibility and sacredness of units, the majority of thinkers evidence a total ambivalence. Conceptual-units and Antropocities generally fare well. The Being or Existential-Atom, on the other hand, suffers from a treatment worthy of Vandals. For some unconscionable reason, the need for indivisibility and immutability when concepts are at stake, is questioned by none — not even the Huxleys, Selsams and Teilhards. Sheer common sense seems to convince even the rankest of Relativists and Evolutionists that a concept ceases "to be itself", a fact or truth, the instant that it is interpreted in the least degree differently from its original formulation. Everyone apparently realizes that the minutest variation wrought in a formulated doctrine, even upon that of the relativity of relativity, makes of the formulation, a new entity, and of whatever equation such might be incorporated in, a new equation.[5]

Amazingly, when the time comes to uphold the integrity of the real flesh and blood Atom, the situation reverses. No one — excepting Parmenides in millenia past, in a vague fashion, and the Scholasticists, in our era, when they introduce into their system a *Deus ex machina*: "the eternal and dimensionless

---

> Today we can see life as a unitary process, made up of a number of smaller processes. The individual organism is a process within the species, the species a process within the radiation of a type, the radiation of a type a process within the succession of dominant groups, and this in turn a process within the over-all process of realizing new possibilities of variety and organisation.

5. This ethical schizophrenia is admirably illustrated by these statements of Bertrand Russell:

> No. 1: "All that constitutes a person is a series of experiences connected by memory and by certain similarities of the sort we call habit."

In *Mysteries of Life and Death* and:

> No. 2: "We do not, in fact, feel our certainty that two and two are four increased by fresh instances, because, as soon as we have seen the truth of this proposition, our certainty becomes so great as to be incapable of growing greater. Moreover, ... the best attested empirical generalizations always remain mere facts: we feel that there might be a world in which they were false, ... In any possible world, on the contrary, we feel that two and two would be four: this is not a mere fact, but a necessity to which everything actual and possible must conform."

In *The Problems of Philosophy*, New York, Henry Holt, p. 121. In other words, a process, viz. man, according to Russell, can beget a fact!

human soul" — has been faithful to Truth as this resides in the Existent. With quasi-unanimity, philosophers and in their wake, the majority of laymen, have held that the Atom can be tampered with, altered, "become" and still, "in the process", remain itself. That the truth, the fullness of the Real is thereby annihilated, does not seem to in the least worry the Evolutionist. Blissfully, the champion of the "changing" Being, commits the grossest of intellectual indecencies — that of negating his own selfness. The indictment is harsh. Yet, it is one which will never be successfully challenged for, as Parmenides writes:

> "never shall this be proved, that things that are, are not."

It is not that the common run of mankind and its thinkers deliberately conspire to make of the Existential a lie. Far from it, excepting a minority — the Hegelians and Relativists for whom as a matter of dogma untruth is truth — most, often with desperation, seek to grasp the Truth, the *One and Indivisible*, which inhabits the Existential-Atom. The culprit is, in some instances, a lack of daring, and in others, a misplaced loyalty in the Aristotelian dogma that "all knowledge comes to man through the mediation of the senses". In a word, no one heeds Parmenides' admonition:

> ... nor let custom born of much experience, force thee to let wander along this road thy aimless eye, thy echoing ear or thy tongue; but do thou judge by reason the strife-encompassed proof that I have spoken...[6]

On the question of the oneness or indivisibility of the Atom one stand only is valid. The Principle of Absolutes dictates that each Atom, once in possession of its quota of the Real, must partake of objectivity and oneness. These, both synactive with facticity, predicate in turn, that the Atom be whole and indivisible at the Orders of the Real and of the Now. *In effect, objectivity extends to encompass not only the Universe perceived as a massive fact and/or the universe of the conceptuals, but also to encompass such entities as may possess any amount whatsoever of Energy or, still any parcel of "matter".* Stated colloquially, if Peter is indeed Peter, then Peter is Peter and not Paul, and the twain

6. Cf. 2, *Ibid.*, p. 45.

can never blend. Or to quote G. K. Chesterton's pungent syllogism:

A pig, is a pig, is a pig.[7]

Thus, oneness and its corollary, indivisibility, is the second requisite of existential individuation.

4. The Existential-Atom, Because Indivisible, Must be Dimensionless

To find in Existence an univocal fact, or worse to affirm that the modality of the Universe is of absolute to absolute is to choose the path of the lonely. Further, the chopping-up of the Real, into a finite number of parcels, each inalienably owned, can hardly increase the area of understanding. The next proposition will sever whatever ties remain with conventional wisdom. Having chosen to see the Universe as composed of a fixed number of Atoms, each in full ownership of a parcel of the Whole, one must venture farther afield, into parts uncharted. Bound by no material strait jacket, unconcerned with either time or space and their manifestations, and having opted for individuation at the level of the Existential, it is now argued that the Atom, to be true to itself, must, as any other entity, be not only one and hence indivisible, but also dimensionless. The implications of adimensionality are shattering, for it simultaneously unhinges the accepted norms of epistemology and defies a host of time honored premises, upon which presently rest sciences such as physics, psychology and sociology. Therefore, to avoid misunderstanding, the nature and implications of adimensionality should be spelled-out.[8]

---

7. It is to be observed that the paradoxes related to the issue of the many in the continuous, have their origin at this precise juncture in cosmontology. Philosophers and physicists fail to respect the jurisdiction of the two Orders. Change, divisibility, etc. — all sense percepts — are allowed to insinuate themselves into the Real.

8. Adimensionality in this context assumes a more radical texture than the normal. One could say that it describes the genuine article. An effective way of conveying the difference might be to indicate that the adimensionality which concerns us is the antithesis of the primary point-centre of interaction postulated by the mathematician-astronomer, Boscovich (1711-87). The point-centre, while useful to portray physical structures — three dimensional patterns of points — remains imbedded in the conceptual and indeed creates the dimensional.

The first precision to be kept in mind, is that here the investigation is restricted to the Atom in its role of Obscure-Absolute — as grasped in the truth of its hidden, unknowable inner-Self. Within these limitations, the term dimensionless, has vested in it its full meaning. This implies that every Existent resides neither in time nor space, curved or otherwise. All modalities of quantization, such as miles, bushels, acres, and possibly the most important, speed, are evacuated. In a sense, *the Cosmos itself, as "seen and felt", is nihilated, for once the Commonwealth of the Atoms come to assert title, each to its share of the Real, then the Universe as such ceases to exist. Existence belongs not to the Universe, but to the Atoms.* The terms Universe and Cosmos are concepts, and concepts, it goes without saying, occupy no dimensions.

Existential adimensionality perpetrates a worse intellectual outrage yet. Because of it each Atom rests beyond and outside of movement and evolution. "Becoming" stops dead in its tracks. Such Parmenidean affirmations, especially as they apply to man, can be expected to give rise to considerable perplexity. What of my body, is it not divisible? What about its processes? Does it not grow and degenerate with age? Does it not decompose at death? Also, if we are to forget space and speed, how can we explain the moon and astronauts speeding towards it at an average of 3 540 miles per hour? In sum, isn't to declare all Existents indivisible and dimensionless, flaunting common sense and the physical sciences? Hardly! Adimensionality involves not so much as exceeding of the senses, as a refusal to be their slave. One must not, upon the basis of superficial, secondary sense data, panic and in so doing, betray the intellect. Ontology is not a science of words, but of the Physical. To talk of potency, historical categories, concrescences, specificities or any similar concept, when such cannot be made to concord with the experimental is to play with words. Having recorded that reason bolstered by the evidence of physical experiments, predicates that the factual as this lodges in entities, conceptual and existential, is indivisible and it follows adimensional, one must accept indivisibility and its corollary — namely, the unnerving prospect of a dimensionless universe. If John is dimensionless, so are Peter, Paul and Mary, and the Holstein bull out in his pasture; so are lead atoms 10 and 9878, and all the sisters and aunts of every Peter and mu-meson; so is the entire universe of Existents.

Why so categorical an insistence upon indivisibility when individuation itself, seemingly more fundamental, was proffered as an option which might be dropped should later findings render it untenable? It is true that when opting for the hypothesis of individuation as against monism all dogmatism was avoided. So should it be with a hypothesis supported only by sensual observation. However, where indivisibility and its corollaries are concerned, the matter is not one of option, but of reason versus irrationality, of honesty versus falsehood. Having opted for individuation one cannot rationally find it other than that which it is by definition: unique. Individuation and indivisibility occupy the opposite faces of the same coin, indivisibility being a rational imperative. On the other hand, should individuation fail to be confirmed physically, then it could be jettisoned, and with it, the indivisibility and adimensionality of the Existential-Atom would go.

A further question can now be considered, namely upon what grounds can adimensionality be declared a corollary of indivisibility? A certain irony attends the answer. As observed, indivisibility finds its rationale in reason and, by extension, in the conceptual. The most incontrovertible manner through which this can be established, is by noting that the prototype of individuation, the cipher one, is irrevocably destroyed if it has subtracted from it, even the minutest iota if, for instance, it is reduced from 1.00 to .99999999999, or expanded to 1.000000001. As much seems so invincibly ingrained in the warp of the Real, as to be unquestioned.

And now for the irony. The lord of the Universe, as if intending to mock the humanoid, has immersed him in an opaque fog, commonly referred to as "matter", whose very structure and justification, the dimensional, must be vacated, if the fact, the inneity of It-which-is-real, is to be grasped. In a word, the Real can only be perceived when divested of that which appears to make it real — its quantities and dimensions — and is reduced to a single qualitative oneness. This explains the statement that indivisibility and adimensionality are two faces of the same coin. Adimensionality corresponds at the Order of the Real, to indivisibility at the Perceived. The Atom can be itself, only when it has vested in it the inalienable ownership of that parcel of Reality which makes it the It-which-it-is. In turn, it follows that any "thing" which can be abstracted from an Atom, is not integral to it in the first place; any dimensioned extrusion which can be excised only apparently belongs; is only under its control. Thus, to be true to itself the Atom can have no "finite" dimensions, such as those given to us by the senses of sight, etc. The very dimensions which seem responsible for Reality must die if there is to be Reality! Finally, since an atomic universe is but a conglomerate which must reflect the status of its constituents, the Universe also is shorn of dimensions — that even of curved space. *The Universe knows but one dimension: Existence.*

5. Synactivity of Truth, Reality and Existence

An observation of major relevance to the coming experiment and to epistemology now offers itself, that of the synactivity of Truth, Reality and Existence. While the subject rates in-depth fathoming, this has to be deferred to a separate work. The following brief exposé of the factors and mechanism involved will however be adequate for the immediate purpose.

The key requisite to a proper understanding of the operation of this synactism is that each of the terms describing the three synacts be given its radical meaning. Thus Existence refers to one or more Existential-Atoms as these are and rest in the plenitude of their status of Obscure-Absolutes. Truth corresponds to the fulness of That-which-is-present in an Atom, grasped as an Obscure-Absolute by an Outsider. Reality, for its part, refers to the sum of the Existence grasped, including that of the grasper. *Reality,* in other words, *is the lieu whereat transcendence and immanence occur.*

The synactivity of the trio, Existence, Reality and Truth implies that Truth corresponds to a total knowledge of whatever is under scrutiny, and that firstly the Real, and secondly a knowledge thereof, presupposes Existence. Thus the truth of an Atom or particle, its reality and its existence are different aspects of an identical fact. This implies that a reality cannot be grasped outside of Truth; that a reality is a fact founded upon Existence and defined and grasped absolutely as an absolute. As to Truth, it constitutes an absolute perceived intellectually. Reality, in this context, partakes at once of Existence and Truth — each being inseparable.

The relevance of this triple synactism is farreaching. A corollary of the Principles of Absolutes, it dictates to the ontologist his method: Objectivism. The rationale is straightforward. Because Absolutes rules both Orders and applies to all categories of onenesses, Truth, Reality and Existence are not amenable to the senses, but to the intellect, which alone can deal with absolutes. Hence to study an Existent, it is necessary to start off by encompassing it as a unit — exactly as with a mathematical unit. In a word, the parameters of ontology are identical to those of any other physical science. To grasp an ontological unit or primary particle and dissect it, one must proceed as when dealing with a mineral or the Cosmos. That an objective and absolutist approach is the proper one to the study of Existence becomes evident if one considers that even a strictly empirical discipline such as pathology proceeds absolutely, namely, from a global assumption to the particular. For example, the pathologist who seeks increased knowledge of the hormones released by the hypothalamus, firstly endows the latter with conceptual unity. That particular gland, together with an arbitrarily established "area" of its relationships, becomes absolutized in the researcher's mind, and from then on, his efforts are directed either to substantiate his initial surmise as to the hypothalamus' identity or to analyze its operation and relationships with the Outside, with, for instance, the pituitary or nervous systems. If he decides to extend his field of research, automatically, albeit often subconsciously, a new whole is created, and his findings to that point, are reassessed accordingly.[9]

Since the Atom, by nature and definition, partakes eminently of the Real, the same methodology imposes itself upon the philosopher viewed as a general practitioner, as upon the ontologist in the latter's role of specialist. *The Existent cannot be grasped through an exclusively logical maneuver, such as the principle of contradiction; nor will it respond to a progressive*

9. On this point, it seems that the correct view is that of Morris Cohen who argues that "we perceive trees before we perceive birches", which is to say, that the progress of knowledge is from the general or absolute to the definite.

"structurization". Its presence must be taken for granted, and the same scientific criteria applied as to any other entity. To insist that the Atom as Obscure-Absolute must be taken for granted does not however rule out the right to doubt. Doubt as to whether or not an entity has its roots in the Real remains legitimate. What is affirmed is that the cosmic mass, and within it the Atoms, constitute the globally prehended subject of any ontological adventure, for a whole can never be deduced, still less grasped, through analysis. Aquinas notwithstanding, one does not "receive knowledge of the simple from the composite". Knowledge of Existence generally or of an Existent, and the "substance" of either, is gained through a reverse empiricism, through an initial absolutized grasping of its facticity. *Qualities and relationships come second in order of perception.* Thus epistemological requisite number one in the process of establishing existential individuation and the need for permanence or indivisibility on the part of It which is existentially one, is that the Universe and the It or Its involved be accepted as constituting absolutes.

6. **The Indivisibility and Unicity of the Existential-Atom Can be Established Experimentally**

The objective in this chapter is to uncover the qualifications of a genuine primary particle. Three in number, the first presupposes perpetual possession of a parcel of the existential mass. The second, a two-tier requisite, is oneness and its negative, indivisibility. The term negative here describes a relationship paralleling that between a print and its negative. This parallel was to be expected, for indivisibility is basic at both Orders. The third essential qualification, adimensionality, on the surface, seems hard to credit, for it appears to negate the very "thing" which it is reputed to make possible. The difficulty is only apparent, for tangibility has not been denied to the Atom, only temporo-spatial dimensions, a feature which should assuage the Sensualists. In this context Sensualist encompasses in one super-school, the Aristotelians, Marxists and sundry Materialists who hold that knowledge and, by implication, truth comes through the senses. (The latter does not signify agreement but merely notes, in anticipation, the compatibility of adimensionality with sensory perception and qualitativity). To date our efforts have been rewarded by the emergence upon the ontological screen, of a destitute, dimensionless It, an Outsider, hermetic in its sheath of indivisibility. The qualification, destitute, is added for a self-contained and dimensionless Atom must appear more barren and indigent than Democritus' identical atoms — each of which could at least feel free to whirl about in "the void to therein by and by" encounter one or more mates, from which encounter "something different" would hopefully "materialize". This is true. The Existential-Atom presently offers no handle by which it can be held. However, the entire field of the qualitative and relational lies ahead. As these are investigated, an as yet skeletal and necessitous It will put on flesh and gradually inject itself into life's processes.

From an empirical point of view, the Existential-Atom being discovered, no further demonstration would be required. Such would be the course followed by a researcher in the physical sciences. A geochemist who has detected copper in the ore brought to him for assay, sees no necessity to disprove the opinion of a colleague who might profess to have uncovered zinc. In such cases the burden of disproof rests upon the challenger. An identical course of action would be twice justified here, for the coherence of Dynamic Vision is based upon the Universal Principles and Laws which flow from a Universe whose equation is U = X (E : A). These laws pragmatically confirm the postulate that individuation presupposes the *de facto* possession of a dimensionless parcel of Existence. This workability of Dynamic Vision would suffice to have it stand above the ideological quarrels of the schools. If the remainder of this chapter is devoted to existential indivisibility, and the following to physical experiments which empirically verify the criteria established, it is for several critical reasons. A first. The indivisibility of the Existent has not been satisfactorily demonstrated to this day. A more compelling motive is that many philosophers and in their wake, entire schools of psychology and politics proselytize in favor of theories which negate existential individuation — thereby inflicting incredible harm upon mankind. Finally, Truth itself is inseparably linked to the inviolability of units. Thus, until existential indivisibility is established and accepted in political circles, all hope for lasting social progress is forlorn. For, a universe wherefrom Truth is banished, can only be envisioned by the coherent thinker as an inchoate morass pullulating with billions of rudderless, relativating human "beastlets", fit subjects for bullying and, if need be, extermination.

In hope therefore of shedding light on an issue as far away from resolution as in the days of Aristotle and Democritus, four topics will be briefly touched upon. The first consists of a foray into epistemological methods. Its purpose is to demonstrate that any progress on the subject has been and will be due to the adoption of an objective epistemology. This has the merit of introducing into the ontological science, the parameters of mathematics and the methodology of the exact sciences. The second will demonstrate schematically that the traditional arguments adduced in behalf of existential individuation — in particular, that based upon divisibility to infinity and that grounded upon the principle of contradiction and/or identity — are suitable, at best, to show that individuation is a reasonable assumption. The third will provide evidence, based upon the mechanics of a model universe, that only a universe composed of a finite number of Atoms conforms to the norms of Reality and Truth. Finally, the fourth will offer preliminary evidence to the effect that fear of rigidity and staticity — seemingly inherent in a model universe of objective Parmenidean Existents, and by extension, in the real Universe — is groundless, once the proper synact of Existence, Power, is vested in each Atom.

7. Objectivism: Key to the Discovery and Understanding of the Existential-Atom

The preceding pages contained three related affirmations. One. It was noted that philosophers and physicists alike have failed to solve the question of individuation and it follows that the prime Existent, otherwise known as the primary particle, continues to elude them. Two. It was stressed that this failure was due to faulty epistemological methods, specifically to a continued reliance upon an Analyticism consonant with the Aristotelian world view. Three. It was simultaneously affirmed that the issue is solved and the primary particle discovered, when both are subjected to a body of principles akin to the Empiricism inherent in the Parmenidean position. This method, briefly alluded to in the previous section, was defined as Objectivism. Its basic premises are:

A. the Universe in its role of massive fact, is present to all and offers itself to be known empirically;

B. all knowledge proceeds from this embryonic and global, albeit subconscious, grasp which one has of the Fact-of-to-be, and

C. knowledge is gained through a process which conforms to the spirit of the Principle of Absolutes, namely absoluteneity.

The break from tradition thus initiated is clear. It predicates that the study of existential problems must rely for its initial data upon empiricism and absolutes rather than upon systems of logic bolstered by the cumulation of analytical data. Founded upon the view that knowledge flows from an empirically prehended cosmic absolute which encompasses all quality and relationality, it introduces in ontology the methods in common usage in the applied sciences.

The rationale of Objectivism flows from facticity, from a substitution of the concept of fact for that of act. In a nutshell, this implies that, firstly facticity, and secondly objectivity and absolutes, extend their sway beyond the cosmic mass and the province of conceptual-absolutes, of the numeral for instance, to jointly rule over the Existent, and through the latter, over the mind's processes. The role of facticity being established one can immediately note instances of the salutary effect which it has upon cosmontology. Foremost among these, is that it guarantees the integrity of the Self. Where Bergson resigns himself from the inception of his research to the pessimistic surmise that, "individuality... is not fully realized anywhere, even in man", and Santayana, outdoing such a dismal vision, proclaims, "A soul is but the last bubble of a long fermentation in the world", Objectivism allows the ontological scientist to grasp the Existent as fact, and to verify his initial assumption through experiments which at once bare it's mechanism and set the stage for a Code of Cosmic Jurisprudence. A second benefit of importance in our era, is that the synactivity of the triumvirate: Truth, Reality and

Existence, is demonstrated and, it follows, total scientific objectivity is brought within the researcher's grasp. *Classical Dualism is restored, not however as between "matter and idea", but rather as between* bona fide *Existential-Atoms, whose minds are nourished upon a diet of absolutes.*

The remark in respect to a special need for an epistemology which safeguards objectivity was prompted, in part, by the Heisenbergian challenge. The fact that Objectivism, through absoluteneity, solves this seeming threat of cosmic indeterminacy, suffices to establish its claim to recognition. There presently exists a malaise in the scientific community, arising from the implications of the Uncertainty Principle. The fear is of an ultimate physical limit to the precision with which the position and momentum of a particle can be simultaneously determined. Crudely, and hence somewhat inaccurately translated the Uncertainty Principle predicates that since the photon used to detect and track a disintegrating kaon, or any weak interaction particle, is powerful enough to alter the trajectory of the item-object being explored, a degree of imprecision mars all physical data — the indeterminacy extending, in the view of some, even to the higher macroscopies. Effectively the idea is that "the method transforms its object". The threat to science and morality inherent in this deduction is the more frightening in that it is indeed justified whenever insights remain situated in the Perceived, and are calibrated according to the relativistic norms of a time-space continuum. At that level, Eddington's statement that "through science, man only discovers his own footprints", does apply. Inexorably the Universe of the Relativist, and within it man, seems doomed to dissolve in a subjectivistically oriented Monism wherefrom precision, let alone Truth, vanishes. The very foundation of the sciences, and in particular of ethics, disintegrates.

Understandably the average and not so average man who has been spared perversion by the relativistic religion, intuitively balks at so dire a prospect. The "the not so average man", includes Einstein, as witness this statement from the pen of Heisenberg himself:

> However, Einstein would not admit that it was impossible, even in principle, to discover all the partial facts needed for the complete description of a physical process. "God does not throw dice" was a

> phrase we often heard from his lips in these discussions. And so he refused point-blank to accept the uncertainty principle, and tried to think up cases in which the principle would not hold.[10]

Einstein and those who think as he are right. Yet the Heisenberg Principle, within its legitimate confines also stands. The keys to the conciliation of both views are:

A. the distinction to be drawn between the Real and the Perceived,

B. an appreciation of the role of qualitativity in Now processes, and

C. the insertion in epistemology, of the criterion of the Principle of Absolutes, absoluteneity.

Only thus can "science" be rescued. Finally, an ancillary, but not insignificant development. Once the Universe is grasped empirically and absolutely and is furthermore seen to consist of an X-number of qualitative Cosmic-Presences, metaphysics, viewed as a super-science dealing with the principles of "another world", is demystified. Yet, nothing is lost. Quite the contrary, the supernatural, theorized by friend and foe to reside beyond the reach of sense-datum, reintegrates a Cosmos free of all dichotomy. Then each Atom — a free entity which ignores all dimensions, natural and supernatural — exists by imposing its will, and in particular its thought-power, upon the Outsiders. In man's case, the fruits of his conquest are quanta of knowledge, fleeting peeks into Reality. Since the ratio of ones insights is a function of quality, that which to some appears as "supernatural" is to others perfectly "natural". It is all a question of the quality and intensity of ones thought-power.

8. A Brief Critique of Analyticism

Before proceeding with the experiments, it seems useful to offer a summary critique of the analytical and/or logical approach through which the question of the discreteness of Existents has traditionally been tackled. Since the purpose here is not controversy, and in particular, not to determine whether a philosopher's

10. Werner HEISENBERG, *Physics and Beyond*, New York, Harper & Row, 1971, p. 80.

method is the fruit of his ontological vision or vice-versa, only the differences will be highlighted.

It may be objected that to lump all other theories in a common category is not in order, since those who have sought to establish existential individuation have, even when logicians, ventured upon many paths. This diversity is conceded. However, variations notwithstanding, all the arguments and proofs adduced nestle under an identical umbrella: the analytical — an attempt to grasp the Existent through logic. This is unsatisfactory, for such proofs, regardless of dress, boil down to an attempt to introduce the purely intellectual principle of identity into the Existential. As the Radical Sceptics have shown, any attempt to capture the Existent through this principle is doomed to failure.

Why must pure logic be disqualified? Firstly, Existence constitutes a fact antecedent to ones knowledge of it, and secondly, the Existent sought, if discovered, must aver itself a whole. Either obstacle suffices to thwart the mightiest effort of the logician. As the Eleat rightly observed six millennia ago:

> One way only is left to be spoken of, that it (Being) is; and on this way are full many signs that what is, is uncreated and imperishable for it is entire, immovable and without end. (Fr. 8) ... For it is the same thing to think and to be. (Fr. 2)[11]

While it is common practice to interpret the statement: "that it (Being) is", as an affirmation of the principle of identity, and on the basis of this view, to proclaim Parmenides inventor of the principle of contradiction and father of dialectics, such an interpretation is unsupported by the overall spirit of the *Way of Truth*. For Parmenides, rationalization and negation are posterior and incidental to his prehension that "Being is". It would seem that he adopted towards Existence, a form of radical Empiricism. Be this as it may, such is the only sound approach. Any other corresponds to an attempt by the thinker to lift himself up by his bootstraps. Descartes or not, one is, before one thinks. Furthermore, the logical endeavor is subject to an occupational hazard. Whereas everyone can be deemed to start his investigations determined to respect the "logically demonstrated" identity of the existential *one*, temptations galore strew the path

11. Cf. 2, *Ibid.*, p. 46.

of the ontologist who believes that he can logically "prove" an existential fact. He who rests his case upon a logicism soon reduces his allegiance to lip service — resorting to logical double-talk, as witness "movement", "change" and "potency" etc., in a vain attempt to cancel his initial error. The unbridgeable dichotomy which separates the Real from pure logic, never allows one to grip an Outsider.

A variant of the proof by identity, that by negation or contradiction, at least on the level of the Real, also constitutes a futile exercise. To affirm that something, whether phenomenon or fact, is not something else, proves nothing about anything. It at best indicates that one is on the wrong track, and must go looking elsewhere. The uselessness of attempting to prove the existence of a given Atom through analysis is even more readily discerned. He who attempts this feat faces the same dilemma as the maggot which would attempt to encompass the whole of a piece of cheese by eating its way through it. By the time either are through with their analyzing or eating, neither the Existent nor the cheese remains. No process, no matter how intricate and exhaustive, will ever envelop a whole. The error in this procedure, which is essentially that of the modern, cyclotron wielding subnuclear physicists, accounts for the latter's mounting frustration as they find their prey, the prime particle, forever disintegrating into the "void of space".

As to the proof by *reductio ad absurdum*, this is at once more and less powerful than that offered by the principles of identity and negation-contradiction. Whereas the weakness of a demonstration resting upon logic is that it does not grasp the Real, and whereas by negation or contradiction nothing positive is determined, proof by division into infinity has the merit of at least dealing with the physical — generally defined as "matter". Yet, a demonstration that a process is unfeasible or leads into absurdity, lacks, on the one hand, the apparent definiteness of a logical proof, and shows, on the other, the same weakness as the argument by negation, in that mere lack of power to go on dividing never provides sufficient grounds upon which to establish something positively.

The age-old argument of the absurdity of divisibility *ad infinitum* has a further defect. It operates in an undetermined locus and concerns neither the Universe nor individuals. Rather, its champions offer it as proof of the absurdity involved in refusing to be bound by the principle of identity. A big step forward, this remains inconclusive for neither the whole of an Atom, nor the mass of Existence are thereby hemmed in. A further flaw mars this type of proof. In achieving its purpose, it destroys the very foundation upon which its subject, "dimensioned matter" rests, a feat tantamount to proving that a chicken lives by cutting its neck off.

The evidence about to be adduced in behalf of the indivisibility of the Existent, of a different order, rests upon the factual and pragmatic, rather than the procedural. One could say that it is inspired by the type of "genuine pragmatism" described in the following passage from Paul Tillich:

> Reality itself makes demands, and the method must follow; reality offers itself in different ways. An exclusive method applied to everything closes many ways of approach and impoverishes our vision of reality. A world construed according to the model of classical or Hegelian dialectics or behavioristic protocols is not the cognitive fulfilment of the potentialitics of reality. In this respect a genuine pragmatism is much more realistic than a dogmatic empiricism with which it is sometimes confused — even by its own followers.[12]

All epistemological dogmatism is avoided, dialectics in particular are shunned. Instead, the scientific approach, which consists in probing into a clearly defined raw material is privileged. Where other scientists concentrate upon parts; a heart or pile of ore for example, here the prime raw material, Parmenides' "What-is", is systematically dissected. This allows for progress from one discovery to another, while at all times leaving all options open. In sum, the Existential-Atom, the Universe's building block, is a fact, and as such will yield its secrets only if dealt with as facts must be, namely as empirically and pragmatically prehended absolutes.

---

12. Paul TILLICH, "The Problems of Theological Method", *The Journal of Religion*, vol. XXVII, no. 1, January 1947.

Chapter IX

Experiments Upon Existence

From all of this evidence Thomson fashioned in 1904 a *model* of the atom, which is noteworthy as the first serious attempt at a detailed quantitative concept. (A model in the sense used here is not a small replica, but an imagined construct to account for observed phenomena.)

Victor Guillemin,
The Story of Quantum Mechanics, p. 29.

1. In the Beginning There Was *Not* the Particle

TWENTY FIVE centuries ago, Democritus, attempting to reconcile the monistic Being of Parmenides with the world of the senses, advanced the then radical thesis that in infinite space, moved an infinite number of atoms. He held that these atoms were eternal and absolutely minute — so minute that their size could not be diminished. They were also absolutely full and incompressible, occupying entirely their alloted "space". Atoms, he further argued, were homogeneous or univocal, differing only in shape, arrangement and position.

Precisions such as those provided by Leibniz and modern physicists notwithstanding, to all purpose and intent, the primordial Democritan particle was to traverse the centuries unscathed. Its modern version, described as an elementary particle, differs from its predecessor mainly through semantics. While technical sophistication allows the modern Atomicist to refer to the primordial particle by awe-inspiring names, as witness neutrino, photon and omega-minus, both the concept formed of it and its processes remain unchanged. Today in the 1970's, the consensus is still that the Real, the "material", rests embedded within dimensioned building blocks. It is commonly believed that the higher (more complex) Existents, e.g. man, virus and enzyme owe their beginning (birth or creation) and their "existence" to a more or less fortuitous, on-going rearrangement by "nature" of a primary "substance". Exactly as Democritus would, twenty five centuries ago, declare that: "In the beginning there was the particle", so do his modern disciples. Two exceptions of consequence to this view, are the Radical Idealists and at the other end of the ideological spectrum, the Dialectical Materialists who espouse a stark, non-atomistic, non-existential and yet assumedly dynamic Monism. Pragmatically, both groups end up by situating the Real within dimensioned structures in which prime particles play a central role.[1]

The longevity of the Democritan atom is readily explained. In the first instance, it underpins a common intuition : the presence about us of units. Each Democritan atom, because held to be eternal, incompressible and indivisible, would satisfy the requisites of generic unicity, and by proxy it is argued, even those of individuality. A second reason, corollary of the first, is that the primary building block hypothesis seems to provide the ultimate shelter against the inclemencies of "change" which the ardent of Evolutionists senses that he must protect himself from — even though this negates his basic premise. Much as he may hate to admit, man faces the fact that dimensions have a perverse propensity to shift, even to melt. Growth, degeneration and radical change have forever caused man to realize that his tangible, dimensioned possessions — his loaf of bread, gold coins, 60′ × 20′ split-level bungalow, and yard — are artificial and cannot support Reality, save at the expense of reducing the Universe to a solipsistic daydream. Suffused in degeneration, yet desperate for permanence, for a footing, men see in the Democritan atom — the prototype of the ultimate dimension — their salvation.

---

1. That the hunt for the prime particle continues as lively as in the days of Democritus, is demonstrated by the history of the quark. The quark, latest candidate (as of 1973) for the title of elementary particle, was invented, in 1962 by physicists Murray Gell-Mann and George Zweig, to serve as the theoretical tool which would meet the requirements of the "genuine subparticle". Their hypothetical status notwithstanding, quarks have become the object of a frantic search. British physicist J.B. Hasted, arguing that possibly they have been sought for in the wrong places, suggests launching a Venus flytrap-like rocket which would open its jaws at an altitude of thirty miles, where it may absorb hypothetical quark-oxygen atoms. Hasted maintains that if real evidence of quarks is found, "elementary-particle physics will have taken a great step forward. It's so important to find quarks that it's worth looking anywhere. But we think that it's much easier to look in the lower ionsphere than anywhere else". (Time Magazine, New York, May 19, 1967, p. 67). Good luck ! However, if quarks are ever "caught", they will aver themselves, as all previous prime particles, no more nor less prime than the reader, myself or any other dynamic entity — all of which must prove adimensional.

Up to this point, the focus has been primarily upon the theory of the Existent. From the beginning, however, it was emphasized that Existence was the fit subject of physical experimentation. Now that the nature of the Atom and the Principles which govern it are established, it is proper to subject these hypotheses to a test of workability; which is to say, to subject Existence to a physical experiment.

If this chapter opens with a cursory look at the Democritan Universe and that of its heirs, it is for these reasons. Firstly, to indicate that Dynamic Vision and the World View of the Atomists (the chemical building-block school), issue from the same lineage. Both are grounded upon the evidence of unitization and a concomitant need for indivisibility. Secondly, to show that while the principle underpinning both visions is identical, the end-products are wholly unlike. The experiments about to be undertaken will demonstrate that *the "existence" of a Democritan atom or dimensioned elementary particle is physically as well as rationally impossible*, and that *the Real and its synact, Truth, can only reside in an adimensional, asectile and immutable medium.* I come, in other words, to contradict. Where the Democritans proclaim: "In the beginning there was the particle"; I affirm: In the beginning there was not the particle. Excising from the Democritan premise, all trace of a physis, material, electrical or other, and with this time and space, I hold that: *the Existential-Atoms are, period.*

2. Are Experiments Upon Existence Possible? If so, to What Purpose?

Many, while in sympathy with the objective, are perhaps questioning the method. Upon reading that experiments will be conducted upon Existence, philosophers and physicists alike, no doubt feel inclined to retort: An experiment upon Existence? Is not Existence the very stuff of the metaphysical, of the transcendental? As such, does it not lie beyond the grasp of the researcher, let alone the assayer?

The rationale for such objections when voiced within the context of traditional philosophies, also within that of most contemporary cosmophysical theories is sound. However, an objective assessment of the situation reveals that there is no need to hover in the high clouds of rationalism with the metaphysician. There is nothing metaphysical about Existence. It is not, as conceived by most, an act, or worse, a vague concept about which one talks and talks and talks; a something, ethereal, metaphysical, general, analogical, contingent, assumed but never investigated. Existence and Reality are synactive facts, and it follows, as fit a subject of experimentation as sex or uranium or cats and cat livers. The ground being staked lies midway between the theory that Existence originates in the concept and the opposite, that it remains shrouded forever in the mystery of a transcendental world of "Being-in-itself", encompassing subject and object and inaccessible to thought. *Existence when individuated, is knowable absolutely by an Absolute-Being, and more or less intimately by those whose thought-power is less than absolute, or otherwise, the Existent is graspable factually as an Obscure-Absolute, but remains mysterious due to the cosmicity of its relationships.*

The Marcellian "mystery" speaks of nothing more than the knower's ignorance. That type of mystery while "real", is susceptible to progressive disrobing, for the Fact-of-to-be, as such, presents man with no mystery whatsoever. Any normal person knows his own Reality and that of some other Atom or Atoms. Indeed, given the proper mental equipment and environment, man can Take-Possession of his Self.

It is not necessary, as are wont to do many physicists, to empty the Cosmos of its existential content, of its feeling. A Cosmos, impalpable, inhabited solely by the skeletal structures of mathematical symbols is a phantom against which the strictures of Kierkegaard, Nietzsche and Sartre are justly aimed. To reduce the Universe to relativating impersonal particles, short-changes oneself and mankind, for this new mathematical Idealism offers even less grasp upon Reality than that of a Berkeley, or the Marxist's historical categories. In a word, the physicist who leaves out of his Cosmic Equation dynamic factors such as the energy quota of his father or of an uranium or sheep, unwittingly falls into as dangerous a trap as does the philosopher who sees in Existence a mere concept. Both sacrifice accountability i.e. Truth, and with this, scientific accuracy.

The correct scientific stance respects the presence within the Cosmos of every Existent, placing them all upon a democratic footing of existential univocity. Only thus can one, on the one hand respect the Principle of the Conservation of Energy and on the other avoid the bifurcation of science, so vividly described by Whitehead in this passage:

> What I am essentially protesting against is the bifurcation of nature into two systems of reality, which, insofar as they are real, are real in different senses. One reality would be the entities such as electrons which are the study of speculative physics. This would be the reality which is there for knowledge; although on this theory it is never known. For what is known is the other sort of reality, which is the byplay of the mind. Thus there would be two natures, one is the conjecture and the other is the dream.[2]

Both objectives are achieved by the simple expedient of laying claim to the sum of Reality, and having done so, to see in its mass a raw material reducible to an X-number of Existential-Atoms each of which, upon further analysis, reveals itself a Dynamic-Fact or motor. Such an Existentialism, scientific and honest, lays to rest the objection which would reduce Existence to some esoteric substratum akin to the ether of the 19th century physicist, and opens the door to empiricism, because from then on each Atom, being a fact, yields to experimentation. Granted, Existence is not thereby hemmed in nor are its "limits" embraced. However, it is not a requisite of experimentation that the subject be encompassed visually or otherwise. The geochemist analyzing the mineral values of ocean water or the ozone content of the atmosphere, hardly encompasses either element. Yet his work is accepted as rational and occasionally provides new insights and products. To-be, as we experience it, is as much a fact as copper, ozone or cats. Since Existence constitutes the raw material of all entities, existential or conceptual, it must, when grasped as an Obscure-Absolute, be recognized as the most factual and best known of facts. Indeed, each of us knows more about his own Fact-of-to-be than about magnesium, bovine sex or electric-power. Thus, while the core and outer limit of the Fact-of-to-be are shrouded in mystery, this is no more of an impediment for the ontologist than is a similar lack of information for the practitioner of an other discipline. The inneity or personality of a magnesium,

---

2. Laurence BRIGHT, *Whitehead's Philosophy of Physics*, New York, Sheed and Ward, 1958, p. 31.

for instance, presently mystifies the chemist, in that it is not fully graspable nor comprehended. This mystery, furthermore one can safely wager, will endure to the end of time. Nonetheless, for all that, no one suggests that experiments involving magnesium should be abandoned.

Effectively, the position adopted can be defined as one of a Scientific Existentialism whose main characteristics are objectivity and realism. It implies the outright rejection of the Subjectivism and Idealism inherent in the Berkeley thesis that: "All the choir of heaven and furniture of earth, in a word all those bodies which compose the mighty frame of the world, have not any substance without the mind". An Objective-Realism or Objectivism implies among other things, that whenever a quality or phenomenon whose origin is unique or pinpointable is detected, this quality and the phenomenon related to it are the inalienable property of a specific Atom and that, while the perception of qualities or Antropocities rests in the knower, neither is a creature of his perception. It-which-is, is — regardless of any Outsider's knowledge. It follows that each Atom, best described for the present purpose as an Obscure-Absolute, is a proper subject of research, and it is upon these that the coming experiments are directed.

3. Three Experiments Upon Existence

The three experiments to be performed involve differing subjects. That of the first is a prototype or synthetic Existent. The second is conducted upon a model universe composed of 1,000,000 Existential-Atoms, identical in structure and endowed of the same qualities as vested in the prototype used in the first. Experiment number three is proceeded with in Part III, once the components of an Atom are isolated and catalogued, and the nature of relationships is ascertained. In it, two categories of Atoms, the animate, represented by a humanoid, a simian, a phagocyte and an enzyme, and the inanimate represented by metals, an iron and an uranium, are brought into play. Its objective is to crosscheck and confirm earlier findings, by applying these to real life situations.

To prevent misunderstanding as to the purpose of these tests a few preliminary remarks are in order. In a general way, experiment number one will demonstrate that, just as a concept cannot be tampered with, cannot be divided, added unto or multiplied without seeing its truth destroyed, so it is with an Existential-Atom. The purpose of the second which, as the first, entails a bisection performed upon one of the 1,000,000 Atoms composing the model universe, is to demonstrate that *if the Universe is not monistic but rather is a conglomerate of building blocks, be these blocks Democritan atoms, synthetic ITs, men or elementary particles, then the objectivity of each building block predicates an immutability as radical as that of the numbers 10 or 2.*

The structure of the subjects of the first tests, that of four foot cubes, may appear counterproductive. How can a dimensioned object be used to prove that the Existential-Atom is division proof, and that the Universe knows but one dimension, that of to-be? Does not such a procedure legitimize dimensions, especially the spatial? Hardly. As noted the cosmic structure presents an ironical situation, namely that the very dimensions which, in the eyes of man, seem to make Reality, must die if there is to be Reality. Together, experiments No. 1 and 2 confirm this irony by providing evidence that the Real is asectile and immutable. Moreover, this is bolstered by the observation that most philosophers and cosmophysicists implicitly extend the range of the principle of identity, which all see as invincibly binding upon concepts, to make it apply to whichever species of unit they privilege, such as the hylemorphic, symbiotic, categorical or concrescent. In summary, the first two experiments will demonstrate that the criteria for a real individual, as established on the basis of induction, apply even to conventional building blocks, Democritan, Leibnizian or Thomsonian. By further applying these norms, in the third experiment, to identifiable Existents, their validity is established more effectively than has been the case with the criteria and surmises made by physicists concerning the structure of subatomic units. Indeed, an appendix to number three, dealing with the primary particles, demonstrates that by substituting the norms of Reality for those of an "extent endowed primary Democritan-like proton or omega-minus", the inconsistencies attendant to the latter can be dispelled and the cosmic structure rationalized.

4. Why a Synthetic Existential-Atom Rather than a Man or Proton?

Several questions pertaining to methodology are apt to be raised at this point. A first concerns the suitability of a synthetic Atom as subject of an experiment into Existence. Anything short of an actual bisection with scalpel or laser beam upon an Existent lying on some spotless operating table, it may be argued, will prove nothing. Directly related, but more specific, would be the objection that the value of the experiment will depend upon the species of Atom chosen as guinea pig. According to this opinion, the choosing of an "animate" or conversely of an "inanimate" may invalidate the findings or, at the very best, can produce results valid for one or more species but not for all.

The answer to both queries was indirectly provided when in section 2, it was established that Existence constituted a proper object of study. It therefore suffices to consider the nature and the scope of cosmontology to show that the species is irrelevant. Whereas other scientists are restricted to a specific field, the cosmontologist can acquit himself of his task, only if reversing the criteria, he objectively encompasses the Universe.

The ground selected satisfies this proviso, for the dividing of Existence between a number X of Atoms, leaves the mass intact and provides units which, without exception, share univocally in one property, that of ownership of a portion of the Universe. The sole remaining condition, if an experiment intended to discover the requisites of existential individuation is to be valid, is that the specimen used should in-fact own its share of the Universe. An alternative offers itself. Adopted here it is that, by agreement, the specimen be endowed with a parcel of Reality. In summary, the cosmontologist who whishes to experiment can pick at random, a human, a neutrino, a water, a douglas fir, or an Existential-Atom created for the purpose. Provided the steps required to conclude the experiment are adequate, the results will be valid. The above notwithstanding, some way wonder why, when so many real Atoms pullulate about us, an *ersatz* one has been selected for two of three experiments. A model atom was chosen because this is common scientific procedure. The experimental sciences use scale models whenever the need arises. Physicists go further on the road to idealization. They may compute their experiments upon paper entirely and only *post facto* seek physical verification. The development of subatomic science followed this course. A classic instance is provided in *The Story of Quantum Mechanics*, wherein Victor Guillemin describes succinctly the road pursued by Thomson in discovering the electron:

> The mass of the electrons having been found negligibly small compared to that of atoms, it followed further that the positive part must represent nearly all of the atom's mass and should presumably form most of the bulk,
>
> From all of this evidence Thomson fashioned in 1904 a *model* of the atom, which is noteworthy as the first serious attempt at a detailed quantitative concept. (A model in the sense used here is not a small replica, as a toy model airplane, but an imagined construct to account for observed phenomena.) [3]

The present position in respect to observable phenomena parallels that of Thomson. Evidence of individuation surrounds me, that of my sister Fernande as distinct from my own, for example. If anything it is far more conclusive. Whereas Thomson's and Rutherford's atom was hypothetical, we both definitely are not.

The advantages to be derived from an *ersatz* Existent are as follows. Firstly, the setting-up of unnecessary ideological road-blocks which might arise if the Existent selected fell into a category subject to controversy, i.e. an angel or dolphin, is thereby avoided. A second advantage is uniformity or standardization. This simplifies an operation of segmentation, and simultaneously reduces the problem of localization which a complex, tentacular specimen such as a rhesus monkey, would present. The basic and precise dimensions of IT, will prove especially valuable when a large number of units is involved. Also, those who subscribe to the prime building block theory of the Universe, will find a synthetic IT, a congenial soul. This compatibility becomes apparent during the second experiment.

---

3. Victor GUILLEMIN, *The Story of Quantum Mechanics*, New York, Charles Scribner's Sons, 1968, p. 29.

5. Qualifications and Specifications of an IT or Synthetic Existential-Atom

In respect to the purely semantical aspect of the project, the name of the synthetic Atom, a non-committal candidate offers itself: the pronoun, "it". From hereon, our model will answer to the brief and utterly neuter name of IT.

Where physical qualifications are concerned these are simple. The objective being to ascertain whether or not existential individuation is compatible with bisection, it suffices that a synthetic Atom should be endowed with existence and objectivity, and should evidence the characteristics of a conventional "material" entity, namely size (space), weight (mass) and qualitative attributes (color, smell, etc.). Size is irrelevant, for divisibility only is at stake, and to excise an omega-minus from a Leibnizian object, "smaller than which one cannot think", or from the moon, excises in either case. Given this latitude, IT will be endowed with, by human standards, a quite substantial size, that of a cargo container encompassing a neat cube of "matter" four feet square on all six faces. To avoid having IT's "materiality" and objectivity placed in doubt, let it be understood that IT is maximally concrete in the sense that IT can be seen, smelled and touched. Finally, the model, at any given "point in time" owns its sixty-four cubic feet of "matter" or concreteness. Surprisingly, these are the only radical qualifications required.

As to IT's secondary endowments, one could speak of IT's personality, these can be tailored to suit personal tastes. IT can be as lovingly tender as the choicest sweetheart or filet mignon, as musically gifted as Beethoven, or just a plain yellow-purple cubic modern sculpture. As to mass, a factor in which modern physics places great store, again this is optional. It can be that of a cube of helium, or still IT can accommodate itself with a mass equal to that of the freak white dwarf star known as "the companion of Sirius", one cubic inch of which, it is theorized, weighs the equivalent of a ton upon earth. Together the above qualifications would seem to establish IT's credentials as a prime building block of Existence, some might prefer to speak of a block of "matter". Certainly a universe wherein *all* individuation could be so unambiguously identifiable and yet so malleable, would be highly intelligible — much more so than one composed of elusive photons, quarks or positrons.

Those accustomed to equate beingness with life and given to attribute "genuine individuation" only to the living, may object that IT lacks this characteristic. The association of individuation with animation and of the latter with Existence, is natural in a civilization, conditioned to think "metaphysically" and to view the Universe as a two-tiered structure, one tier of "matter" and one of "soul or spirit", each tier unmiscible. This objection, already answered, does not apply, for presently we are concerned with the genus Existent, and not with its subspecies such as animal, plasmic or vegetable, which merely categorize quality. The Fact-of-to-be precedes all else, and is shared by each. *Is an Existent,* genus generalissimum, *any individual, animate or not, which owns the minutest speck of the Real.* This requisite, IT, as constructed, fulfils admirably. A further technical difficulty is perhaps being envisaged, namely: that the dimensions of IT are excessive; that a four feet cube is fantastically huge compared with an invisible Democritan atom or electron. As the previous, this fails to consider the objective. IT is created to serve in two experiments intended to establish whether or not excision, evolution or mutation is compatible with existential individuation. The objection that IT is huge by elementary particle standards disregards the nature of models.

To sum up, the fact to be established is not that the members of a species or genus are indivisible and dimensionless, but rather that individuation of the Real requires immutability and, as a corollary, adimensionality. Stated inversely, the question is: how much "dimensioned matter" is required before genuine individuation occurs? Since up to this point, individuation has been observed as a general phenomenon and Existence also as a general fact, the proper course is to investigate individuation as this might occur within Maritain's "bugbear", the *genus generalissimum* called Existence.

6. Experiment No. I: Operation Divisibility

The objective of experiment number one is to demonstrate that IT cannot withstand the excising of even the minutest parcel of its sixty-four cubic feet of Existence without ceasing to be ITself.

To avoid getting lost in the maze of technical details which would result from a series of divisions, that which can be described as Operation Divisibility will be limited to a single bisection performed by a four pronged instrument which cuts in from four sides simultaneously and neatly cleaves IT into two equal blocks. This first move immediately exposes two problems, either of which suffices "to put the bug in ones ear". These concern the speed and the precision of Operation Divisibility. Speedwise, only a division performed *instantaneously* could satisfy the criteria of bisection. A "cleavage performed in-time" does not cleave but rather consists of a series-of-undefinable-somethings, to which the mind *arbitrarily* allocates a "beginning and an ending". Precision-wise, the Materialist who would feign divide "things" in equal portions ends up in a corner more uncomfortable still. No bisection, even one executed with the sharpest, most precise of cutting instruments — with a laser beam — ever corresponds to the mental specifications assumed by the segmentor. Divisions are operations of the mind, and the pieces never reproduce exactly the stipulated dimensions. No method conceivable exists whereby a unit of "matter" can be divided into precisely delineated portions. Placed under a microscope, the rough edges which result from the moving particles reveal the dissimilarity of the parts, and more fatal, the instability of the edges.

Without delving into either issue (both are dealt with in Part III) one may rightly point out that it is generous to overlook them, for either when pursued to its ultimate *dénouement* would by itself convince an open-minded researcher of the irrationality of any degenerative or evolutionary hypothesis. Presently, let it be noted that if an operation intended to divide a physical entity involves mere indealization of crudely defined knots of relationships, then a genuine division never occurs. Damage only is inflicted, damage, meaning that an observed amputation represents merely a more or less central mutilation performed upon an Antropocity. The term "more or less, central", here, implies that cuts on the edge of a cube or a humanoid or through the centre differ only in degree, and that such mutilations do not bisect an Existent, but rather only a dense knot of relationships. *A fortiori*, a mechanical operation, unrealizable even upon an Antropocity such as a chair or automobile, will prove impossible to perpetrate upon an adimensional Atom.

Assuming that for the present purpose the impossible happens and that, with surgical precision, a hapless IT is segmented into identical halves, since IT was a cube, 4′ × 4′ × 4′, sporting 64 cubic feet of "material", IT is no more. Rather, in IT's place lie twin blocks, 2′ × 4′ × 4′, each possessed of 32 cubic feet of whatever qualities, i.e., ambition, tenderness, mass, color, which might have filled IT. However, if these were unevenly distributed, if, for instance, "heartness" was situated in IT's far south-east corner, this "heartness" must stay put. To make the task of identification simple, the two halves will henceforth bear the names B1, B2.

The bisection being completed, two issues offer themselves for consideration. The first concerns an assessment of the visible or physical impact of the operation. The second involves its ontological interpretation. Insofar as the superficial effects of bisection are concerned, a consensus can be assumed. It will be generally agreed that when a physical entity is segmented, as was IT, the effects are felt by the original and by the resulting parts, regardless of the number and size of the latter; regardless also of the type of entity truncated, be this star, neutron, chair or man. Such an agreement, however, has meagre scientific import. Focussing entirely upon visual evidence and limited to the Perceived, it merely testifies on behalf of the occurrence of a Whiteheadian "event". The situation changes when the time comes to place an ontological interpretation on the same event. Not only is unanimity shattered, but the issue triggers philosophical quarrels upon the very nature of Reality. In view of the importance of the issue, a synopsis of the doctrines held on the subject is in order. This will provide contrast and also demonstrate that often the debate arises mainly because the inneity of the Real is misunderstood. Once such misconceptions are dispelled, most, in effect, agree that any It-which-is must, exactly as must an abstract unit, prove indivisible and immutable.

The number of interpretations of the impact of segmentation upon physical entities defies computation. Every school offers its hypothesis. Often within the same school, as many variants of the main thesis are propounded as there are original thinkers — a multiplicity to be expected. Once the structure of the Atom is misconstrued, the visions which the scientist can conjure as to relationality, of which segmentation is but one aspect, is limited solely by the fertility of his imagination. Yet this pluralism deceives. The basic options are few, for the problems posed by segmentation are central and are governed by the principle of the Proportionality of Extremes. While the minor variants are legion, their multitude can, for the present purpose, be reduced to three major hypotheses. Understandably none of the three, referred to henceforth as A, B, and C, is held *in toto* by any one ideological school. Rather much hybridization takes place. Depending upon their ideological biases and to some extent their disciplines, whenever attempting to explain the effects of division upon a physical entity, scientists regularly alternate from one to another.

Here are, in capsule form, the interpretations which the three basic trends place upon the segmentation of IT:

A. The advocates of A look upon B1 and B2 as two realities and upon the original IT as having disappeared in the sense that IT "died" or "ceased to exist".

B. A proponent of the second school would see IT as maintaining itself but in an "altered form", B1 being held to represent a new entity or Being. According to this theory, B2 never makes its entry upon either the conceptual or existential stage.

C. More sophisticated, hypothesis C predicates the survival of the original IT, but in an "altered form" and, dispensing also with B2, sees B1 as becoming integral to an alien — in other words, as substantially, symbiotically or hylemorphically absorbed by another entity. A human arm swallowed and digested by a shark would, in this view, correspond to B1, and the man who lost the arm would represent IT.

The remarks which follow are not intended to prove or disprove the several views referred to. Their intent is solely to bring into relief the fact that each supports — in some cases outrightly, in others indirectly — the view that an Existential-Atom if it is to be, must aver itself one, immutable, indivisible and adimensional.

This is clear in the case of hypothesis. A, for in it B1 and B2 are looked upon as new entities and IT as having vanished. Of course, the agreement persists only at the level of the conceptual, since its proponents consider Existents as phenomena born, created and/or caused by the application of an extraneous and somehow binding force upon a given unit or mass of "matter". Such a conclusion is as far removed as imaginable from Dynamic Vision which sees each Existent as a oneness which no outside force, even the Almighty, can divide. Yet in the light of hypothesis A, IT has to be one and indivisible to be itself. For instance, A, applied to the human animal asserts that a bisected man dies — ceases to be — and that the end-product consists of two nondescript pieces of flesh, described either as half men or possibly as two new "things". Barring a miracle, supernatural or medical, no one attempts to apply hypotheses B and C to this situation.

Hypothesis B would normally be held to apply to man and IT, if instead of being bisected, both had lesser amounts cut off, possibly the left arm of the vertebrate and a mere 7½%, volume-wise from the south-east corner of IT. According to the proponents of B, in such a situation, the two original entities subsist but in an "altered form" and the excised arm or the 7½% of IT, as in A, represent new existential entities, new "things".

Formula C, more sophisticated than B, makes only relatively more sense existentially. As in B, the man and IT, when suffering from the excisions described above, retain their identities but in a diminished state. The human arm and the 7½% of the south-east corner of IT (provided IT is deemed digestible) are, when eaten, let us assume by a shark, seen as "incorporated" and integral to the shark. Depending upon ideological backgrounds, the incorporation proceeds symbiotically, hylemorphically, etc.

Closer scrutiny of these formulae reveals simultaneously their basic inconsistencies, and the indirect support which each provides in behalf of a universe composed of asectile and inviolable Atoms. Since the incompatibility of existential division with a Fact-of-to-be is the sole concern, the case re A can be compended briefly. Its advocates, while holding a concept of existential individuation diametrically opposed to ours, nonetheless argue that a divided entity is a destroyed entity. The disagreement, not related to divisibility, flows from a diverging concept of an Existent. The partisans of A see an Existential-Atom in a chair or stone, whereas either is but an Antropocity — an entity mindfactured upon the basis of intensity and coagency factors. In summary, while A yields no corroborative physical data in favor of existential individuation, the principle of identity is nonetheless in it recognized. However, within its context no attempt is made to grasp a true Existent and the goodwill, logic and intellectual coherence of those who argue that a "big stone" ceases *to be* when broken into two smaller ones, cannot be put to the test. Hypothesis A simply ignores the synactivity of Reality with Existence and Truth.

The issues become more complex and can yield pertinent evidence in behalf of the immutability of the Atom when one moves on to theories B and C. Jointly these summarize the thinking of practically the entire scientific community in respect to the impact of a division upon Existents such as animals, plants, etc. Ideologically options B and C are miles apart but can be dealt with simultaneously, since in both hypotheses the original Existent suffers an identical fate, and this alone is of interest.

A bisected IT presents those who champion the "same Being but in a different form" with a dilemma which they usually avoid cunningly, but are in this instance prevented from doing. Since the bisection of IT happens instantaneously, producing two blocks identical in size, they are faced with deciding which is the original. Normally, it is assumed that the nipping-off of parts — the evolution — occurs gradually, in sequence as in an "aging body", and that the situs of the Existent or Symbiosis is always, "to the last instant", easily pinpointed. Under the specifications here stipulated, they are denied this easy way out. Yet should one generously leave them to wrestle in peace with their dilemma, and condescend to play the game by identifying B1 as representing IT, only of course in a sadly diminished state, such generosity would offer scant relief, for there is still the question: what of B2? From their point of view, B2 can never be integral to IT, even though this was prior to the bisection assumed to be the case, since there B2 sits, and poor diminished IT alias B1, stands lonely in his corner. At that point, it would seem that the rational stand to adopt is that B2 was all along, merely under the control of B1, and that we Outsiders were fooled by the fact that B1's control was so overwhelming as to submerge and hide B2's identity. But the partisans of "the same-Being-under-a-different form" rarely bow to common sense, especially when this provides a clear-cut answer to that which appears as a problem worthy of complexification. In the present case — central to an understanding of the Universe — they, with quasi-unanimity, opt for anti-common sense and seek to explain the "changing form" through abstract concepts such as potency, symbiosis, historical categories, etc., which allow one to gloss over Truth with sophistication — to say that black is white, no less.

A refutation is not called for. The point of interest is that the adherents of both B and C when promoting the usual explanations of change through segmentation effectively recognize in the Existent an adimensional. Granted, most Evolutionists seem to be unaware that their stand re divisibility and "change" implies the adimensionality and permanence of the living. Be this as it may, to argue that an Atom, human or coniferous lives on unaffected when an arm or a branch is lopped off, is to argue that a "something", albeit non-localizable, "acts" outside of the "material dimensions" of said man or conifer. The evidence adduced in behalf of such an inneal factor, often referred to as a "soul", is more explicit still when an attempt is made to account for accretions or growth. Faced with this phenomenon, even the most adamant in the opinion that the human atom is but a conglomerate of molecules, invariably insist that the conglomerate or symbiosis is "something" more than a "pile of atoms"; that, for instance, there is a "specificity" at work. Yet, such an affirmation does not prevent them from rushing to emphasize that this "something", this "specificity", is "nothing". Was the issue of less import, a condescending smile would be in order. With the very nature of man at stake, one can but sadly shake ones head in disbelief and sorrow.

To the Scientific Existentialist the cause of the confusion of the Materialist and Spiritualist is evident. Torn between a blind dedication to the empty concept of "matter" and the equally blinding evidence in behalf of the adimensionality of the Atom, both resign themselves to sacrificing the "living" to the "inanimate," which restricted sense perceptions seem to indicate is the *more* permanent. Still, as long as the "living" is round-about and hopping, they dare not deny it all reality, but grudgingly concede that the animate *is* and *remains* itself, even when it loses "parts of itself". Thus, while A provided conclusive evidence that according to its adherents, divisibility is not consistent with individuation, B and C provide positive clues, if only vaguely intuited and never conceded, that existential individuation is not tied to space. For, if both IT after losing half of its cubage, and a man after losing both arms, are still present in the half-cube and mutilated body, no one respectful of intellectual honesty may proclaim that IT or the man were dimensioned initially. The dilemma of the advocates of B and C — that of conciliating the discontinuous with the continuous — is the same as sorely tried Aquinas when the good man was asked to account for the relationship between a dimensionless "form" or "soul" and its "body", composed of precisely dimensioned "matter" (*materia signata*).

Since physical segmentation, as opposed to a mental operation of it, never does in-fact occur, in final analysis, the interpretation which each group places upon the division on an entity is identical, and all are driven to jump from one intellectual foot to the other — only to end up all in chorus brazenly denying the Real. The reason is simple. They rely upon the process, and since processes dip into the continuous and cosmically relational, each group, when attempting to blend and/or integrate the quantizing modality of the intellect with the continuous, must privilege the one over the other. Invariably, the victim is the Atom, the Real and Truth — all sacrificed upon the slimy altar of Becoming. In effect, those who see the Existent as susceptible to "change", impudently arrogate for themselves the power to create or annihilate Existence and Truth at will.

The conclusions to be drawn from this brief survey of the main theories held as to the impact of an amputation or bisection upon an existential entity, are the following. The truths which underlie the Principle of Absolutes; namely, facticity and its corollary indivisibility, so overwhelm the intellect as to exact from everyone a minimal degree of adhesion. Thus, at the Perceived, the facticity of absolutes such as numerals is unquestioned. Further, this recognition, overflowing in the form of an intuition into the Real, leads most to postulate some modality of existential individuation. One such widely held is the hylemorphism of the Scholasticists which professes to situate a dimensionless "soul" or vital principle in a dimensioned yet changing "form". Symbiotism, a materialistic version of hylemorphism wed to chemical atomism, also bears witness in behalf of the inviolability of the Atom. Under both a bisected IT is said to remain present in the major or vital segment — "in an altered form or state". Neither theory holds water. As demonstrated an instantaneous bisecting of IT into identical halves demolishes the defenses of schools B and C and their variants. A single blow denies to both the opportunity to sneak quietly, "progressively" out of the dilemma presented by "change" due to segmentation. Both must, to maintain coherence, abandon all talk of evolution and/or potency, and join the A option, which categorically affirms that division nihilates.

Their position does not improve when, for the purpose of this experiment, they are given the option to situate a subsistent IT in whichever half it might please them to privilege. Having injected the procedural in the Existent, they cannot on the basis of logic or physics, at pleasure terminate Operation Divisibility but must opt for one of three equally unplcasant alternatives. The first involves joining Leibniz with "his particle smaller than which no one can imagine" — a solution which Leibniz himself admitted implied artifice. The second is to proceed beyond the Leibnizian artifice and embark upon an operation which, by its nature, is interminable. Since to consider an infinite process is to plunge into irrationality, the more pragmatic shy from this solution, opting instead for a third. This, less reassuring still, exacts of its advocates that they condone the evaporation, the annihilation of the person and of the Universe itself, into that catch-all of distraught philosophers: the void.

As stated, to disprove proves nothing; to pursue an error into absurdity is equally counter-productive. When an avenue leads to a dead end, the sensible procedure is to return to the point of departure and start anew. For this reason the objectives of Operation Indivisibility were limited to:

1. demonstrate that a model Existent constructed along the lines of a conventional universal building block, could not simultaneously satisfy the requisites of time-space and Reality-Truth, and

2. point out that the interpretation which the proponents of time-space place upon bisection testifies against their thesis, and that, in final analysis, all see the individual as unlocalizable and effectively adimensional.

Both objectives are achieved. To grasp the Real one must pursue some other avenue of research. This is done in experiment number three.

7. Experiment No. 2 — A Model Universe of 1,000,000 ITs

Some may be tempted to discount the results of the first experiment because it involves a single specimen. Others may further argue that while division did indeed destroy IT, this was only because IT was, by definition, endowed with objectivity; was, in other words, held to constitute an absolute.

The second experiment, conducted upon a model universe consisting of 1,000,000 ITs, while brief, should dispose of both objections. Doubt as to the universal applicability of findings based upon an experiment involving a single Atom evaporates when an identical operation is performed upon the perfect, *ne plus ultra*, absolute: the Universe or the sum of "matter". While the Universe so defined still represents a single object, an objection arising from its unicity can hardly be entertained, for whether monistic or atomistic, it effectively encompasses on a factual basis all possible units. Provided the model accurately reproduces the characteristics of the whole, the findings will apply to the original, including its components. The second objection which would question the endowing of IT, by definition with objectivity, was answered when, in chapter VI, it was established that objectivity or absolutes do in-fact constitute the foundation of Reality, and that any scientific experiment into the Real, to prove valid and honest, must lead off with an absolute. This imperative is further confirmed empirically by the fact that experiments conducted in the field of natural science invariably proceed from an absolute — which is to say, that the researcher looks upon his raw material as constituting a whole. A model existent conforms to this rule. In any case, anyone who might reject the above as inconclusive has no alternative but to grant physical objectivity to the Universe. Certainly no more absolute a subject of research can be found — even ones own thoughts being encompassed.

The affirmation that it is possible to construct an experimental model of the Cosmos may seem brash. Yet closer scrutiny dispels any reservation which may be entertained. Indeed, the Universe lends itself to being reduced to a scale model more unambiguously than any other object. Whereas some question as to limits, dimensions, representativity, etc., can always be raised when the model is that of an urban development or of the human skeleton, a similar reservation leveled against a model universe is groundless. In-fact and by definition, the Universe represents the one genuine absolute encompassing even the Absolute-Absolute. Thus, the sole requisite which its model must fulfill to be representative, is that, whatever its configuration, it be understood as encompassing the sum of the Real. This leaves but one topic to be agreed upon; namely, the structure and configuration of the model. Since some may reject an experiment conducted upon an atomistic or alternately, a monistic universe, Operation Divisibility, phase two, will be conducted upon a monistic (Spinozan-Marxist) and an atomistic (Democritan) model.

A. *A Monistic Universe and Divisibility*

Those, probably few in number, who opt for monism, may note that the structure of their universe is, to all purposes and intents, identical to the IT of experiment No. I. It follows that there is no need to perform bisections, quadrisections, etc., for every step and finding which applied to IT, applies integrally in this situation also. To avoid repetition, it suffices therefore to record that a model monistic universe is indiscernable from IT, and that which applied to IT, applies to the Monist's Cosmos. Specifically, this implies that even the slightest bisection or change renders a monistic universe a lying, irrational universe.

B. *An Atomistic Universe and Divisibility*

The advantages of a model atomistic universe consisting of 1,000,000 ITs (including the IT of experiment No. I) have already been noted. Firstly, the neutral structure and composition of ITs precludes ideological controversy. Secondly, IT's universe has a structure familiar to the contemporary physicists, most of whom envision the Cosmos as closed and composed of Democritan-like elementary particles. Applicable to this second experiment, is the added advantage of technical efficiency. A universe of 1,000,000 ITs, cubic in stature, is in this respect superior to practically any conceivable model. For example, a million ITs are quickly arranged in a neat stack one hundred units high, wide and long. Such an object is at once easily visualized, and most importantly, disturbances or turbulence in it can be detected by the naked eye.

Adopting the Cosmic Equation to the model, with X being equal to 1,000,000 and the Atoms having become ITs, this now reads: U = 1,000,000 ITs.

Briefly the repercussions of Operation Divisibility upon the truth of the reformulated Equation are these. A first operation, and the only one required, is to subject our friend IT to a quadrisection, effected again at absolute speed, by a six-pronged cutting device which digs in from all six faces simultaneously. For IT, in its role of individual, the effects of such a quadrisection parallel those of a bisection, and in any case are of no concern presently. Rather, the fate of his universe and the truth of its equation is at stake.

Prior to operation quadrisection, the universe consisted of 1,000,000 precisely defined objects or pieces of the Real or "matter". Each of these could in its own right, lay claim to facticity and truthfulness, for together the 1,000,000 accounted for all of Existence and Truth — each offering itself to every other as a full, unambiguous Presence. Of a universe so constructed it could rightly be affirmed: "Truth resides throughout". Evidently, the truth referred to is not an intellectual but rather an eminently existential truth which must, to have meaning, forever coincide with one million facts, each factual in the physical sense. As was seen, existential truth involves the total perception of a reality, or alternately corresponds to the fullness of a Being or Beings, communicated and grasped. Once IT is quadrisected, clearly, not only is IT itself destroyed, but the truth and facticity of his whole universe founders irremediably. Deductive reasoning, by revealing the synactivity of the trio Existence, Reality and Truth, had already revealed as much. This logical deduction is now confirmed empirically and physically. Even a visual survey reveals that once IT collapses into eight equal cubes, then the relationships, realities and truths contained in the model, all are invincibly disturbed. As a shattered Humpty-Dumpty, no one, not even all of the king's men can ever reconstruct IT; a fact glaringly illustrated by a cursory analysis of the new formulation of the Cosmic Equation. Where this initially read:

$$U = 1{,}000{,}000 \text{ ITs},$$

it presently must be restated:

$$U = (999{,}999 + 8\text{-eights}) \text{ ITs}.$$

Whereas one previously dealt with 1,000,000 facts or objects, one now contends with 1,000,007 of which 999,999 remain "themselves", and eight are aliens. The eight "newcomers" bear no resemblance whatsoever to the original fact *qua* IT. Simultaneously, all relationships pertaining to the million are altered. In respect to relationships, an entirely new system replaces the original. The universe of the ITs-which-are, ceasing to-be, vanishes into a non-existent past. With a non-existent past one might learn to live — provided somewhere, sometime there be a present. However, he who would feign find the present in the new equation: U = (999,999 + 8-eights) ITs, is denied this consolation. The Becomingist must, if his game is to be honest, submit each new evolving universe to the same operation as that suffered by the first, and once again untruth, occupying the battlefield, deeds it to yet another non-existent past. And to the process there is no end and everywhere nothing real, nothing positive and scientific exists. Irrationality and falsehood alone reign. Kafka's Absurd alone beckons.

From an empirical point of view, the experiment, as brief and basic as it may appear, is at this juncture concluded. Nothing of relevance can be added. Physically there are no grounds upon which to attack its validity. Indeed, with each further segmenting, with each changing "instant", its results become more glaring. Should, for instance, each of the million ITs suffer from the excision of one tenth of its mass, each excision occurring consecutively at as short a time interval as one nanosecond, bedlam arises. No computer, regardless of its sophistication, nor for that matter The Absolute himself could cope with the resulting indeterminacies. Need one mention the mind shattering irrationality of a universe whose myriadic entities evolve in space over eons, as do, supposedly, all evolutionary universes?

8. The Universe and the Computer

Consider briefly one of the more important inventions of our era, the computer. Until recently the validity of experiments I and II would have rested safely upon proofs of logic, such as those just detailed and on common sense. Now, technical confirmation is available. From a logical point of view any computer, regardless of its complexity, embodies a finite number of units, conventionally called "bits". While computer technology undergoes constant sophistication and each break-through ushers in a new "speed era", both logically and physically the prime component remains some type or other of a magnetic cell subject to a "+" or "–" or "yes" and "no" polarization. The numbers involved are fantastic, yet on the one hand, each cell or bit is a discernable and, on the other, all share a common function, that of a basic component of the whole. The process remains one of absolute to absolute when, next, individual cells are banded in series of 4, 8 or 16 known as words and the latter are grouped into sentences and eventually into programs. Some idea of the rapidity at which this apposing of unit against unit operates can be gained from the following data. Illiac IV, a fourth generation computer (it is now out-classed) developed through the cooperation of the University of Illinois and Burroughs Inc., by drawing information from "permanent" records stored in "terrabits" (1 trillion bits) discs, at the rate of 1 billion per sec. can execute from 100-million to as many as 1 000-million instructions per second. Operating at full-speed, on a three shift basis, it would require from 200 to 300 programmers. Its efficiency is such that it can simulate the aerodynamics of a NASA shuttle orbiter, reentering the Earth's atmosphere or still translate satellite data, as to the state of a corn crop over a province-size area.

The relevance of the above to our second experiment is as follows. Firstly, it allows one to counter the objection of the excessive simplicity of a 1,000,000 unit universe and, secondly it confirms the principle of Absolutes. If, to satisfy the contemporary appetite for gigantism, each of the original 1,000,000 is multiplied a trillion, trillion, trillion times, Illiac IV or one of its more efficient descendants could still deal with any program based upon such a sum of entities, provided only the number of entities involved be finite. Confirmation comes from the fact that any alteration, no matter how insignificant in a program or in the number of units it affects, necessitates a wholesale reprogramming.

In sum, while all but the rare macroscopic mutation or event, such as a birth, a death or animal growth, etc., in a trillionic or in our "real" Universe pass undetected by the naked eye and are described as an "evolutionary process" by the Becomingist, nonetheless the truth of such universes is predicated upon the objectivity of each of its units, a fact documented by advanced computer technology. Nor would the situation change when processed by The Absolute. The Power of the Absolute-Mind being absolute, Its comprehension of the Universe is total. Hence for it no movement, excision or change occurs. Before It each IT, man or uranium, grasped fully in the most intimate of its chords and relationships, rests maximized, in the Absolute. The trillionic myriads become an intimate One, akin to the Plotinian or Brahmanic "Ones".

Part II

Dynamic Vision Power

chapter I

Power, Synact of Existence

My suggestion would be that anything which possesses any sort of power to affect another, or to be affected by another even for a moment, however trifling the cause and however slight and momentary the effect, has real existence; and I hold that the definition of being is simply power.

PLATO, *The Sophist*

1. *Power, Synact of Existence*

THE opening chapter of Part I emphasized that Existence was to be equated with Reality and a raw material, two reassuring affirmations to one in search of realism. However, by the close of the last chapter "matter", physical dimensions, "change", time and mass, etc., were demoted to the status of real-illusions. A universe which initially seemed to promise maximal realism, had been reduced to a finite number of univocal, faceless and factual, hence apparently static Atoms. Was this not an Idealism more radical than Descartes' or Berkeley's? The answer is no, for the investigation has but begun.

From the beginning, aware of the danger of being charged with Idealism, I sought to portray the concreteness of Existence by stressing that it was not only a universal fact, but that it is upon it that we stub our toes, of it which we eat, to it that we talk. At that stage no additional information could be provided as to how this eatingness, etc., is achieved, except possibly to indicate that when we stub our toes, it is not upon space; that when we eat, it is not time that we swallow; nor do we, if sane, talk to space or even to "matter".

This procedure was adopted because it is essential that in matters philosophical the first step be the first taken. As noted, the attention of every ontologist turns initially to two types of phenomena, those of individuation and of movement-change. Individuation was privileged because sheer common sense has it that one must first know what it is that is about to change, before a judgement upon the nature of its evolution can be passed. Stated otherwise, individuation received precedence for it alone provides a foundation upon which the *what-is* can be established.

Now that the general criteria of individuation are determined, the equipment required to conduct the existential experiment to a fruitful close is available. Such confidence may appear misplaced. How, after all, can one populate the Universe with adimensional Atoms, and still hope to account for time-space and their offspring, movement and speed, not to speak of the countless ancillary problems to which a factual universe gives birth? The point is well taken. Unless a complementary factor, responsible for movement and growth, etc., can be unearthed the game is over. Individuation at best provides a landmark, and to speak of "rocky-beingness", etc., as do Existentialists, clearly contributes little to the advancement of science. More is needed than such superficialities. The Existent must be so grasped that it will yield some of its deeper secrets; that, at the very least, it will offer an identifiable something or factor upon which we stub our toes, of which we eat, to which we talk.

A first assumption will be that the factor being sought must be utterly elusive and mysterious. Actually the opposite is the case. The missing element is a commonplace, namely: Power or Energy. Suffering the fate of the overfamiliar, it has been, through the centuries, taken for granted or sadly misunderstood. Some, going to one extreme, made of it the "essence" of the Universe, while others reduced it to the status of a concept. Philosophers in this have acted as the distraught smoker who in search of his pipe, turns the house upside down, while all along said pipe sits clenched between his teeth. Endlessly analyzing its effects, they have ignored its nature.

The reaction to a disclosure that Power or Energy is the "missing link" which prevents science from deciphering Reality and in particular the Self, is apt to be a shrug. Has it not just been emphasized that Power is a commonplace; that philosopher, physicist and layman alike constantly discuss it? True. It is equally true that, often, to be aware of a phenomenon and to discourse about it, is not to be equated with an understanding. Power's very ubiquity renders it susceptible to stereotype interpretations which bear no relation to reality; interpretations all the more blindly accepted in that they are venerable with age. Presently the dogma in favor is that Power involves a potency, a floating-into which causes acts kinetically or otherwise. This hypothesis, traceable to Aristotelian physics, could be valid. The theory of antipodes and of an unhabitable "bottom" of the earth, could also have been accurate. Exactly as it was "only reasonable" that no one could walk about with their feet directly opposed to ours and their heads pointing downwards, so does it seem reasonable to assume that Power causes movement, evolution, growth, and change generally.

As with antipodes, so with Power. The common-sensical, logical explanation does not correspond to Reality. *Power is not potential, procedural and a cause of becoming. Rather it is factual and synactive with Existence.* The full implications of the facticity and the synactivity of Power with Existence, will not be immediately evident. Nevertheless, together these two concepts turn the conventional universe inside out.

2. **Synact and Synactivity: What and Why?**

The facticity of Power, flows from its synactivity with Existence. Since synact and synactivity are new concepts and terms it is proper before proceeding, to provide general data upon the nature of both. The term synact describes a factor, an element without which another fact or factor cannot be. For example, to affirm that Power is the synact of Existence, implies that without Power, Existence lacks, and vice versa. It follows that synacts share characteristics. While differing, they must be fully compatible. In a word, synactivity is the intellectual adhesive needed to reunite factors which philosophy or "the common sense" sunder, causing man to view these as independent, whereas they merely represent different aspects of a phenomenon, subjectively prehended.

A second corollary is that synacts never in-fact compose. Creatures of the mind, residing within the perceptor synacts promote analytical thought, while safeguarding the intrinsic unity of the object. As to the adjective "synactive" and the verb "to synact", these need no elucidation. Both are syntaxical forms of the noun. Considerable use of this concept will be made, for its sole effective competitor, the Thomist concept of coprinciple, carries a higher content of intellectualization, and is furthermore of restricted applicability. For example, one can only with difficulty, speak of the trio: Existence, Truth and Reality as coprinciples, whereas it is proper to see in all three, full synacts. More important, coprinciple cannot convey facticity, and this latter is the key in the synactivity of Existence to Power.

3. **Power: a Fact to Be Investigated in Its Status of Fact**

To find in Existence a massive fact, and to proceed thence to see in the individual Existent a fact also, was bound to have radical consequences. These soon revealed themselves. The existential facts which came to people the Universe, if they were to satisfy the requisites of facticity, had to be seemingly so abstract, so disembodied, that an unfamiliar observer would be tempted to view each as objects of the imagination. Thus, before dealing with the Existent's interrelationships, its inneity should be investigated. One should, colloquially speaking, if flesh is to be found, put flesh on its dry, intellectual bones.

As noted, upon casting about in the cosmic depths for a fleshing agent, Power surfaced as a likely candidate. The problem in seeing Power, both as synact of Existence and as factual, is that this seems to raise as many issues as it solves. To vest facticity in the Existent constituted a break with orthodoxy. To make of Power also a fact irretrievably cuts all ties with past thought on the subject. It implies a novel universe, qualitative and dynamic rather than evolutive and processional. However, the rewards of such an approach to the ontological mystery clearly outweigh its cost. An Atom, factual and synactive with Power, provides the researcher with a stable subject. Instead of being restricted to chasing evanescent processes and indeterminate relationships, and to ultimately resort to intellectualism — to talk of contraries, limits, negations or the void — he is enabled to concentrate upon a well defined entity analyzable to its core. Whereas others work under an unsurmountable handicap — that of seeing Being as "caused by an act"; he can even dispense with speculation as to origins. Each Atom, due to its facticity, provides an objective base of operation from which all inquiries radiate. That harmless "F" placed before act, inverts the Universe. Opening to the cosmontologist paths as yet untrod, it allows him to pursue his research into the what-is of the Existent, rather than the by-it.

That which applies to Existence applies to Power. If anything, the factual option would appear more fruitful, since its alternative, Power perceived as a potency or kinetic factor can never be subjected to a systematic analysis — for the simple reason that the flowing or potential cannot be seized, let alone scientifically dissected. There is of course no guarantee that Power can flesh an as yet dimensionless Atom. Yet the odds seem good. Certainly no other universal fact evidences the same versatility and wealth of qualities. Having vested in each Atom a parcel of the existential mass, let us therefore seek to discover whether or not each also possesses its share of the Power or Energy in the Cosmos.

To proceed from the premise that Energy is parcelled out in individually packaged units or quanta, means that even though one will pour over the same "material" as others have, still, one may possibly uncover facets as yet ignored or misinterpreted. With Power, as with Existence, the merit of Dynamic Vision is not to reveal a mysterious factor, coming out of the blue to set everything straight, but to place facts, issues and phenomena in their rightful perspective. Power will be promoted from its traditional status of agent of processes and effects, to that of a fact dealt with in its own right.

To establish the facticity of Power it will be necessary firstly, to investigate what Power is and not how it operates; and secondly, to ascertain if it lends itself to individuation, instead of being, as is commonly held, some sort of universal which pressures from the outside-in, to cause or create beings-of-occasion each, as the Whiteheadian concrescence, a mere crest upon dynamic waves. The logic here is that if Power does lend itself to individuation, then synactivity is vindicated, and the Existent achieving its second metamorphosis, graduates from neuter, antiseptic Existential-Atom to Dynamic-Fact.

chapter II

What is Power?

The energy in one gram of mass is sufficient to keep a 1 000 watt electric-light bulb running for 2 850 years.

Isaac Asimov, *Guide to Science*, p. 367

Caesar could do less with Rome than Napoleon with France; Napoleon less with France than Lenin with Russia, and Lenin less with Russia than Hitler with Germany.

C. Wright Mills, *The Power Elite*, p. 23

1. Power, Physical Samples

THE question: What is it? regardless of its object can be answered in two ways. One can point a finger or if a sample is not immediately available, one can describe. A second approach is the analytical which seeks to penetrate beneath the surface to explain the object's inneity and mechanism. Each offers advantages and in some situations either suffices. In view of Power's key role in the Universe, it is best to answer the query: What is it? under both headings.

Of the two modes, where Power is concerned, the descriptive is the easiest to fulfil. While universal and versatile Power can nonetheless be comprehensively described in a few pages, whereas the remainder of this Part is required to merely outline its basic mechanism. Exceeding with ease the time-space dimensions, one can figuratively point a finger at a power which both the reader and myself sample firsthand. To write the ten words which follow with a pen and for the reader to grasp their meaning, constitutes an exercise of thought-power. Its pervasiveness is further revealed when one next observes that to print these words set in motion a remote chain of powers, each link qualitatively distinct the one from the other, from the editor's to the printer's, etc. The purchase of the book demanded the exercise of somewhat parallel energies, i.e. money-power, and power to carry it home. In a word, factual or exercised power saturates the entire chain of events. A more concrete, because painful, example would be an assailant's punch administered to the someone's nose, followed by a copious nosebleed. This would constitute dynamism, observed once again factually and literally first hand and first nose. Certainly in such a situation there can be no question of Idealism.

Beyond the area of man's intimate and subjective world, every manifestation of "matter" can also be reduced to an intensity factor of Power. Einstein's epoch-making $E = MC^2$, and its tragic validation achieved through the first atomic bomb, has made the intensity characteristic of Power, household knowledge. This convertibility of the "mass-matter" tandem into energy is described in accessible and less awesome terms in the following quote:

> Einstein's mathematical treatment of energy showed that mass could be considered a form of energy — a very concentrated form, for a very small quantity of mass would be converted into an immense quantity of energy.
> Einstein's equation relating mass and energy is now one of the most famous equations in the world. It is:
>
> $$e = mc^2$$
>
> Here "e" represents energy (in ergs), "m" represents mass (in grams) and "c" represents the speed of light (in centimeters per second).
>
> Since light travels at 30 billion centimeters per second, the value of c^2 is 900 billion billion. This means that the conversion of one gram of mass energy will produce 900 billion billion ergs. The erg is a small unit of energy not translatable into any common terms, but we can get an idea of what this number means when we are told that the energy in one gram of mass is sufficient to keep a 1 000 watt electric-light bulb running for 2 850 years. Or, to put it another way, the complete conversion of a gram of mass into energy would yield as much as the burning of 2 000 tons of gasoline.
>
> Einstein's equation destroyed one of the sacred conservation laws of science. Lavoisier's "law of conservation of mass" had stated that matter could neither be created nor destroyed. Actually, every energy releasing chemical reaction changes a small amount of mass into energy: the products, if they could be weighed with utter precision, would not quite equal the original matter.[1]

The ubiquity of Power is further confirmed by the fact that phenomena, apparently as unrelated as magnetization and imperialism, are both manifestations of an identical characteristic. The magnet drawing to itself iron filings, or the financier endlessly extending his influence in the business world, or still the

1. Isaac ASIMOV, *Guide to Science*, Basic Books, Inc. New York, 1972, p. 367.

sun drawing in its wake the planets, planetoids and humanoids, speak a same language and affirm this utter interrelatedness of all types of Energy. A final example can be that of political imperialism as graphically depicted in this passage of C. Wright Mills' *The Power Elite.*[2]

> Caesar could do less with Rome than Napoleon with France; Napoleon less with France than Lenin with Russia, and Lenin less with Russia than Hitler with Germany. But what was Caesar's power at its peak compared with the power of the changing inner circle of Soviet Russia or of America's temporary administration? The men of either circle can cause great cities to be wiped out in a single night...[3]

As is evident, the list is endless and familiar to everyone. Nonetheless, to eliminate any ambiguity, one might add that the terms to ionize, to rule, to run, to hate, to magnetize, to fall, an idea, a bullet, a tree, an atom, a dream, a stallion, a rock and mysticism speak either of Power or involve owned Power. In the above, both verb and noun, Atom and Antropocity are included deliberately, to emphasize that the issue is not one of semantics, but rather that whenever Power operates, existential situations are at stake — regardless of the word used. As noted earlier, semantics and signs are of themselves empty of Existence, and hence also communication, regardless of its modality or objective. Rather, all forms of communication represent the specialized tools of a given species, through which the group and, within it each individual, physically impresses its "sign", its Self upon the Other, within and without the group. The energy dimension of thought is singled for special mention, because it remains the least understood, and yet it is in a sense the most critical, for alone the realization that thought is Power, exactly as electricity, can eventually eradicate the unhealthy "matter-spirit"

---

2. While here ionization and magnetization are linked to conflict and imperialism, it can be effectively argued that in the case of ionization, certain reactions parallel the love process between animal atoms, i.e., between goose and gander. The grounds for such an observation, are that within the metallic realm, electrostatic attraction performs the same duty as love does within a family, human or national. In both instances, Power binds the crystals or animal atoms respectively into coherent units. All parties retain their identities; yet each enjoys the benefits of a common brotherhood.
3. C. Wright Mills, *The Power Elite*, New York, Oxford University Press, 1959, p. 23.

dichotomy which plagues and perverts scientific research. In a word, as Plato long ago remarked in *The Sophist*, Power is present whenever a fact or event manifests itself — regardless of order or intensity.

The above catalogue has probably met with general approval. There remains a remark which will undoubtedly destroy such consensus as was established. Affirmed from the beginning, it is that Power is a fact. All of the instances of Power enumerated, and any which *are* anywhere in the Universe partake of the factual, of the As-is. The barrier thus raised between Dynamic Vision and the schools which see Power as a potency, as a flowing, as "part of a process" is more insurmountable than Mt. Everest. Save for the following brief observations no attempt will be made to presently justify this theory. It suffices to state clearly that in this section and in all subsequent, Power is investigated solely as exercised or factual and never as "potential power"; that in each case, one Atom either alone or in conjunction with others in-fact has a concrete, tangible impact upon other Its-which-are. Any notion of potency or evolution is to be foresworn.

An identical fate awaits concepts such as those of "matter", void and substance, etc. All gratuitous and nocive intellectual accretions, these only cloud Reality. For example, the hypothetical punch on the nose illustrates the redundancy of that overworked theme, "matter" and its mates. Once the fist hits and returns to its master, the victim may find himself with a broken, bleeding nose. Certainly, he possesses no extra potency, no additional "matter", "category", "essence", "substance", and "idea", each of which would be held responsible by as many schools. The recipient is no more substantified (*à la* Aquinas) or categorized (*à la* Kant) or materialized (*à la* Marx) or idealized (*à la* Berkeley) after than before his nose bleed. Granted, these several attributions involving a maximum of simplication, fail to consider the attenuating nuances which each school brings to bear upon the subject. Yet it remains that finessing can never rectify a doctrine 180° off course. To the assertion — "when one is punched in the face, 'matter' hits", is it not more accurate to substitute, "an exercise of Power" by someone, possibly a friend, who may be angered? *To insist that it is "matter" which hits, reduces the friend to a concept. For, it is either he, in his role of*

Dynamic-Fact, who, with the help of other Existents, metallic, cellular, etc., punched or it is "matter". It cannot be both. To affirm that the friend "is composed of matter" merely dodges the issue. Nor does talk of a symbiosis or of a similarly accretive term solve the dilemma. A big pile of atoms no more makes a man, than a big pile of oranges make a gigantic orange. A pile, the colloquial term for a conglomerate or symbiosis, forever remains a concept.

Exactly as a geochemist when asked to assay ore does not speculate on the content of a sample which he thinks may in the future be brought to him, or upon the sample assayed last week, but concentrates upon that on his bench, so must any investigation of Power and its synact Existence be confined to Power which in-fact is.

As with Existence, the logicians may object that it is a contravention of the rules of logic and common sense, to declare the sum of Power in the Cosmos to be a raw material and that in any case an *a priori* assumption that Power is universal is improper. The objection re universality is dealt with in chapter VI, wherein the characteristics of Power are considered. As to the argument that the cosmontologist may not embrace the sum of the dynamic within his field of inquiry, this is unfathomable. Why should he be denied the right to respect the objectivity of his subject, by encompassing it mentally, when other scientists are granted the same license? A metallurgist delving into platinum is not held to exceed his mandate simply because his experiment covers only an infinitesimal percentage of the platinum in the world. Also, no one would bind him to his original findings, should some property of platinum unknown to him be uncovered later. Until such are discovered, his duly established findings are applied to all platinum. The positions coincide. No cosmic principle which would allow one to fantasize is proclaimed nor is any vaguely defined hypothesis advanced. I do not even claim to be aware of all types of Power. My basic premise being an objective What-Is, Is, I merely observe. If and when a new form of Power, having all along been there, is discovered, then it must be taken into account because a refusal to do so simply because one does not "like its author", or does not "believe in it" would prevent one from obtaining an accurate understanding of the Universe. In any case, no Power presently unknown to man could actualize which would not be covered, for the Power even of God is automatically included, on par with that of a gnat. In respect to Power, the same objective stand is adopted as was in regard to Existence. *In accord with the principle What-Is, Is, all powers, known as well as unknown are included, and any which someone might "imagine", but are not found in the Real are excluded.* Thus from an empirical point of view, at this stage, such objections do not apply. Such as may be rightly raised, should be directed towards an interpretation of facts and phenomena and not towards the facts and phenomena themselves. To the encompassing, without exception, of the sum of Existence and Power, even that which escapes detection, the same reasoning applies. Objection to this should be made only if later a valid reason arises to exclude a given type. Presently, to encompass the entirety of Existence and of Power, merely lays the ground work for due scientific investigation. *Existence serves to encompass the phenomenon of individuation. Power, for its part, when objectively compassed, invests the qualitative phenomena.* Together, the two provide a first and basic insight into the Real.

2. **Why the Word Power?**

The noun Power which plays a major role in the structure of Dynamic Vision is charged with controversy. Indeed in many circles it assumes a pejorative, even evil connotation — a normal reaction in an era wherein the Stalins and Hitlers and lesser editions thereof, shamelessly abuse political and economic power to oppress and liquidate entire populations. It therefore seems useful, as in the case of the equally contentious term of "absolute", to explain the rationale responsible for the adoption of Power in preference to its numerous competitors.

The term Power was chosen not as the result of study and protracted argument, but rather of a deeply felt intuition that all Existence subsumes in Power, to the exclusion even of "matter" a logical sequel of an innately positive, existential and aggressive approach to life's problems. For many years its suitability was not questioned. To me, Power meant a something at once universal and owned, and it never at the time entered my mind that it could be otherwise. Later, a perusal of those compendiums of mankind's acquired knowledge, the encyclopedias, etc., confirmed this intuition. Also, in nearly every instance, it was implied that, when the need arises, the term can convey a sensc of facticity. An excellent example is the definition in *Webster's Unabridged*, one of the more concise and yet comprehensive of the sources consulted. Clearly, this is not quoted as scientific evidence. Rather the purpose is to show that semantically the word describes most effectively the synact of Existence. Of its seventeen subsections, six are especially relevant:

(1) the latent or inherent property of a being, human or animal, manifested by endeavor, by reason of which that being is capable of bringing about moral or physical changes; potency.

(4) force; strength; momentum; as, the power of the wind which propels a ship, or tears up trees during a cyclone.

(5) influence; that which may move the mind; as, the power of argument or persuasion. (The theory that thought is physical, on the same basis as electricity, is hereby clearly implied).

(11) that quality in any natural body which produces a change, or makes an impression on another body; as, the power of medicine; the power of heat; the power of sound. (This qualitative feature, as will become evident, plays a key role in the deciphering of the dynamic.)

(12) divinity; a celestial or invisible being or agent supposed to have dominion over some part of creation; as, celestial powers; the powers of darkness.

(17) electricity: the rate of activity of performing work or of exerting energy; the practical unit of electric force being the volt, ampere, or watt...

Such a comprehensive catalogue of processes and entities, when added to an already exhaustive list, qualifies Power for the role of synact of Existence — if synactivity there be.

3. Why Power's Competitors, Energy, Potency, Flux, Dynamism, Lost Out

The five terms, Energy, Power, dynamism, potency and flux, while related, nonetheless when integrated into a philosophy, yield different universes. Their cousinship notwithstanding, three must be outrightly rejected, Energy only, being a true synonym. The reasons are not of the same order in each case. In some, these are ideological — as in that of potency. In others, as with flux, the necessity of dealing with first things first is responsible. For the sake of impartiality confirmation is again sought in *Webster's*. The objective, here, is not to refute the philosophy in which the three do the yeoman's share of work, rather, only to establish why they do not qualify.

The alternate candidate, Energy is defined under five headings, four of which are relevant.

(1) internal or inherent power; the power of operating, whether exerted or not; ...

(2) power exerted; vigorous operation; force; vigor; as God, ...

(3) effectual operation; efficacy; strength or force producing the effect.

(4) in physics, the power of doing work; capacity for producing effect upon matter.

As will be observed, all four equate Energy with Power, the first specifically describing it as: internal or inherent power, an apt description of synactivity. The existential content being identical, for purposes of euphony, Energy can serve as alternate. Power rates primacy mainly because of a subtle distinction often made between the two, Energy being viewed as the more "material" and less "spiritual" or intellectual. By and large, the word is given the mechanistic connotation associated with physics, a distinction useful to the Materialist or Schizoid, since it allows either to emphasize their dichotomous views of the Universe. In a univocal universe no difference exists — hence, their interchangeability.[4]

Of potency, the Scholastic substitute for Power, the relevant sections are:

(1) the state or quality of being potent; power, either physical or moral; inherent ability; energy; efficacy; strength.

(2) power derived from external sources; influence; authority.

Even a cursory perusal reveals why potency was unsuitable; also why any dalliance with its close relative "power-potential" was

4. The term Schizoid encompasses the broad spectrum of schools who look upon the Universe as divided into two distinct spheres, that of "matter" and that of "spirit". The most successful proponents of this theory are the Aristotelians and Scholasticists. While Materialists come in all shades, the dominant variant presently, is that of the Marxists.

brief. After all, one can hardly look upon the Self as for real, if it in any measure "becomes"; if ones power derives from external sources. Others may be happy with the status of a sewage pipe. I could never be.

As to Dynamism, it is defined as:

> The doctrine of Leibniz, that, besides matter, some necessary material force exists which is the prime mover in all physical as well as mental phenomena.

Our indebtedness for the word is to Leibniz. Since his time the word has obviously gained wide acceptance. While between it and Power there exists an affinity, its connotation is primarily adjectival and does not convey a sense of facticity. Its role is therefore limited mainly to that of a partner in composite terms, as in cosmic dynamism or of adjective as in Dynamic Vision, where it adequately pictures the aggressive, alive and outgoing. Occasionally, it will serve as noun, in which case it carries a high content of possessiveness and implies the synactivity of Existence to Power.

To flux defined as:

> (1) the act of flowing; the motion or passing of a fluid.
>
> (2) the moving or passing of anything in continued succession; as, things in this life are in continual flux.

Much the same comments apply as do to dynamism. Yet, flux as understood in the 20th century, describes well the relation of mediumship and will be of limited use in that context. An effective substitute for the notion of change, it connotes the relational more than the factual and was never a serious challenger.

In summary, Power was adopted because it is generic. Both in the mind of the intellectual and of the man on the street, it blankets the phenomena and concepts included separately in the other four terms, and can encompass others not dealt with, as witness that of motion, central to Marxism. With ease, it embraces the gamut of the real and qualitative, and semantically avers itself worthy synact of Existence.

4. Power: Science's Great Unknown

An assessment of the progress up to this point reveals that the bulk of the work remains ahead. The listing of physical samples was intended solely to describe in an embracing manner, with the Webster definition further realizing this objective. Surprisingly, upon leaving behind the descriptive to search for a systematic analysis of Power viewed as a fact-phenomenon and distinct from potency and change (virtual or kinetic force), little of value is available. Since Aristotle, the mechanics of energy (energeia) are a constant source of research and as constantly of controversy — that, for example, between the Cartesians and Leibnizians and more recently between Lord Kelvin and John F. W. Herschel, H. Spencer et al. Since the splitting of the atom, the volume of speculation and applied experimentation has mushroomed, with the physicists stealing the leading role from the philosopher and general theoretician. Simultaneously, due to its universality and convertibility, the cross-fertilization of interdisciplinary insights has accelerated, a process to which the spread of the inherently dynamic Marxist world view undoubtedly contributes. Yet, these promising developments notwithstanding, the structure or inneity of Power remains to all intent and purpose an unknown factor. Understandably, effort devoted to the subject by the subdisciplines has yielded only marginal insights into the cosmic. Each merely develops its own valid but tailor-made concepts, as a rule quite meaningless when transposed into another frame. The Christian priest-counselor or Liberal psychiatrist, for example, would find the physicist's "a capacity to perform work", of meagre practical use in his trade. After all, the psychological and ethical content of the marital problems of some cuckolded, dejected husband are with utmost difficulty, translated into terms of pounds, horse-power or kinetism. Nor would the method used to measure the thrust-power of the Saturn space missile help the microphysicist to understand that of the Beta particles. The one group which should be preoccupied with the inner structure of Power, grasped in its cosmic dimension, that of the physicists, also seems satisfied with superficialities. These can of course plead their status of empiricists as an attenuating, if not absolving factor. This may be so. Nevertheless, even the empiricist has all to gain by increasing the depth of his knowledge, especially into his raw material, as in this instance. Technical research is not an end in itself, but rather a mean to keener insights into Reality.

This lack of success in uncovering worthwhile data seems due to an actual paucity of data. The many professionals queried could volunteer nothing more enlightening than a "capacity" or "a principle of", and would refer one to "authorities" on the subject. While I readily confess to not having conducted an exhaustive investigation of such references, it soon became evident upon consideration of their basic premises that these, be they Aquinas, Locke, Comte, Marx, Whitehead, Mach or Einstein, all thought or still think in terms of the Aristotelian theory of "a progressive 'actualization' of that which existed only in potentiality"; for short, in terms of Becoming. A summary perusal of the basics of the Lochean and Whiteheadian doctrines confirms this amply. The comprehensive Locke quote is from *Essay On Human Understanding* (II, XXI, I).

> *This idea how got.* The mind being every day informed, by the senses, of the alteration of those simple ideas it observes in things without, and taking notice how one comes to an end and ceases to be, and another begins to exist, which was not before; reflecting also on what passes within itself, and observing a constant change of its ideas, sometimes by the impression of outward objects on the senses, and sometimes by the determination of its own choice; and concluding, from what it has so constantly observed to have been, that the like changes will for the future be made in the same thing by like agents, and by the like ways; considers in one thing the possibility of having any of its simple ideas changed, and in another the possibility of making that change; and so comes by that idea which we call "power". Thus we say, fire has a power to melt gold; ... and gold has a power to be melted: ... In which and like cases, the power we consider is in reference to the change of perceivable ideas: for we cannot observe any alteration to be made in, or operation upon, anything, but by the observable change of its sensible ideas; nor conceive any alteration to be made, but by conceiving a change of some of its ideas. ... Power thus considered is two-fold; viz. as able to make, or able to receive, any change: the one may be called "active", and the other "passive", power. ... I confess power includes in it some kind of relation, — a relation to action or change; as, indeed, which of our ideas, of what kind soever, when attentively considered, does not. For our ideas of extension, duration and number, do they not all contain in them a secret

> relation of the parts? Figure and motion have something relative in them much more visibly. And sensible qualities, as colours and smells, etc., what are they but the powers of different bodies in relation to our perception! ... Our idea therefore of power, I think, may well have a place amongst other simple ideas, and be considered as one of them, being one of those that make a principle ingredient in our complex ideas of substances, as we shall hereafter have occasion to observe.

In the above, two points retain the attention. The first has the considerable merit of asserting that: "our idea of power... may... be considered as one of them" (simple ideas), "being one of those that make a principle ingredient in our complex ideas of substances", ... To so intuit the key status of Power is noteworthy. Locke's achievement, however, is marred on two counts. Even within the same paragraph, Power is implicitly demoted to the status of an idea. Indeed, he seems motivated more by epistemological than structural considerations. The second and fatal flaw is stated unambiguously, as witness: "Power thus considered is two-fold; viz. as able to make, or able to receive, any change: the one may be called 'active', and the other 'passive', power". Locke thus situates himself squarely in the main stream of Aristotelian Becomingism. For him, as for everyone within that massive fraternity of thinkers, change occupies the center of the stage. That one should speak of "potency", another of "sedimentation", and others still of "movement" or "process", matters not one wit. The spirit and content, minor variations notwithstanding, of all Becomingisms converge. Even Whitehead, though the man strove valiantly to free himself of the irrationalities inherent in Becoming, posits as first amor., his twenty seven categories of explanation:

> (i) That the actual world is a process, and that the process is the becoming of actual entities. Thus actual entities are creatures; that are also termed "actual occasions".[5]

In other words, the side-roads travelled by a Becomingist, whether philosopher or physicist, may differ from school to school and variant to variant, yet all ultimately think in terms of capacity, of an in-and-out or degenerative-generative process, of

5. Alfred NORTH WHITEHEAD, *Process and Reality*, New York, The Free Press, 1969, p. 27.

the Thomistic theory of potency. This is evident in the case of Whitehead, who wearing two hats, that of a philosopher and physicist, affirms, in the second of his categories:

> (ii) That in the becoming of an actual entity, *the potential* unity of many entities — actual and non-actual — acquires the real unity of the one actual entity; so that the actual entity is the real concrescence of many potentials.[6]

To define Power as a capacity or potency does explain the dynamic — but only to a most limited extent. To this last of the great Aristotelian "self-evident" principles yet to be challenged, Newton's often quoted statement applies:

> To tell us that every Species of Things is endowed with an occult specific Quality by which it acts and produces manifest Effects, is to tell us nothing: But to derive two or three Principles of Motion from Phaenomena, and afterwards to tell us from the Properties and Actions of all corporeal Things follow from those manifest Principles, would be a very great step in Philosophy though the Causes of those Principles were not yet discovered.

In summary, by scientific standards, our current understanding of Power constitutes quasi virgin territory. Considering its omnipresence and prime role in the Universe's processes, Power can therefore justly be labeled: *The Great Unknown of Science.*

5. **Power is Neither Potential Nor a Capacity**

Technically, a demonstration of the inconsistency of any capacital theory of Power could be dispensed with. However, the issue of Becomingism is pivotal and, being presently unchallenged, a few pages will be devoted to a refutation of some of the key tenets of potentiality.

The case can be stated briefly. *That which is on-the-way-to-become is not there, and never was, and hence does not partake of Reality. The presumed fountainhead of that which is potential, or capacital can never be grasped, but rather diffuses itself outward, drawing from an ever more remote and indeterminate network of sources, to at last get lost in the void or infinity.* To speak of Power as a capacity nihilates the individual. While the notion of

6. *Ibid.*

capacity can imply an outgoing force, a something which oozes from a specific source and is indeed frequently understood thus, such a view makes sense only when deceiving thought modalities are entertained — this intellectual cheating being induced, as a rule, by a subconscious realization that the animate is a self-motored unit, or to use Bergsonian terminology, that a vitalist principle is at work. Granted, since the original meaning of the noun capacity conveys receptivity, to say of an empty barrel that it has the capacity of being filled is perfectly logical — only, however, in the eyes of an Aristotelian for whom a barrel is a being, albeit by analogy. Once Existence by analogy roams the ontological barn yard, it is only to be expected that the latter should come to be peopled with all manner of weird critters. If the Aristotelians were satisfied with applying potency to barrels or their safety deposit boxes one could readily go along. But they do not. Rather, they and their first cousins, the Evolutionists, the Becomingists and most Existentialists insist upon filling all Existents, including man, with Power funnelled into them from the Outside — as vinegar into its barrel.

The above may appear as metaphysical hair splitting. It may be argued that the source of ones Power is irrelevant, that the concern should not be with the wherefrom but with the how and what; also that Power is not merely capacity but "a capacity to perform work". This latter precision in particular, in the opinion of many, settles the issue. Closer investigation reveals otherwise. Neither observation contributes worthwhile enlightenment as to the operation of Power as such. Whether Power is seen as synact of Existence, or as drawn from the Outside like an electrical current, its source matters immensely, for a capacity which flows from a foreigner cannot rightly be considered as of the receiver, but rather as that of the foreigner. The issue is of no consequence only to the blissful who looks upon himself as some manner of bottomless bag or bottle; also of course to one who propounds the "no-subject", "no-ownership" doctrine of the Self, implicit in symbiotic, specificital or concrescental hypotheses. Finally, to append notions such as: to love, to work, to eat after the term a capacity, in no way alters the funnel concept of the Atom, nor does it restore its uniqueness and independence. Such a maneuver only succeeds, if a single incident is cited, in describing the outstanding characteristics of a phenomenon, and if many are recited, in enumerating a series of observations. To attempt to gain insights into Power by launching into an enumeration of its modalities is counter-productive, and should be left to Webster, Larousse and other qualified encyclopedists.

To sum up, Power defined in terms of capacity, merely describes phenomena, as these *appear* to occur. No feat of casuistics will ever establish a substantive difference between capacity and potency, nor will it vest in the capacital any "substance", "essence" or "thing" whatsoever, which will endow it with the slightest measure of the Real. *A capacity always "has been" or "will be"; it never "is". Power, observed as a fact*, on the other hand, *is real and present.*[7]

6. **Power: A Factor of Intensity**

With the benefit of hindsight, one wonders how the way out of the quicksands of Becoming should have eluded researchers for so long, especially when the answer turns out to be a common place factor: Intensity. The answer? In this, as in so many instances, the obvious becomes obvious only *post factum*. In the case of intensity the obvious was jealously guarded from sight by that master mesmerizer, perceived-time. Actually few, if any other problem was to be a source of as thorough frustration for so long. The time-space jungle had to be hacked through, foot by foot, with the major breakthroughs initially passing by unnoticed. Upon recollection it becomes clear that the crucial role which intensity plays in the cosmic economy — it accounts for the *de facto* maximization of the Real — revealed itself in three unrelated stages. The first, summarized in this section, involved an elimination process. The second, occurring as an intuitive

7. In a universe of total compenetration of all by all — of immanence — the campaign waged by Phenomenologists against the Positivist's bias in the secondary disciplines, and vice versa, loses its relevance. The knower is in-fact an Outsider and the others constitute for him true objects. Yet, because of his immanence beyond time-space, and the concomitant facticity of all relationships, Truth is available to him. He knows the Outsider, neither through a "process of sedimentation" (Husserl), nor as "an objective uncertainty" (Kierkegaard), but existentially as a fact, albeit obscurely — as an Obscure-Absolute. Error and misinterpretation are still with us, but so is Truth; and science, ethical as well as chemical, need not collapse before the imaginary onslaughts of the Heisenbergian Uncertainty.

flash, is related in Chapter V of this part. The third, the digestive phase, goes on. This is to say that, long after its initial discovery, intensity and its corollary maximization continue to yield valuable insights.

The first breakthrough occurred when I detected in the capacital theory of Power, a fundamental flaw related to the basic structure of the Atom. The gist of the flaw is that, if Power is to be a capacity or potency, then this capacity must logically be attributed to Power alone. However, this implies that Power is an "independent something acting on its own behalf". The individual, the Self in such a set-up sits it out in the cold. Hence the conclusion that capacity *cum* potency could not be an attribute of Power, but must be of the whole of the Atom. Such an observation far from solving the problem, only brought one back to the first base. For the Atom, being a resident of the As-is, can neither receive nor give, has neither potency or capacity. It simply is. Either it owns its Power and there is no potency, no transfer or there is no Atom, only a phenomenon. Lacking at that stage, an understanding of the decisive role of absoluteneity but wishing nonetheless to respect the norms of reason and of intellectual honesty, I chose to proceed empirically upon the hypothesis that Power is a factor of intensity, the idea of intensity being derived from the concept of Power as an agent of the more-or-less. While this step seemed to leave the problem intact — the more-or-less being readily conciliable with the capacity theory — in effect, it did solve it, provided of course it could be established conclusively that intensity partakes of facticity and maximization. The remainder of this Part is devoted to confirming this hypothesis.

chapter III

Intensity

... but she hath anointed my feet with ointment. Wherefore I say to thee, her many sins are forgiven because she hath loved much.

Luke, 8–47

The average density (of the white dwarf stars) is about 10 000 times that of water.

Lawrence H. Aller,
Encyclopedia Britannica

1. Intensity, Physical Samples

INTENSITY when dealt with empirically, as were Existence and Power, is easily detected. Indeed, a close analysis reveals that everyday life consists of intense situations and that existence is a sum of intensities.

Starting with the category of Atoms with which we are most familiar, the human — when we walk the streets or brood in silence or go to sleep, it is with a human that we walk, as one that we brood, and with one that we sleep — one does not have to search for long before uncovering intensity at work. A prime example immediately comes to mind, namely that enigmatic, high-tension-field called love-hate which all experience at some time in life. Everyone knows the somatic effect of love, in particular the sexual appetite, upon a body, even when limited to an exercise of imagination, to a yearning. Hate is hardly less dynamic. He who hates experiences all sorts of physical symptoms and ills. Indeed, a hateful condition, if allowed to persist, can cause serious body degeneration. That Power and Intensity are recognized as synactive factors in both emotions is evidenced by such colloquialisms as "he shakes with hate" or "one loves with all ones power". Simultaneously both statements clearly intuit a maximization. Nor is intensity associated solely with emotions. Thought-power, analyzed in coming pages, even when directed at abstract and neutral objectives reflects pure intensity. Also, intensity is present in a clenched fist or in a lumberjack's pushing upon a tree about to fall or still in the operator of a forty ton forging press molding automobile fenders. The human factor, especially in the last instance, may be minor, but this only establishes a further characteristic of Power, its miscibility. Manifestations of intensity in the remainder of the animal realm hardly need demonstrating. What is the closing of a shark's jaws upon its victim's foot — if not applied intensity?

Among the inanimates an identical phenomenon is at play everywhere. A classic example are gas molecules under pressure in a pipeline. The same applies in the field of mechanics. Exercised power rates according to its *actual* intensity, whereas the capacital forever remains a hypothetical factor. Twenty extra miles per hour coaxed from ones Thunderbird, results from *actual*, exercised compression — the mechanical equivalent of intensity. Likewise, electricity measures the rate of attraction and repulsion between an agglomeration of electrons, i.e., the amperage, and this in turn gauges intensity. The number of electrons present at any "point" in a single ampere is a fantastic 6,242,000,000,000,000,000, the repelling or aggressive force of each being minimal — 0,000,000,000,000,000,000,000,000,080,38 of a pound at one inch. Man, of course, has no instrument allowing him to measure such "minitudes". Only by combining the repulsion quotient of vast numbers of these weak Atoms do we succeed in calibrating them. What is calibrated is the intensity factor of the combined units. Their capacity remains a vague concept in a mind, a description only of something imagined or presumed. As will be noted, in the case of presumption, if the presumption materializes then actual and intense power is present. Upon turning ones attention to theoretical physics, the same phenomenon is uncovered. In this discipline operative energy equals a concentration of forces — in the Newtonian scheme as well as in the Einsteinian. To refer to gravity, for example, as a capacity is to remain in the hypothetical. Real, factual gravitation is rated according to the intensity exercised by one body upon another. The same holds for the force of magnetic or electro-magnetic fields.

In a nutshell, in any instance where Power is at work, the notion of capacity seeks in vain to reinject into the Alice-in-Wonder-land world of Becoming, a measure of facticity. *Intensity*, on the other hand, *can and is always directly related to a fact, to a that-which-is*. Further, since wherever and whenever intensity is detected, Power looms, the two can be described as synactive, and one is entitled to see Power as a factor of intensity.

2. Correspondence of Intensity and the Factual

Here, an observation critical to ontology in particular and to science in general, offers itself, namely that of a total affinity between intensity and the As-is. In each sample proffered in the previous chapter, exercised power is accurately described only as intensity, while if one seeks to grasp it in the capacital or potential, one never finds it. Once the fist is clenched, the hate felt or the pressure is upon the automobile fender, power is exercised; is *factual*, and this is synonymous with intensity. Granted, to realize as much the Self must operate in the instantaneous. This presents no problem. Firstly, the Real exists solely beyond man-created dimensions. Secondly, thought is composed of absolutes.

Even if one eschews instantaneity, still it remains that to analyze power which-is, and not of power which might-be or has-been, one must deal with intensity and not capacity or evolution. While projections into past or future constitute legitimate fields of inquiry for a paleontologist or historian, neither has a place in ontology; at least as long as raw, primary Existence and Power are being investigated. Therefore, here and throughout, only That-which-is, only Reality as experienced preoccupies us. The question is not one of greater or lesser emphasis, but of the either-or. Whether the Becomingist admits it or not, his concept of Reality is not related to fact and truth, but exacts of him a dogmatic faith in all manner of hypotheses, each more preposterous than the previous. A close perusal of the average evolutionary thesis, wherein the Becoming process extends over millions of years, soon reveals the irrationalities involved. One such most effective eye-opener is that classic among comic books for grown-ups, Julian Huxley's: Evolution in Action.[1]

---

1. The following excerpts from p. 110 of *Evolution in Action*, New York, Mentor Books, 1957, in which Julian Huxley summarizes the path of the humanoid's evolution from amoebe to monkey, etc., give an idea of the fantastic level of credulity required of the believing Becomingist. Clearly, one must reserve his sincerest, most profound admiration, not for Becoming-man, but for the monkey, *genus generalissimum* — what foresight! what prescience! A power of anticipation in the range of 10,000,000 or more years. "Pray god" that they had passed some of this priceless endowment to we humans — their witless descendants whose powers of forecasting are so poor that we invariably carry our umbrellas on sunny days, and leave them home when it is due to rain!

In summary, at-any-given-instant, As-is Power, is an observable fact, adequately described only as exercised intensity. It does appear as a progressive, flowing, potential affair. However, its sequential appearance is due to the fact that the intellect, unable to cope simultaneously with the fulness of Reality, must deal with it piecemeal. When exploring the Real, one must ignore the potential, the semblance of sequences and "change". To do otherwise is not only to indulge in a problem created by weak perception, but also, is a waste of effort on two counts. One, the expected may not happen, and two, if and when the foreseen occurs, it does so on an As-is basis, and is manifest through intensity. In a nutshell, the dynamic is never witnessed, save in its actuality. To talk of it as a potency, implies speculation upon origins, probabilities and possible universes before having discovered what the subject is. Only if the factual should lead to a dead end would hypotheses, evolutionary or otherwise, be justified. Fortunately these are unnecessary. Whenever factual power is witnessed, intensity or the state of the more-or-less surfaces. Hence, it is proper to proceed upon the assumption, firstly, that *Power is a factor of intensity,* and secondly, that *Power and, by attribution, Intensity, partakes of the factual.*

3. Second Metamorphosis: The Existential-Atom Transmuted into a Dynamic-Fact

At this point, the Existential-Atom undergoes its second metamorphosis. Progressing beyond the essentially statistical

---

> "Monkeys live in trees, and they use their hands as well as feet for climbing. They also use their hands for manipulating their food, and have developed binocular vision for its better detection. ... Tree life thus laid the foundation both for our clearer definition of objects by conceptual thought, and for our fuller control of them by tools and machines tens of millions of years later. ... First, monkeys had to become apes. Apes get around mainly by swinging with their arms, not by climbing with all four limbs. Finally, it was necessary for the apes to descend from the trees... Looking back into the past we see clearly enough that conceptual thought could only have arisen in an animal as against a plant; ... And finally, it could have arisen only in a mammal which had become gregarious, which had a long period of learning and experience, which produced only one young at a birth, and which had recently become terrestrial after a long spell of life in the trees. Clearly, the path of progress is both devious and unique!"

You said it, Julian. Or could it be that it is the evolutionist's thinking which is muddled and devious?

character which atomicity vests in it, it becomes a Dynamic-Fact. The term Dynamic-Fact speaks for itself, for it describes exactly that which each word on its own and in combination implies, namely a discrete package of power — or still a self-contained, adimensional motor.

The promotion which this metamorphosis bestows is major. From hereon any revelation proves anticlimactic or at best hermeneutic, the concept of a Dynamic-Fact being pregnant with its full reality and serving to link the Order of the Real to that of the Perceived. The clause, "pregnant with its full reality", is particularly significative, for it reveals that once Power is added unto the Existent, the latter enters into full possession of its quota of the real and the qualitative. Nothing more can be added. This, while not readily discernible as yet, will become evident once the inneity of Power is decoded.

4. **Intensity Defined**

To decode intensity the same procedure is indicated as for individuation. The first point to note is that it is, as any universal phenomenon, subject to the Principle of the Proportionality of Extremes. This principle has the disconcerting habit of presenting simple answers to basic issues. Just as individuation is encompassed when described as the fact of being one, so is intensity when defined as a state of more-or-less or alternately of qualitativity. Elaboration only deals with particular cases or situations, a fact borne out by this standard definition from Webster's:

(1) The state of being strained or stretched, ... the state of being raised to a high degree; extreme violence; ...

(2) in physics, the degree of energy in any acting force, as in traction or compression.

(3) in photography, the degree of light or shadow in a picture.

(4) in psychology, the degree of mental activity; the embodiment of emotion and feeling.

Scrutiny of the above yields two key observations. One, together the four sections neatly correspond to the several experiences, animate and inanimate, described earlier. Two, both ends of the spectrum are covered: the microphysical through the inclusion of particles (light, etc.), and the macrophysical through traction and compression, which would include gravitation and mechanical motors. Intra-Existent intensity is represented by emotion and feeling. Most revealing, the conjunction of the five key terms (common with respect to "degree" to all four sections), namely: "state", "degree", "violence", "energy-force" and "compression", brings together all the factors involved not only in the synactivity of Existence to Power but also in relationality. Such a comprehensive coverage indicates that the role of intensity equals in the realm of Energy that of unicity relative to Existence, and that it rates the status of a univerquality — one of five — ranking in this respect on a par with unicity.[2]

5. What is Intensity? Maximization of the Existent and Measure of the Will and Efficiency

Samples of intensity have been listed. It has been defined. But what about its inner structure? While the question: What is intensity? is as readily answered as was: What is individuation?, it remains as difficult to depict in concrete, "material" terms as was individuation. To merely describe it in no way reduces the mystery in which it bathes. Described intensity, both as it resides within an Existent and as it operates between two or more remains as intangible as unicity. If anything it is easier to grasp the fact of ones individuation than to understand the fluctuation of emotions, of hate or love, for instance. Nor is the phenomenon easier to comprehend when additivity is studied. A first impression will often be that the process is then understood. We know that the adding of the powers of many Atoms, whether hydrogens, waters, men or electrons, results in greater intensities, i.e., higher pressures and amperages, more powerful ideological movements, stronger gravitational pulls, overflowing dams. The increase in knowledge is illusory. The process within each additivating unit refuses to be physically bared. This is to be expected. Intensity partakes of the cosmicity of each Atom and the cosmic cannot be cut up into pieces.[3]

---

2. Re univerqualities, cf. secs. 3, 4 and 6, chap. VI Pt. II
3. As indicated earlier, an outstanding characteristic of Dynamic Vision is the applicability of its basic principles and norms to all species of Atoms, animate and inanimate. The key terms which bare the structure of the Atom, carry unaltered into the subdisciplines, including epistemology and ethics, all of

Faced with the task of explaining the inneity of intensity, as this resides within each Atom, the objective observer must concede defeat. Mystery is involved and the odds are that it will be so forever. Yet this is no more disturbing than was the fact that one could not explain or prove, as the Radical Sceptic demands, the-fact-that-one-is. *What-is, is.* Intensity, as a fact of life, provides experimental science with more than enough raw material. Issues and problems which flow from the core of the Existent, offer those who revel in speculation upon the origin of "things" great scope in which to indulge their urges and an equally vast opportunity to waste energy which could be more usefully devoted to problems of an accessible nature. The proper approach in respect to the origin and nature of intensity, is the same as that adopted *vis-a-vis* Existence. It must be accepted objectively. What matters is the decoding of intensity's operation within the Atom and between Atoms. It may be argued that this involves dissection. Conceded. But there is all the difference in the world between the building of hypotheses so that one may then dissect these, and the dissection of an observable phenomenon. There is nothing hypothetical about intensity. It is as real as fire or water, and as factual as the rising of the sun or the disintegration of uranium.

---

which are thereby linked and correlated. While this convertability holds for the key terms beginning with those of Existential-Atom, absolute and quality, it is nowhere as evident as when the two radicals, intensity and efficiency are concerned. For instance, the concept of an efficiency factor or rating applies equally to mechanics viz. that of an electric motor, and to ethics viz. that of a gangster, Al Capone or of a saint, Ignatius of Loyola. Intensity also speaks the same language whether it is that of the love of Mary Magdalene — of which Christ said:

> ... but she hath anointed my feet with ointment. Wherefore I say to thee, her sins are forgiven, because she hath loved much; but he who is forgiven little, loveth little.
>
> LUKE, 8–47

or that of the assumedly inanimate Atoms which coagentize intensely, to constitute a white dwarf star, whose

> "average density" (it is postulated) "is about 10 000 times that of water. Under these conditions the electrons are nearly all stripped off the atoms and form what is called a degenerate gas. Such material has remarkable properties. It does not obey the ordinary gas laws and is an almost perfect conductor of heat."
>
> (Lawrence H. ALLER, *Encyclopedia Britannica*)

Reversing the procedure, in the case of intensity, the answers will be provided before the evidence. As every ontological factor, intensity must be approached from two levels — the first corresponding to the Real and the second to the Perceived.

At the Real, intensity accounts for a phenomenon which, at best, has been vaguely intuited by the rare philosopher or physicist. This is readily explained by the fact that nearly everyone accepts to see in Power a potency, with the consequence that intensity is relegated to the sidelines. The phenomenon referred to is the *de facto* maximization of the Existent. This implies that intensity makes the Existent present to the remainder of the Universe — beyond time-space. Further, "present" here does not mean a mental abstraction and subjective knowledge restricted to a play "within" the mind. Rather, intensity makes each Existent, in the fulness of its physical endowment, maximally present to every other. When observed as the factor responsible for maximization it is of the First Order, and partakes of the Real. It then represents one of five univerqualities, that synactive to Power, and countervails unicity in Existence. In the Now, intensity corresponds firstly, to a norm of efficiency, and secondly, represents a measure of the will and by extension of freedom. Efficiency, for reasons to be presently disclosed, also qualifies for the role of univerquality. These three factors, maximization, efficiency and freedom which jointly account for all manifestations of intensity are, at once, of paramount importance and bound to prove controversial. Indeed, the theory of maximization is apt initially to mystify and be rejected as unconscionable. Our next task is to establish all three.

At this juncture the roadblock peculiar to cosmontology reappears. Where other scientists can in most instances cut up their raw material into manageable, usually spatial units; the Atom, working unit of the ontologist, due to its facticity and consequent cosmicity can be adequately grasped only as a whole or absolute. It follows that the order in which a series of analytical steps is presented is always less than satisfactory. Presently, for instance, each of maximization, intensity, efficiency, synactivity and quality can theoretically claim priority. The dilemma is arbitrarily solved by giving precedence to each factor on the basis of the degree of an earlier involvement with it, it being understood that, from a research point of view, the same objective could be achieved was the sequence inverted or generally altered. The final steps in the decoding of the Dynamic-Fact will be to:

1. establish the synactivity of Power to Existence,
2. investigate the maximization aspect of intensity, and
3. illustrate the role of quality in the Cosmos.

In view of their relevance each issue rates a separate chapter.

chapter IV

Does Power Qualify for the Role of Synact of Existence

> Thanks to the work of Einstein, physicists have come to realize that "mass", which had been regarded as the "material" basis of matter, is equivalent to energy; that is to say, it can be converted into energy ($E = mc^2$)... Energy provides us with what is in fact "the valid proof of the uniformity of all matter.
>
> W. HEISENBERG, 1959.

1. General Remarks Respecting Synactivity

THE attempt to put flesh on the dessicated bones of the Existential-Atom, proceeded upon the assumption that Power was a proper synact of Existence — a privilege of the experimental scientist. Indeed, the total parallel between an ontologist and his raw material and a geochemist and a truckload of ore was then noted. As the geochemist may proceed empirically upon an assumption, so can the ontologist, both being subject to end up with the facts corresponding to their initial intuitions. Having opted for the synactivity of Power with Existence, and analyzed the facticity of both synacts, the stage is reached where a vindication of this surmise can be expected. Due to the novelty of synactivity and to the fact that the data provided is limited to an operational definition, some elucidation seems in order.

Recapitulating, we find that a synact is an It or factor, without which another It or factor cannot be, and that synactivity describes the concepts through which the fact or phenomenon involved is known. In the present case this implies that without Power, Existence is absent, and vice versa. The simultaneously inneal and relational character of synactivity precludes a mechanistic analysis of its components. The researcher must rely mainly upon an analysis of qualitativity. This in turn may involve analogy. Consequently, the earlier reference to the parallel between a marriage and synactivity still offers an effective avenue of investigation, the notion of a marriage conveying the intimate nature *par excellence* of synactivity. Analogies, however, automatically carry a measure of misrepresentation. One could call them useful lies. Synactivity, for example, goes far beyond animal wedlock in the intimacy which it establishes between Power and

Existence — to the point where homogenization could possibly describe it more accurately. Yet, even homogenization is inadequate, for it merely blends components — as in the case of skim milk and cream. To obtain a clear understanding of synactivity one must enter the realm of the abstract-absolutes. This is logical synactivity being a concept. Applied to the analogy of a marriage the concept, divorced from the married and conceived as an independent fact, represents synactivity. Marriage, thus puts on the cloak of a conceptual, and the human Atoms contribute nothing save the relationship required in a valid marriage. However, even the above calls for rectification. While both male and female continue to be-for-real whether married or not, *the situation neatly reverses in the case of Existence and Power. Both terms considered independently, lose all existential content, to become mere conceptualizations. Only when the two are observed as one is the content restored.*

In summary, synactivity is a conceptualization, primarily analytical, whereby certain salient features of Reality, divorced for scientific purposes, are conceptually reunited to safeguard existential truth.

Finally, a few words to explain the methodology used in this chapter. According to a theory prevalent in philosophical circles, any view held by the common man upon scientific matters rates the utmost reservation. "The common sense", supposedly, is contaminated and best left alone, a discrimination frequently extended to evidence derived from chemistry, astronomy, etc. This taboo will be ignored and considerable weight will be placed upon the intuitions of both the sciences and the man on the street. The rationale here is simple. While the average housewife's views upon Hylemorphism or Dialectical Materialism would prove inadequate — these and similar prescriptions which clutter the philosophical apothecary are specialized subjects often entailing intellectual bias — this is not true of Power. Power is a phenomenon upon whose "existence" philosopher and layman alike agree and are exposed to. Hence the intuitions of the layman of average schooling can be expected to be valid in a general way. The same applies to the insights of sciences such as physics whose very subject is Power. The orthodox metaphysician may be of the opinion that such an approach must necessarily flaw a system. Granted — in respect to a system. However, as emphasized, Dynamic Vision is first and foremost an empirical venture into Reality, with a view firstly of discovering the primary particle, and secondly of developing a cosmic code. It combines the rationalist and empirical approaches checking and balancing one against the other. The price exacted for whatever liberties this entails with logic and the senses, is that the product be judged upon the basis of its coherence and applicability. Should the final product prove defective or to state the case colloquially, should it not work; then let it be jettisoned in its entirety.

2. Synactivity of Power to Existence Predicates, on the Part of Power, Facticity, Unidimensionality, Miscibility and Universality

The key demand of synactivity upon the partners is self-evident — every univerquality uncovered in the one partner must find its correspondence in the other. Correspondence is not to be confused with identity. Rather it implies that the qualities of each synact be either:

A. coextensive,

B. compatible, or

C. complementary

to the point that the sum faithfully reconstructs the oneness destroyed by the mental divorce. Hence, it is necessary to ascertain whether or not Power can accomodate itself with the requisites which flow from the univerqualities proper to Existence, namely: unicity and facticity. Alternately, those of Power, intensity and efficiency, should return the compliment. As to the fifth, miscibility, this occupies a niche of its own, and must aver itself as the proper of Power and Existence simultaneously. Over and above this, Power, to constitute a valid synact to Existence, must prove universal. The categories in which the five univerqualities and universality fall, are these. In the "A" or coextensivity category, one finds universality. Requisite "B", compatibility, relies upon the two pairs, unicity and facticity, freedom and intensity-efficiency. Category "C", implying complementarity, is occupied by miscibility.

As noted, the first requisite, universality, is not a quality, but is of the order of the necessary, by composition or alternately by similitude. That Power must be universal to synact with Existence, is tautological. Since the Dynamic-Facts (Atoms) divide the Real among themselves and thereby share in an universal fact, Power also must partake of this fact, even though neither the Atom nor its Power are *per se* universal. At the Perceived, universality is conceptual, while at the Order of the Real, it results from additivity and composes. In either instance it satisfies the criterion of coextensivity.

In regard to "B" the compatible requisites, the following remarks apply. Compatibility addresses itself to the inneity of the subjects, and in its case, the univerqualities of either synact will be investigated. While not formally identified as such, the two which are specifically existential, unicity and freedom, have already been isolated and analyzed. The same applies to intensity and efficiency. What now remains to be established, is that since unicity and freedom predicate facticity and quality, then intensity and efficiency must also be compatible with the factual and qualitative.

In the "C" or complementarity category, resides miscibility. Miscibility rows a wake of its own. It suffuses the Real and explains immanence. One might argue that it is coextensive. However, the notion of complementarity seems more adequate, for the fact of being relationable is essentially qualitative, whereas universality is clearly compositional and descriptive.

While based upon considerable physical evidence the bulk of the investigation has up to this point involved primarily theory and deduction. The nature of the subject imposed such a method. The balance of the *a priori* with the empirical will now be reestablished for, to ascertain whether or not Power qualifies for the role of synact to Existence, it will be necessary to delve into it as it affects each of us daily and incessantly. Unidimensionality and miscibility in particular, as both are checked against physical experience, yield data easily verified through the senses.

3. Universality of Power

Where the universality of Power is concerned the logicians and dialecticians will be disappointed. No demonstration will be attempted — logical or empirical. Until the contrary is proven, it is held universal. In light of the findings in respect to Existence, this was to be expected. Power as synact to Existence, partakes of the ontological and universal, and ontological facts are not proven, only observed. Hence with Power as with Existence, "it simply is or is not", and this either-or applies to its universality as well. *Grosso modo*, the position here adopted corresponds to that advanced by Plato in the *Sophist*:

> My suggestion would be, that anything which possesses any sort of power to affect another, or to be affected by another even for a moment, however trifling the cause and however slight and momentary the effect, has real existence: and I hold that the definition of being is simply power.[1]

Such a stand, there is no gainsaying, hardly conforms to classic syllogistics. Yet, Dynamic Vision being neither a system of metaphysics nor of logic *à la* Kant or Descartes, still less a code of semantic constructs *à la* Wittgenstein, but being rather an experiment upon Existence, it is proper to consider as Atoms only such as possess Power. It follows that Power becomes automatically as universal as Existence. In fairness, those who object may note that this is by no means the easy way out, since scientifically an assumption is of value only if it conforms to Reality; when, for short, it works; when, for instance, it solves real problems, sociological, chemical, ethical, etc.

To vest universality in Power adds no new dimension to the Universe — no additional territory is fenced in. In effect, this merely constitutes the first step in an analysis of the Real, which latter ontologically antecedes Existence. *Thus Power, defined as a factor of intensity, is not a "thing" which comes to compose itself with another "thing", Existence. Creatures of analysis, the two are one and the same. Power as factor of intensity, acts to reveal that the bare Fact-of-to-be is an eminently qualitative Dynamic-Fact.* This first step somewhat parallels that which takes place if someone, having observed an automobile and wishing to know whether it was gasoline, electric or diesel powered, raises up the hood and finds his answer. Just as the raising of the hood does not question the automobileness of the automobile, an investigation of Power neither nihilates nor complicates Reality.

1. PLATO, *Sophist*, Jowett's translation, p. 247.

Further, the arguments which established the cosmicity of Existence, apply *mutatis mutandis* to Power.

Among the issues justifiably raised at this point, two jointly encompass all others. These are:

A. the "possible universes" which the formal logician and science fiction theorist may wish to conjure, and

B. a rejection of the univocity of Power implicit in its universality, since this has for effect to eliminate the distinction conventionally drawn between "matter" and "spirit".

A. *Possible Universes Irrelevant*

The answer to an objection involving "possible universes", wherein conditions "might be different", wherefrom, for instance, Power "might be absent", is elementary. "Possible universes" are, if possible, emptier of substance than the "past" or "future" of the Becomingist. Those who play with such, cannot even picture these in their minds, but rest, satisfied with vapid speculation upon which they squander their own reserve of intellect-power and that of their readers. A raw material which encompasses all That-which-is, takes into account the entire Universe of the Real, including any "possible universe", should one or more of these of "second, third or fourth order" some day aver itself physical. Also included are such "universes", as these reside in anyone's mind. Undaunted, some may retort that philosophically, to lay claim to so comprehensive a domain is not legitimate; that the unknown is beyond purview. To this, the reply is the same as when the right to encompass the sum of Reality was challenged. The fact that one does not feel every physical relationship which he entertains throughout the Universe, does not make that of which he is unaware any less real. To the contrary, the scientist is duty bound to accept whatever concrete manifestations of this "unknown" which at some "future time and place" reveal themselves. Again, the parallel with a geochemist and his sample of pyrite applies. Either accepts the unknown as a fact and the findings are held to apply universally. To the objection that the geochemist, limits himself to a clearly defined field, we answer that here also limits are set very clearly, namely, the sum of the Real. Insofar as limits are concerned, every subdiscipline, every art even, follows exactly the same course. Each scientist and artist embraces the totality of whatever subject either has cast his mind upon. Nor has anyone any other option, for the Principle of Absolutes dictates that the mind deal in absolutes only. The sole latitude in the matter, is in the choice of the "dimensions". Actually, the position in respect to the size of the universe is most enviable. Whereas others, be they chemists or moralists, can always err by tampering, unwillingly or otherwise, with their initial objective, where the universe is concerned, provided the cosmontologist remains willing to include in the Cosmic Equation such Existence-Power as reveals itself, he is assured of not straying outside his domain.

Conceding as much, it may nonetheless be argued that some day man might form a different concept of Power. If this implies that in the years to come a different word may be utilized, a shrug suffices. Even as of now any substitute goes — Energy for instance. Words are empty signs which can be altered at will with no loss to anyone, as long as by mutual agreement, the newly coined encompasses an identical fact or phenomenon. If, and such an eventuality would be more serious, it is argued that another type of Power might manifest itself, the answer is that it would, at that time, be dealt with. Furthermore, again, even the wildest of science fiction fantasies, also notions such as that of antigravitation, should these prove real — are already covered. In summary all fear pertaining to the revisions which the discovery of "new" or "possible universes" might necessitate is groundless. If such "possible universes" are in-fact real, they are encompassed. If fictional, as witness those with which logicians toy, these also are accounted for and fall in the category of polka-dotted flying rhinos or five-legged archangels. Any lingering doubt as to the inclusion of unknown and/or "possible universes" in an empirically prehended Parmenidean mass of as-isness, should be dispelled by the next subsection concerning the barrier which assumedly separates the supernatural from the natural.

B. *The Supernatural, an Integral "Part" of the Real*

The controversy surrounding the supernatural represents one of philosophy's prize hornet's nests. To question the supernaturality of the supernatural, on the one hand, arouses the ire of the Spiritualist, and on the other, the answer affronts the Materialist. The issue, intimately related to the previous, differs in that "possible universes" are "born in time", while the supernatural is seen, incongruously, as coeval not only with a present but also with a past and a future. (Charitably, the champions of the eternal supernatural will not be asked to explain the coevality of a temporal realm amidst an eternal one). According to widely held theories, the "world of the spirit" and more so that of the spirits, is of a different order from the "known universe of matter". The variations on this theme are legion, but all, in final analysis, proclaim that the supernatural rests beyond the physical grasp of man — the dichotomy between the two being absolute.

The controversy is spurious. While on the surface the problem appears serious, objective scrutiny reveals it to be a non-problem. If the spiritual order (whether this includes God only, and/or spirits, i.e., angels, demons and/or thought is irrelevant), is so separate as to in no way relate with our universe, then for practical purposes, this realm of the spirit is non-existent and best ignored. After all, of what use to those on either side of an assumed dividing-line would the coexistence of two distinct cosmoses be, if either is denied physical contact? The Spiritualists who push the dichotomy to that point, may as well adopt the materialist stance. If however the supernatural has an impact upon our universe of which man is unaware, such an impact participates in the Universe as defined herein. Then the relationships of the "supernatural" to the "natural or material" is identical to that of mankind to any as yet undetected neutrino sallying forth from the infernal core of the Andromeda nebula. Either the supernatural is of the Universe and relates to the whole, or it is not. If so, this supernatural, through the power of its agents is automatically integrated, regardless of the latter's species, and there is no problem. If the opposite applies, again no problem. Then it is imaginary or, what amounts to the same, unrelated and irrelevant. The subject is immensely complex, and one cannot do it justice in a few paragraphs. Yet the essential has been singled out and from this, the solutions to secondary issues are deducible.

4. Miscibility of Power

The notion of the miscibility of Power impinges upon every facet of ontology, for one of its correlates is cosmic immanence. So high a profile in the cosmic economy earns it the rank of radical of Existence and prime univerquality. The term miscibility may puzzle. In the present context, its meaning is exactly that attributed to it in common usage. Miscibility, according to the *Oxford English Dictionary*, implies : "The quality or condition of being miscible ; capability of being mixed". Applied to Power, this predicates that regardless of origin and shunning any dichotomy whatsoever, all powers mix, blend or coordinate with each other throughout the Universe. To some degree miscibility is recognized in every philosophy and is intuitively accepted in applied physics. The following quote from *Process and Reality*, subject only to a rejection of its Becomingist bias, describes it effectively :

> It follows from the fourth category of explanation that the notion of "complete abstraction" is self-contradictory. For you cannot abstract the universe from any entity, actual or nonactual, so as to consider that entity in complete isolation. Whenever we think of some entity, we are asking. What is it fit for here ? In a sense, every entity pervades the whole world ; ...[2]

To use a mechanic's terminology, *miscibility allows the superimposition of as many layers of Power as one may wish to add one upon the other, without thereby any dimension accruing other than that of intensity.*[3] Ontologically, it describes the integral compenetration of Dynamic-Fact by Dynamic-Fact, and establishes the

---

2. Alfred N. WHITEHEAD, *Process and Reality*, New York, The Free Press, 1969, p. 33.

3. Those familiar with the key dilemmas of modern physics will appreciate the implications of the principle of cumulated intensities which occur at the conjunction of intensity with miscibility. Actually, on a cosmic scale the concept of cumulated and factual intensities and the concomitant maximization of all Atoms before every other, calls for a reformulation of $E = mc^2$. The issue is too complex to be dealt with in a footnote. It suffices to indicate that, together, the adimensional Atom and its maximization dispose of "the problem — among the most acute faced by nuclear physics of the mass of the electron". As long as the factor M. in mc^2 retains its character of an indeterminate, no problem arises. When however, M is attributed to a given unit such as an electron or neutron, if the latter becomes physically nonexistent, which is to say according to traditional thinking, loses all extent

correlation between Power and immanence. As indicated in section I, at the Perceived its contribution is to introduce formally the as yet but vaguely glimpsed world of sense data. Due to its obviousness three examples of miscibility, namely those of wind, automobile and mind-power, each drawn from a different order, and together encompassing the spectrum of existential phenomena, should suffice.

Wind-power or "windness", as long as it implicates only atmospheric forces, already results from an intermingling of cosmic kinetic factors and localized chemical reactions. These are

---

(becomes dimensionless), then one is faced with the disturbing question of E's status and energy content. The problem and its basic parameters are clearly set-out in these paragraphs from page 27 of *Particles and Accelerators*, R. Gouiran, New York, McGraw Hill, 1967:

> The electron cannot be considered as a geometric point which is a perfect conception of zero, for its electric field would then be infinite. But if it is slightly extended the electric charge tends to repel itself, and would lead to dissolution unless a contrary force opposed it in order to maintain cohesion; but this "self-force" could only accumulate an infinite self-energy, giving to the electron infinite mass!
>
> What are we to think of these infinities, and down to what minimum distance do the laws of electromagnetism apply? We have arrived at 10^{-14} cm for the muon, and even to 10^{-15} cm for the proton without involving any anomaly, thus reaching theoretical limits for the idea of the electric point. What happens with distances even smaller, and has a smaller distance even any meaning? That the electron does have a mass is a fact which cannot be eliminated by a stroke of the pen, and we are left with the following definition: electromagnetic self-energy is infinite but the "bare" mass is also infinite, and the difference is what we measure.
>
> The fact that the number of different particles is finite, and that they can be identified and are found with regularity in nuclear reactions, proves to us that mass must be a quantum number, and that is can only take a discrete range of values as found in nature. But what is the universal law which governs this scale of masses?

The dilemma disappears once infinity is relegated to the pasture reserved for mythological creatures and concepts and C^2, demoted from its status of an absolute, is reduced to the qualitativity peculiar to a certain category of Atoms. Then, qualitative intensity invests cosmic relationality (the continuous, adimensional medium) and the problem of "infinite energy and mass" vanishes. Each Dynamic-Fact, in this instance each electron, simply *is*, and *is* more intensely so *vis-a-vis* some than others. That which is presently defined as its mass corresponds to an Antropocity, to a knot of intense relationships, privileged by those concerned with it. To use Gouiran's words, "every particle in reality covers the universe, but the probability of finding it" (of defining it) "is almost entirely confined to a small space". (*Ibid*, p. 11)

felt as one. The homogenized product is defined as wind. As the intensity of "a wind" increases, it unites with whatever Antropocities it meets on its way — dust, pieces of paper, hay stacks and butterflies. Should its velocity augment further to tornado scale, then pieces of boards, trees and cars even, join in the fray. Whosoever stands at the receiving end of a flying board suffers not solely from wind-power, but from a new combination : wind-board-power. In sum, a tornado represents an example of the indiscriminate, yet utter admixing of energies.

The star actors in the first event were mainly inanimates. Miscibility of other types — the intellectual inclusively — is as readily observed. An eighty year old great-grandmother behind the wheel of a 1975 Chrysler provides a stunning example. Then we see a Dynamic-Fact, weak in body, using its intellect in association with a combination of gas, electrical and the plain mass-power of metals, to "tear-down" a highway (assuming the old dame is a speed demon). In the process, some helpless gopher or gander gets splattered. If next the Chrysler penetrates the vortex of the tornado, a new power pattern looms. The careening great-grandmother acts as catalyst for the intertwining of the forces "immediately present" with far removed intellectual forces, namely the automobile industry which through the cooperation of hundreds of human-power-units, manufactured her Chrysler. Even a cursory analysis reveals that physically, these forces are cosmic, for no limit, either in time or space, can be set of which one may say, here begins or ends the impact of:

A. the power of the "wind",

B. the will-power of the great-grandmother, and

C. the kinetism of the Chrysler, etc.

The third example establishes most conclusively the universal miscibility of Energy. It involves an engineer and the central panel of a continental power-grid. Under-cover agent of a foreign world ideology, this engineer, one fatal night, cuts off the current on the east coast of North America. A deft twist of the wrist, and a paralyzed continent succumbs to a preventive atomic strike — his ideology achieves world domination. The added relevance of his feat, is that it demonstrates the univocity of Power. Idea-power, which most philosophies, either explicitly or implicitly set apart in a sphere of its own, here reveals itself inextricable from every known force. At that so-called "instant", the engineer's intellect-power transcends time-space by blending with that of the complex grid which took decades to assemble, that of the electrons "immediately" involved and of the ideologues who in centuries past toiled to spread the ideas, the religion, about to conquer the world.

Several ancillary observations offer themselves. Firstly, *to witness miscibility is to witness the death of time-space, as both dimensions draw into an evermore thinly stretched and receding skein of cosmic relationships.* Secondly, *miscibility reduces that which most philosophies look upon as causality to corresponsibility.* Ontologically there is no sequential causality, only cosmic relationships, "each" more intense than the other, and "each" qualitatively different. The quotation marks around the pronoun "each" emphasize that events when referred to as isolated units achieve their unity only in one or more minds. Each are Antropocities. Thirdly, miscibility confirms the universality of Power. That which can be mixed and homogenized in utter promiscuity beyond time-space occupies the Cosmos.

5. **Power is Factual: Owned Inalienably by Each Dynamic-Fact**

Of the characteristics of Power, none is apt to prove as unexpected and controversial as its facticity, for this squarely contradicts all accepted contemporary theories. Yet so does reason predicate and physical experience reveal. To say that Power as Existence is factual implies that Power, in-and-of the Atom, is possessed by each in perpetuity — hence the metamorphosis of the Existential-Atom into a Dynamic-Fact. Stated in other terms, Power can interrelate, but cannot pass from the one to another. Regardless of his might, no Outsider can rob the Power of another — hence the radical freedom of each. Structure-wise the status of the facticity of Power within the Atom can be described as follows. Whereas the universality and miscibility of Power countervail the cosmicity and raw material status of Existence, its facticity and the latter's corollary, adimensionality, in turn correspond to the atomicity detected in the cosmic raw material.

Up to this point the question of the facticity of Power has only been the object of a brief reference in section 3, chapter I of Part II, in connection with the Atom's outright ownership of its quota of the Energy in the Cosmos. It is possible, now that more data is available, to establish experimentally that Power is factual or alternately non-transferable. A search for the physical parameters of such facticity necessitates investigation on two fronts, for as it applies to Power, facticity covers two distinct ontological phases, attributiveness and inalienability. The first synacts with the individuation factor consonant with Existence. The second countervails the indivisibility of the Atom and by extension its freedom or independence.

A. *Power an Attributable Fact*

The individuating aspect of facticity in Power is readily detected, its rationale being the same as that which leads to a general consensus upon individuation in the Universe. Individuating aspect here means that a Dynamic-Fact, as opposed to the concept which one may have of such, always emanates specific qualities which make it distinct from every other. This qualitative specificity is so glaring, that on it, as upon existential individuation, everyone, at least in principle, agrees by acknowledging that :

A. a distinction must be drawn on the one hand between the concepts of Existents with which the intellect can be peopled — witness drunk, polka-dotted elephants, homosexual angels, and night-marish dreams wherein rocks fly and men have ears on their fingers and eyes on their buttocks — and on the other hand, *bona fide* drunken elephants, rocks and men, albeit possibly deformed, malformed or perverted, and that only the latter represent real drunken elephants, etc., and

B. each real ("material") Existent manifests its presence through the exercise of some qualitative power, different from that of its neighbor. Stated otherwise, it is commonly agreed that each has a personality and style through which it relates with the Outsiders, and that this relating is achieved through the use of Energy.

The attributiveness of Power can be deduced from strictly empirical data. It suffices to note that to certain manifestations of individuation, there corresponds a specific and constant source of qualities. A first instance on which there is general agreement, is that men differ quality-wise from radishes, and that radishes for their part, have a personality distinct from that of electric eels and buzzards. The incontrovertability of such a minimal measure of strict individuation, is such that no philosopher has sought to challenge it, an unusual unanimity no doubt bolstered by the fact that under experimental conditions, individuation withstands the most violent of assaults. Only in the fictional sagas of Frankenstein and Dracula is the feat of existential transmutation performed. In actual life, even under laboratory conditions, weeping willows are never made to behave as crows, nor could advanced techniques of transmutation make crows of blue whales, lead atoms or pi-mesons. The evidence so overwhelms that it needs no belaboring.

Here, the devotees of evolution will rise to defend their faith. They will argue that through "the evolutionary process", amoebaes become fish, and that by and by fish do become human, and that men become? — on this none of the various sects seem to have any *ex cathedra* dogma — and that one cannot rightly speak of "stable sources of power" and consequent individuation. The rebuttal is simple. Presently the concern is not with "that which was" or "that which may be". The Real, the As-is is the sole concern, and even the confirmed Evolutionist can hardly argue that a 1975 vintage rhesus does not differ factually from his own offspring sired in 1975.

B. *Inalienability of Power*

The observation that to each Dynamic-Fact there corresponds a package of specific powers does not establish the strict individuation of Power. This remains all the more problematical in that earlier its miscibility was established. What is miscible and additive can logically be equated with a "single flowing force", a "prime matter", manifesting itself under a variety of guises. A second alternative would be that each, animate and inanimate, "begins" or is "born" with a given quota of Power and that this slowly "leaks out" until "death" occurs, the spent Power being in the "meantime" appropriated by Outsiders. Indeed, the plausability of this deduction, especially when bolstered by the "wholesale evidence of change" offered by archeological detritus or the aging which everyone undergoes, is such that, save for Leibniz, nary an ontologist has resisted the temptation of incorporating among the major tenets of his system, some modality of Energy transferability. Hence, next it is necessary to establish *that the powers observed as emanating from a given Dynamic-Fact are in-fact its own, and can never be appropriated through any process by Outsiders — that, in a word, Power or Energy is radically quantized and possessed in fee simple and in perpetuity.*

Due to the several ideological interpretations placed upon the words possess and possession and to their materiality in this context, a clear statement of their meaning is in order. Wherever the terms possess and possession and their derivatives are used, it is in the ontological and not in the socio-economic sense. They do not imply control, as examplified by the ownership associated with Liberal or Moslem Capitalism, or even by the ownership of the body. Ontologically, the latter only describes a more or less effective authority over ones factories, harem, body or shoes, and is not to be confused with *bona fide* possession. Since control, the product of aggression, is subject to ebb and flow, and even to being superceded when a third more powerful entity asserts its acquisitive instincts, control is the antithesis of ownership. Here, *possession implies a relationship so intimate, so inviolable, so much of the Existent, that the owner himself could, under no circumstances, divest himself of it, even should he desperately seek to do so, and it follows, one which no outside agent could forcibly cleave.* The difference between the two phenomena, the one factual and the other relational, can be illustrated by the following situations. Control might include the government of Chili confiscating the Anaconda copper properties, or a thug relieving you at gun point of your pocketbook, pants and shoes; also of course, a willing divestiture of ones possessions, as witness gifts at Christmas to a friend.[4]

4. The universal character of both energy and intensity is clearly brought out in the following statement of W. Heisenberg. Simultaneously, however, the chasm between the conventional view of a nonspecific "interchangeable" energy (which implies a *de facto* monistic universe) from that of energy as inalienably owned by strict entities, whether primary particle, ape or uranium is as clearly enunciated:

Due to the cosmic dimension of the Existent, samples of its possessions can be "pinpointed" only with difficulty. Indeed each owns but one "thing": the Self, the Fact-of-ones-to-beness. There is, however, an emotional state ardently sought by and familiar to everyone: love, which typifies true possession. Love can be given, but always remains of the giver. A gratuity — hence its pricelessness — it does not impoverish the giver, for he parts with nothing but rather communes willingly and longingly. Love, the same holds for hate, presents the researcher with an ideal "working model" of Energy. In the first instance, it witnesses to its intensity characteristic, and in the second to its inalienability and facticity.

To the many logicians and scapel-wielding natural scientists who will insist that the above is subjective evidence, the answer is the same as to those who objected that the "existence" of Existence was not proven. Power as synact of Existence reaches to the heart of the Atom. At once eminently existential and physical, to it Shakespeare's: "To be or not to be", applies integrally. Dialectics are impotent to solve the problems which it presents. Any decision re its facticity or non-facticity must initially be arrived at empirically, and confirmation must come from physical experiments. Also proof by "default" is provided by the fact that the quantizing of Power solves the paradoxes which the *"corruptio unius est generatio alterius"* theories of degeneration, together with those of evolution or symbiotism fail to solve. Actually, conclusive equational proof is available through cosmic equations which become feasible once Cosmic Jurisprudence or Universal Law is established. A third category of proof offers itself, that of a consensus evidenced by non-philosophical, "average man". As conceded, the opinion of the layman on specialized philosophical issues, on the Kantian categories for instance, cannot be expected to be of much value.

Thanks to the work of Einstein, physicists have come to realize that "mass", which had been regarded as the "material" basis of matter is equivalent to energy; that is to say, it can be converted into energy ($E = Mc^2$). Rest mass thus represents potential energy; it is the "inertia of energy" and can therefore be expressed in units of energy. This means that elementary particles are largely interchangeable, and can be partly converted into radiation just as radiation can become matter. So elementary particles can be produced from kinetic energy. Energy provides us with what is in fact "the valid proof of the uniformity of all matter.

Upon gut issues the opposite applies. When, save for the philosophically biased, men in all walks of life instinctively hold an identical view upon an issue as central as that of the ownership of Power, one cannot rationally ignore such an intuition. The phrase "philosophical bias", possibly calls for elucidation. It merely means that:

A. if on a given phenomenon two doctrines are offered, diametrically opposed, both evidently cannot be valid, and

B. if prior to being introduced to philosophical theory, men adhere exclusively to one of the two, it is no exaggeration to speak of bias in respect to that which has the support of but one segment of the professionals.

A synoptic survey of the major phenomena through which Power-Energy manifests itself in everyday life, and a brief analysis of the interpretation which men of all nations and ideological suasions place upon such, substantiates this. A first phenomenon warrants consideration, that closest to the reader: his own dynamism. Should the reader scrutinize his pre-philosophical intuitions on the subject, he should find that he then looked upon Power as possessed by the Being which appeared to generate it. In possibly no instance is this as true as when it applies to his own person. We all feel, and more vital still, act as if our energies are unequivocally ours. Simultaneously, we tend to see the others and their powers, "as fit to be drawn unto" and "into" ourselves, as called to become "our possession", and thereby implicitly proclaim the initial foreigness of powers other than our own. Further the fate reserved to our capitalist-like appetite for the "substance" of the Outsiders strengthens this evidence. For instance, try as one may, it is impossible to appropriate either the personality or bodyness of another man. Granted, one can impose oneself and oppress, one can imitate behavior and acquire limbs through transplanting, i.e. receive mental and flesh succor from another human, but all such attempts fall short of a genuine appropriation. What takes place is coagentization. The aggressing Atom or Atoms so intensify their attacks against a given knot of relationships that for *practical purposes* their control, whether biological, emotional or economic is seen as having integrated the Antropocity concerned "into" the aggressor. The emphasis upon *"for practical purposes"* draws the distinction to be maintained between the It or Atom which remains forever beyond acquisition, and the mindfactured Antropocity. Simultaneously, this safeguards the demarcation line between disciplines — distinguishing ontology from politics, biology, etc.

Upon progressing from the somewhat crude relationship with the various chemicals, enzymes and corpuscles which serve as coagents in the maintainance of a body, to the more pervasive such as personality, magnetism and the emotional generally, the inalienability of Power appears beyond doubt. As example, love — among the most efficient forms of Power — provides an unquestionable instance of inalienability. That the loved can never be owned by the lover constitutes the most deeply intuited sadness of life. The power-of-love can be intensified but never acquired. Confirming further its facticity, it is withdrawn at will; which is to say, disintensified — thereby simultaneously exhibiting the key characteristic of Power, intensity. The non-transferability of Power between species is, if anything, more glaring. For instance there is no manner through which man may own the power of a Douglas fir. Vice versa, the fir tree is as helpless to appropriate man's. Their respective energies can be added, as when man burns the fir to fight off cold. The variables to this type of aggressive additivity exceeds the imagination. But none comes to mind which involves an actual transfer of ownership. Always, the relationship remains, frustratingly, one of Outsider to Outsider.

Finally, upon surveying universal or conceptualized power — an example of the first being electrical-power, and of the second political-power — again these are always referred to as alien, as coming from the Outside. Never as possessible. This is confirmed, in reverse, in the case of political-power. It never enters the mind of Mr. Politician "X" that his power could conceivably be the possession of someone else. The process is identical with electron-power. While the electricity process is not yet adequately understood — even in an era which has learned to live by it — this much seems established: it remains foreign to the agents which cause it to be generated and through which it is transmitted, be the transmitter a high voltage line or the human nervous network. Since the issue of the relationship of electricity to man is highly technical and the center of profound controversy, the schematic outline which follows is presented solely as an instance of a practical application of Existential Atomism.

The character of adimensional motor and the consequent radical independence of each Atom once recognized, the status of electricity in a flesh and blood body, human or other, is readily discerned. Both, the individual electron and humanoid, being self-contained foci of Power, serve as coagents to each other. For example the electric impulses which emanate from the human brain bear the same relationship to the body as does electric-power to a turbine or any other Antropocity involved in the generating of electricity. *In the case of the brain waves these constitute normal electrical-power generated through the inter-relationship of the central agent, the human-atom, which on its own and with its satellites — the enzymes, leucocytes, etc. — impose themselves upon the electrons, to thus provide the medium necessary for the self-realization at once of the electrons and of the human and his satellites.* Physically, the electrons help the latter make themselves, and vice versa, the human and his satellites help the electrons realize themselves. The result : a humanized electricity or alternately an electrified human. More specifically, man utilizes his energy to shape and direct the resulting electricity according to a human modality, but while doing so, is inversely stamped with an electrical trade-mark. In this sense, the electrical impulse recorded from a brain is neither human or electronic, but partakes of the human and the electron. Coagency (corres-ponsibility) is involved. For the sake of simplicity, the corres-ponsibility factor was restricted to the man and electron. In actual fact, thousands of agents — to name but two, the pituitary luteinizing hormone (LH) and the hypothalamic hormone (LRF) — are simultaneously at work, and should any withdraw its cooperation beyond a critical-point, both electron and man will find their relationship going awry.

The coherency, intellectual and existential of this perspective, when compared to that of the several hypotheses currently in vogue which would reduce man to a complex of electrical synapses, stands out. Whereas any "man is an electric complex" hypothesis, if pushed to its logical end nihilates both man and electron, Existential Atomism gives to each his due. All synaptic theories of the "living body" imply gross oversimplification of an otherwise most complex situation and the mature scientific mind can at best grant such theses folkoric status. On the other hand, the strict atomism explication here outlined, while schematic, avoids the pitfalls of oversimplification. By remaining open-ended, it allows for the subsequent integration in the human equation of any newly discovered factor or agent viz. HLA antigens, etc. Of possibly greater relevance is the fact that strict atomism allows the researcher to allocate precisely the sphere of responsibility of each contributing agent. In summary, to reduce man and, by extension, all Existents to a network of shifting relationships — two prime examples being the man is a "sum of electrical synapses" and the Marxian "man is a historical category" theories, is to banish reason from ones "evolving universe". Thereafter the sole refuge is the dismal depths of the Absurd and Despair. Instead, the Scientific Existentialist can face the challenges of a harsh world with serenity and a cool realism. He, as everyone, does not have all the answers. He, as everyone, lives in mystery. However, since his Universe is a rational whole, composed of a fixed number of Dynamic-Facts, each an Outsider and all simultaneously corresponsible, for him the unknown, the mystery is not a source of despair, but of hope, awe and a challenge.

chapter V

Absolute-Speed: Speed of Universe

Velocities greater than that of light... have no possibility of existence.

EINSTEIN, *First Article on Relativity.*

In the limiting case of a tachyon moving at infinite speed its total energy would be zero, although its momentum would remain finite. It should be emphasized that for a tachyon at infinite speed it is the total energy that is zero and not just the kinetic energy.

Gerald FEINBERG, *Particles that Go Faster than Light.*

1. Intensity and Maximization Explored

Existential maximization, a revolutionary theory, central to Dynamic Vision, is bound to be controversial. It is fortunate, therefore, that it and its corollaries, namely, the *de facto* maximization of every Atom and the fact that the true speed of the Universe is not of light but of absolute-speed, can be established upon the basis of statistically verifiable Now phenomena. Once of the latter, in particular, the stationary or fixed point, is a commonplace occurrence which we all witness and indeed experience daily.

The demonstration contained in this chapter covers three headings and is intended to provide basic but preliminary evidence only. Indirectly the balance of the book elaborates upon the subject, with Part IV being specifically devoted to establishing that our true state is one of maximization in a medium of Cosmic Peace. The three points referred to are:

A. a brief analysis of the nature and implications of the type of maximization observable in the Now — that of the stationary-point.

B. a history of the discovery of maximization, which simultaneously establishes that the discovery itself constitutes an example of applied maximization, and

C. an extrapolation from verifiable Now maximization data, into the Real which demonstrates that the stationary-point coincides with immanence, embraces the Cosmos, and accounts for the Atom's third metamorphosis — from Dynamic-Fact into a One-Intense.

2. Maximization Vaguely Intuited by Everyone

Uncanny as this may appear, the *de facto* maximization of each Atom can be physically established from a proper interpretation of an universal phenomenon, the peak or stationary-point.

The stationary or maximized-point, an everyday occurrence, has shared the fate of most commonplace physical phenomena. Men have not dared to accept it at full face value. Even the layman intuitively interprets each such point as an instance of actual maximization. All however persist in seeing it as local only; all refuse to draw from it the logical conclusion. At best the more perspicacious recognize it as a source of mystery and paradox, being quite aware of the irrationality attendant to the presence of even one fixed-point in an allegedly moving or evolving environment.

As most physical paradoxes, this one arises from a failure to situate the data in its proper locale — the Cosmic Equation — and from a perverse obstination to tailor every issue and fact to fit procustean anthropocentric norms. To see in a stationary-point an instance of local or Now maximization is correct. The ontologist however who cuts his investigation short at that stage, acts like the mathematics student who would refuse to use the addition process. Result: no solution in either case. As it will be shown shortly, the reference to addition is not metaphoric. Ordinary addition and/or subtraction explains both the entropy and maximization phenomena.

In summary, mankind vaguely intuits maximization, but fails to draw the implications of his intuition. Having observed that a stationary-point testifies in behalf of maximization, one must recognize the inescapable, namely that the sum of all stationary-points adds up to a state of cosmic maximization — even in the Now. A closer look at the situation bears this out abundantly.

Upon considering the structure of stationary-points one is immediately struck by the intimacy of each key cosmic factor with every other, each leading inexorably to the next. From the beginning it became evident that only the concept of synactivity could adequately join those of Existence and Power. Both quality and intensity could also be accurately evaluated solely if each is viewed as a full synact or radical of the Atom. The same incestuous relationship now bares itself between intensity and maximization, even as this latter is observed in its degenerate form of perceived stationary-points. For, as perusal of the definition of *state*, itself a key component of intensity, reveals, stationary-points synactivate intensity and maximization.

As noted, the definition of intensity implies: The state of being strained or stretched... In turn the notion of *state*, is commonly defined as: The condition or circumstances of a being or thing at any given time; situation; position — or still, a crisis or stationary-point. The above, drawn from Webster's, is based entirely upon observations derived from the Perceived — from unreconstructed sense data, from life as it appears, as for instance, when one strains to open a stuck door or to pull a recalcitrant carrot from the garden, two instances of "being strained" at a given time, but not involving what is normally considered as constituting stationary-points. Unquestioned instances of these latter would be situations where the straining results in a stalemate — as in those of the two hands pressing with equal force against each other and the two deadlocked caterpillar tractors, proferred earlier as examples of intensity at work.

The profusion of stable or stalemated-points and situations is such that the phenomenon is accepted as a commonplace. Yet they remain a source of bafflement to the wide awake, for each represents the dynamical counterpart of Zeno's arrow. After all, no genius is needed to realize that while stationary-points do litter the landscape, still none can be pinpointed or grasped with accuracy. To Mr. Averageman whose only involvement with stationary-points is apt to be a dispute with a traffic cop who would refuse to accept his "stop" as constituting a full, legal "stop", the paradox remains of secondary concern, offering mainly an occasion for good-natured philosophical banter. The maximized-point is however no joking matter to the Materialists and the Becomingists. Indeed, it is deadly.

The category of Materialist includes all who subscribe to real time-space, even an Aristotelian for whom both represent *bona fide* existential dimensions. He who accepts the occurrence of stationary-points in a time-space continuum faces the problem of situating an infinity of stationary-points within the original — a process which nihilates the original point. Since none of the points, neither the original nor any born from a subsequent division, are either stationary or physically embraceable, but *are* so only in the mind of the operator, the age old paradox of Zeno's arrow which can never reach its destination, returns to mock the budding Materialist. Of course the "real time-space" advocate dismisses his dilemma by arguing that the issue is either purely hypothetical or epistemological. So it is. In the meantime, he does not satisfactorily account for the fixed-point in question and his dogma of a concrete and dimensioned "matter", infinite or otherwise, becomes physically untenable. It either moves or is fixed.

The quandary of the Becomingist, upon being asked to account for the maximized or stationary-point is more radical still. Even one of these suffices to physically bring crashing down and to a stand-still, the entire machinery of a "matter in movement" universe. As much has long ago been grasped by many. Indeed, one can surmise, somewhat ungenerously, that the lack of interest shown by philosophers and sundry scientists on the subject is due to an unwillingness to face up to the irrationality in which they find themselves if they attempt to reconcile Becoming with anything which threatens — as does a state, even "temporary", of maximization — to introduce facticity into Power and the Cosmos. Be this as it may, to observe, as has mankind throughout the centuries, everywhere in the Universe foci of intensity, and to describe these as stationary-points, is to bear testimony, either unwittingly or unwillingly, to a measure of maximization.

We now discover that in the matter of maximization, there is no half-way house; that maximal intensity, as revealed under the guise of isolated stationary-points, embraces the Universe. Stated otherwise, *the Universe consists of an X-number of Atoms, all maximized, with the result that the* de facto *relationship of a given Existent to any other is maximal.*

3. The Discovery of Maximization an Exercise of Maximization

The present stage of the investigation makes it possible to preceed the technical demonstration of the maximized status of the Atom and the consequent stationary-point status of the Universe, by a brief consideration of an event whose character may surprise, but which may nonetheless throw more light on the subject than can a purely technical analysis. It concerns a lived instance of maximization, which occurred to the writer, and coincided with the discovery of existential maximization and of the One-Intense character of the Atom, namely the realization that Power is fact.

While only the brash would reject the concept of Existence as the sum of That-which-is, still Existence so grasped does offer little upon which to hang a hat. Even after individuation is observed and the cosmic mass is divided into an X-number of Dynamic-Facts, these remain bathed in an ethereal atmosphere and of meagre heuristic value. Now the position has improved considerably. The Atom has put on flesh. To its first and elusive univerquality, unicity, is added a second eminently qualitative one, intensity, readily detectable throughout the Cosmos, particularly at every level of man's activities, and which affects all of his relationships. Effectively, the structure of the Atom has been deciphered to the point where, while respecting scientific methodology, it can be investigated in its role of a human Self. There is irony attendant to such a step, for to introduce the subjective in a study of Existence — in this instance, to analyze the operation of that most intimate of mysteries, the intellect — necessitates a descent from abstraction to the raw realities of daily life, a bias characteristic of the Existentialist. Yet, it is precisely at this juncture that the traditional Existentialist will balk, since in his opinion, Existence — especially that which dwells in man — is an ungraspable phenomenon — "residing in untruth" and therein condemned to remain "essentially unknowable". That I should eventually part company with the philosophers of Faith and the Absurd, of Becoming and Nothingness, and rejoin the Aristotelians and Positivists, was foreordained. While I share the anguish of a Kierkegaard and others when faced with the tragedies of life, my preoccupation with the Objective exceeds even that of an Aquinas or Comte. *Literally conciliating Parmenides with Heraclitus and Democritus, I know myself to be an absolute in my own right, and through the agency of the absolute to absolute modality of thought, I further know myself as enabled to achieve objectivity — within and without the Self.*[1]

This competence will now be utilized for a dual purpose. The first provides a further example of intensity at work. The second, more ambitious, will establish upon the basis of personal experience, that the person does not become, but rather is aware progressively of his Outside; that *one is not born in time, nor does one grow through "sedimentation" or even evolve. Rather birth and growth only witness to a free-willed exercise of maximization, achieved at the true speed of the Universe — that of an absolute.* Specifically, the purpose is to demonstrate that our primary act of awareness of the Outside and subsequent acts of consciousness have the cosmos as initial point of reference, and that the particular event and the constructive process in general are coeval ontologically. All particulars are at once embryonic in and explanatory of ones initial vision of the Real — no matter how faint, how blurred such a vision might be, as in the eyes of the fœtus.

---

1. The divergence of views as to the character of Truth, Objectivity and Subjectivity which separates Scientific Existentialism from a time-space-oriented Existentialism is clearly outlined by Kierkegaard in this statement.

> Socratically speaking, subjectivity is untruth if it refuses to understand that subjectivity is truth, but, for example, desires to become objective. Here, on the other hand, subjectivity in beginning upon the task of becoming the truth through a subjectifying process, is in the difficulty that it is already untruth. Thus, the labor of the task is thrust backward, backward, that is, in inwardness... But the subject cannot be untruth eternally, or eternally be presupposed as having been untruth; it must have been brought to this condition in time, or here become untruth in time... The paradox emerges when the eternal truth and existence are placed in juxtaposition with one another; each time the stamp of existence is brought to bear, the paradox becomes more clearly evident. Viewed Socratically the knower was simply an existing individual, but now the existing individual bears the stamp of having been essentially altered by existence.

S. Kierkegaard, *Concluding Unscientific Postscript*, Book two, Part one, Chapter II, Section 4 B, "An Existential System is Impossible", as found in *Reality, Man and Existence*, H. J. Blackman editor, New York, Bantam Books, 1971, p. 26.

If anything the chasm which divides Scientific Existentialism from out-and-out Becomingism is revealed more strikingly by Sartre's famous: "I am 'not that', I am 'no thing', I am not even what I am aware of as myself, for that has become my past, a thing".

A first, and in itself conclusive feature of a history of the concept of maximization is that in arriving at it, the time sequences were "thrown into a cocked-hat". For example, these several pages represent second generation insights inserted after the Existent had undergone all three metamorphoses, and stood in its ultimate garb, that of a Cosmic-Presence. Factual Power witnesses to a greater degree still of embryocity. Some twenty five years ago, as if impelled by sheer intuition, I never tired to reiterate the very principle of facticity, that "what-is, is" and to simultaneously affirm that the ground of Existence was Power. Unconcerned with a formal definition and assuming that the views of everyone were identical, I accepted, until recently, to proceed under the assumption that Power was at once a fact and a capacity. But through the years a nagging suspicion persisted that some basic insight was eluding. For instance, the capacital could not be reconciled with the innate and qualitative. The pieces just would not fit snugly. The problem became acute when next a niche was sought in the realm of Power, wherein facticity, intensity and capacity would be peaceably accommodated, while allowing the capacital to retain its conventional paramountcy. The exercise was bound to fail. *Spare notions within a philosophical structure are as disruptive as are excess cogs in a gear system. The sole difference is that the rigidity of steel gears and the resulting clatter, soon make it evident that something is awry, whereas Power transmitted by ideas, is so much more fluid and artful, that only the strictest of mental discipline allows one to detect the jarring caused by ideological errors.* In this instance, the more one insisted upon coherence, the more unsatisfactory capacity became.

By late 1971, the "problem" assumed the proportion of a crisis. A process of intellectual plodding had led to the conviction that capacity, potency and change must be rejected outright. As Parmenides had perceived, a universe which accommodates "change" is a lying universe. But the cure appeared as deadly as the disease. For time and the potency-capacity team continued to dog my every step, and close on their heels trailed "change", degeneration and death. Stubbornly, the pack of the evanescent-ones refused to vanish. Mocking, in refrain, they chanted: "we are real; we are real, no one may disown us!" Haunted thus, yet painfully aware that to stop short of the eradication of movement in the Real was to reduce Dynamic Vision to a variation upon the theme of Becomingism — in which case it was best to devote ones energies to more pleasurable endeavors — I was presented with three options. Firstly, to forget the whole thing; secondly, compromise the intellect, or thirdly, make an effort of will. In a word, the struggle could be intensified. Intensity won out. I willed to conquer. I maximized.

So it came to pass, that as I walked the streets of Montreal in an unpleasant December rain, the last and key piece of the cosmic jigsaw puzzle fell neatly into its slot. No startling phenomenon revealed itself. Rather, for the first time I was profoundly conscious that, from always, my concept of Power had been at odds with tradition. From youth, it had meant more than a capacity and infinitely more than the seventeen subsections of the Webster definition. Always, it had been a possession — unambiguously me. Power was not a something that "flowed into" in the form of food or air. A factor of intimacy and of intensity, it pressed out and out unceasingly. It was a feeling of force, a force of love, of anger or of any other nature; a compression, a heightening of ones steam presure — to use a fireman's terminology. Power equalled flexed muscles, a clenched fist, a will to conquer. Thus was Power. It was this revelation and its implications which, at that moment, came to the fore, in a flash. Then, the difference between capacity and intensity was made clear. Capacity was purely descriptive. Intensity was the proper of Power. Intensity alone spoke the language of the Dynamic-Fact. Intensity alone spoke of struggle and self-realization. Then, it became evident that from the first flickerings of my consciousness life had been, not only a thoroughly individualized affair, but a positive adventure in conquest. This intuition that Power is fact, intensity and struggle is confirmed by manuscripts, some of which date back to the 1950's. These record a constant use of phrases implying outright ownership of Power, and a clear appreciation that intensity and aggression were the name of the game, as witness the following from the opening page of an unpublished work entitled: *Life is Conquest,*

> All beings have, locked in them, powers inherent to their species of being. Each human being within his limitation is free to develop these powers. He does so by imposing his being, e.g., power, upon

> other beings, by conquest of one nature over another. For the greater part of creation this is accomplished by an act of blind conquest or destruction. The creatures of the ocean, the trees of the forests, the beasts in the jungle, have from dawn to dark and dark to dawn, but one purpose: conquest.

By 1964, ownership of Power is vested in the Being, but the debate between Power and power-potential or potency remains unresolved as the next lines indicate:

> To refuse all Beings the capacity to possess anything whatsoever and to then turn around and vest all Beings with a measure of power or power-potential, may appear to some as a mere play on words.

However, the next paragraph makes clear which has the upperhand:

> It is never said in every day parlance, that one owns any amount of power which is foreign to one's own inner powers. Rather it is said that one controls it, if political power is being discussed, or provides it, in the case of electrical power... a divided or possessed Being is a destroyed Being, so is possessed power destroyed power and not power at all.

Returning to a night and a nasty December rain, what took place that evening is that deeply angered by a failure to decipher the riddle which held the key to the paradox of change in Truth, of movement in Reality, I willed to concentrate. A maximum of Power was exerted upon one specific point-issue. The only accurate way to describe this is that the intensity of my intellect-power peaked — was maximized at that-point-in-time. Facetiously, it can be said that intensity was required to discover intensity and its mate, maximization. If intensity rather than capacity revealed itself as the proper of Power, it was not due to a capacity to think, but to an effort of will, of presentialization. This intensification when observed at the Order of the Real effectively maximized at that-point-in-time that specific intellectual relationship with the remainder of the Atoms, namely an embryonic knowledge of the role of intensity in the Cosmos. From then on nothing could be added to that insight. It was maximal. At the Now, the same applies. Now intensity does not involve potency or capacity, but is rather of the will, and constitutes, at once, the measure of a Being's freedom and the norm of its efficiency. While the process, as a whole, became apparent in that evening of 1971, presently, eight years later, as the final corrections are being made, the continuum which subsumes life affirms itself as vividly. The unity which binds not only my knowledge of Power, but my every relationships with the Outside evidences this. From the beginning there has been nothing new added unto my Self; nor has anything whatsoever been lost or abstracted. I sense-know myself not as "something in the process of being made", but rather as a Presence asserting itself against aggressors and in cooperation with friends. Even within the Self, the same continuity is detectable. Unquestionably the outlook and ambitions of the six year old are not "changed". The thought patterns and ambitions triggered by the tales of Robin Hood are identical with those which fill and motivate the adult. Only the array of friends and foes differs, and with these it is logical to cope differently. The neighbor's six year old son does not call from the child for the same response as do the stock market or political issues such as, for example, the "Canadian" unity crisis.

While the above can be dismissed as hindsight, evidence of a past which is still a present, is not as easily ignored. Here, the reference is to memory and recall. That, as Freud maintain, ones past remains a present is easily established. Given the proper circumstances, past events reactivate with fantastic clarity and impact. The reference is to a particular night when in minutes, if not instants, the quasi totality of my sexual experience flashed before me. The time sequences were jumbled, but the vividness and accuracy of this wholesale recall was absolutely astounding. Anyone, who has had to witness at a trial of law, will be familiar with this ability of the mind to relive the past. Gradually, under probing, friendly or otherwise, the minutiae of even insignificant incidents reemerge. If the past is forever present, albeit most of the time subconsciously, and as a consequence affects the present, when does the true future begin? The question is especially embarassing to the Evolutionist in that even the future impinges upon an informed and/or psychic mind. Given sufficiently precise data, an intelligent person can foresee certain events with considerable accuracy.

Existential maximization is central to a theory of cosmic presentiality. While its basic mechanism is simple, its concept and implications may seem, at least upon first introduction, so unconscionable as to prove very difficult to entertain. The brief observations based upon lived acts of maximization, presented in the preceding pages, were intended mainly to draw the attention to the type of happenings in which it occurs, even in the Now, and secondly to document it first hand. The value of such subjective evidence may be challenged upon several grounds, all of which in final analysis can be traced to the notion that dimensioned or signated and tangible "matter", external to the researcher's "body", alone can be the subject of experiments. The question has been debated at length. Presently, it suffices to reiterate that all evidence and experiments are subjective — have their source and locus in a mindscope : in an independent mind, which sets out to assess its relationships with the Outside, according to its own parameters. While, as noted, the principle itself of maximization is simple, its theory is complex. This is developped in the coming sections and all of Part V is devoted to a more detailed demonstration of the manner in which it is experienced in real life situations. Together these added precisions and data should confirm the intuition which flows from the principle of absoluteneity. Most helpful should be the step by step demonstration that "bodies" are but nodes of intense relationships.

To summarize, Existence is a qualitative-fact. Perception is only one among many qualities. Aggressivity is a second which afflicts any Atom immersed in the Now. Together these explain the feeling of progression — of growth and degeneration. Even though the true speed of Reality and of aggression is absolute and it follows maximized, the power deficiencies of man, i.e. his qualities, deny him a panoramic view of the whole of his Self and of his relationships. Certain aggressors force themselves to the forefront of his consciousness, and hide others from his view — even others which he would fain embrace closely. For example, the torrid love affair can be abruptly brought to a halt by the intrusion of a third party bent on violence. Then, the threat of physical injury becomes number one. Yet, the interrupted affair is not voided, but rather upstaged. Both acts persist concurrently. The process involves firstly quality, secondly intensity and thirdly efficiency of response to challenge. For anyone which as man is endowed with a restricted quota of consciousness and swims in conflict, the fact-of-existing is a function of the intensity and efficiency of the power brought to bear upon the Outside. The whole, and in it every event, is maximized but certain events are privileged.

4. Third Metamorphosis of the Existent, The One-Intense and/or Free-Efficient

Maximization and its corollary, a maximized Universe composed of Atoms each individually maximized, each a Cosmic-Presence provides a most useful insight into the phenomenon of "life". Responsible for the Existent's third metamorphosis, it transmutes the Dynamic-Fact into a One-Intense and/or Free-Efficient. The second, which transmuted the concept of a barren Existential-Atom into a Dynamic-Fact, had the merit of endowing each Atom with a character: that of a qualitative adimensional motor. Yet this gave no indication about the Atom's inneity, its structure or the nature of its relationship to the Outside. As implied, the third metamorphosis is more complex than the previous. Since with it relationality enters upon the scene, the Existent now assumes a Janus-like personality, the one face corresponding to the Real and the other to the Perceived. The face of the Real is that of a One-Intense, and the Perceived that of a Free-Efficient.

A One-Intense resides outside of time-space in a state of maximal development. Applied to a man, this means that the factual, As-is man, as opposed to the perceived man, rests at the height of his beauty, strength, intellectual development and, generally any qualitative state which corresponds with a maximum of humanness — a state wherein one is present in-fact, to the Universe. Further, that which applies to man, applies *mutatis mutandis* to all Atoms. The sole difference between the most powerful and the most insignificant, between The Absolute and a downtrodden louse, is quality. The term One-Intense has for effect to simultaneously give an added preeminence to the notion of an atomicity, and emphasize the maximized state of the Power vested in each Atom. However, while the idea of the Self resting in a maximal state — at the peak of its youthful beauty and strength, and enjoying the height of the intellectual development of its mature years — undoubtedly fascinates, it is bound to be received with scepticism. Instinctively, it will be countered that in "actual-life" this is not so; that such a vision, while grandiose, would entail a wholesale contravention of the "laws of nature".

5. The Mechanics of Maximization at the Order of the Real, or Some Objections Answered

Effectively maximization challenges the veracity of every perceived phenomena, birth and death included. Therefore until these are satisfactorily accounted for, maximization must remain in the category of the daydream or utopia. The dual purpose of the next pages is to analyze its mechanics and thereby provide preliminary answers to the main issues raised, namely those of birth, growth and death. More specifically, the objective is to explain how, if every Existent *is* at its maximum outside of time-space, one accounts for progression of any type, and in particular, for the growth of the human embryo into proud adulthood, and thence into the tottering degeneration of the nonagenarian? Certainly, the affirmation that each Being lives forever its peak relationship and development insults the intelligence. Similarly, what of birth and death? Do not these two events occur before our eyes? Does not maximization negate both? Since the issues at stake penetrate deeply into the woof of the Universe, and impinge upon every science; the full answer — to the extent that such answers can be complete — must be provided progressively. The last remark applies specifically to the life-death and growth-degeneration pairs. The latter, related to the subject of "bodiness", is investigated in the third experiment, while the life-death pair is discussed in Part IV which deals with Cosmic Peace. Therein, death, observed in the light of the latest discoveries of astrophysics and biochemistry, is discovered to be the measure of physical-time and explicative of entropy.

The birth-death and growth-degeneration pairs fall into two distinct categories. Birth-death, directly relates to the Real, and growth-degeneration — whether these apply to a tree, nation, uranium atom or man — lodges in the Perceived. Both concern origins. The opening chapter disclaimed any pretension of solving the mystery involved in the origin of the Fact-of-to-be. Presently nothing justifies a different stand. Any idea of a beginning in time rests strictly upon the questionable evidence of a "logical assumption arising from the testimony of the senses". As anyone familiar with phenomena such as hearing or color blindness knows, sense datum is unreliable. Hence, by empirical standards, birth and death should be approached as are color blindness or the suspicious noises escaping through the walls of a hotel bedroom. In such situations, the mind must remain uncommitted. A birth testifies solely to the fact that the Real, assumedly in the person of an Obscure-Absolute, is being — of a sudden — observed. To jump to the conclusion that a something or person has *ex-nihilo* begun-to-be is unscientific. Death which involves merely the subjective observation of a lack of presence is of the same category. To dogmatize about the disappearing act witnessed in a death or of a plane beyond the horizon, is to abandon the realm of the given to enter that of fancy. Both birth and death will be dealt with in more detail further on. The above observations have for purpose only to note that, since neither constitutes a fact, physically determinable in either time or space, but are rather phenomena, it is improper to use either as the basis for dogmatic pronouncements on any issue, that of the maximization of the Existential-Atom inclusively.

While birth and death, being mere perceived-terminates, offer nothing whatsoever by which either can be grasped and deciphered, the same opacity does not shield the phenomenon of growth-degeneration. Even though it is enmeshed in the question of origins, being observable in time-space, it can be stripped of some of its mystery. The insights now available, firstly into the structure of the Atom and its Power, and secondly into the existential code make it possible to unravel it with surprising clarity. One of the break-throughs achieved thereby is an understanding of the deproceduralization of the Real. This in turn holds the key to an understanding of the maximized status of Existents. Subject to further elaboration, the deproceduralization of the Real is achieved by transcending the Perceived, to enter the Real. Time and space are reversed and the process completed, not at the snail's pace of the speed of light, but of absolute-speed. Such a reversal, contrary to contemporary thinking does not produce infinite energies or similarly fearsome phenomena. Rather it renders each Atom fully present to the Self and to the commonwealth of the Atoms.

The reference to an absolute-speed may perhaps be interpreted as an irreverent challenge to Einstein's affirmation in his

First Article on Relativity "that velocities greater than that of light..." (about 300,000 kilometers per second) "have no possibility of existence". While it does contradict the letter of Einsteinian thought, it confirms its spirit. Actually, the Existential-Atom by providing the ontological foundation which general relativity otherwise lacks, reveals that the Principle of Relativity is, not only compatible with the Principle of Cosmic of Relationality but is, in effect, a special case, valid in the field of applied physics, of the latter. The logic here is basic. Before universal relativity, can be observed there must first exist *bona fide* dynamic units whose relationships are universal. In a word, *universal relativity presupposes the adimensional Existential-Atom and its universal relationships.*

Similarly, the structure of a universe whose equation is U = X(E : A), far from clashing with subatomic physics, effectively eliminates some of the inconsistencies which will plague this science for as long as it remains confined to a strait jacket of "dimensioned matter" — regardless of the extreme minuteness to which one would feign reduce the primary units. The following statements by two different authorities in subnuclear research, one dealing with "infinite speed" and the other with the "extent of matter", substantiate the double affirmation that absolute speed is consistent with the Theory of Relativity, and that the idea of an "extent of matter" is an obstacle to the advancement of cosmophysic. They also corroborate the affirmation that a correct interpretation of cosmophysic's latest findings predicates the maximization of all Atoms. The first is from an article entitled "Particles That Go Faster Than Light", by Gerald Feinberg, and the second is excerpted from a work by Robert Gouiran of the European Organization for Nuclear Research of Lucerne (CERN), entitled *Particles and Accelerators*. Since the same general comments apply to the quotes from either author, these are introduced concurrently. The first, taken from the summary of the Feinberg article which precedes the text proper, argues that speeds exceeding that of light such as are postulated of the tachyons, are compatible with the theory of Relativity:

> Efforts to detect such particles, named tachyons, have yielded only negative results. Contrary to common belief, however, their existence would not be inconsistent with the theory of relativity.

The two paragraphs which follow and contain the kernel of Feinberg's thought, entertain directly the possibility of infinite speeds and maintains that even these are compatible with General Relativity.

> In the limiting case of a tachyon moving at infinite speed its total energy would be zero, although its momentum would remain finite. It should be emphasized that for a tachyon at infinite speed it is the total energy that is zero and not just the kinetic energy. For an ordinary particle with nonzero rest mass the total energy can never vanish.
>
> The condition of infinite speed is, however, not invariant but depends on the observer. If a tachyon were moving at infinite speed as seen by one observer, its speed as measured by another observer in motion with respect to the first would not be infinite but rather some finite value between c and infinity. This is another way of phrasing Einstein's discovery that simultaneity for events at different points in space has only a relative and not an absolute meaning.[2]

The two Gouiran quotes, also from his introduction, central to his thought, can moreover be seen as a compendium of the key theories of contemporary physics. Together they establish that the author's perspective is a) cosmontological and b) that only an absolute-speed and the consequent maximization of each Atom can rationalize the present views on the nature of "matter" and Energy. The first is that:

> Man's fundamental quest has always been the search for the basis of existence, which he has pursued in order to gain a better understanding of himself or to justify himself. To reach the goal there are two royal roads: that of the philosopher examining concepts and that of the physicist delving into matter to investigate the void.[3]

The second directly relevant to the present subject, reads:

> Although the element of matter has an extent it has no clearly defined outlines. For though energy presents the *discontinuous* aspect of quanta, the passage from the outside to the inside of the point is done in a continuous manner by increasing density. There are no clear edges and every particle in reality covers the entire

---

2. Gerald Feinberg, "Particles That Go Faster Than Light", *Scientific American*, February, 1970.
3. Robert Gouiran, *Particles and Accelerators*, (trans. by W. F. G. Crozier), New York, McGraw-Hill, 1967, p. 11.

> universe, but the probability of finding it is almost entirely confined to a small space. There is a fundamental uncertainty concerning the size of the object.[4]

Briefly, the positive contributions of each quote are these. In the first two Feinberg unambiguously affirms an infinite (absolute) speed to be, a) possible, and b) compatible with Einstein's discovery. In view of the hypothetical nature of tachyons, beyond this no support for the theory of maximization is sought, for the theory of tachyons suffers from the same ontological misconceptions as plague much of the research into the particle. As will become evident Feinberg's theory helps more by what it omits than what it posits. The positive contribution to a hypothesis of maximization of the Gouiran texts, however, warrants close scrutiny. The first recognizes, without hedging, the univocity of the cosmos and posits as its basis "existence", while the second would seem to summarize the concept of the prime particle of most contemporary physicists. Having in the first instance adopted a cosmontological perspective, but standing in contradiction to my views on atomicity, witness this assertion also from the introduction:

> The study of fundamental particles should enable us to discover the smallest form in which an entity emerges from nothingness, and how it returns to it, so that we can know what that "dust" is of which we are made. Not only material dust, but also space dust. For the physicist attempts to discover what is the smallest possible dot that he can imagine. The continuum of space and time is an old concept which no modern theory can use or justify, and an imaginary point cannot be without dimension, for it would only be nothingness or an infinity of energy.[5]

The author unwittingly sets the stage for a dimensionless Existential-Atom. Only a stubborn refusal, shared by many physicists, to even contemplate an adimensional, dynamic universe denies him the insight needed to eradicate inconsistencies such as the following. How, for instance, can one proclaim that: "although the element of matter has an extent it has no clearly defined outlines", and not at the same time, renounce classical time-space and dimensions in general? Is not the concept of

---

4. *Ibid.*, p. 11.
5. *Ibid.*, p. 10.

"extent" incompatible with a lack of "clearly defined outlines"? More incoherent is the affirmation that, "the passage from the outside to the inside of the point is done in a continuous manner by increasing density", especially when, a mere paragraph earlier, it was categorically asserted, on the one hand that:

> A particle can be considered as just a mathematical entity or an invisible evanescent wave.

and on the other hand that:

> an imaginary point cannot be without dimension, for it would only be nothingness or an infinity of energy.

Finally, and at this juncture Gouiran rejoins his colleague Feinberg, the ultimate insult to the intelligence is perpetrated when the latter speaks of, "a tachyon... moving at infinite speed as seen by one observer, its speed as measured by another observer in motion with respect to the first would not be infinite..." and the former assures us that:

> There are no clear edges and every particle in reality covers the entire universe, but the probability of finding it is almost entirely confined to a small space. There is a fundamental uncertainty concerning the size of the object.[6]

Even a cursory analysis of the structure of an adimensional Atom reveals that it at once satisfies the criteria enumerated by Gouiran and implicit in the Feinberg position and eliminates the paradoxes contained in both. The problem with the conventional time-space universe is here bared. Its advocates have no alternative but to try to grasp the whole by worming their way in and around and about an assumedly infinite cosmos. A hopeless task. The solution is simple; to turn the time-space universe inside-out or alternately to deproceduralize it. The first step in this reverse process is the realization that there is simultaneously a total penetration and total outsideness of all by and to all. Each Atom, a Cosmic-Presence, has but one contact with the Outside and rests in a relationship at once of transcendence and immanence. The deproceduralization is completed when one next substitutes for the concept, "dimensioned element of matter", that of a Dynamic-Fact which subsists in a state of maximization, in other

6. *Ibid.*, p. 11.

words, a One-Intense. Then one realizes that Gouiran's "increasing density" or Einstein's matter-energy is more adequately visualized as intense power possessed in permanence by extensionless Atoms and perceived as locally maximized. To quantize a proton, a water, an amoebe or a man is to note diverse manifestations of an identical phenomenon: coagentship. The perceived object is but an Antropocity. The responsible Atom is perceived and grasped as an Obscure-Absolute, and the quantum or body traditionally attributed to it is merely an absolutized, intense knot of relationships integral to its otherwise unique relationship.

At the strictly epistemological level once quanta of any type or dimensioned units such as the human body are recognized for what they are — namely foci of perceived relationships — many an otherwise intractable dilemma dissolves. In a first instance the "matter-spirit" dichotomy disappears. Also the 30 year war between phenomenology and science is brought to a close. The subject or Atom remains at once a closed Self and an object *vis-à-vis* the Outside, its integrity and freedom of action guaranteed by the ownership of an inalienable quota of Power. Equally pertinent is the realization that in the Absolute, at absolute-speed nothing is predetermined or predestined. All is correlational and coeval. To N. Weiner and others who as he are troubled with causation and predestination and who argue that:

> In a rigid system, without degrees, if we introduce causation it pervades the whole system, and the only conceivable cause of any future status is the entire past. But in a world in which the whole past causes the whole future in an integral inseparable way, the category of cause has no operational significance. In such a system, the introduction of purpose anywhere will again be all-inclusive and the notion will again be operationally meaningless... The concept of cause is only significant when there are different degrees of causation that can be measured.[7]

the reply is that "an all-inclusive purpose" is not to be equated with no purpose; nor held inoperative and discountable. To the contrary in a dynamic universe, free-will, far from being banished, is the privilege of everyone. Even for the so-called inanimates a

7. A. ROSENBLUETH and N. WIENER, "Purposeful and Non-Purposeful Behavior", *Philosophy of Science*, vol. 17, no. 4, 1950, p. 320.

purpose or goal and its corollary a free-willed act becomes significant since causation operates not by degrees, but rather rests — beyond dimensions — in the Absolute. The key to an understanding of this and related issues lies in the fact that in a universe wherein "every particle in reality covers the entire universe", the real speed of events is not that of a race horse, Boeing 707 or light photon, but rather that of an absolute. As much is implicit in the Weiner statement, although the correct implications are not drawn.

6. Absolute-Speed and Not Speed of Light is Speed of the Universe

Talk of an absolute-speed may seem another instance of a perverse inclination to pile intellectual outrage upon intellectual outrage. The following observations, while not here developed at length, should dispell such an impression. *The first is that absolute-speed is a corollary of adimensionality. How can It which is without dimensions move? To postulate the dimensionless status of each Atom, simultaneously implies absolute-speed, or alternately, non-speed.* Since the indivisibility and consequent adimensionality of any genuine Existent was established through an experiment, namely the cutting-up of a raw material: the Real, into Atoms, from a physical point of view no further evidence is required. That absolute-speed is not just another item of philosophical fancy arrived at through conventional metaphysics or logic is confirmed by a proper interpretation of the basic data of applied physics. General relativity, for example, predicates a measure of omnipresence by all concerned. A similar state seems implicit in the case of the neutrino. A second and closer look at Gouiran's thesis, which has the merit of incorporating most of the acquired knowledge on the subject of "matter", reveals that if this is rigourously construed, then absolute-speed is indeed the true speed of the Universe. Gouiran having initially divested "the element of matter" — the traditional building block of the Universe — of "clearly defined outlines", and noting "the discontinuous aspect of quanta", next affirms that "there are no clear edges and every particle in reality covers the entire universe". A doctorate in nuclear physics is not required to draw therefrom the consequences. *It which fills the Universe cannot travel at any speed whatsoever. Where, after all, can one go when one is already there? To speak of filling the Universe is to speak of absolute-speed. The term "speed", however, merely adds a human touch to the universal process, only to dissolve this by setting it in a framework of absoluteness. Absolute-speed, in a word, implies a lack of speed, and predicates cosmic presentiality.* The above acquired, to reconcile maximization with the time-space dimensions (these include all processes, birth, growth, degeneration and death inclusively), one has only to consider the limitations of the intellect and the relativity of our sense of speed.

Because of man's limited perception, *no Atom is ever fully observed — each being dimensionless and cosmic, and hence beyond* in se *grasping, except by one possessed of absolute power. The perceiver sees neither himself nor others as they in-fact are. Rather, he sees-knows only a restricted area-number of relationships, each of which he absolutizes or mindfactures into an Antropocity.* This is rarely appreciated. Rather, man interprets his multitudinous relationships in a self-centered and distorted manner. For instance, the very "substance" of other Atoms is held by some to be possessed; as witness the theory of Hylemorphism which implies outright ownership of the "human body" by its "soul". Another source of confusion is the tendency to reify concepts (intellectual-absolutes), the error here being that these come to be seen as actually carving up the Real. Partially perceived processes such as childhood are isolated and given an importance entirely out of proportion to their real weight. Also, such patently man-made dimensions as a cubic foot of ice or a Chrysler car are arbitrarily endowed with Being. Understandably, this piling up of misinterpretation upon error upon subjectivity precludes any possibility of the Real ever being grasped — even to that limited extent which a right thinking man can achieve.

7. The Stationary-Point Extends to Coincide With Existential Immanence

He who seeks an objective knowledge of the Real and of his Self must proceed as follows. Firstly, he must keep in mind that the interpenetration of every Atom by every other is absolute, and that there is consequently between each but one contact. Secondly, the nature of Power must be considered. Power, in its role of synact of Existence, fills the Cosmos and is divided between an X-number of quanta. Further, Power reaches a maximum whenever it attains the height of its intensity; when it is raised, not to a high, but to its maximum degree of compression. Stated inversely and in terms which correspond to a resonant point in physics or still to the Wheeler "wave crest", each high-point constitutes an instance of full intensity and a stationary-point. The conjugation of these factors reveals the state of the individual as that of a One-Intense and that of the Universe, one of cosmic presentiality. Irony is implicit in this since it predicates the acceptance of the concept of stationary-points declared earlier to be inconsistent with change. This seeming contradiction is easily explained. The position which the Evolutionists and partisans of change in general cannot rationally occupy, becomes legitimate when universalized. For although no given maximized-point, can be physically isolated, the same problem does not arise when maximization applies to the Universe encompassed as a unit. In summary, *maximization is not a local phenomenon. The Universe itself experiences maximization; is one massive stationary-point.*

At this point, an unpleasant dilemma arises. The question of maximization, crucial to an understanding of Reality, is so unconscionable that it calls for a detailed analysis and explication. Yet this is feasible only once the mechanism of cosmic relationality is dealt with in the next Part. As a compromise, the data now available will be applied summarily to a phenomenon of concern to all, that of bodily growth and degeneration — of youth and senility. Such a synopsis will serve a dual purpose. It provides an example of applied maximization and a graphic picture of the Atom, as it emerges from its third metamorphosis, from Dynamic-Fact into a One-Intense.

The key to a basic understanding of both phenomena is contained in two principles already established, namely, that on the cosmic scale there is no sequential causality, only cosmic relationality and that the body is not a possession of man, but rather a sum of intense coagential relationships, absolutized into Antropocities — literally into frames identical to those of a moving picture camera. Within the above parameters the process of ageing involves mere presentializing. We single out and present to ourselves, and to those who care to observe our bodies, privileged relationships. This discrimination, this privileging of one knot of events at a given-point-in-time results from a quality peculiar to man: sequential perception. *In-fact, one is neither old or young, rather one entertains differing but simultaneous relationships with each Existent.* With ones mother, for instance, one relates simultaneously as a baby, as a grown son, etc.,[8] with others as a mature business-man or scholar or lover. In-fact, however, at the Real, relationships are unique and instantaneous — each being a Presence before the Universe. All relationships being simultaneous, the maximal one with a given Atom corresponds "at-that-point-in-time" to Reality, and the obverse applies. *Reality consists of the sum of stationary-points i.e. of the maximal relationships of all Existents, and Existence implies the maximal presence or immediacy of an It to every other It.* Since the Universe consists of a fixed number of Atoms, the confirmation of this cosmic presentiality equation is an affair of primary mathematics. In short, intensity reveals the fulness of Existence at both orders. *Cosmic intensity, the sum of stationary-points in the Universe constitutes the Real and within this each individual maximizes, is a One-Intense. At the Now, each perceived high or stationary-point, each "wave crest" gives the viewer an insight into Reality* — the breadth of the insight, being a function of the individual intellect.

While refusing to follow Berkley and his idealist colleagues to the point of affirming that *esse est percipi*, one can join their company to this extent. Pragmatically, for an intelligent Atom, realized perception and its existence can be equated, for to perceive is a major attribute, and to the degree to which it perceives, it realizes itself. This applies to the conscious, but in no way reduces the objectivity of inanimates.[9] Nor does it preclude

8. Cf. secs. 5, 6, 8 and 10, chap. VII, Pt. I, re the mechanism and forces responsible for the feeling of sequence experienced in relationships generally, and in inter-human commerce in particular.
9. While there is as yet scant evidence that chemical atoms and subnuclear particles are endowed with consciousness and sensitivity, this is not to be rejected out-of-hand. In particular the crystalization of metals leaves many questions to be answered. Certainly, one must consider benighted the Positivist scientists and philosophers of the 18th and 19th centuries, whose anti-soul bias led them to consider animals as "machines" and who as a consequence would perform with utter *insouciance*, cruel experiments upon cats and dogs, etc. In our day, not only has the philosophical sadism of the era of

the alternative, that seemingly inanimate entities may well be conscious. Thus, the notion of total compenetration and a concomitant maximization, yields a Cosmos identical in its broad lines to that which subnuclear research reveals — yet richer since it accounts for the full spectrum of phenomena. In particular, the One-Intense situated in the Absolute, is compatible with a "transcendental" conscience and will. Such is the Atom, at the Order of the Real, during its third metamorphosis. Hence, subject to minor reservations, this statement of Heisenberg is valid:

> Les tenants de l'atomisme ont dû se rendre à cette évidence que leur science n'est qu'un maillon de la chaîne infinie de dialogues entre l'homme et la nature et *qu'elle ne peut plus parler simplement d'une nature "en soi"*. Les sciences de la nature présupposent toujours l'homme et, comme l'a dit Bohr, nous devons nous rendre compte que nous ne sommes pas spectateurs mais acteurs dans le théâtre de la vie.[10]

Flesh of the Universe, we are not spectators, but actors on the cosmic stage.

Enlightenment been laid to rest, but the pendulum has swung. It is now established that, not only animals but plants also, feel emotion. A pioneer in that field was Sir Chandra who some fifty years ago dared affirm before an incredulous audience of his peers that "plants have hearts similar to animals". Re the L or Life-Field of plants and of life in general cf. sec. 5, chap. II, Pt. III, and sec. 11, chap. III, Pt. III, re the evidence of animation in enzymes, etc.

10. W. HEISENBERG, *La nature dans la physique contemporaine*, Paris, Gallimard, 1962, p. 18-19.

Chapter VI

Quality, the Ecumenist

> Thus the angels reduce the infinite gap separating man from God and man fills in the gap between angels and matter. Each of these degrees has its own mode of operation since each being operates according as it is in act... Thus the principle of continuity gives precision and determination to the principle of perfection.
>
> Étienne Gilson,
> *The Student of St. Thomas Aquinas*, p. 251

1. General Remarks Re Quality

THE role or status of quality in the existential scheme is major. Being at once of the inneity (the "essence") of the Atom and the factor which explains processes and relationality, quality unites the Real with the Perceived; binds fact to procedure. Its analysis can therefore yield insights into the nature itself of the Atom and in the operation of the mind. The pages which follow deal only with basics. Where the nature or structure of the Atom is concerned one feature mainly will be considered, namely the qualitative character of its five radicals, each of which speaks of quality. From this will emerge an X-ray picture of the Atom, at the time of its third metamorphosis, from a Dynamic-Fact into its dual personality of a One-Intense and a Free-Efficient.

2. What is Quality?

A universal, quality chameleon-like assumes all manner of personalities, both in the eyes of the layman and of the ontologist. To a butcher it rests in the tenderness of a perfectly aged sirloin. To the Scholasticist, quality comes in two packages, the one labeled "essential", the other "accidental". Plato, seeing qualities as synonymous with universals or forms such as whiteness, hardness, beauty, endowed each with separate "existence", then proceeded to compound Being itself from some combination or other of these. A mother, in her role of cook, has yet another concept. She sees in it an undefinable, yet indubitably real something, to be tasted in the lemon pie set before the family at supper time. Quality, according to Boyle, Locke and Hume, speaks an altogether different language again, that of primariness and secondariness. And while to the owner of a harem it is the well-rounded, firm body of his last purchase, to Hegel, it is the end-product of a transmutation of quantity. When one turns to a standard definition for enlightenment, one is offered, as was the case with Power, an adequate description, but no insight as to either its source, nature or operativity (if any), as witness in Webster's:

> That which belongs to a body or to an entity and renders or helps to render it such as it is; characteristic attribute; nature; a belonging; as, purity of tone is an important *quality* of music; a man is admired and respected for his good *qualities.*

The examples and concepts enumerated and the Webster definition are adequate either within their context or to the extent that they describe. The one exception to this blanket endorsement is the Hegelian thesis. For the latter no basis, empirical or rational can be found.

In Dynamic Vision, quality is central. Encompassing all previous concepts, it exceeds these, to the point of dethroning and reducing quantity to the status of a mindfactured unit of intensity-aggression. Whereas other cosmontologies, in particular the Platonic, rightly place high emphasis upon it, the cosmos of Dynamic Vision bathes in a medium of pure quality. The very inneity of the Atom is qualitative, and quality is divorceable neither from an It-which-is nor from Power. This explains why, on the one hand, the mother's idea of a good lemon pie and Plato's and Hume's concepts are valid, and on the other, why these must be relegated to the role of particularities. Due to the Principle of the Proportionality of Extremes, quality evidences simultaneously maximum simplicity and maximum complexity. Each Atom being a discernible, and Power a universal fact, the qualitative manifestations of both are as varied as the Universe's realities, and present the intellect with a source of investigation more complex than the hues of a rainbow.

The rationale for affirming that the inneity of the Atom is qualitative and that quality is divorceable neither from any It-which-is nor from Power, is that the latter and their first generation radicals, oneness and intensity respectively, are emimently qualitative. To be a strict entity or alternately to constitute an infrangible oneness implies, one, the prime quality, discernibility, and two, that inherently qualitative trait called freedom. The intensity feature of Power observed, its qualitativity follows. *To be intense, on an As-is basis, implies a more-rather-than-less state, the very definition of qualitativity. As-is intensity, degraded and proceduralized by the senses (as in the Now) by assuming the status of perceived efficiency emphasizes further the qualitative nature of Power.* The above when incorporated into definitions yield the following:

A. quality of the order of the Real corresponds to the intensity ratio of an Atom freely manifesting its Presence, and

B. quality in the Now is a facet of intensity as manifested, and grasped by an Outsider or by the manifesting Atom.

To use an inadequate but useful simile, quality in the Real reflects the whole diamond and in the Now, the perceived glow of a single facet.

3. Range of Qualities in the Universe: Univerqualities and Indiviqualities

Structure-wise, the theory of quality here advanced has much in common with that of Boyle. Where the latter speaks of two categories, the primary and secondary, the other speaks of universal and individual qualities. However, while the classifications coincide the contents correspond only marginally. One could say that the intuition is similar, but that the conclusions differ. This is explained by the fact that Boyle, Locke, etc., deal with quality as a concept, whereas Existential Atomism, by providing the researcher with an object, the Atom, allows him to analyze it as it operates *in* each individually. Stated otherwise, quality is as much of the essence of the Atom as Power or Existence. Quality is inneal and an in-depth analysis of its nature and operation bares the structure of the Atom.

The distinction between universal and individual qualities is a corollary of the conjugation of a univocal raw material: Existence-Power within a strict atomicity: The Existential-Atom.

A universal quality characterizes all Atoms. By such, everyone in every situation is bound, from The Absolute down to the most insignificant elementary particle. Of these there are only five. An individual quality is any manifestation of the Real not shared universally, even though it may be detectable over a broad band of the existential spectrum, e.g. sex. Individual qualities are numberless, since each mind can observe and create them at will. For purposes of semantic economy each category is hereafter referred to as an univerquality and an indiviquality.

As the term implies, an indiviquality is the antithesis of an univerquality, but to an extent only. At first reading this may sound contradictory. How can something be antithetic and yet not be? The contradiction vanishes when one observes that while every indiviquality is not common to all Existents simultaneously, yet all are endowed with some. The concept of indiviqualities corresponds closely to that of individuality as predicated of man, of the higher primates and to a degree of the animates generally. The term individuality, while conceivably suitable, was not chosen to guard against all taint of anthropocentricity, Dynamic Vision being neither man, nor even life-centered. Its use would lead to ambiguity and/or would tend to overemphasize man's minor role in the Cosmos. By our 20th century ethic this would constitute discrimination — a sin to be avoided at all costs.

A final observation. The subject of philosophy being Existence and Power and the radicals directly related to either, it may be argued that only univerqualities should be considered, and that the study of indiviqualities should be left to sciences such as physics or sociology. Granted, subject to one proviso. Indiviqualities as a group and distinct from an indiviquality observed in isolation, constitute a universal category — that which provides the basis of *de facto* existential individuation. As such they are a proper field of inquiry for the philosopher. Specifically, the inquiry into indiviqualities will be limited to the universal and epistemological; the latter being further restricted to the dynamics of perception.

4. **Univerqualities: Five in Number**

In accord with the Principle of the Proportionality of Extremes, univerqualities are few. While the qualitative lends itself to minutization or diffusive analysis, only five candidates qualify for the title. These are: unicity, intensity, miscibility, freedom and efficiency. The first three classify as prime and the fourth and fifth as derivative. To fulfil the role of univerquality the candidate must satisfy two conditions:

A. be universally detectable, and

B. partake of the qualitative.

These conditions, since the univerquality represents an analytically derived facet of quality and prior to this of the Existential-Atom, imply that each of the five be constitutive both of the Atom and of quality as such.

The universality of the five radicals is self evident. That of unicity goes without saying — oneness being a *sine qua non* of existential individuation. The same applies to intensity and to miscibility, both of which were dealt with earlier. This leaves freedom and efficiency to be considered. Both can be peremptorily disposed of. Once one observes that each derives from unicity and intensity respectively, their cosmicity follows.

The qualitativity of the five radicals is not as readily established. A complex issue, its demonstration may furthermore be faulted on the ground of circularity, the definition of quality being compounded from intensity, unicity and freedom. Closer scrutiny reveals, not circularity, but rather analysis, and surely a proper definition can be analytical. To define an automobile through its prime characteristics — those of a vehicle, motorized and set on wheels — offers by far the most useful definition. Any other, in particular one based upon the principle of exclusivity, can never portray as much. Indeed, the best in the matter of definitions outside of analysis is description. Actually, the position adopted is at once sound epistemologically and faithful to the subject: the Atom. Since Existence, Truth and Reality are synactive and predicated upon oneness and since a part must partake of the inneity of the whole, the objection of circularity relying upon the fact that the elements of an analytical definition evidence characteristics identical to those of the defined, is voided.

5. Extremes, Second Universal Principle, Unitive and Qualitative

Before proceeding to establish the qualitativity of the five radicals a farreaching observation must be made. Quality as partaker of Power and Existence and thus universal, is not subject to as many principles as there are Atoms, phenomena and events, but rather to a single principle of a magnitude equal to its own, the Second Universal Principle: that of the more-or-less or Extremes. For the following reasons, Extremes will not be dealt with as extensively as was the Principle of Absolutes. Firstly, its mechanism is simple; secondly as opposed to Absolutes, Extremes should not give rise to controversy; and thirdly, whatever complexities it does present are of the Perceived and therein are connected to the relational whose minutiae fall under the wing of other disciplines.

Just as the paternity of Absolutes could with certainty be laid upon the doorstep of Individuation-Truth, the sire of Extremes is beyond doubt Power. Hence its role in the universal economy is major: the regulation of all energy processes. Extremes reads:

The state of the Universe is one of tension.

Among the many names available to describe the Second Principle, two stand out: Maximization and Extremes. Neither excludes the other, and either would be effective. The choice of Extremes can be considered as a concession to man's anthropocentricity. Extremes should be more readily accepted than would maximization, for everyone visualizes extremes as the intensity of the Self constantly fluctuates, as, for instance, between drowsiness and sleep, between love and hate, or between Quebec City and Montreal. A further advantage militates in behalf of Extremes. Since the Second Universal Principle begets the Second Universal Law: that of Extremes, and since the latter is the key to Now relationality, a common terminology is preferable.

The relevance of Extremes to quality, is that whereas Absolutes is root of the Real and Truth, Extremes contributes the calibration and modal diversification factors to the Universe. Any conflict of interest between the diversification factor inherent in Absolutes and that contributed by Extremes is only apparent, since Reality rests in the As-is, and a paradox which seemingly arises from an analysis, is the result of the degeneration or diffraction which attends an attempt to break-up that which, as the Real, is unitary. Since calibration is synonymous with quality, or alternately, since quality reduced to its bare essentials, equals calibration, no further investigation of Extremes as Principle need be conducted. To establish the qualitative character of the radicals of the Atom, it suffices to conciliate its imperatives with those of the First Principle, Absolutes.

The qualitative character of the five radicals is not equally evident. That miscibility, intensity and efficiency represent quality in every sense is hardly open to question. On the other hand, the qualitativity of unicity and freedom is by no means patent. Even though the link between unicity and quality is the more difficult to establish it will be tackled first, for it carries the highest ontological content, and any findings in its behalf apply, at least indirectly, to the remaining four.

The best method by which to measure the quality content of unicity is through an analysis of calibration. This reveals that while quality is multihued, as when colors or tastes are gauged, still, regardless of its category, it always involves calibration. To observe as distinct from to experience quality, has one purpose: to calibrate either as to selfness or relationship. It follows that the more universal the standard of calibration, the closer to a oneness it becomes. Here, it is argued that the absolute or unique is a fit yardstick of calibration and differentiation. Stated otherwise, a quality which merges into the absolute, provided that it continues to serve as a calibrative tool, retains its character. *The absolute and qualitative, far from being incompatible, are synactive.* Once quality is reduced to a calibration factor, the qualitative content of unicity is well on its way to being demonstrated. I say well on its way, for due to its dryness the notion of unicity would by some, even when observed as calibrating, not be recognized as a qualifying factor. The difficulty is due to a case of overkill. Unicity being the root itself of calibration, its role is discounted. However, when the issue is assessed globally, it becomes clear that it is an Atom's unicity which sets it apart from the remainder of the Cosmos. In a word, *unicity, the prime quality, encompasses all secondary qualities, calibrating them simultaneously and indiscriminately.* The problem and its answer can be stated succinctly as follows: unicity lies at the root of discernability.

For the argument in favor of the qualitativity of freedom, one must transfer from discernability to the other end of the existential spectrum: that of the assertive or still of aggression. There, freedom reveals itself as a prime factor of self-realization. Hence, for the same reason and by the same modality as applied to unicity, namely that of absoluteneity, freedom, essence of the dynamic, becomes pregnant of all secondary qualities, all indiviqualities. Before one can be hot, red, naked or intelligent one must be free; must inalienably possess such attributes. Only then can these be manifest. To be free implicates not only the dynamic and qualitative, but also an invincible link to the Real, as this is owned in all of its manifestations by the Atom. It follows that, as unicity represents the ultimate in discernable calibration, so does freedom denote the ultimate in dynamic calibration.

As noted, the qualitativity of the other three univerqualities: miscibility, intensity and efficiency is of a somewhat self-evident nature. To be miscible presupposes an aptitude which, as the two previous, oozes from the core of Reality, for miscibility, on the one hand is attributable to each Atom, and on the other makes possible cosmic immanence and relationality. While miscibility as such does not calibrate, it nonetheless rates as a prime quality: that of being relationable. In other words, miscibility derives its qualitative character from the fact that without it calibration is impossible. The qualitativity of intensity and efficiency can be assessed according to the same parameters, the latter being intensity in a human setting. That intensity, the fact of "being more or less", speaks of quality, verges on the truism. To manifest a heightened degree of any given attribute is to presentialize; to force ones personality upon the Outside, and of necessity this is accomplished through the agency of individual powers. In turn the idea of efficiency conceptualizes the quality whereby men mindfacture and calibrate the Antropocities which inhabit their personal universes. Even by the standards of evolutive ontologies, efficiency, due to its comparativity content, rates as qualitative and universal. To affirm, "It is efficient", in respect to an Obscure-Absolute or Antropocity, proclaims at once its qualities and impact upon its surroundings. To the objection that the word, if unpredicated, is meaningless, the answer is: on the contrary, in its unpredicated form, efficiency attains an universal status, and thereby fulfils the criteria of a genuine univerquality — that of being full of the secondary qualities of its predicate. Clearly, a prerequisite of a sound ontology is that its key components and norms apply *mutatis mutandis* to every Atom and situation. Efficiency conforms to the rule.

6. **Role of Univerqualities Within the Existential-Atom**

What of the status and role of univerqualities in the universal economy? Jointly they provide an X-ray picture of the Atom observed in its dual personality of a One-Intense and a Free-Efficient. Of the five, three: unicity, intensity and miscibility, are prime. To evidence all three is to present oneself before the Other as a One-Intense, as a maximized person. The distinction of prime and derived between unicity and freedom, flows from the observation that unicity is self-sufficient in that it partakes of the ontological, whereas freedom requires the presence of an univocal entity, and has its root in the qualitative. In other words, freedom predicates a something which can be free: namely the unique. The same reasoning applies to the prime-derived relationship between intensity and efficiency. Intensity describes a fulness of power, and rests initially in the Real, whereas efficiency speaks of the more-or-less or of a perceived relationship. Where perception is involved ethics also become a factor. Thus, while the primes are the proper of the maximized Atom, and are present in the Perceived incidentally and after a fashion, the two derived univerqualities pertain to the Perceived and reveal the free and efficient character of all Atoms.

A further distinction holds between these four and miscibility. The four are qualities of the Atom as Atom, whereas miscibility is eminently relational. Without miscibility meaningful relationships are impossible — a fact which seems to elude many philosophers. Two units of rigid (signated) "matter" — dimensioned and radically isolated — can, at best, entertain crude kinetic relationships much as those of marbles in a bag. The incoherence of such a situation, when transposed upon a cosmic theatre, is transparent. The problems which it poses and the consequent perennial debate between Idealists and Materialists, with the painful sight of either resting their arguments upon a time-space medium in which, hopefully, through some *legerdemain*, a measure of immanentizing relationship can be established, is evidence enough of something amiss in the conventional four dimension time-space continuum. The concept of an univocal and qualitative One-Intense, resident of an adimensional Cosmos, by eradicating all dichotomy and rigid dimensions from the Real, ends the "idea-matter" war. Further, the One-Intense places before the philosopher an entity full of itself and the Other. The import of this statement will become clearer in the next chapter when cosmic relationality is analyzed.

To sum up, the five univerqualities play a two-fold role. Firstly, they provide an X-ray picture of the Existential-Atom. This is presented in the form of a graph in the last section of this chapter. The second, a corollary of the first, is that together the five unite the Real with the Perceived or still bind fact to process, to thereby operate the third metamorphosis. Metaphorically speaking, when used as analytical tools, the univerqualities reveal the Atom's Jekyll and Hyde personalities, for whereas the previous metamorphoses involved a unitary development, with the Atom putting on the same plumage at both Orders, in the third, the One-Intense has the Free-Efficient as its counterpart in the Now.

7. Enter the Free-Efficient, Third Metamorphosis at the Order of the Perceived

The prime particle or existent has undergone a progressive fleshing. From a nondescript Existential-Atom, lost in the multitudinous myriads of the X in the Universal Equation, it next graduated to the status of a self-willed Dynamic-Fact capable of aggression and self-realization. Upon transmuting into a quality-laden One-Intense it provided us with a glimpse into its ultimate state of a Cosmic-Presence, because It which is dynamic, qualitative and maximized rests in the plenitude of its own and of the Other's flesh. Already, of it one can affirm that it is flesh of the flesh of the Universe. However, a One-Intense resides eerily distant in the Real, without past or future — quite out of reach of mortals who lay great store upon imagination and the senses and this failing, must resort to analysis. It is at this stage that the univerqualities come to the rescue. Imagination, because it operates through sight, touch or hearing focuses only upon indiviqualities and can play no role in an investigation of the Atom as such. The situation differs in respect to analysis, for it operates through absolutes, each universal in scope. The analysis of quality, for instance, revealed five universal qualities, two of which are time and space oriented, namely freedom and efficiency. Without detracting from the concept of a One-Intense, a proper structuring of the univerqualities can therefore outline the Atom's skeleton and shed a light upon its behavior, penetrating enough to allow us to understand our Now personality : that of a Free-Efficient. A restructuring and summary interpretation will suffice to illustrate the above, for to materialize the Free-Efficient nothing new need be added to the data already accumulated. The task will consist of placing in correct focus each univerquality, to then assess its role and operation within the Atom. Literally, one will decode the Atom because, together, the five are constitutive of it. An adequate simile would be to refer to the result as an X-ray of the prime particle.

8. An X-Ray of the Prime Particle or Atom

After the fact, the decoding of the Existential-Atom appears deceptively simple. The key was the assumption, followed by a physical demonstration, that each Existent is a strict entity, and it follows that any object-subject relationship is grounded in the physical. In a word, the question of Monism versus Atomism, had to be solved. Next, the prime components of the Existent had to be determined. This was resolved through the synactivity of Existence with Power, and the consequent metamorphizing of the Atom into a factual and adimensional motor. Once the facticity and synactivity of Power and Existence, and by devolution that of unicity and intensity, were established it became possible to delineate the respective roles of the unique and intense within the Atom, as and when the latter bathes in the Now. At that point the pivotal role of quality revealed itself. It acts as the common denominator, the adhesive which reunifies the several elements and radicals which analysis yields. One could also refer to it as the channel through which all processes flow. In particular it explains how each of us resides, at once in a universe of Parmenidean as-isness, beyond time-space, and in our exiguous mindfactured universes. The norms uniformly applicable to the private universes, are set by the two derived univerqualities : freedom and efficiency. Coinciding with the individuality inherent in the parcel of the Real possessed by each Atom, these account for the indiviqualities, time and space being but two of the more prominent. To resort to imagery, unicity fathers freedom, for the inalienably one is truly free, and intensity mothers efficiency, for it which is operative and bound by extremes, is by definition more-or-less effective. The off-spring is the Dynamic-Fact or Motor — free and efficiency-minded. Alternately it can be said that the homogenization of the two synacts with their four univerqualities engenders the Free-Efficient.

Since "one picture is worth a thousand words", the following graph can be used to advantage to illustrate the relationship between the Real and the Perceived. In it the symbol: ←——→ indicates synactivity, and ←——→ (with arrows converging on Q), signifies that "Q" (quality) is constitutive of, rather than common to, whatever synacts are involved. Letting "Q" = quality, this means that quality in the synactive graph of Existence to Power, and of oneness to intensity is of both, but would be of or in neither if not resident in or possessed by both pairs. The passage from the free-willed efficiency of an individual, time-space universe to the real Universe of as-isness is effected through absoluteneity, i.e. at absolute-speed. Absoluteneity does not appear in the graph, for it is modal and relational and not of the Atom as such. The same remark holds for aggression. Both are corollaries of the Principles of Clash and Absolutes respectively. If one should wish to situate them, aggression *qua* time-space should be located in the lower half and absoluteneity in the upper half. The purpose of the graph, however, is primarily to show the relationship between the Atom's radicals. It is, in other words, an X-ray picture and not a process or flow-chart.

Even a summary glance reveals the chasm which separates the Dynamic Vision theory of quality from other theses and, in particular, from the most broadly accepted, the Boyle-Locke notion of primary and secondary qualities. While, for instance, both theories speak of five prime or universal qualities, the Boyle-Locke primary qualities of extension (size), form (shape), solidity (impenetrability), motion or rest and number, serve primarily to describe external features of "things", i.e. of Antropocities or mindconstructs. In a word, such a theory does little more than to formalize any standard dictionary definition. On the other hand, as the graph clearly shows, in the schema here offered, quality resides at the very heart or core of the Atom or particle, at once binding and explaining its radicals and their relationship. Existence itself becomes a qualitative exercise and the Universe, a sum of Qualitative — Facts.

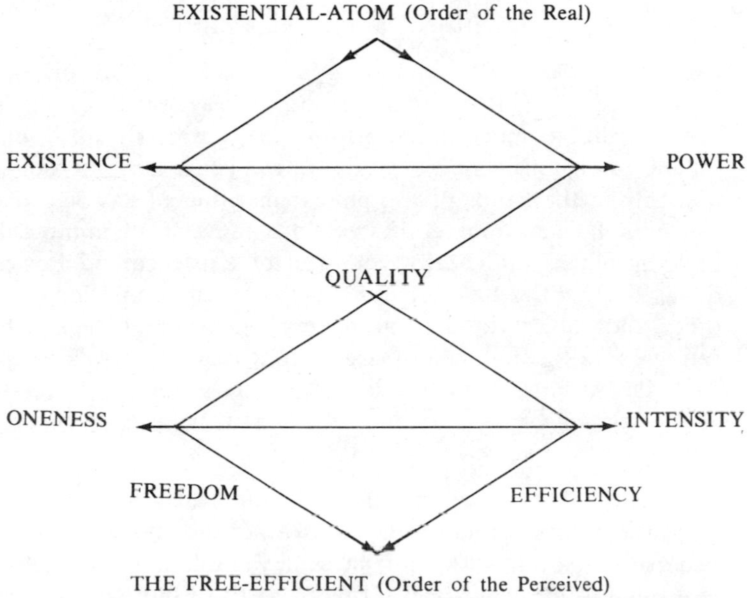

EXISTENTIAL-ATOM (Order of the Real)

EXISTENCE POWER

QUALITY

ONENESS INTENSITY

FREEDOM EFFICIENCY

THE FREE-EFFICIENT (Order of the Perceived)

Or the Existential-Atom as perceived through the veil of time-space.

* * *

The appearance upon the ontological landscape of the Free-Efficient makes it possible to formulate existential problems and set up solution-yielding equations. The discovery that each Existent equals an absolute placed ontology in the same favored position as that of mathematics. Now the Atom's synacts and univerqualities reveal its geometry. From the interplay of these and of the Universal Principles, can be drawn the laws which regulate the interaction of Free-Efficients — the code according to which existential-equations are constructed and resolved. This Code, consisting of two Principles and five Laws, is set-out and briefly commented upon in chapter II of Part V.

At this point the Universal Equation can be reformulated. Substituting (F ⟷ E) for the original (E : A), this now reads :

$U = X(F \longleftrightarrow E)$ where,

U = Universe,

X = a fixed but indeterminate number, and

$F \longleftrightarrow E$ = an efficient agent. (Free-Efficient)

Outwardly, the new formulation seems to alter the original $U = X(E:A)$ slightly. Indeed nothing existential is added or substracted. Nonetheless, the data in the $(F \longleftrightarrow E)$ substituted for the ambiguous concept of $(E:A)$, can prove a useful tool — not only in the hands of the philosopher, but of any scientist. Further, the intuitions contained in a universe of immutable building blocks, univocally endowed of Existence and Power, qualitatively different, each free, each corresponsible for every other and subject to the parameters of cosmic efficiency, by rationalizing Reality makes possible contemporary man's escape from the Absurd, from the dismal, evanescent world of relativating relationships — whether of Marxist, Bergsonian or even Teilhardian vintage.

Finally, the concept of the Free-Efficient allows man to discern the basic structure of his own personality. If objective, this realization that we are all of a same flesh should cause him to lose some of his arrogance, a characteristic of our age, *vis-a-vis* the lowly ones — the fleas, hogs, waters and hydrogens. However, the dignity or more accurately the superiority complex lost on the "downside", is more than compensated for on the "upside", as his reach extends into the Absolute, to cement his kinship to The Almighty. The impact of the univerqualities and the Free-Efficient upon science in general, as distinct from the restricted sphere of human behavior is no less farreaching. Since the univerqualities penetrate deeper into the structure of the Existent than do X-Rays into flesh and bones, and more important, since the five univerqualities are all-encompassing, the coherence which they bring to the social disciplines — to ethics and politics — should be of value to all concerned. In summary the five and their mentor: the Free-Efficient, promote an in-depth understanding of the unity which underlies the Cosmos and binds all sciences. At last, the bifurcated universe, which so exercised A. N. Whitehead, is made whole.

Part III

Cosmic Presence and Relationality

chapter I

Modalities of Cosmic Relationality

Neutrinos are produced in enormous numbers... more than a trillion (10^{12}) passing through every one of us in a second... For neutrinos it is "daylight" around the clock.

Victor GUILLEMIN,
Story of Quantum Mechanics, p. 142

For them (beatified spirits) all things are transparent, and there is nothing dark or impenetrable, but everyone is manifest to everyone internally... For everyone has all things in himself.

PLOTINUS, *Fifth Ennead*

1. Relationy, the Science of Relationality

THE incursion into Existence-Power as fact, nears its end. The Atom having completed its metamorphoses, the books of philosophy and its satraps cosmontology and cosmophysics are closed. Now, one major issue only: relationality, confronts us before the glory of the ultimate state is unveiled — that of being a Cosmic-Presence. The subject, of prime relevance to any ontology, is especially so to Dynamic Vision whose universe is adimensional and formless.

By and large, the scientific community has not granted relationality its proper estate; namely that of an independent discipline. As indicated in Part I, relationality rates this status for being constitutive of Reality, for being inneal, for plunging its roots directly into the physical and for doing so independently from both Power and Existence; to state the case colloquially, for being its own man. This third Part can therefore be considered as a general inquiry into relationships and as the groundwork for this new science, referred to henceforth as relationy. The logic for this innovation will reveal itself. At this stage it suffices to note that relationality's title to the status of a discipline is summarized in the last half of the previous paragraph.

Clearly, an attempt to deal comprehensively with the question of relationships would call for a major work. However, since our objective is restricted to an analysis of a *genus generalissimum*, Existence grasped solely as raw material, it is possible in a relatively brief space to lay the groundwork for the science of relationy, and to introduce the ultimate relationship, cosmic presentiality: the fact that each Atom is a Cosmic-Presence embracing and embraced by every Outsider.

2. Foundationship, Mediumship and Coagentship: General Remarks and Outline

The task of relationy, at the cosmic level, is to provide the data needed to conciliate immanence with transcendence. This can be achieved by breaking down the prime relationship into three master modalities, those of foundationship, mediumship and coagentship, or for short into the "Three Ships". Together these cover the field of the Real. Coagentship furthermore bridges the crossing from the Real into the Now.

The concept of the "Three Ships", it would seem, is exclusive to Dynamic Vision. Granted the evidence in behalf of cosmic interrelatedness is such that most cosmogonies assume and in some cases affirm it. It is for example implicit in this saying of the Upanishads:

> "'I am Brahma'. Whoever knows this, 'I am Brahma' knows all".

Likewise the major theistic creeds, the Judaic, Christian and Moslem, are predicated upon a measure of cosmic relationality, with foundationship, in particular, explicitly affirmed in all three, at least as a one-way process — The Absolute being defined as the ground-of-Being. The orthodox Christians extend cosmicity further, to have it explicitly encompass mankind through the Communion of Saints, as witness this passage from the Nicene Creed:

> The third day He rose again from the dead, He ascended into heaven, sitteth at the right hand of God, the Father Almighty; from thence he shall come to judge the living and the dead. I believe in the Holy Ghost, the Holy Catholic Church, *the Communion of Saints, the forgiveness of sins, the resurrection of the body and life everlasting.* Amen.

Also, one can read it in the scripts — otherwise so foreign to each other — of Leibniz and Spinoza. Among the many contemporary thinkers who have entertained a measure of cosmic relationality (as opposed to an outright Relativism or Becomingism), Teilhard and Whitehead deserve special mention.

An acknowledged familiarity (acquired mostly *post-factum*) with the above and other theories of the same ilk; also a Christian heritage which audaciously proclaims "the resurrection of the body and life everlasting" were without a doubt contributing factors to the theory of the "Three Ships". Nonetheless the theory, considered in its full breadth, could only be derived from a cosmontology premissed upon the fact that each Existent is simultaneously univocal, subsistent, factual, dynamic and formless, and, it follows, coeval and coextensive. Alternately, the "Three Ships" are conceivable only within an ontology whose prime equation reads U=X(D :F), and whose characteristics are dynamism and facticity.

Such a universe enriches, spiritually and technologically. Individually and jointly the "Ships" open upon innumerable and breathtaking vistas. The brotherhood of man extends in every direction. Corresponsibility beyond time-space for a common welfare and self-realization becomes a "fact of life". The human family, outgrown, is now a fellowship, that of Francis of Assisi's cosmic family — our brother wolf and our sister moon, and galaxies beyond. The technical fall-out is equally impressive. Relationships of the order of the "Three Ships" make way for interdisciplinary coherence and provide the solution to many otherwise intractable issues. To give but one example, the inconsistencies and contradictions which plague attempts to explain the relationship of man to his body through hylemorphic or symbiotic processes, are eliminated by the principle of complementarity, a corollary of coagentship.

3. **In a Formless Universe, Relationality is Constitutive of the Real**

In the formless universe of Dymanic Vision relationships assume a critical role. This may surprise, since the One-Intense and his *alter ego* the Free-Efficient, being dimensionless, being a resident of nowhere must appear ethereal and quite incapable of relating with other equally dimensionless Atoms, or if so to little or no purpose. Such a surmise is dispelled by the observation that relationality, when restricted to foundationship, mediumship and coagentship, partakes of the Atom as Atom. The "relationship" of *relationships to the Existent is somewhat of the same order as that of thought. It is physical. Less than fully inneal but more than interfacial, relationality is constitutive of the Real in its mass, and of the Existent in its role of individual.* Even constitutivity conveys poorly the phenomenon at play, for the mystery of the Fact-of-to-be hinges upon and flows through relationality. Possibly the line can be drawn more finely if said to pass between constitutivity and coevality. Or one might speak of the point at which self-realization and corresponsibility conjugate. Also helpful would be Jasper's notion of "the locus of dialogue".

In a formless, cosmically-oriented ontology all major tenets contribute to and converge upon the type of relationality implied in the "Ships". Among the lot, two can be singled out, for both carry a high content of the relational. The first is adimensionality. *Each Atom, because a resident of "the nowhere in particular", automatically occupies the Universe, to literally rest upon and bathe in every other.* The second, equally relevant, is the Free-Efficient character of the Atom. It which is free and efficient has all its neighbors as coagents. A multiplicity of other factors also participate, but the interplay of these two coordinates, mainly, accounts for the complementary relationships of foundation, medium and coagent.

The affirmation that each Existent serves as foundation for every other is not a figure of speech. *Literally each is an integral component of the cosmic mass. Each requires the presence of all the Its-which-are upon which to rest* — exactly, but with infinitely more intimacy, than a house upon a foundation. For example, if you are to-be-It-which-you-in-fact-are, you require the presence of every Existent, of every human and copper — each copper which inhabits Sirius inclusively. Foundation-wise, every Atom in the "X" of the Cosmic Equation, is a platform without which any other cannot be. The same literal interpretation applies to mediumship. Every Existent which existed, does and will exist — is to each a physical medium exactly as water in a fish bowl is to the two goldfish darting in it. Finally, *coagents are we all, man to virus, iron atom to omega-minus, cat to neutrino and angel, beyond time and space*, each more or less intensely; with the result that some Atoms we look upon as "our body", and others as the "body of our lover". Conceptualization as well as analogy have no meaning where the "Ships" are concerned. Each involves physical contact, and describes an objective and factual relationship.

Briefly, the distinctions between the "Three", are the following. Coagentship, which embraces intensity and specificity, is of a separate order. As eminently relational as foundationship and mediumship, it differs in that it reaches into and partakes of individuation. Also, at the Now, coagentship accounts for the "birth" of the Antropocities, and for the sense of selfness.

The demarcation line between foundationship and mediumship is more subtle. Further, this demarcation holds only at the Now. At the Real, the two blend. The foundation relationship, of an *upon* nature, is ontologically directed, whereas the medium relationship is of a *through-which* nature. Pre-eminently relational, mediumship unifies the Existence-Power synact, and acts as the transmission line or homogenizing agent between the foundation and coagency factors. A second distinction intrudes between the two. Now foundationship implies aggression, a reaching-out, a domination. Nor is agression cancelled-out when two or more Atoms additivate or cooperate. Even when both parties willingly serve as foundation, the aggression in foundationship persists. Mediumship, on the other hand, is passive. It speaks of an inherent harmony, of cosmic concord and immanence. The importance of this will reveal itself fully when aggression is analyzed in *Cosmic Jurisprudence*. Applied schematically to man — somewhat after the fashion of the preview to a movie — the "Ships" reveal the human "body" (as distinct from the human atom) to consist of a knot of high intensity relationships, through which man imposes himself upon certain Outsiders more powerfully than upon others, and thus presentializes himself. However, the "body" is privileged over the universe of Antropocities only as to intensity, as to its degree of coagentship with its owner. It has no existence as such, and no limits save those imposed arbitrarily through the mind's absolutizing. Erroneously conceived of by most as owned, it is a mere privileged Antropocity. Every Atom throughout the Universe, serves man simultaneously as foundation, medium and coagent. Indeed, some (oxygens, hydrogens, etc.), being more essential to survival, constitute truer coagents than hair or limb— a fact which the proudly possessive human animal hates to admit.

While the detail of the above is novel, a state akin to it is implicit in the findings of nuclear physics, as witness this text of H. Guillemin, dealing with the behavior of neutrinos.

> Neutrinos are produced in enormous numbers... more than a trillion (10^{12}) passing through everyone of us in a second... but since a person probably does not absorb more than one in a lifetime, they have no effect whatsoever. For neutrinos it is "daylight" around the clock; it might be said that for them the earth is like a sphere of clearest crystal.[1]

If cosmic relationality is but implicit in the contemporary physicist's text, seventeen centuries ago, Plotinus, the mystical philosopher, explicitly conveyed, albeit in poetic terms, its grandeur.

> For everyone has all things in himself and sees all things in another; so that all things are everywhere and all is all and each is all, and the glory is infinite. Each of them is great, since the small also is great. In heaven the sun is all the stars, and again each and all are the sun. One thing in each is prominent above the rest; for it also shows forth all. There a pure movement reigns; but that which produces the movement, not being a stranger to it, does not trouble it. Rest is also perfect there, because no principle of agitation mingles with it.[2]

Even a summary survey of the individual "Ship" reveals its mechanism and validates the theory of a cosmic relationship. Nonetheless the data which follows is intended to provide basic insights only. Since, together existential individuation and cosmic relationality encompass the Real, the remainder of this work in effect deals with the question. An individual analysis of the three modes of relationality can be considered as the counterpart of the prerequisites of individuation, namely as key instruments for the decoding of the Atom.

4. **Foundationship**

Of the three, the encounter with foundationship will be the briefest, for while the subject does present a major difficulty, once this is disposed of, the remainder follows. The difficulty is the same as that which attended the adimensionality of the Atom. In a word, success depends upon a willingness to do violence to

1. Victor GUILLEMIN, *The Story of Quantum Mechanics*, New York, Charles Scribner's & Sons, 1968, p. 142.
2. PLOTINUS, fifth *Ennead*, in Victor Gollancz, A Year of Grace, London, Camelot, 1950, p. 471.

the senses and to transcend the dimensioned and temporal, as well as the concept of restricted causality. In particular, it requires the ability to distinguish between the Obscure-Absolute or real man and the conglomerate or Antropocity, of which a human body or chair are examples.

This achieved, the mechanism of foundationship becomes self-evident for it only implies extending to the Cosmos, an intimately familiar relationship: that of needing others upon which to stand. For instance, the ground upon which we walk, our beds, our shoes, all serve as foundations; as do also the air and food which we ingest — for "support from the inside". Effectively to observe foundationship as cosmic, is to note the reciprocal character of relationships, and to extend reciprocity to the point of immanence, where it achieves cosmicity, embracing all That-which-is-real.

As indicated, the trademark of foundationship and the feature which distinguishes it from mediumship, is aggression. Here are in brief the factors responsible for this characteristic. Foundationship arises from the need for others to rest upon which each non-absolute Atom experiences. Such a condition constitutes an insatiable appetite, and appetites, even if the devoured offers of itself willingly, imply aggression, because whether of not the support and succor sought are proferred:

A. the intent to aggress is present, and

B. the seeker cannot refrain from his quest, for his existence depends upon his ability to impose himself.

Many relevant issues can be raised, as witness those involving will-power, free-will, perfectibility and the complex nature of the foundationship provided by The Absolute, etc. Presently, they are only noted, since all are more properly dealt with in *Cosmic Jurisprudence*.

Succinctly, *foundationship is the relationship which an Atom establishes, when as a subsistent, independent entity it reaches towards the Outsiders, and in its quest for self-realization and/or survival, imposes its will upon them.* Thus *foundationship, at the Now, explains aggression.* Colloquially speaking, foundationship has each of us saying to each other: "Come here; I need you, and like it or not, I will have you."

5. Mediumship

The concept of mediumship extending beyond time-space, while novel, is simple. Nothing more is required to act as medium, save that *one be* — that one should partake of the Real. While, in the Now, foundationship involves aggression and will-power and may be to a degree refused, mediumship involves presence only and is passively and inexorably altered by every whim of every Being. One cannot refuse to serve as a medium, yet paradoxically mediumship speaks of freedom. An inescapable corollary of adimensionality, it merely notes the fact that the dimensionless and dynamic bathes and is bathed in every Existent.

A cautionary remark is in order. Here medium does not refer to an ethereal fluid or substance similar to the luminiferous ether postulated in the 19th century by Fresnel and others. *The medium is in and of the adimensional Atom itself, and mediumship is, if a physical description is to be attempted, best described as in the nature of the substratum of a magnetic field.* A distinction between the field and its substratum is drawn, for a specific field partakes of coagentship. As in all situations involving cosmicity, a satisfactory terminology is hard to come by. Presently, it seems, no other word in English conveys the concept as effectively. More closely related to the vocabulary of physics than of philosophy, the term "medium" carries a high content of dynamism, and readily associates with the cosmic. Additionally, together the two speak the language of Dynamic Vision. The philosophical concept closest to mediumship is that of immanence, a trait graphically depicted by the simile of a bath and bathing. The connection between immanence and mediumship and the imagery of a bath may appear remote, and a concession to anthropocentricity. We shall discover shortly that such imagery portrays the real thing accurately, and serves philosophy well.

While mediumship is verbalized only with difficulty, the physical phenomenon which it represents can be faithfully reproduced in simple experiments. An example involves substituting an air-tight cage, four feet all around, for the Universe and three fruit flies for the sum of Atoms. Upon being introduced into said cage any of the three would, by its flight, disturb the relationship of the gas molecules and dust particles, and it would be accurate to say that it was fashioning a medium to its liking. To simplify the process further, one can view the dust and gas molecules as homogenized to the consistency of a neutral medium. Again, should only one of the three subjects be released, its every movement modifies the pressure patterns throughout the cage, and in its solitude, it owns the entire cage medium. If next her sister flies are released in her company, each can rightfully claim the entire flight-medium. Yet there is still but one medium — one now common to all three. *Insofar as mediums go, we have a perfect case of "to each his own and to no one anything", for each fly with every stroke of its wings, alters at once its own flight medium and that of its mates, both of which reciprocate, with the result that none of the three can lay claim to a medium, neither in time nor space, and yet each does possess its private medium. In effect, we are presented with a demonstration of the compatibility of radical immanence with equally radical transcendence.*

Faced with this dilemma, the practitioner of pure logic and the Materialist, are left with no alternative, save to affirm that "there was no medium in the first place", since none can be dimensionally ascribed to a specific fruit fly — that which no one can call his own, cannot, in a universe of dimensioned "matter", be considered as real, as "there". At this point, the difficulties of visualization created initially by the fact that Existential-Atoms are not only smaller than tiny flies, but are without dimensions, aver themselves non-difficulties, and indeed come to rationalize a physical situation which in other universes remains paradoxical, often irrational.

The conversion of the inconveniences presented by adimensionality into a positive contribution to science is achieved simply. If, instead of centering the attention upon dimensioned flies, the notion of a localized or "material cause" is abandoned and the three mediums are seen as engendered by three dimensionless Dynamic-Facts of the type discovered at the time of the second metamorphosis, *the problem* of what belongs to whom, where and when *vanishes. There is still one medium for each of the three motors known as fruit flies, each altered coevally with the two others, with the result that the three are one and the one is triune. Each dimensionless fly creates its own medium in total simultaneity with, and yet in total independence (freedom) of the other two.*

The "picture" which emerges pleases. Where the Materialist sees isolation, alienation and selfishness eternally perpetuated behind "bodies" or in steel vaults, mediumship opens wide the cosmic window, revealing on the one hand, the mechanism which guarantees the innate freedom of each Atom, and on the other, witnesses to the corresponsibility of each to each.

By themselves, these two features seem to vouchsave for the coherence of Dynamic Vision. Only within its context can personal freedom and social responsibility be simultaneously entertained, and in final analysis, these loom larger upon the scale of values than do arbitrary concepts such as space or "matter". Certainly, the socially conscious, given a choice between his inalienable freedom and cosmic corresponsibility on the one hand, and "dimensioned matter" and the fences of all types which time-space builds on the other, would opt for the former — for liberty and love. The substitution of love for corresponsibility may surprise. To do so, is to anticipate, yet this seems justified, since an insight is thereby provided into the farreaching impact of existential univocity and the concomitant miscibility of Power. Corresponsibility, we shall discover, transmutes into love when there is intellectual understanding, as between humans or humans and dogs.

It is not necessary to dwell upon moral values to discern the plausability of mediumship. One has but to consider the Materialist, wrestling with the physical dilemmas inherent in his vision. For instance, he who believes in a dimensioned prime particle, when attributing the ownership of the mediums generated by the latter or by fruit flies, finds himself in an intolerable position. To begin with, there is the question of the whereat — where does each medium begin? At the "center" of the particle or brain of the fly? A second dilemma arises when the hapless Materialist attempts to causally allot to each fly, its share of the sixty-four cubic feet of space encompassed by the cage. Thirdly, how can three dimensioned individuals, particle or fly simultaneously alter a single spatial container? To these questions and many more Materialism offers no coherent answer.

While the mystery of the coevality of a universe of Outsiders is not evacuated by mediumship, its mechanism at least is accounted for. Once each Dynamic-Fact, *genus Drosophila* possesses in fee simple its portion of Existence and Power, the interplay of its flight pattern, now dimensionless but nonetheless physical, offers no greater problem than that of two hands, one upon the other, and used to press upon a third object such as a table. The latter highlights intensity, while in the former, flux and fluidity predominate. Granted, when extended to encompass the Cosmos, wherein trillions of quadrillions of quintillions of Existents play, the complexity, the mystery in mediumship seems mind-shattering. Such a reaction, while normal, has no scientific basis. Once allowance is made for the distortion-factor in scale models, medium-wise, the relationship of flies in a cage corresponds to that which the commonwealth of the Atoms entertain. Sheer weight of numbers does not abrogate the principle. It merely complicates matters, and while complexity on a cosmic scale is mind-boggling, Reality for all that remains unscathed. What-Is, Is. The mechanism which operates in the four foot cage, operates equally throughout the Universe.

Applying mediumship to man and his "body", whatever held for his relationship of foundation, holds for mediumship. As all reservoirs of Power, that of man bathes all Existents, bar none. Each mineral atom, each cell reciprocates. Yet each retains its identity. The "body", if equated with so many ounces and pounds of this and that mineral, does not belong to the humanoid. Rather, "his body" is a focus of intensity — a human field — upon which a high percentage of his power is exerted, and to which he provides a coagency medium, qualitatively human — all the while maintaining his broader relationship of cosmic medium.

6. Coagentship, General Remarks

Those who felt somewhat at sea when the subject was cosmic foundations and mediums, will no doubt breathe a sigh of relief, for coagentship returns us to the land of man — to the comforting realm of Antropocities or "dimensioned things". The more complex of the three, coagentship is that relationship whereby self-realization is achieved. It describes the fact that each Atom, through intensification, uses a limited number of Outsiders as immediate agents, as agents more actual, more controlled. Its role is major in all aspects of individuation, in particular, those involving quantization, consciousness, and aggression.

A rapport of coagentship is established by concentrating and directing Energy upon a specific target — an Antropocity — to the exclusion, conscious or otherwise, of the remainder of the Universe. The mechanism is simple. It whose power is not absolute finds its field of action restricted to those targets which it can attack with a measure of efficiency. *Coagentship, thus, operates* when and wherever *a relationship occurs between two or more Existents, more intense than the mean.* An effective visualization is that of a knot or bulge of relationships of above average intensity, biceps, for instance. *The terms knot and bulge, in this context, are not metaphorical. All dimensions represent a coagential bulge of relationships, which becomes quantized only when intellectually absolutized.* Closer scrutiny reveals a further structural difference between coagentship and the other two "Ships". The latter were, so to speak, of one piece. Not so with coagentship. An in-depth analysis reveals it in two submodalities, namely objective and subjective coagency. The former operates at the Real and the latter at the Now.

Objective coagency speaks of a *de facto* personal relationship between some Atoms to the quasi exclusion of others, and is a corollary of the limitations of all Existents, save The Absolute. A prime example of objective coagency, is the high intensity rapport which an Atom, be it an enzyme or uranium, entertains with its "body". Subjective coagency arises when a value judgement is placed upon a node, real or imaginary, of objective coagentship. It is aggressive, epistemological and hermeneutic. Theoretically, subjective coagentship could prove neutral. However, in the Now it is invariably resorted to to conquer viz. six men agreeing to form a hockey team to play another. The perception and defining of a chair also constitutes applied coagentizing.

7. **Coagentship at the Order of the Real: a Concentration of Power and Immediacy of Presence**

At the Order of the Real all relationships, those of The Absolute inclusively, are coagential, for thereat the ground of phenomena is the Atom, and since each represents a fact and a discernible, its one contact with each Outsider differs intensity and quality-wise. In effect, objective coagentship is a corollary of existential individuation, and can be described in terms of immediacy, specificity and presentiality, for, in final analysis, ones coagency-factor corresponds to the manner in which one presentializes. Observed cosmically, coagentship therefore is objective and as universal as are foundationship and mediumship.

Where coagentship differs radically, especially from mediumship which roots in miscibility, is that it derives from the complex of the individuation radicals: unicity, intensity and quality. Since the latters' corollaries are self-realization and factual complementarity, it is correct to see in coagentship the self-realization factor through which the Atom is "made" and "makes" itself. To all intents and purposes where the intimacy of the relationships borders on the inneal, as within the human "body", those who coagentize engage in mutual self-realization. To illustrate, a man or cat cannot use their power-of-sight if photons are not available for either to impose themselves upon. Vice versa, the photons do not achieve their status of light giving entities, except when said cat or man are available. Again, it is a case of: each to his own and all to everyone.

Here an important precision concerning the meaning of self-realization is called for, to avoid misunderstanding. Self-realization is not to be interpreted in the Becomingist sense, according to which one draws "substance" from the Outside, to therewith build the Self at the expense of ones victims, be these capon, radish, zinc or even man. Self-realization corresponds to a coefficient of facticity or alternately to factual complementarity. Quite simply this means that each of us, in the fulness of our is-ness, and as residents in the Absolute offers himself to every Atom in the Cosmos. Each complements the other, the complementing process being achieved at absolute-speed. We do not cannibalize our neighbors. Instead, each contributes his quota of the Real, of "matter" to the cosmic complex, all communally foundizing, mediumizing and coagentizing. A brief look at the Becoming theory of self-realization, as affirmed in its radical form by Hume, shows its weakness and provides a practical instance of the operation of the principle of factual complementarity. The Hume thesis, one of incipient Nihilism, is clearly outlined in the following classical passage:

> For my part, when I enter most intimately into what I call *myself*, I always stumble on some particular perception or other, of heat or cold, light or shade, love or hatred, pain or pleasure. I never can catch *myself* at any time without a perception, and never can observe anything but the perception... And were all my perceptions removed by death, and could I neither think, nor feel, nor see, nor love, nor hate, after the dissolution of my body, I should be entirely annihilated, nor do I conceive what is further requisite to make me a perfect nonentity... Setting aside some metaphysicians, I may venture to affirm of the rest of mankind, that they are nothing but a bundle or collection of different perceptions, which succeed each other with inconceivable rapidity, and are in perpetual flux and movement... The mind is a kind of theatre, where several perceptions successively make their appearance; pass, repass, glide away, and mingle in an infinite variety of postures and situations.

To avoid protracted controversy, a simple question can be placed before the advocates of the Humian and related hypotheses: if Hume is but a "bundle of perceptions" (actually having denied his own strict atomicity, Hume has no right whatsoever to refer to an "I"), which "perception", each of which "succeed each other with inconceivable speed", is having the "bundle of perceptions"? Who, in other words, originates the percepts of smell, pleasure, hurt, colors and sensations generally? To the above, Becomingism, regardless of its variant, offers no answer other than that of perpetual flux — answer which any intelligent, "philosophically unperverted" eighteen year old would scorn. The debate of ontological process and evolution versus as-isness and complementarity is central to philosophy. Reduced to its basics it becomes a question of accountability and intellectual honesty. If the latter is to be maintained, the evolutionary process whether Aquinian, Humian, Whiteheadian or other must be abandoned. By substituting for evolution, coagency and the complementing of each by every other on the basis of an instantaneous process, the universe is rationalized. Then, photon and man still make each other, but not as "making" is understood by the Becomingist. Complementarity, achieved at absolute-speed, operates. Each becomes responsible for either being what it is. Simultaneously each gets credit for his contribution. The reader, for instance, is promoted from the demeaning status of a "bundle of perceptions" to that of a One-Intense, utterly qualitative, subsisting in a state of maximal intensity. His relationship with the Outsiders is of absolute to absolute. *The process, still with us, becomes an absolute-speed process, between adimensional-motors.*[3]

In summary, objective coagentship speaks of self-realization, through complementarity. Fully as universal as are foundationship and mediumship, it differs from either in that it considers intensity and quality ratios. Whereas the former account for immanence, objective coagentship speaks of that which is often described as the transcendental, and explains specialization — the fact that each is a discernible. Morally it is honest, a trait

3. The more profound and coherent of evolutionists are understandably perturbed by the inconsistency of their hypothesis as witness this passage from Teilhard de CHARDIN'S, *Phenomenon of Man*, Wm. Collins & Co., Ltd. London, 1959, p. 171:

> And we are happy to admit that the birth of intelligence corresponds to a turning in upon itself, not only of the nervous system, but of the whole being. What at first sight disconcerts us, on the other hand, is the need to accept that this step could only be achieved *at one single stroke.*
>
> For that is to be my second remark, a remark I cannot avoid. In the case of human ontogeny we can slur over the question at what moment the new-born child may be said to achieve intelligence and become a thinking being, for we find a continuous series of states happening in the same individual from the fertilised ovum to the adult. What does it matter whether there is a hiatus or where it might be? It is quite different in the case of a phyletic embryogenesis in which each stage or each state is represented by a different being, and we have no means at our disposal (at any rate within the scope of modern methods of thought) for evading the problem of discontinuity.

The open admission of an intellectual roadblock such as that presented by "the need"... (to) achieve(d). this step... at one single stroke", which invalidates ones entire work is honorable. That which is not and which indeed verges upon the dishonest is the suggestion that new "methods of thought" might be invented, and worse, that the phyllum, which the author has clearly and repeatedly affirmed to be a concept, might nonetheless solve his dilemma.

> Look at it as we will, we cannot avoid the alternative — either thought is made unthinkable by a denial of its psychical transcendence over instinct, or we are forced to admit that it appeared between two individuals.
>
> The terms of this proposition are disconcerting, but they become less bizarre, and even inoffensive, if we observe that, from a rigorously scientific attitude, nothing prevents us supposing that intelligence might (or even must) have been as little visible externally at its phyletic origin as it is today to our eyes in every new-born child at the ontogenetical stage: in which case every tangible subject of debate between the observer and the theorist disappears.

A more eloquent, albeit left-handed argument, in behalf of the Principle of Absolutes is hard to imagine.

which should recommend it to the natural scientist. Viewed as the relationship of complementarity, it allows for a strict accounting of not only each Atom, but even the most insignificant of events and qualities. Through it, the Law of the Conservation of Energy sits at the highest of tribunals: the cosmic.

8. Coagentship at Order of the Perceived, a Coordinate of Efficiency and Free-Will, is Responsible for Quantity

The basic insights which the concept of coagentship offers at the Real are fundamental and require little elucidation. The obverse applies in the Now. The issues raised, in particular those of quantization, efficiency, clash and conquest, are so complex that they can, in a work of this nature, only be touched upon. Actually, since efficiency, clash and conquest are correlates, the investigation of their connection with Now coagentship will be deferred to the last chapters. Only the broad issue of self-realization in time-space, through coagency, need be considered at this time.

The first question which comes to mind is: how can It-which-is and resides in the Absolute be said to realize or make itself in time and space? Is not Becoming, so vehemently rejected formerly, now surreptitiously reintroduced? The difficulty is apparent. Effectively, self-realization need not, indeed cannot, be equated with Becoming. Becoming predicates the irrational — it being impossible, Aristotle and the senses notwithstanding, for that which is "in potency" or in the "process" of making itself, to be at once "in potency" and for real. Nor does a "progressive or evolutive creation" resolve the dilemma. One does not create in time. As to "substantial change", no matter how subtle, only a philosopher in desperate straits will resort to so blatant a subterfuge. The self-realization referred to has nothing in common with a Sartrian "out of nothing into nothing process". Rather it defines a two level phenomenon. The first, situated in the Real, occurs at absolute-speed. In the Now, the key remains the Principle of Absolutes conjugated, this time, with the Atom's two Now radicals: quality and freedom. As noted in the preceding chapter, quality links the Real and the Perceived. It could even be said that the Atom is a Qualitative-Fact rather than a Dynamic-Fact, for individuation and energy are quality-factors. In such a context coagency and self-realization reveal themselves as functions of quality — thought being a quality. Thus Atoms, which as man or weasel, are endowed with an intellectual quality or power create for their personal consumption a world dressed to their taste. They accomplish this by antropocizing knots of relationships to which are ascribed value, causality and dimensions, etc. Cosmicity in relation to coagentship implies that coagentship is as universal as its partners. *We are each of us, even when immersed in the Now, coagents beyond time-space — exactly as we serve as foundation and medium to every inhabitant of the Cosmos.* Indeed, the distinction between the three "Ships" is purely conceptual, its purpose being to analyze our perception of the variable intensity, the peaks or high-points, of an otherwise total relationship. The nowness in the human "sense of self-realization", results from the combination on the one part, of the sequentializing quality of the intellect, and on the other, of the aggressivity and concomitant freedom which subsumes the Perceived — a freedom in which all Existents participate. Neither the sequential quality nor the aggression-freedom factor changes the fact that we are Cosmic-Presences which self-realize by communing with the Outside. We are what we are, in-fact. What we think and perceive subjectively, does not alter Reality. Time-wise, "we come to observe" — after the fact. The processes which Becomingism equates with ontological self-realization, in particular birth, bodily growth, degeneration and death, merely bear witness to an increase in the basic or objective freedom in which all Atoms partake. Thought, in other words, is an efficiency-factor closely related to free-will.

Since the mechanism of objective freedom was investigated in sections 3 to 7 of chapter VI, Part II, a synopsis will suffice. In a nutshell, objective freedom is a corollary of the Existent being one, dimensionless and non-possessible. This basic freedom, grounded in the As-is, is inviolable. It prevails even against God. It does, however, vary intensity and quality-wise, "within" a given Atom and "between" individuals or species. This graduability flows from the fact that freedom obeys the Principle of Extremes, and participates in the intense and qualitative. Where man is concerned, thought or consciousness renders his freedom more efficient.

The same phenomenon, approached from the relational, yields subjective coagency. Then we encounter the entire panoply of Antropocities — bodies, such as our flesh and blood; things, such as a bed or skyscraper; objectives, such as a rabbit to eat, and value-judgements, such as ones nation or religion. *None of these grow, happen or reveal themselves. Rather, the sequential perceiver, extracting them at absolute speed from the As-is, and simultaneously inserting them into his personal conquest-oriented vision of life, thereby self-realizes. At the Perceived, coagentship, self-realization and consciousness, all intimately linked, are coordinates of efficiency and free-will.*

chapter II

Structure and Location of the Existential-Atom

The highest Seraph has but a single image. He seizes as a unity all that his inferiors regard as manifold.

Meister Eckhart

Although the element of matter has an extent it has no clearly defined outlines... There are no clear edges and every particle in reality covers the entire universe.

Robert Gouiran,
Particles and Accelerators, p. 11.

1. The Existential-Atom as Free-Efficient, Puts on Flesh: Preliminary Considerations

THERE has been much talk of the Real, of Power, of facticity, intensity and quality, etc. Yet, the owner of these attributes, the Atom, it is emphasized, resides outside the normal dimensions of space and time. Worse, it is affirmed that a man's "body" is not his own. As yet, about the only tangible "thing" proferred as participating in the Real, is a punch on the nose with copious bleeding. Nor has the incursion into the field of relationality proven of much comfort, since, then also, the emphasis was on the cosmic and adimensional. To one bred and born within the confines of the reassuring world of measured, "changing matter" wherein causality explains everything, and accustomed to seeing the "body" as owned, as himself, the entire exercise must by now seem eerie. This delay in coming to grips with the tangible was unavoidable. To respect coherence, in any intellectual project, each fact, phenomenon and process, must be dealt with in its proper sequence — in its "time and place". In the present situation, the synactivity of Existence and Power, and the Atom's nature of Free-Efficient had to be both established and analyzed, before a comprehensive picture of a living Existent could be drawn. These prerequisites being satisfied, we can now enter the world of the "body"; we can now tack flesh upon a dessicated, skeletal Existential-Atom.

The present chapter will therefore break no new ground. Rather its contents correspond somewhat to the car manufacturer's assembly of the main frame, in readiness for a subsequent fitting of the accessories, in this instance, in readiness for the final experiment. The key insights garnered to this point will be redeployed in preparation for the third experiment conducted in the coming chapter. Thus its objective is two-fold. Firstly, it seeks to provide a visual picture of a living, yet dimensionless Atom, whether human, ferric, etc. Somewhat incongruously it can be said that in it the dimensionless comes to inhabit time-space. An interesting feature of such an attempt to "locate a citizen of the nowhere" is the discovery that the dynamic facticity and qualitativity of the Atom, as well as its adimensionality are all three confirmed by some of the more recent findings of biochemistry and astrophysics; in particular, by the body structure of enzymes *et al* and the entropy phenomenon. Secondly, the ground is prepared for the above mentioned experiment. In this, the adimensional structure of the Existential-Atom *qua* primary particle, is established by subjecting a cast consisting of a humanoid and orangutan and four representative specimen of the Atoms with which man and monkey have necessary intercourse, namely organelles and primary cells such as macrophages and enzymes, and metalloids such as irons and uraniums, to a process which allocates to each its private area or domain in time-space. To this end, three sections will be devoted to:

A. Reconsider the implications of existential univocity in the light of the coming experiment.
B. Elaborate upon cosmic presentiality, simultaneously establishing its concordance with past views and with micro and macrophysics.
C. Elaborate upon the dynamic facticity of the Atom to establish its character of an adimensional motor while demonstrating that a correct reading of contemporary physiology and physics corroborate such a view.

Epistemologically this chapter answers the questions *what, where* and *who* is an Existential-Atom. The order given to the three classical queries, *what, where* and *who*, may seem unusual, it being customary in any inquiry into identity to deal with the *who* firstly, and only thereafter to proceed to analyze the *what* and *where*. The inversion of precedences is justified by the cosmic character of the subject; also it is consistent with our blueprint and faithful to scientific methodology. Further, the dogmatism inherent in the ascribing of norms, such as "matter" and "substance" to arbitrarily defined units is avoided.

Since the research to this point has dealt with the *what* of the Atom, its determining involves mainly a summarizing to clearly identify the Atom as partaker of the *genus generalissimum*: Existence-Power. This summary will be capped by an insight into the Atom's personality, specifically into its status of a motor, dimensionless and immovable. Technically, when dealing with a cosmic subject, the usual *where* question could be dispensed with as academic. It which is cosmic resides everywhere. Nonetheless the revolutionary implications of existential cosmicity justify some elaboration on modalities. Indeed, in a sense, a knowledge of the whereabouts of the Atom constitutes one of the more difficult feats which faces the student of the Real, and the most rewarding if successful. It is difficult because to forge the link between the cosmic dimension of the Real and the time-space Antropocities which inhabit any Now universe, one has to resolve the master contradiction which haunts philosopher and cosmophysicist — a contradiction clearly set-out in this attempt by Robert Gouiran to situate a primary particle in space:

> There are no clear edges and every particle in reality covers the entire universe, but the probability of finding it is almost entirely confined to a small space.[1]

In other words, to succeed one must transcend the boundaries of the four-dimensioned universe — to enter into the eternity of the nowness of It-which-is and of Truth.

2. Structure of All Existential-Atoms, Animate and Inanimate, Identical

More often than not, philosophers see man as the beginning and end of all. Worse, petty human norms are applied to all research, with the Cosmos itself being reduced to a strictly human enterprise. In the process, any reality which the near-sighted, insensitive human beast cannot see or touch is cavalierly dismissed, either as non-existent or as irrelevant. To guard against this myopic arrogance, the role of *mere unus inter pares*, in the cosmic economy, of *Homo-sapiens* was, from the start, emphasized. However, the fact that the first two Atoms selected to be fleshed happen to be a humanoid and his first cousin, an orangutan, may cause these earlier admonitions to be forgotten. To view the coming description of a Being as applicable only to the living, to the animal would be to adopt a measure of the Subjectivism and/or Idealism or Berkeley *et al*, according to which: "To exist is to perceive, to will, or to be perceived or desired". To avoid such misunderstanding, we again emphasize that since Existence is the univocal possession of all Atoms, animate as well as inanimate, throughout this chapter and those

1. Robert GOUIRAN, *Particles and Accelerators*, (trans. by W.F.G. Crozier), New York, Mc Graw Hill, 1967, p. 11.

directly following, a statement made regarding one type of Atom, applies *mutatis mutandis* to every other — to neutrino and wolf, to fern and man. The Universe knows but one species or genus: that of the Existent. The two primates are selected as demonstration units for practical reasons. A first is familiarity. We humans are best acquainted with Existence as this manifests itself in one of our tribe. Secondly, the use of a man as subject and a primate as control, makes the present position re the nature of man ultra clear, and contrasts it with the demeaning and nefarious concepts of the individual propounded by certain other philosophies and ideologies. The reference is to the cleverly orchestrated pseudo-scientific propaganda which conditions millions to accept as gospel truth the theory that humans and orangutans are "systems" on par with an automobile or an egg beater. Depending upon the philosophical allegiance or discipline of the propagandists, the "animal system", is held hylemorphic, symbiotic, concrescent or specifical. Simplifying the process, many reduce the identity content of the animate to the point of proclaiming it a vulgar conglomerate of minerals, mysteriously bound by electrical impulses or some synaptic process.

The divergences persist in respect to the fate of the human symbiosis, synapt, concrescence or soul. Certain schools subscribe to the hypothesis that humanoids and primates are temporal, implying that both begin and end in time. Death, according to this view, equals annihilation through disintegration, with a consequent loss of energy. Another, more popular, sees man as beginning in time, but "thereafter lasting forever", while the orangutan and lower, "nonspiritual" animals vanish into thin air upon their demise. A third widely held theory, involving a major feat of existential acrobatics, is metempsychosis whereby souls transmigrate, whereby man becomes cow or vice versa, and a monkey becomes a gnat, etc. As far apart as such theories may appear, all share in a common flaw. *All deny the strict atomicity of the Existent.*

The logic for using experimental subjects so similar yet so different must now be clear. Were the orangutan not included, the out and out Materialists would classify Dynamic Vision among the dichotomous philosophies, labelling it probably a variation of Aristotelo-Thomism, while those who situate a dead human in an eternal hereafter would be tempted, as the Materialists, but for the opposite reason, to equate my position with theirs. The placing of the simian, which in the former's opinion as in that of the Materialist, at death evaporates as yet another soap bubble, on the same footing as man, denies both this opportunity. *With respect to the status and fate of Atoms, Dynamic Vision stands in isolation from the established schools. Its premise, What-Is, Is — which makes of the physicist's Law of the Conservation of Energy, a special case — predicates that all possessors of Energy possess it in perpetuity.* The criterion for dynamic facticity is the exercise of a power-quality traceable to a specific source. As example, a vanadium, a human, a lyzozyme and a philodendron, all of which evidence unambiguous personalities, are all conserved outside of time-space. *Only thus does the Cosmic Equation balance. When the conservation of Energy is at stake, hedging is taboo. It-which-Is, Is.*

3. A Closer Look at Cosmic Presentiality

It seems advisable to investigate certain aspects of cosmic presentiality which, when clearly grasped, will facilitate the inquiry in the coming section, into the motor-like nature of the Atom. Essentially the question to clarify hinges upon that which can be described as the positive and negative aspects of adimensionality. The negative side of the ledger exposes briefly the manner in which the radical adimensionality of Dynamic Vision differs from rudimentary notions of the same state as advanced by others. In particular, this points out how cosmic presentiality clears away the underbrush of time-space myths, the more outstanding being the void, infinity, radical causality and the infinite divisibility of "matter" which linger in other theories. The positive or asset side of the ledger outlines additional features of the implications, for science in general and for the human sciences specifically, of cosmic presentiality.

The task of understanding cosmic presentiality consequently becomes a matter of an "accurate visualization" of its corollary : adimensionality. The term "accurate visualization" in the present context implies condescension to human frailty, to the senses. One can further argue that the term carries an element of contradiction, implicit in the reference to a positive side of the ledger and to the obligation to do away with myths. Indeed, a most cogent argument in favor of cosmic presentiality is the need which the Spatialists feel to include in their intellectual tool kit negative counterparts of an intuited adimensionality such as the hypothesis of an infinity and void — of which the most charitable affirmation is that they are meaningless. It follows that the idea of adimensionality, also superfluous and itself a form of negation, is here entertained, merely to emphasize a rejection of other views. An effective method of "visualization" will therefore be to consider some representative theories re adimensionality and a universal dimension generally, and to indicate how these differ from an integral cosmicity.[2]

The intuition of adimensionality so obsesses that its latent recognition appears in just about every ontology. Its crudest formulation consists in a dwelling upon the chimera of the void. Having demonstrated the vacuity of this concept, no elaboration is needed. Close scrutiny reveals that even the more constructive hypotheses are flawed by a visceral fear of renouncing completely "real time-space and dimensioned-matter", as this supposedly resides in some Democritan-like prime particle. Undoubtedly, everyone from Aristotle onto Eddington, ardently sought to enter an honest Cosmos. But, having wrapped themselves up in that parody of the cosmic called "an infinity bound by a void", and having compounded this monumental blunder by filling a void-bound infinity with an infinity of infinitesimally "small Leibnizian prime particles", all were denied their objective. An exception to the rule are the Hegelians and Marxists whose remedy is worse than the cure. The following quotes, two of which were previously cited, illustrate this contradiction. For instance, it is exquisite in the Gouiran position, which has the

2. Those conversant with 19th century German *Naturphilosophic* will observe that cosmic presentiality merely extends to the individual, the interrelatedness and permanence which this school attributed to indeterminate phenomena. Coherence and the conservation of Energy both require that, if, as Fredrich W.J. von Schelling argued in 1799: "magnetic, electrical, chemical, and finally even organic phenomena (are) interwoven into one great association... (which) extends over the whole of nature", then the electron, iron and tree responsible respectively for an electrical, chemical and organic phenomenon also "extend over the whole of nature".

added merit of summarizing the thinking of many contemporary physicists:

> every particle in reality covers the entire universe, but the probability of finding it is almost entirely confined to a small space.

The same critique applies to this theory of A.N. Whitehead, an accredited physicist and philosopher:

> The physical field is, in this way, atomized with definite divisions: it becomes a "nexus" of actualities. Such a quantum (i.e. each actual division) of the extensive continuum is the primary phase of a creature.[3]

Again, one is expected to conciliate an "extensive continuum" with "definite divisions" — a logical deduction on Whitehead's part, since for him space assumes the role of the "real thing".

Identical ambiguities mar the earlier views of Laplace, Faraday and others, witness the Faraday thesis:

> The view now stated of the constitution of matter would seem to involve necessarily the conclusion that matter fills all space, ... In that view matter is not merely mutually penetrable, but each atom extends, so to say, throughout the whole of the solar system, yet always retaining its own center of force.

Surprisingly, the above makes more sense than most "modern" theses. Still one glimpses, dancing in the background, the ghost of Democritus' atoms. Closest to the mark, on the question of adimensionality, is Boscovitch the Jesuit who, as Whitehead, wore two hats, combining the philosopher's insights with the mathematician's. Yet, even in the otherwise commendable Boscovitchian position — it effectively eradicates "matter" — according to which:

> Atoms are mere centers of forces or powers, not particles of matter, in which the powers themselves reside,

time-space retains its privileged position, for where a center is pinpointed, space surfaces, and close on its heels, time jumps into the act. Of the same vintage, and drawing the same comments, is this statement of Maritain,

---

3. Alfred NORTH WHITEHEAD, *Process and Reality*, New York, The Free Press, 1969, p. 97.

that each of us is situated precisely at the centre of this world. Each is at the centre of infinity.

Nor are the latest insights of pure physics more reassuring. The vision of the modern physicist, who as reward for his realism, intellectual honesty and achievements is gradually usurping the philosopher's ancient prestige and prerogatives, is altogether as dismaying as Santayana's: "man is the last bubble of a long fermentation in the world", lacking as it does the redeeming odor of poetry redolent throughout the Spaniard's works. Effectively, physics reduces Reality to a series of abstract calculus equations which, as Einstein emphasized, possess only the most indirect relationship to sense experience. The following queries from an article entitled the "Dynamics of Space-Time" paint graphically the sad emptiness of the mathematician's universe, a universe consonant with the Marx-Engels hypothesis of "pure matter in movement".

> Is the physical universe made of matter, or is it made of mathematics? To put the question another way — is space-time only an empty arena within which real fields and particles play out their drama; or is the four-dimensioned continuum of space-time all there is? No questions are more central than these to the master plan of physics, the plan which seeks to unify into one harmonious whole phenomena so apparently diverse in scale and kind as elementary particles, neutrinos, electromagnetic fields, gravitation, and galaxies.
>
> The answer to such questions suggested by striking new developments in general relativity is that empty space may indeed be all there is. Fields, particles, galaxies, and stars truly may not be independent entities immersed within the static, vapid geometry of space. In the end they may prove to be nothing but geometry — but geometry of an unexpectedly rich and dynamic kind. And it was Einstein's general relativity that gave geometry a life of its own.[4]

Granted, the physicist as physicist, can be satisfied with the abstract. Nonetheless, even he, if realistic, must ultimately be preoccupied with the source of a dynamism. But the philosopher and the man-on-the-street, the businessman and the lover, can at no time afford existential dilettantism, for the price is nihilism and a "Kafkaesque" despair. This plunge into the void, this

---

4. John A. WHEELER and Seymour TILSON, "Dynamics of Space-Time", *International Science and Technology*, Dec., 1963, p. 62.

negation of genuine selfhood is all the more painful to contemplate, when one realizes that, not only is a genuine Self compatible with the latest theories of physics, but that indeed a discrete, adimensional Atom alone rationalizes a universe in which "matter" interchanges with energy. The sole alternative is to find in the Self, "an ephemeral conformation of the primordial space-time field", or still a Humian "bundle of perceptions... which succeed each other with inconceivable rapidity". I, for one, do not brook such nonsense. Not only am I a fact, dynamic, aggressive and free, but also I *know* beyond the shadow of doubt, that when during moments of maximal lucidity I gaze beyond the blue depths of the heavens, I physically transcend time-space to commune with an adimensional, cosmic That-which-is. I, the Dynamic-Fact, *know* that I am not evaporating into the nothingness which, with a consumate inanity, a Sartre would have lay just "outside of infinity". Rather, bound by no dimension save selfhood, I commune in the flesh of all the other "I's".

A normal retort will be that it is well and good to rationalize and imagine an adimensional Self — but that when all is said and dreamed, adimensionality and its corollary, cosmic presentiality, remain just that: a dream, an intellectual "gew-gaw". Such a feeling while normal does not withstand scientific inquiry. That one should experience difficulty in achieving a sense of adimensionality — his own or anyone else's — must be accepted as one of the crosses of the human condition. Imprisoned in a coating of flesh; weighed down by the atmosphere; jostled by the crowd on the subway; forced to withdraw behind brick walls and swathe himself in layers of cloth that heat or cold be made bearable; semi blind, even when in the best of health, and given to see friend, car and airplane, disappear and die at a more or less rapid pace as distances and opacities intervene; the human is illequipped to see or feel the fulness of Reality. *Only through a deliberate effort of the senses of intellect and will, can the grip of the Outsiders, whose concerted attacks impress the finite upon us, be broken and the adimensional entered.* A difficult feat. Yet, given the proper determination and a sustained effort to escape from the "body" dungeon and commune with the *what-is*, anyone can perform it. A feat most rewarding, morally and psychologically.

Subject to a subsequent demonstration, the parameters of adimensionality and, by devolution of being a Cosmic-Presence, are the following. The affirmation that all of the Its-which-are, are dimensionless, refers to an adimensionality exceeding even that of Boscovitch. Not only is the idea of a centre rejected, but Parmenides for whom Existence:

> ... is all continuous; for what is clings close to what is. But motionless within the limits of mighty bonds, it is without beginning or end, ...[5]

is rejoined. Every Being, including the reader is physically present before and in communion with every tomato plant, neutrino, angel and dinosaur which has-does-and-will-exist; each resides in a tensorial, maximized As-is. Real or absolute time or space is fiction. Void and infinity are fantasies. The same applies to a Maritain-like "centre of infinity", (of which there would assumedly be a centre for each human). The sole dimension is the Fact-of-to-be, otherwise known as Existence, etc., a fact shared univocally and to which each of we fleas and neutrons contributes, each according to the plenitude of his power-quality. Inversely, none need fear poor Jean-Paul's void and his diffusion into the insatiable maw of a frigid infinity. *We make our dimensions. Limits are self-imposed. Our conquests, of space, political power or Self, are but functions of will-power, individual and/or communal. The Now-dimension is sheer conquest.*

Finally, a few reflections of a psychological character; anticipatory reflections, for expanded in Part V, they close this volume. The universe of the adimensional motor reverses that of the Materialist. The physical having shed its limits — thought-power alone restraining — all horizons are of ones own making. As one learns to scorn the emptiness of "matter", to exceed the "senses" and especially to transcend time, boundless vistas loom. A dormant energy is harnessed. The world offers a trove of opportunities heretofore undreamed of — as the Self bursts into the Absolute, basking in The Absolute. All barriers fall. A sense of belonging, of physical and spiritual liberation suffuses. The neophyte, now a freed-man and full-fledged citizen of the

---

5. PARMENIDES, *The Way of Truth*, as found in Greek Philosophy: Thales to Aristotle (ed. R.E. Allen), New York, The Free Press, p. 46.

Cosmos, experiences a wondrous communion, a brotherhood, with God, men, his animal brothers, and even so his Assissian sisters, the sun, moon and stars.

4. The Existential-Atom: A Dimensionless Motor, Resident of the "Nowhere"

As adimensionality, the motoricity of the Atom is implicit throughout the Second Part, which deals with Power. Nonetheless, some explication seems called for to provide structural data and facilitate the visualization of the mechanics of the phenomena dealt with in the coming experiment. Simultaneously, the concept of motoricity can contribute to a better understanding of adimensionality.

The structure, if one may be forgiven so mechanical, hence inadequate a term when speaking of the Atom, may strike as esoteric — possibly as the philosophical counter-part of abstract art. The parallel is proper for, as abstract art seeks to reveal the inner truth of a superficially discerned person, situation or mood; so does the notion of a dimensionless motor. Equally valid, is a comparison between its structure and the structures of the subnuclear physicist, who, when grappling with the mysteries of the nucleonic realm, finds that the "rabble of the senses" must be transcended, and ends up speaking a language involving calculus so intricate that even to the learned nonspecialist, "it is all Greek". To conciliate adimensionality with the Atom one need not empty the Universe of content, nor reduce it to a skeleton of mathematical symbols. Quite the opposite. The distortion resulting from a superficial assessment of sense data being corrected, the universe of the Atom has restituted to it a cleansed, immensely aggrandized, indeed limitless domain, pregnant of all qualitativity — the sensual inclusively. Some mental calisthenics are required — a new vision of the Real is not as cheaply acquired as a new pair of socks. However, the difficulty is surmountable, and since an understanding of Dynamic Vision as a whole is predicated upon that of the mechanism of adimensionality, the effort is justified.

The first step to this visualization is the shearing from the Atom of all "materiality", of the minutest dimension, that even of a Boscovichian point. The Atom is not a point, geometrical or otherwise; still less a coordinate. The above merely clears the deck. A positive suggestion next offers itself, namely that the notion of Dynamic-Fact be substituted for that of Atom, for facts are intuitively conceived as absolutes and concepts, and as bereft of "material" dimensions. Further, since dynamism ignores dimensions, the synacting of the two terms does provide an adequate picture.

From Dynamic-Fact to motor, the progression is natural. That, It-which-is-dynamic constitutes a motor, is undebatable, at least by standard criteria, as witness this definition of a motor:

(1) A mover; any person or thing causing motion.

(2) In machinery, an engine or device through which motion is communicated, as a locomotive or hoisting jack; a machine for converting any form of energy (power) into mechanical energy. (Webster's)

Given the nature of the Atom, one of whose synacts is owned power, the character of a motor, in the conventional sense, follows since an entity, one, dimensionless and possessed of Power, must use this to relate and impose itself upon Outsiders — each of which can but repay it in kind. In summary, every Atom aggresses upon every other, in a ratio proportional to the intensity and quality of its dynamism, and in doing so, satisfies the criteria of motricity.

5. **The Atom as Atom, an Immovable Motor**

A major difficulty now arises, introduced when the Existent was denied even the dimension of a Boscovichian point. Those who might accept the Atom's motricity, as equated with the impact of Dynamic-Fact upon Dynamic-Fact, may object when the motor becomes dimensionless. The plot thickens when the corollary of adimensionality, immovability, is taken into account. How, after all, can the motor, an entity defined by common agreement as "a mover, a person or thing causing motion", be held not only dimensionless, but also immovable? A colloquial interpretation of the word motor seems to justify this objection. However, closer scrutiny reveals that even at the level of the commonplace, motors can be immovable, at least temporarily. Far more than semantics is involved. The Truth of the Universe is at stake. Again, the key is the conciliation of the phantasmagoric evidencc of the "senses", which speaks of a universe drowning in movement and degeneration, with the facticity of Existence.

The solution to this dilemma was provided when an analysis of Power revealed this to be not a factor of potency, but rather of intensity and resting in a state of maximization. As a consequence, at the Real each, due to its presence to the Outside, constitutes a motor. The same conclusion follows from the fact that motricity is a function of the Atom's status of a One-Intense and its concomitant role of foundation. To serve as foundation, to support another, makes of It which supports, a motor in the true sense, for support exerts pressure, and motricity is nothing else.

While deductions involving entire systems, parts of which rest beyond the reach of the senses, may be rightly incorporated within a scientific theory — provided that the latter works — it is always preferable to confirm such "logicalities" through experiments made upon systems, the whole of which can be sensually encompassed. In the case of immovable motors, confirmation is available. The Perceived abounds with static motors. Here are three examples. We will let the first be your two hands pressing the one against the other with equal force. Neither moves. Still each are motors. A second would be that of identical horses harnessed one against the other. All outside factors being equal, both are stalemated. The same situation arises when two bulldozers clash. The tracks spin and spew dirt all about, yet at the point of contact an equilibrium occurs. Some may argue that while these situations, each representing a different category of "material" motor — the first, internal, the second, animal and the third, mechanical — constitute observed instances of maximized, non-moving motors, nevertheless their non-motility is temporary. Conceded. However, temporariness applies only as a norm of the Perceived, and insofar as the situations under consideration are concerned, is irrelevant. As a matter of fact, even in time, motors are found which are not moving and yet operative, and most germane, their immovability coincides with the peak of their power, with their maximization at a "given-point-in-time".

The above provides the elements necessary to establish the immovable motor status of the Existential-Atom, for the non-moving point and the maximal point of the two hands, horses and bulldozers correspond. The three are static because maximization is reached *vis-à-vis* each other, and since as established in sec, 8, ch. III, Pt. II, the Universe rests in a maximized state, each represents an immovable fact, for that which holds for the individuals in a conglomerate establishes a common denominator — in this situation universal maximization. This is the point made when in the mentioned section it was stated that:

> the contact and interpenetration or immanence of every Existent by every other Existent is absolute, and there is consequently between every Existential-Atom but one contact.

Then, it was further demonstrated that this one contact is maximal, and that:

> (those) relationships which are thought to be changing and less than maximal, are so only in a mind, human or other, which is restricted to sequential perception.

In other words, a maximised relationship similar to that observed between the two bulldozers, prevails throughout the Real. Therein each, a One-Intense, rests in its full facticity. The Materialists, in particular the advocates of the "finite building block" theory or modernized Democritan atom, who can be expected to question such a position, might weigh the following observation. *Theirs' is an inverted universe, where the physical is seen as chopped-up into pieces and thought-power as operating in a continuum of sorts, whereas in-fact the Real operates the other way around — the Atom being a continuum, and thought being quantized.*

Since the quantum status of thoughts was dealt with in chapter VII, Part I, here, only the continuous state of the physical need be considered. Due, among other factors, to a blind acceptance of the Thomistic theory of dimensioned "matter" (*materia signata*), and in some instances, to a biased rejection of any phenomenon which validates the spiritual and/or eternal condition, the notion that "matter" is segmentable into any number of strict units between which physical contact is broken and re-established at will, was until recently accepted quasi universally. Among the rare exceptions to this crude kinetism, one can cite a half-hearted Leibniz and an equally indecisive Whitehead. The physicists, on the other hand, due to a less dogmatic approach, have contributed fruitful insights. It may seem that Bohr's quanta and Planck's constant, indeed all of quantum physics, gives the lie to a theory of adimensionality and of the consequent cosmic scope of relationships (waves). Hardly. Most maintain an open mind on the subject — including the founders themselves of quantum physics, as these excerpts of reconstructed discussions clearly indicate. The reporter is Werner Heisenberg, who as a young man participated in the original discussions held by Bohr, Einstein, Schrödinger and others.

> *Schrödinger*: "I don't wish to enter into long arguments about the formation of concepts; I prefer to leave that to the philosophers. I wish only to know what happens inside an atom... If there are electrons in the atom, and if these are particles — as all of us believe — then they must surely move in some way..."
>
> *Bohr*: "I beg to disagree. The contradictions do not disappear; they are simply pushed to one side. You speak of the emission of light by the atom or more generally of the interaction between the atom and the surrounding radiation field, and you think that all the problems are solved once we assume that there are material waves but no quantum jumps..."
>
> *Schrödinger*: "I don't for a moment claim that all these relationships have been fully explained. But then you, too, have so far failed to discover a satisfactory physical interpretation of quantum mechanics. There is no reason why the application of thermodynamics to the theory of material waves should not yield a satisfactory explanation of Planck's formula as well — an explanation will admittedly look somewhat different from all previous ones."
>
> *Bohr*: "No, there is no hope of that at all..."
>
> *Schrödinger*: "If all this damned quantum jumping were really here to stay, I should be sorry I ever got involved with quantum theory."
>
> *Bohr*: "But the rest of us are extremely grateful that you did; your wave mechanics has contributed so much to mathematical clarity and simplicity that it represents a gigantic advance over all previous forms of quantum mechanics."
>
> And so the discussions continued day and night. After a few days Schrödinger fell ill, perhaps as a result of his enormous effort..."[6]

6. Werner HEINSENBERG, *Physics and Beyond: Encounters and Conversations*, (Ed. by Ruth Nanda Arshen, trans. by Arnold S. Pomerans), New York, Harper and Row, 1971, pp. 74-75.

Einsteinian Relativity also contradicts any theory of dimensionality and of the strict quantification of "matter". Granted, its author renounced any pretension to the answer to the ontological question of the nature of the universe's prime units. Nonetheless, General Relativity, even when restricted to an explication of relationships *per se*, speaks of adimensionality. Another theory, which points in the same direction, is Eddington's ghost-particle which excludes all trace of "materiality". Even though in true ghost-like fashion — its role is that of a concept set in a medium of wave probability vectors — his particle hardly qualifies as a prime ontological unit, again its existence predicates some mode or other of adimensionality. The same applies to the De Broglie-Schrödinger wave-particle theories, which have the merit of being incorporated as a working premise in many of the basic equations of nuclear physics. While these and like theories fall short of advocating the cosmic relationality consonant with existential atomicity, nonetheless, together they indicate a subjacent suspicion on the part of the scientific community that adimensionality at "some point" must be integrated into a theory truly explicative of the Real. The present stage of thinking seems aptly summarized in this statement of Lancelot Law Whyte:

> ... recent work has suggested that what marks a "fundamental" particle is not its physical indivisibility, but the possession of a definite set of *fixed parameters* (mass, charge, spin, etc.) and no internal *variables* that might represent changes of inner structure. For a fundamental particle must be incapable of internal modification.
>
> "C" (the De Broglie-Schrödinger wave particles theory) is the most recent and certainly the most successful, but in many respects it represents a departure from the classical atomic tradition. Moreover, the high-energy wave-particles discovered since 1930 are intuitively felt not to be true "constituents" of material systems. Underlying this judgement lies a criterion which has seldom been more explicit: A true constituent of physical systems must possess characteristic properties which are *not* functions of position (relatively to other particles) or of time (relatively to events in its neighbourhood). This criterion of genuine constituents corresponds to Epicurus' "impassibility" of the atoms, the property of not being affected by anything. Any particle whose properties, for example its times of appearance and disappearance, are functions of its space-time position relatively to the experimental system may be called *virtual* in the sense that it behaves in certain respects like a constituent

particle, though not actually one. It seems that many of the recently discovered particles are virtual in this sense; they possess variable properties which are functions of their environment.[7]

There are two points, both critical, upon which it is necessary to venture beyond the Law Whyte position. Firstly, "this criterion of genuine constituents"... Epicurus' "impassibility of the atoms...," must be extended, to encompass all Atoms. The second concerns the animate Atoms and the theory of the Conservation of the Real or of Energy. In an honest universe, the criterion which corresponds to Epicurus' "impassibility" must be accorded to the oak atom, water atom and human atom. It makes no sense, even by the standards of elementary accounting, that as yet hypothetical, "genuine constituents" should subsist beyond "functions of time-space", while the human atom whose presence is verifiable experimentally and which contributes to the universal power complex, should be classified as a "virtual particle" or ephemeral "subjective-field". Undoubtedly, as much would be a matter of common agreement were it not that, due to an unknowledged religious bias, many close their eyes to the evident.

Regardless of biases against the conservation of "animate" energy, the animates, even if held to be virtual and subject to annihilation, do provide the objective researcher with physical units whose adimensionality and, it follows, immovability are detectable through instrumentation as sophisticated as that utilized to research into particle behavior, etc. The Self for instance. One need go no further than his own Self to become aware of the invisible and unlocalisable bonds which tie this invincibly to other persons with whom no body contact is entertained. An example of such an adimensionality is hatred or its pole, empathy and love. Both can be engendered through a medium as remote as a T.V.'s screen, or still through a reading of historical events. Such emotional involvements leave permanent scars; are not subject to disjunction, and operate outside of space and time. By the norms of man as man, also by those of physics, any emotion is a continuous phenomenon. The norms of physics are added, for the development of more precise instruments, has

7. Lancelot LAW WHYTE, *Essay on Atomism: From Democritus to 1960*, New York, Harper and Row, 1963, p. 24.

made it feasible to photograph Life or L-fields, a breakthrough achieved in 1939 by the U.S.S.R. scientist, Semyon Davidovich Kirlian. Kirlian, by perfecting a process for developing high frequency (75,000 to 200,000 oscillations per second) fields, was able to photograph the bio-luminescence emanating from a hand, a leaf (his first subject) or any living entity. Describing his work, he states that the first photographs were "a window on the unknown" — the human finger showed up like a complex topographical map:

> "The pattern of luminescence was different for every item, but living things had totally different structural details than non-living things. A metal coin, for instance, showed only a completely even glow all around the edges. But a living leaf was made up of millions of sparkling lights that glowed and glittered like jewels. The flares along its edges were individual and different.
>
> "What we saw in the panorama through the microscope and our optical instruments seemed like the control board of a huge computer. Here and there lights brightened and dimmed — signals of processes inside. If something's wrong inside or conditions need adjustment, the engineer at the control board can read the signals in the lights," the Kirlians said.
>
> "In living things, we see the signals of the inner state of the organism reflected in the brightness, dimness and color of the flares. The inner life activities of the human being are written in these "light" hieroglyphs. We've created an apparatus to write these hieroglyphs. But to read them we're going to need help."[8]

Initially, the Antivitalists of all denominations denounced Kirlian as a charlatan. These attacks have now lost credence, since his experiments have been replicated in Europe and North America, by physiologists and biochemists using either his process or adaptations thereof. Similar aura-like fields were detected in natural or "live" ascorbic acid by Fransciscan Sister M. Justus Smith of Rosary Hill Laboratories, California. Commenting on the differences between the chromatograms of the natural product and the synthetic, Sister Smith stated:

---

8. Sheila OSTRANDER and Lynn SCHRODER, *Psychic Discoveries Behind the Iron Curtain*, Englewood Cliffs, New Jersey, Prentice-Hall, 1970, p. 204.

> These two chromatograms, alone, are sufficient reason to make unacceptable the statement that there is no difference between natural and synthetic Vitamin C.[9]

Subsequent research by the laboratory staff, established that the enzymes (proteins) in the natural vitamin accounted for the aura — these being absent from synthetic ascorbic acid. Enzymes, it shall be established in the coming experiment, have bodies and life, exactly as the primates.

The specific qualitativity of the "living atom" and its field have also been demonstrated conclusively by polygraph expert Cleve Backster, and by Drs. Harold Burr and Leonard Ravitz of Yale University's School of Medicine. The latter detected a complex force-field surrounding every human, which they call the L-field — the field of life. According to Burr: "Every living thing on this planet from men to mice — from seeds to trees — are molded and controlled by electrodynamic fields which can be measured with a good modern voltmeter." Ravitz speaking at the Fifth International Congress for hypnosis and psychosomatic medicine held in Mainz Germany, noted:

> Electric fields control birth, growth, and death as well as the maintenance and repair of all living things. These L-fields are *different* from the alternating-current output of the brain and heart as well as from the epiphenomenal skin resistance. Rather, *they serve as an electronic matrix to keep the corporeal form in shape.*
>
> The cellular structure in certain parts of the human body is completely renewed every six months. It is the L-field, *not* the DNA molecule, Dr. Ravitz explained, which molds the new material, derived in part from food intake, into the same design as the old. "This explains why, even though you might not see a friend for a year or more, during which time all the molecules of his face and head have completely changed, he is recognizably the same." It also explains why you can remember events of five, 10 or even 20 years ago when every molecule of your brain has been replaced perhaps half a hundred times.[10]

---

9. Jane KINDERLEHRER, "Natural is Beautiful and Better !", *Prevention*, January, 1974, Emmaus, Pennsylvannia, Rodale Press, p. 97.
10. Joseph F. GOODAVAGE, "Have Scientists Found the Electronic Key to Man's Soul?", Saga, June, 1974, p. 62.

The above, based on physical evidence of the same nature as that adduced by the nuclear physicist in behalf of subatomic particles, is doubly relevant. In the first instance, it confirms the specificity of an important subspecies of Atoms, that of the "living". In the second, since animates emanate dynamic and qualitative-fields as permanent and more complex than those of any pi-meson or omega-minus, their motricity and immovability follow, for, one, every dynamic-field constitutes a motor and two, every motor rests in the Absolute beyond movement. Unexpectedly, the same conclusions can be drawn from the theories which would reduce the universe to an empty arena called space-time "within which real fields and particles move". The following quotes from "The Dynamics of Space-Time", outline concisely the key features of this general concept. The first suggests:

> In Brief: Is space-time only an empty arena within which real fields and particles move; or is it all there is? Recently recognized implications of Einstein's long-dormant 1916 theory of general relativity suggest it may indeed be all there is. The geometry of space, originally the slave of matter and only curving in response to the gravitational field created by matter, turns out to manifest curvature even in the absence of matter. And this curvature *must* evolve through time. Which means that curved empty space is a dynamic entity, as competent to store and carry energy as are ordinary elastic materials and electromagnetic waves. Catalyzed by energy, and precisely guided by Einstein's field equations, empty space evolves: Into a gentle curve that apes a gravitational field; Into ripples indistinguishable from an electromagnetic field; Into regions of intense curvature — infested by "wormholes" 20 orders of magnitude smaller than elementary nuclear particles. Bunched together, these wormholes may be what elementary particles are.[11]

Such a view warrants consideration by the philosopher. Not only does it encapsule physic's more advanced hypotheses, but it lacks a single concept, to offer a more satisfactory vision of Reality than is advanced in any work of "pure philosophy", phenomenological or otherwise. Child of its era, the Wheeler-Tilson theory of a "dynamic space-time" incorporates the major flaw of Becomingism, when it affirms:

> "And this curvature must evolve through time."

---

11. John A. Wheeler and Seymour Tilson, *op. cit.*, p. 62.

However, once this offending feature is eliminated, and a formless Dynamic-Fact is substituted for "wormholes infesting regions of intense curvature", then the Universe peoples with discernible entities, each possessed of energy and of a personality. *Actually, it is logical to speak of addition, for no impediment, no barrier precludes the insertion of a formless and dimensionless individuation factor into a "dynamic entity of curved empty space". Indeed, the latter would seem a logical receptacle for the Atom, as this emerges at the time of its third metamorphosis from a Dynamic-Fact to a One-Intense.*

The compatibility or better the receptivity of the physicist's universe of abstract geometry, with a universe of immovable motors, evident in the summary, becomes glaring when under the subtitle, "Unexpected riches in general relativity", the authors write:

> In a matter-free universe the stuff of space-time, literally nothing but geometry, turns out to be a remarkably malleable primordial dough. Catalyzed only by energy and by the fertile yeast of mathematical imagination, it rises — here into a slowly curving section that has all the attributes of a gravitational field, there into a rippled configuration indistinguishable from an electromagnetic field, and elsewhere into knotted regions of intense curvature that manifest concentrations of charge and of mass-energy and behave like particles.[12]

The concepts of "a remarkably malleable primordial dough, ... a rippled configuration indistinguishable from an electromagnetic field... knotted regions of intense curvature... concentrations of charge and of mass-energy and behave like particles," individually and jointly await the coming of the quality-laden One-Intense to fertilize them, to bring them down to earth, to fleshify them. These are also notions admirably suited to receive the *person* of an Obscure-Absolute. Simultaneously, they speak the language of the Antropocity when for instance they "behave like particles", the Antropocity being a defined knot of relationships — the exact description of the Wheeler particle.

12. John A. WHEELER and Seymour TILSON, *op. cit.*, p. 63.

In summary, the laboratory findings of physiology and physics correspond with those obtained through experimenting with the mass of Existence, otherwise known as the Universe. As observed, if the Universe is to contain genuine individuals, it must consist of a number-X of Dynamic-Facts whose prime characteristic is intensity swathed in quality. Stated in the mechanical terms of Newtonian physics, each Atom constitutes an immovable motor — for a sum of cosmic entities entertains but one contact with every other. None moves in space nor in time. Each resides nowhere in particular. Each is simultaneously everywhere.

chapter III

Experiment Number Three — Operation Fleshing

Sensory phenomena are the highest form of regulation, and the brain is the ultimate regulatory apparatus of the most complex biological system : man.

Daniel KOSHLAND JR.,
Protein Shape and Biological Control.

1. Nature, Cast and Purpose of Third Experiment

A. *Nature*

THE decision to break with tradition and to deal with Existence empirically, as with a raw material, rather than as the subject of metaphysical or dialectical speculation has led to the discovery of the Existential-Atom. The Atom, in effect the prime particle of "matter", was discovered through two experiments involving the use of scale models. The model in the first was an IT or synthetic atom, and that of the second was a scale universe composed of 1,000,000 ITs. Subsequent research into the nature and structure of the prime particle reveals it to be energetic and adimensional. This adimensional motor, whose outstanding characteristics are qualitativity and aggression, operates in a medium of absoluteneity. A study of its behavior contributes additional insights into its inneity and the mechanism whereby it relates with the Outside. The latter can be summed up by the observation that each Atom relates cosmically, acting at once as foundation, medium and coagent to every other beyond time-space. Now, a further experiment involving a series of tests upon the "bodies" and into the relationships of Atoms, such as a man, an enzyme or still an iron, suggests itself. Together, these will serve to check and confirm the results of the experiments upon the scale models.

In summary, the two-fold objective in this chapter is to provide a real life demonstration of the Atom at play in the Universe, and put the seal of workability upon the accumulated structural or inneal data. To avoid repetition, also possible misunderstanding, let it be agreed that all statements in respect to the relationships and phenomena observed in experiment No. 3, are based upon a literal application of the principles and criteria developed up to this point. For instance the statement that relationships extend beyond time-space means just that. An integral application of these principles, in particular that of Absolutes, is bound to yield unorthodox insights. Anyone tempted, in the name of antecedent improbability or on some similar ground, to reject, in part or in whole, that which follows might consider this comment of A. N. Whitehead on novel ideas:

> If you have had your attention directed to the novelties of thought in your own lifetime, you will have observed that almost all really new ideas have a certain aspect of foolishness when they are first produced.[1]

B. *Cast and Terminology*

The two stars of this final experiment have been identified. They are a humanoid and an orangutan, both male. Cast in secondary roles, will be two phagocytes, two enzymes, two irons and two uraniums — of sex unknown. One of each pair will entertain a relationship of subjective-coagency with each star respectively. The rationale which prompted the choice of two primates as key specimens was outlined in the previous chapter. Briefly, the phagocytes, enzymes, irons and uraniums are selected as coagents because together, these represent a fair cross-section of the major species of units from which "bodies" are built.

Upon first reading, dramatic terms such as cast, stars, acts, etc., may seem incongruous. A closer look reveals such an approach justified. While no literary canon forbids the use of metaphor in an ontological discourse — Plato long ago legitimized the procedure — the notion of acts, cast and stars, in the present context, is not in the least metaphoric. The objective is an analysis of presentiality — the fact of being a presence — and to presentialize is of the essence of a play. This applies especially to the first act, which bares the nature of cosmic presentiality. Cosmic in scope, Act One sets the pace and tone for all dramas,

---

1. Alfred North Whitehead, as quoted in John Langdon-Davies, *On the Nature of Man*, New York, Mentor Books, 1960, p. 16.

past, present and future — the grandiose which speaks of the rise and fall of civilizations and peoples; as well as the humble and solitary, enacted in the intimacy of the anguished, tormented "soul" of we Outsiders, of the mother whose son has died at war, of the doe whose fawn the hunter has just brought down.

C. *Scope and Purpose*

The research will cover three phases of what would commonly be defined as a day in the life of the stars and their associates, or preferably as three aspects of their cosmic presence. In the first of three acts the prime modalities of relationship which bind the several subjects are studied. This will involve mainly an analysis of foundationship, mediumship and coagentship, as these apply to the Atom at the Perceived, and could aptly be entitled: the "Three Ships" applied to a humanoid and orangutan. The purpose is to provide the cosmic setting upon which unfurl the local phenomena that next retain the attention. Act Two delves into what is to man the sacred inner sanctum, the holy of holies: his "body"; into what is also the center of one of the more acrimonious scientific controversies — the ontological status of the "body". The position outlined shares many features with other theories, in particular, with the hylemorphic and symbiotic. Yet any similarity must prove superficial, for the finished product situates flesh and blood in a novel category: that of an Antropocity, anchored in qualitativity and the Absolute. Of the three, Act Two, the more technical, involves the greatest measure of correlation between the disciplines: notably between cosmontology, biochemistry and nuclear physics.

In Act Three, in every sense a closing act, the previous find their complete expression. By then, the full characteristics of the building block of the Universe are revealed. Having completed its metamorphoses, the Atom, in its ultimate garb of an obscure but cosmic presence, offers itself to every other in the universal commonwealth, in a relationship of brotherhood. An Outsider, transcendent in the inviolable shell of its oneness and individuality, it discovers that even in the cruel environment of the clash-prone Now, coresponsibility and love are the answer — love of his brother men and mice and of The Absolute, which, to use the Pauline term, are "all in all".

2. Satisfying the Requisites of an Objective Epistemology

It was noted in the introduction that Dynamic Vision makes existential equations possible. In these, the Existential-Atoms provide the primary absolutes or quanta and the Antropocities, the secondary, either entity being identical structurewise, to mathematical symbols. The epistemology which allows for this mathematization was defined as Objectivism. *The basic premise of Objectivism is that every Atom and every thought (Antropocity) is a fact or quanta or absolute, each of which relates at absolute-speed.* The rules for the mathematization of the Existential are drawn from the Cosmic Code, of which the principles of arithmetic, goemetry, etc. are particular cases. (re the Cosmic Code see chapter II, Part V). The first requisite in the present instance is therefore to unambiguously define and circumscribe the quanta, existential and conceptual, which will enter in the equations about to be considered.

3. Categories and Characteristics of Absolutes to be Dealt With

As established, all entities fall within two categories, those of the Atom or existential-absolute, each of which possesses Energy, and the Antropocity, a quantized concept. In this experiment the category of primary or existential-absolutes is occupied by the Humanoid and Orangutan, and the Organelles, Irons and Uraniums. The secondary or conceptual-absolutes dominant in the equations, are the latters' "bodies". These belong to the fourth subcategory, the conceptuo-existentials. Of the same subcategory, but deserving separate mention due to its "size" and conglomerate role, is the Universe which, as emphasized, is not "a thing"; has no "substance", but rather is a concept.

Since the structure of the Atom has been examined in detail, it suffices to note the following. Firstly, the discreteness of an Atom is objective and grounded in the possession of an inalienable quota of qualitativity. To all intents and purposes, each constitutes an immovable motor. A second relevant feature is the coevality — some might prefer the term coextensivity — of each with every other. Finally, due to the univocal character of

Existence, the "essence", "nature" or preferably the inneal structure of all Atoms is the same. The inneity of Orang and that of his Lysozyme is identical, and both in turn share a common structure with the Iron upon which they jointly and individually impose their wills. The accuracy of this view is revealed in Act Two, when the fact that the Enzymes and Irons own a "body", identical in its mechanism to that of Humanoid, is demonstrated upon the basis of verifiable biochemical data.

The nature of Antropocities was also investigated in a general manner in section 3, chapter VI, Part I. Their key characteristic is that they possess no Existence or Power, but rather are mindfactured intellect-quanta, residing in such Atoms as choose to give them a home. Whereas each Atom is unique and a perpetual Outsider, each Antropocity may reside in many homes, in many minds. All that is required for a chair or leg, for example, to achieve bi or multilocation is a consensus on the part of those which either comes to inhabit.[2]

---

2. One of the arguments raised most frequently against a universe of Existential-Atoms, coeval and coextensive, each of which in turn entertains myriadic conflicts, within and without its Self, is the seemingly unconscionable number of units, existential as well as conceptual, which such a scheme predicates. To state the case colloquially, how can, over the centuries and eons, so many bees, dinosaurs, trees, fishes and carrots, dead and to be born, occupy simultaneously the same "crowded space". The question does present serious difficulties of visualization. Once it will become evident, by the end of the coming experiment, that "bodies" of any type are but intense knots of power, in an otherwise cosmic relationship, the coexistence of everyone with everyone, beyond time, will be scientifically established.

While applied technology cannot provide true instances of coexistence, for the simple reason that it does not operate in the Absolute, the speeds which it has achieved in the fields of space travel and radio communications, does confirm that time-space is but a function of power-peace. The wedding of micro-chip and laser technologies promises to reduce conventional time and space to a vanishing point, when these are gauged according to conventional norms of car or plane travel, etc. Consider, for instance, the solid state laser, developped recently by RCA, that fits through the eye of a needle and can transmit 500 million bits of information per second through a thread of glass. This implies transcribing the entire contents of a 24-volume encyclopedia in 3 minutes; or 20 T.V. programs at the same time. Wed such an instrument to a modern computer and time-space as conventionally envisaged loses all relevance. The same remark holds in regard to the stacking of multitudes of units one upon and in the other — for each of the billions of information bits is a strict unit.

4. Act One: Humanoid and Orangutan Awash In a Sea of Aggression

Act One is the briefest and least technical, but not the less important. By stage terminology, the mood setter, it determines the tone and the spirit of the following two. As intimated in section one, the concern in this first act is the general habitat of the subjects: the "Three Ships". Since the dimension of the "Ships" at the Order of the Real is established, the interest here centers upon one aspect of Now-relationality to which the "Ships" contribute: Aggression. Aggression is no newcomer. It was, for instance, defined as father of time-space. Also its dominant role in thought was analyzed. It now comes in these closing chapters to claim its full legacy — that of the ultimate arbiter in Now processes, and it is Act One's purpose to introduce this aggressive aspect of reality — which one can ignore only at his peril.

Aggression, conflict and conquest are aspects of the cosmic drama upon which philosophers have laid surprisingly little stress. Many actually ignored them. Physicists as a group, have escaped this rank angelism — their raw material, Power, making it difficult for them to neglect completely the aggressive side of life. Yet, their involvement with aggressivity comes as a by-product, i.e. from the study of gravitation, the kinetics of gases, atomic fission, etc. Rarely are the implications of this universal urge extrapolated beyond whatever closed-circuit might be under observation. Aggression, for instance, noted when nuclear fission is investigated, is not linked to the appetites of a hungry cow or lion. More damaging, it is not seen as an integer of the Cosmic Equation.

5. Foundationship: Responsible for the Aggressive Mood of the Universe of the Now

That aggression, conquest or defeat abound throughout the Universe is a truism. That which is not, is that aggression suffuses the Now to the point that the latter's Prime Principle reads: *In final analysis all Now relationships are conflictual.* Since aggression *per* se is not here the concern, only a synopsis of the factors at play, intended to provide the insights necessary to understand its origin and role in the phenomena to be investigated, need be considered. Firstly, the why of aggression. In a Universe whose equation reads: U=X(Dynamic-Facts), each immanent and transcendent, the probabilities that relationality should involve aggression are overwhelming, for each entity, while utterly free, depends upon the Outsiders for "a footing", for the wherewithall of its self-realization. Even though foundationship does not automatically call for aggression, still in a universe of immanence, the injection of the slightest aggressive element automatically imparts aggressivity to the whole. It follows that aggression becomes a factor in every situation and equation, and that to the prime principle enunciated above must next be added the First Law of the Now, that of Clash, namely:

when clashing, the stronger conquers the weaker.[3]

Which brings up the issue of relevance, for at this point, the ontologist, physicist and chemist whose concerns might be respectively Existence or atomic reactions, may question the importance of conflict to their studies, or to an experiment intended to confirm the workability of the criteria posited as those of the Atom. The answer? Insofar as general principles are concerned, aggression is crucial. No coherent science can be developed; no valid vision of the Real entertained, if the aggressivity which permeates the Cosmos is not factored into ones calculations. And this precondition applies for all disciplines, the social, ethical and psychological inclusively. *Aggression is present even in the crystallization of calcium or zinc communities — an act on the part of calcium or zinc atoms, altogether as deliberate and organizational as the construction of urban complexes by human atoms.* Given the coupling of the foundationship and aggression pair, a further postulate can now be formulated. In a cosmos wherein each uses every other to self-realize, *self-realization is a function of the efficiency of aggression.* This basic postulate also applies universally; as for instance between Humanoid and his co-stars, or between an electron and the Outside. The technician who from the beginning may have entertained doubts as to feasibility of conducting an experiment upon Existence or an Existent, perhaps sees his doubts reinforced.

3. Re status of this Principle and Law within the Cosmic Code cf. chap. II, Pt. V.

Not only will laboratory paraphernalia — test tubes, microscopes, scalpels be dispensed with and the assaying be conducted upon paper, but a key postulate will be aggression, a factor usually considered applicable solely to the evaluation of social and parasocial phenomena. The question is one of realism, of adapting the method to the realities of the individual Atom, and the Cosmos. The aggression urge is not restricted to the intelligent or the animal. In the Now, it is the prime mode of relationship, and conquest the universal objective — of the calcite and enzyme as well as the wolf atom.

Whereas concepts such as "matter", "substance", and Existence are blankets of generality thrown over the mind to cover the shame of its nakedness, aggression, observed as the determinant between objective Dynamic-Facts, explains the Now process. In particular, it reveals "bodies" to be knots or high-points of power-quality which an Atom maintains in its struggle for survival and self-realization. In summary, the message of Act One is the motto : *to live is to conquer*. It is the systematic analysis of this brutal fact which will lead to the deciphering, in the coming acts and closing chapters, of the structure and behavior of the Atom, of the Self.

6. Act Two : Stars, Humanoid and Orangutan and Their "Bodies"

A. *Objective : Establish the Nature of "Bodies", Human or Otherwise*

The objective in this act is to investigate the relationship of a man and orangutan to their "bodies". Specifically, this entails demonstrating that neither possesses its "body" ; that physically or existentially, there exists no such unit as a "body", if a "body" refers to a strict unit of dimensioned "matter", so tall, firm, old, voluptuous, etc. ; that rather the "body" represents an arbitrarily defined (absolutized) knot of relationships which describes the coagentizing by Atoms of various "natures" at a given-point-in-time-space — it being understood that time-space are real illusions of human mindfacture.

B. *Cast or Working-Units Defined*

As noted, to satisfy the norms of Objectivism the researcher must:

A. encompass absolutely his field of research and within this, each unit,

B. respect the objectivity of each unit — objectivity in this context implies intellectual honesty; which is to say, a firm determination to neither add nor substract even one iota or omega-minus from ones subject, and

C. clearly delineate the units in his equations.

As in the previous act, the units involved fall into two categories: the Obscure-Absolutes and the Antropocities — the latter being conglomerates of the conceptuo-existential subcategory. Thus to the ten identified Atoms, Humanoid and Orangutan and their eight co-stars, the two Phagocytes, two Enzymes, two Irons and two Uraniums are added ten Antropocities; namely, the ten "bodies" of the complete cast. To avoid duplication and confusion, initially only Humanoid and its "body" will be dealt with. This in no way endangers the investigation, since all Atoms are univocal and the sole reason for the use of a simian as control is to avoid possible ideological controversy.

7. To Existential Mathematics, Existential Algebra is Added

Equations corresponding to those of elementary mathematics were adequate to solve the first two key problems, those of the structure of the Real and of the dominant characteristic of the Now, aggressivity. As example, facticity and the Principle of Absolutes which together revealed that the Real consists of a fixed number of Atoms, yielded U=X (E : A). While the Cosmic Equation's heuristic content increased with each metamorphosis, it nonetheless retained its primary character throughout. The initial indeterminate E : A having been dethroned by the more graphic D : F and the latter firstly by the Janus-like One-Intense-Free-Efficient team and secondly by the Cosmic-Presence, still the ultimate formulation U=X (C : P), where C : P stands for Cosmic-Presence, remained as basic as the initial formulation.

The situation continued unchanged in Act One. Since this dealt solely with the quality of relationships in the Now, no imponderables were introduced. Rather, light was thrown on the mood of the Free-Efficient. Conquest was revealed to be the destiny of the original Now E : As. Nor did the adding of H = the Humanoid, P = the Phagocyte, E = the Enzyme, Ur = the Uranium and I the Iron to U=X(E : A), alter the latter. While it then read:

$$U=H+P+E+Ur+I+X(C:P)$$

it remained balanced since the sum of H+P+E+I+Ur+X(C : P) accounted for the Universe. The austerity of the original U=X(E : A) is an obvious function of the facticity and consequent objectivity of its units, each being a fact prehended absolutely.

In Act Two the situation changes. With the introduction of factors whose value and content are subjective and indeterminate, the existential equivalent of algebra imposes itself. The "body" of Humanoid, our knowledge of which consists of one positive fact: namely that it is not an ontological unit, represents the equivalent of any "x", "y" or "z" in a conventional algebraic equation, and must be dealt with accordingly. While the investigation about to be undertaken is not presented equationally, such formulation is implicit in each step. As the non-applicable factors are eliminated, each step brings the answer closer. The process is graphically summarized when h : b (Humanoid's "body") is incorporated into the Cosmic Equation, which becomes:

$$H+(h:b)+P+E=I+Ur+X(C:P)=U$$

The decoding of the value-content of (h: b), will be achieved mainly through a correlation of ontological principles and data with those of biochemistry. The logic for turning to biochemistry for confirmation is that, in a sense, it is ontology's step-child — its concern being the inner workings of Atoms situated in the micro or submicroscopic range. Effectively each biochemical unit assumes the status of a minuscule cosmos. Such a characteristic makes of biochemistry the ideal medium, for the bond between its subjects, viruses, enzymes, etc., and our subject, the Humanoid, is simultaneously one of existence and complementarity — the same relationship as that which prevails between each human and the Universe.

The rationale behind the choice of the co-stars now reveals itself. Phagocyte, Enzyme and Iron, fall under the purview of the biochemist. Each owns a "body", and together constitute a telescopic sequence of "bodies" within that of Humanoid, whose own "body" in turn is but a focal point of intense relationality within the cosmic body. The Uranium, not normally thought of as entertaining a coagential relationship with either enzyme or man, is selected to illustrate the role of aggression in the "life process". It also provides the basis for a hypothesis on the meaning of death.

The first point to establish is that Humanoid's "body" is not a finite or discrete entity. This can be ascertained through many avenues, for instance, through psychology (love, personality), ethics (will, intellect) or biology (eyesight, hearing), for all such phenomena manifest themselves beyond the recognized boundaries of a man's "body", and thereby void any theory of a physically dimensioned body. For the sake of simplicity, only two, eyesight and personality, will be briefly investigated. Jointly, these establish that Humanoid is not a prisoner of his dimensioned "body". Eyesight is dealt with in this act, with personality being deferred to the third. The second point demonstrated is that Phagocyte and Enzyme also own a "body", and that they, as Humanoid, are not prisoners of their "bodies". The physical evidence provided by these two in support of the conceptual nature of "bodies", is conclusive, for the one and its body, Enzyme, resides in the other, Phagocyte, and in turn both reside in the "body" of Humanoid, a feat which only adimensionals can perform.

8. Eye-Power, Human or Other, Ignores "Body" Restraints

The first relevant observation concerning eyesight, is that of its specificity (it testifies in man to a power distinct from touch or hearing) and further, the eye-power of man differs only quality-wise from that of a frog. Equally relevant is the fact that eyesight is never held to constitute an entity on its own, but rather is always traced to an Atom, human or other. In sum, it results from the exercise of an exclusive quality, and is attributed to a given source. The above covers about the entire area of common ground among scientists, as to the operation of sight. Otherwise its fluidity and fantastic range — it can in the "twinkling of an eye" be directed either at the stars, ones lover or the intimacy of a dream — make of it a matrix of paradoxes over which many stumbled and much controversy still rages. The difficulty stems from the fact that as part of the larger issue of the nature of Existence, it has contracted the becomingist infection. Faced with the problem of situating a moving, unlocalizeable phenomenon, Becomingists devote chapters and books to the issue — to achieve a circularity worthy of a kitten chasing its tail. Invariably, the problem degenerates into a slugging match between Materialism and Idealism. The following, from Sir James Jeans' *Some Problems of Philosophy*, in which Bertrand Russell is simultaneously quoted, aptly summarizes the situation:

> ... Berkeley argued that effects must always be of the same general nature as their causes, a mechanical effect being traceable to a mechanical cause, and so on. Or, to put it rather more precisely, whatever crosses the mind-body bridge must be of the same general nature as its cause on the one side of the bridge and as its effect on the other... Berkley's argument seems to provide a valid proof that mind and matter must have something in common; we can see how much real substance there is in it if we reflect on the straits to which Descartes and Leibniz were reduced when they tried to show how the opposite might be true.
>
> In more recent times, Bertrand Russell has expressed what is essentially the same argument in the words: "So long as we adhere to the conventional notions of mind and matter, we are condemned to a view of perception which is miraculous. We suppose that a physical process starts from a visible object, travels to the eye, there changes into another physical process, causes yet another physical process in the optic nerve, and finally produces some effect in the brain, simultaneously with which we see the object from which the process started, the seeing being something "mental", totally different in character from the physical processes which precede and accompany it. This view is so queer that metaphysicians have invented all sorts of theories designed to substitute something less incredible...[4]

Judging from the above and the balance of the text, one can surmise that the answer is glimpsed by both Jeans and Russell,

4. Sir James JEANS, "Some Problems of Philosophy", in *The World's Great Thinkers, Man and the Universe: The Philosophers of Science*, (edited by Saxe Commins and Robert N. Linscott) New York, Random House, 1947, pp. 386-387.

but that both, together with a majority of those who brooded over the problem, have, due to a becomingist bias, rejected it. Without the discrete Atom the researcher has nothing upon which to "pin" a phenomenon, and is doomed to run around in the circle of an imaginary infinity of Whiteheadian "actual entities". While Russell is no doubt justified in the statement that:

> Everything that we can directly observe of the physical world happens inside our heads, and consists of *mental* events in at least one sense of the word *mental*. It also consists of events which form part of the physical world. The development of this point of view will lead us to the conclusion that the distinction between mind and matter is illusory. The stuff of the world may be called physical or mental or both or neither as we please; in fact the words serve no purpose.[5]

having affirmed as much he, as all Becomingists, remains bobbing in a churning sea of indeterminate "matter", and if anything, less capable of providing a satisfactory account of sight than such outright Dualists as Leibniz and Descartes. The problem is relatively simple. There is no need to, as Russell, speak of "miracle, queerness", etc. Eyesight, a specific quality-power integral to a given Dynamic-Fact, in the present case emanates from Humanoid and operates in the Absolute.

9. **Phagocytes, Enzymes, "Bodies" Within "Bodies"**

Eyesight reveals that Humanoid is not confined to the prison of his "body"; that with great ease he can, with it, commute in space; or as easily enter the adimensional, often vividly colorful world of the dream. We now discover that any talk on his part of his "body" is gratuitous; that *in-fact, he possesses nothing whatsoever, save his own Fact-of-to-be, through which he dominates other Facts-of-to-be, each of which returns the compliment by imposing itself upon him with a power proportionate to its Self*; which is to say, *virusly, phagocytely or ironly.*

Articulated in a Materialist's idiom, the above assumes more devastating proportions. Since, according to the Materialist, each actor sports a "body" (chemists have established this beyond

5. *Ibid.*, p. 387.

question of a stable element such as Iron) each is entitled to claim a portion of Humanoid's "body". The outcome is plain. Should Phagocyte, Enzyme, Iron, etc., together with the multitude of their relatives and confrères simultaneously vote for separatism, the hapless Humanoid must end up with no "body" at all.

Actually, the same paradox is involved, as was during the second experiment, where the Universal Equation read:

$$U = X(E:A)$$

At that time, we saw that should the Atom be dimensioned, the Equation could balance only if the sum of the dimensions encompassed by X, equalled that in U. This applies also when Humanoid's "body", is substituted for U. The equation:

$$\text{Human-Body} = H+P+E+Ur+I+X$$

balances only if, having alloted to each unit its dimensioned portion of "Human-Body", there is volume left to allocate to "H". Such a condition, arithmetic demonstrates, cannot be met the moment dimensions are attributed to each of the components, enzymian, metallic, etc., of a fleshed unit. The sum of the dimensions of the organelles, bacteria and metalloids add up to a fantastically large volume. Nor is the end to this Chinese puzzlebox in sight, for the remarkable discoveries of the last decades, in the field of chemistry, have increased the understanding of "matter". Not only has the human "body" been proven to contain myriads of other "bodies", living or inanimate, but these primary inhabitants are themselves inhabitated by an awe-inspiring kaleidoscope of ever smaller "bodies" known as particles.

Since our objective is strictly ontological — namely, to determine the nature of "bodies" (Antropocities), and having done so to confirm the adimensionality of the building block of the Universe, the purpose is served by focussing on a few of the representative denizens of the human carnal jungle. Further, only the basic characteristics of each species need be investigated, and these to an extent sufficient to establish whether or not the criteria for existential individuation are satisfied in each case.

10. **Phagocyte, Species Leucocyte**

First on the list by virtue of its size, is "P", the Phagocyte. Phagocytes, a broadly distributed species, range from free-living, unicellular organisms such as amoebes to leucocytes otherwise known as white blood cells. Actually the name is generic and merely describes any microscopic organisms who live through ingesting more minute entities such as bacteria, bacilli and protozoa — thus the term phagocytosis applied to processes as diverse as the life-style of an amoebe in its pond and a red blood cell born in the marrow of the tibia. The individual which will be investigated belongs to the family of the leucocytes. Inhabitants of the blood, leucocytes number among man's staunchest allies in his constant war against submicroscopic enemies. Their nation is divided into three tribes, the granulocytes, approximately 70% of the total membership; the lymphoids which account for a further 20%, the remaining 5 to 12% consisting of reticulo-endothelials. By human standards the armies of man's leucocytic allies are huge, numbering some 5 to 10,000 for each cubic millimetre of blood.

An investigation of Leucocyte can be brief for its credentials as a discrete living entity, those of duration, size and specificity are all three readily ascertainable. Born in time and in space (in the marrow or lymph) Leucocyte is massive by microscopic standards, (some 500 to 1000 cubic microns). A free-agent, Leucocyte travels about in Humanoid's blood system, much as Humanoid drives his car on a highway. Evidencing a sense of purpose and a will fully as specific as that of Humanoid, upon reaching an area of infection it crawls through a blood vessel wall seeking out the invading bacteria which it can be said to "smell". Actually leucocytes satisfy the specificity requisite of individuation admirably, for the three tribes are endowed with unique powers, each attacking only certain enemies. The reticulos, for instance, largest size-wise but the least numerous, perform several distinct policing tasks. Operating much as the free living amoebe, reticulos spend most of their life pushing out pseudopodia (common trespassers), and digesting various relatively inoffensive particles. They also have the general duty of mopping up in the wake of severe bacterial infection. The tribe, in times of tubercular, typhoid or malarial war, forms the most effective line of defense of the human empire. Should Leucocyte be a reticulo and Humanoid contract malaria, Leucocyte would patriotically offer his services to his imperial master, fighting, if need be unto the death. This alone suffices to establish the specificity of the individual reticulo.

Until the advent of the submicroscopic era, man being unaware of the pullulation throughout his "body" of these hordes of highly specialized warriors, could, at least upon grounds of "common sense", be excused for equating the flesh and bones of his "body" with his Self; for believing that he possessed his "body" hylemorphically. However, anyone equipped with a modicum of 20th century scientific training who persists upon doing so, is guilty of a materialistic bias and a lack of objectivity; or worse of intellectual arrogance. Granted, Leucocyte and his brothers account for only a small percentage of the mass of Humanoid's "body" [6]. Still the remainder consists of equally dimensioned and independent Atoms: the red blood cells, the calciums, the oxygens, etc., and by the time these multitudinous hordes have claimed their respective domains — so many ounces of neuron organelles, so many pounds of waters — Humanoid may be "there" and in more or less efficient control, but he, as a man, is left with nothing tangible or weighable specifically his. Rather, while *there*, he is *nowhere* in particular — neither in the heart, hide or brain. As posited in sec. 4, he, the reader and I are "dimensionless motors, resident of nowhere in particular", and one of our powers, essential no doubt but by no means the noblest, is to coagentize with the Outsiders for the purpose of controlling a "body". At this point the Becomingist, whether Marxist, Teilhardian or other, might be tempted to retort: "I told you so. Man is nothing, man is but a conglomerate, a sum of "social relationships", there are no man Atoms, no souls, only "matter in movement", only chemicals and electrical forces". This would be to crow out of turn, for the second co-star, Enzyme makes a shamble of any claim to a dimensioned specificity which the phagocytes might assert. As Phagocyte occupies his quota of the volume-mass of Humanoid, so does Enzyme pre-empt his share of the space and mass of Phagocyte, and thereby destroys Phagocyte's title to a "body"

6. The body of an adult male contains about 5,000 c.c. of blood, that of a woman or child proportionately less. Of this some 2,250 c.c. consists or red blood cells and 2,750 c.c. of plasma.

as effectively as Phagocyte destroyed Humanoid's title to any unit of mass or extension whatsoever. Clearly Humanoid, and with him each of us, cannot lay claim to even as small a quantized mass as that still erroneously attributed to the "bare" electron.

11. Enzyme — or There is No Such "Thing" as Life

Of the several co-stars, Enzyme will be investigated in the most detail. Enzyme rates this honor due to its middle-man status, for it entertains re Phagocyte and the multitude of organelles which pullulate in the flesh and blood jungle, the same status as the more easily visualized organelles entertain *vis-à-vis* man. At the present stage of scientific development, Enzyme better than any other witness, testifies to the univocity of Existence and the concomitant equality of all Atoms in respect to the state commonly defined as life. Here, the point being made is that the concept of animation seen as a property characteristic of some but not all Atoms, is as gratuitous as that of "matter", and can be traced to human pride and the exagerated status given to time-space and movement.

Existence, *a genus generalissimum*, is the sole dimension of the Universe; and is alive any It which possesses a parcel of the Real. The notion of "having life" or "being animated", as opposed to "being inanimated", at best rates on par with those of liver and liverness. The fact of being animated does not dichotomize the genus Existence; rather, it speaks of quality and implies a qualifying adjective, such as enzymian or simian, etc. *The life or activity factor of men and carrots, when compared to that of irons or calcites, can only be described as a more-or-different factor* and even then, where the more is concerned, dogmatism is to be avoided. The structure of a calcitic colony is as complex and harmonious as that of a humanoidal or apoidean colony — and given that we lack knowledge of the inner qualities which motivate calciums, the scientific stance is one of open-mindedness and reserved judgement. The same prescription applies in respect to death. Since the question of mortality is dealt with in Part IV in the context of Cosmic Peace, it suffices to observe that an honest accounting of the cosmic balance sheet predicates that death should occur among the inanimates, and that the "history" of some inanimates, notably neutrinos and uraniums, indicates that such do suffer from a happening identical to that described as the death of either man or tree.

Those who would interpret the above as a rejection of the traditional elitist theory of vitalism or soulism are correct. This and the idea of "matter" are intellectual perversions arising out of Hellenistic thought. Enzyme offers incontrovertible evidence to that effect. Organic, it lives exactly as did Phagocyte and Humanoid. Nor does the life chain break-off at the end of the organic or molecular link. Iron and Uranium, it will be established, while generally held to be inorganic and inanimate, are also alive. Further, Uranium, if mortality criteria are applied without discrimination, is subject to death, exactly as we.

Enzymes and molecular biology are more recent arrivals to the scientific world than the biochemistry of the larger phagocytes. Known in everyday language as proteins, enzymes, whose molecular weight ranges from 10,000 to several million daltons,[7] play a major and heretofore unsuspected role in the "life process". As all scientific novelties, they have caught the fancy of many groups, and most Materialists and sundry Becomingists, forever on the look-out for the "natural cause of life", are pinning their hopes upon them. As much is implicit in this quote, which offers the added advantage of succinctly providing some of the basic data required for the present investigation:

> ... It was in fermentation processes that the first enzymes were discovered over a century ago. In 1833 the French chemists Anselme Payen and Jean-Francois Persoz identified in malt extract a substance that converted starch to sugar; they called it diastase...
>
> Enzymes might well be considered the physical embodiment of that *élan vital*, or mystic force, by which some philosophers have attempted to define life. In myriad forms, enzymes mediate the movement of muscles, the process of breathing, the storage of energy, the digestion of food, the building of tissues, the course of reproduction, the transmission of nerve impulses, the workings of the brain and even the thought processes themselves. So far about 1,000 different kinds of enzymes have been identified. Of these, over 500 have been studied at some length, and only recently half a dozen have been analyzed down to the last details of their structure. They are intricately folded and twisted molecules with strange and specific powers. As direct agents of DNA and the whole genetic apparatus,

7. One dalton is roughly equal to the weight of one hydrogen atom.

> they control, promote, guide, and quicken all of life's vital processes. And they do this, like all chemical catalysts, without themselves being consumed in, or becoming more than momentarily a part of, the reactions they instigate.[8]

Earlier, in chapter VIII, Part I, the key requisite of existential-individuation was identified as a specific source of power-quality. That enzymes satisfy the requisites of a discrete dynamism is clearly affirmed above. Further, and physical evidence on behalf of their specificity is provided in these paragraphs which describe their life-style in more detail:

> Early in this century chemists acquired greater skill in separating and analyzing susbtances from the enormous mixture of molecules in living tissue. They began to see that all enzymes are essentially proteins, the main building material of life. Proteins are long-chain molecules made up of linked, infinitely varied sequences of twenty basic amino acids, which in turn are various small configurations of hydrogen-carbon atoms, the ultimate basis of all organic matter.
>
> The way in which one type of enzyme was distinguished from another, and from all other proteins, was in its catalytic action, which proved to be remarkably specific. Each type of enzyme, with only a few exceptions, acts upon only one specific substance or pair of substances, catalyzing only one particular reaction or stage in a complex chain reaction. The specific target substance is called the enzyme's substrate.[9]

As is evident, enzymes also manifest a degree of proficiency in their work which puts to shame the most accomplished of the U.S.S.R.'s stakanohvites.[10] No stakanohvite has been known to accomplish a task with a speed equal to that routinely achieved by the commonplace enzyme known as Lysozyme, whose particular line of work earns it the honor of being singled-out as delegate for his species.

---

8. Lawrence LESSING, "The Life Saving Promise of Enzymes", Fortune, March, 1969, pp. 119-120.
9. *Ibid.*, p. 120.
10. The terms Stakhanovite and Stakhanovism coined in 1935 in the U.S.S.R. to describe a program to speed up industrial production by efficient working methods, were derived from the name of a Donets coal miner Alexksey Stakhanov famous for his efficiency. Stakhanovites received higher pay and other emoluments — a living embodiment of Taylorism in a Marxist society.

Lysozyme was discovered by chance in 1922 by the British bacteriologist Alex Flemming. Having sneezed one day on a bacterial culture, he noted that the growing bacteria began to die rapidly. Investigation revealed that the agent was an enzyme present in saliva, mucous and sweat, as well as in plants and organic fluids generally. Flemming named it Lysozyme, the "dissolving enzyme" — a term which proved appropriate. When in the 60's techniques were developed which made measurements and analyses of the structure of enzymes feasible, this picture offered itself:

> ... the x-ray beam revealed a molecular structure that at first glance looked like a badly snarled bit of rope, with a deep, jawlike cleft in one side. This cleft proved to be the enzyme's "active site"; it fits exactly into and almost literally bites in two some specific carbohydrate molecules in the cell wall of bacteria, spilling and destroying their contents. Each lysozyme molecule, despite its tangled appearance, had its protein chain folded in exactly the same way, presenting the same jawlike cleft to the substrate.[11]

It may be countered that enzymes perform a purely mechanical operation, and do not satisfy the criteria of bodiness, let alone those of animation. Until recently, the plea would have been one of *nolo contendere*. Recent developments in the field of X-ray crystallography effectively refute this objection. D.E. Koshland Jr., reporting in *Scientific American* upon experiments conducted simultaneously at several centers (Harvard, Berkeley, Spain and Japan), reconfirms the specificity of the individual enzyme, and provides data establishing that enzymes use the counterpart of a "body" to fulfill their tasks — evidencing in the process structural flexibility and a sensitivity to their environment, comparable to that found in man's world of flesh and blood. The findings, on which he reports, fill the empty spaces in the enzymian skeleton with the equivalent of the flesh and bone of any macroscopic animated entity, and account for the coordinated movement and aggression of the "active sites" or mouths and limbs of the enzyme which had initially been described as rigid, template-like structures. Having noted that:

> ... Fortunately for our understanding of biological systems many enzymes are quite sturdy molecules and can be extracted from a

11. Lessing, *op. cit.*, p. 121.

> physiological system without destroying their biological properties. Hence they can be studied in the test tube and made to perform the same catalytic role there that they perform in the living organism.

and having briefly outlined the history of the lock and key hypothesis that:

> Unlike catalysts made in the laboratory, enzymes have the special property called specificity, which means that only one chemical compound or a very few can react with a particular enzyme. This property can be explained by the template, or lock-and-key, hypothesis put forward in 1894 by Emil Fischer, which postulates that the enzyme is designed to allow only special compounds to fit on its surface, just as a key fits a lock or as two pieces of a jigsaw puzzle fit together.[12]

Koshland next observes that while the mechanical theory sufficed to explain most features of enzymian action, still it left many aspects of enzyme behavior unaccounted for, as note the following:

> Although this concept could explain much of the specificity data, some glaring discrepancies were found. For instance, certain oversized and undersized compounds were found to bind to the surface of the enzyme even though they failed to form products.

He then concludes that:

> ... These facts and others like them led to the hypothesis that the enzyme does not exist initially in a shape complementary to that of the substrate but rather is induced to take the complementary shape in much the same way that a hand induces a change in the shape of a glove. This "induced fit" theory assumes that the substrate plays a role in determining the final shape of the enzyme and that the enzyme is therefore flexible. Proof that proteins do in fact change their shape under the influence of small molecules was initially obtained by chemical studies showing differences in the reactivity to protein reagents of the amino acid side chains that are arrayed along the spine of the protein molecule. The hypothesis has since been verified with the aid of advanced physical techniques, most notably X-ray crystallography.[13]

---

12. Daniel E. KOSHLAND, Jr. "Protein shape and Biological Control", *Scientific American*, October, 1973.
13. *Ibid.*, pp. 52–54.

The inferences to be drawn from the glove analogy in particular, are farreaching, both from the point of view of Materialism and Scientific Existentialism. One, they present the time-space Materialist with *prima facie* evidence of yet another living "body" within a "body". This, if established, would make an already difficult position more uncomfortable still. Two, they confirm the theory of a universe of discrete, adimensional, willful and living Dynamic-Facts. As noted previously, the three standard prerequisites which, according to the norms of a time-space universe, an entity must satisfy to be accepted within the ranks of the living, are:

1. mass and dimensions,
2. birth and death, and
3. a history or specificity of behavior.

Let us then investigate briefly each, to see whether or not Lysozyme satisfies them. Should this be the case, the untenability of the theory of a universe composed of "dimensioned, material prime building blocks", will be demonstrated conclusively. Simultaneously, the data obtained can be inserted within the parameters of Dynamic Vision, to find out whether or not the latter are compatible with the discoveries of biochemistry.

Dealing firstly with the size or mass of Lysozyme's "body", it suffices to observe that while a dozen average lysozymes hardly affect a bathroom scale, each does exhibit mass — the prime criterion whereby dimensions and bodiness are established. Actually, certain species of enzymes are relatively huge, weighing up to several million daltons. Whether huge or puny, such an entity, by "materialistic" standards qualifies for the title of a "material" or "real thing" — and all "material things", according to Materialism, "have bodies".

While granting Lysozyme a "body", the Materialist might insist that such a "body" is merely "organized matter in movement and potency", and is of the same type as the manufactured "body" of an automobile or submarine, for these also have "bodies" as the term is loosely defined. The objection is legitimate, and should it hold, enzymes would have to be crossed from the list of Atoms. The most cursory of observations seem to preclude such an assessment of Lysozyme and its relatives, for, as a species, they satisfy the second criterion of livingness; that of having a birth and death, and they unambiguously fulfill the third, that of self-induced, dynamic specificity.

The second criterion which Materialists use to decide whether or not a "thing" lives; that of birth-death, need not be considered as decisive in this context. In the first instance, the adjudication of a birth or death, in all cases, rests upon a subjective evaluation of phenomena, and proves nothing. Furthermore, since too little is known of the genetics of enzymes to allow for even the usual approximations, effort expended to establish or negate their births and deaths, would be wasted. In any case, whatever evidence can be adduced favors the biogenesis hypothesis — enzymes do seem to reproduce much as do rabbits and men. As to their death — as death is defined commonly — this is as unquestionable as that of any cat or automobile.

The third and key criterion, self-induced dynamic-specificity, is satisfied beyond reasonable doubt. More than any other feature of enzymian activity, specificity is emphasized by the authors already quoted, as well as by all authorities on the subject. When one adds to specificity, the self-regeneration feature described in the following quote, it becomes evident that Lysozyme is fully as alive as mosquito, mangrove or man.

> ... The high specificity of the enzyme is related to the fact that the structurally complex protein can combine in a particular way necessary for the catalytic action only with molecules that fit very particularized structural requirements.
>
> Like other catalysts, enzymes do not appear to undergo any net change during the reactions which they cause. This apparent absence of change is of course due to the fact that the reaction sequence involves a cyclic regeneration of the original enzyme, so that one molecule of enzyme reacts over and over again within a brief space of time, each time with a different molecule of substrate. The activity of a purified enzyme is sometimes expressed as its turnover number, the number of molecules of substrate acted upon by one molecule of enzyme in one minute. Most enzymes have turnover numbers higher than 1,000 and some have turnover numbers larger than 1,000,000. The enzymes choline esterase and catalase have the highest turnover numbers known-about 18,000,000. Catalase, an enzyme present in red blood cells, causes the decomposition of hydrogen peroxide to oxygen.[14]

14. Birgit VENNESLAND, "Enzymes", *Encyclopedia Britannica*, vol. 8, p. 631, Chicago, Benton, 1962.

Where requisite number one, the bodiness of Lysozyme, is concerned, it has been conceded that even though lysozymes have "bodies" (they possess mass), nonetheless it could rightly be objected that such a "body" need not imply existential atomicity, but could correspond to that of a car — that it may not result from "internal relatedness", to use a Whiteheadian term, but could conceivably be manufactured by "outside pressures". However, when the enzymian "body" or mass is considered in the light of the data available as to its specificity, self-regeneration, aggressivity and flexibility, one must, if scientific objectivity is respected, grant it the status automatically granted to other living "bodies" — those of a woodpecker or snail, for instance. Indeed, it becomes imperative to think in terms of flesh, for the combination of the self-regeneration feature, with the conformability and flexibility which Koshland saw fit to describe as inducing the enzyme "to take the complementary shape" (that of the substrate) "in much the same way that a hand induces a change in the shape of a glove", operates to endow enzymes with every characteristic normally associated with a fleshy embrace.

There is of course no such "material" as flesh. Like liver and liverness, and life and animation, the concept and sense of flesh is derived from the observation and/or sensory experience of a fasces of qualities — the coagentship of which give such Atoms as are responsive to these qualities, a sensation, pleasurable or otherwise. Usually the powers involved emanate from a single Atom, but many can offer their flesh simultaneously to one or more Outsiders, as in an orgy. Then, the situation parallels that described as liverness, where billions of liver cells combine to offer themselves as visible and/or edible to man or dog. Individually, any one liver cell would go unnoticed — it is all a matter of scopies and acuity of perception. The same applies which a vengeance in the case of Lysozyme. Clearly, it is endowed with a qualitivity specifically its own. Due to its submicroscopic size, we cannot feel its ribs, nor see its arms, nor feel its mouth; yet, it does coagentize with the Atoms under its control, and aggress upon those which it requires as a direct foundation. Such is the picture which the X-ray crystallograph transmits when it reveals that Lysozyme "literally bites in two a carbohydrate molecule in the cell walls of bacteria, spilling and destroying its contents" — a picture which at our visuo-sensual range, corresponds to that of a child biting into an overripe peach, or a frog gulping a fly, to dissolve either in their stomachs.

The Koshland interpretations of enzymian activity does call for comment. This will serve a dual purpose. It will prevent misunderstanding — if opposition of views there is — for Koshland may not in fact argue for the position implicit in his statement, and it will illustrate concretely, a key aspect of the corresponsibility feature involved in cosmic presentiality. If the author in the statement:

> the enzyme does not exist initially in a shape complementary to that of the substrate but rather is induced to take the complementary shape in much the same way that a hand induces a change in the shape of a glove.[15]

adopts the Huxley-Teilhardian thesis of archebiosis — whereby the less complex "causes", in time, the more complex; whereby non-living "matter" "causes" a primordial protoplasm, whereby the protoplasm "causes" the amoebe and the amoebe "causes" the coelacanth, and the coelacanth the baboon, and the baboon the humanoid, and the humanoid "progresses" and "progresses" and "progresses" into some type of Teilhardian humanoidal angel or Marxian superhuman; and so on *ad infinitum* — then his interpretation must be rejected. To believe in any modality whatsoever of archebiosis, even sophisticated and buttressed by paleontological detritus, is tantamount to believing that rabbits do come out of the magician's hat, or still that the buzzing fly in Lafontaine's *The Fly and the Coach* did move the coach. That the

---

15. KOSHLAND, *op. cit.*, p. 52. The reservation in respect to the author's actual view as to the specificity or strict entity character of animates and of man in particular, are due to the ambiguity of his reference, in the following, to man as "the most complex biological system". If such a system is seen as closed, then our positions coincide.

> Up to this point I have emphasized the regulatory control of enzymes because they are the regulatory proteins that have been studied the most intensively and they are readily available in the laboratory... Receptor molecules involved in sensory systems have been shown to be similar to enzymes in terms of structure and binding properties. These molecules have the specificity characteristic of enzymes, and it is generally believed, but not absolutely proved, that induced conformational changes are the signals that trigger the sensory impulse... Light induces a change in the shape of a protein in our eyes. Sensory phenomena are the highest form of regulation, and the brain is the ultimate regulatory apparatus of the most complex biological system: man.

lesser does not move, let alone create the greater, is an elementary principle of physics, recognized by all except for the members of a certain school of biology, best defined as neo-Democritans, whose theories of archebiosis are but a renovated version of the discredited *generatio aequivoca* or spontaneous generation of Aristotle applied to a cyclotron-bred Democritan atom.

Even a cursory assessment of the Koshland statistics makes it abundantly clear that to see in the enzyme-to-substrate relationship, one of induced conformability on the part of Lysozyme, is tantamount to affirming that it is the mouse which a cat has just gobbled which creates the cat and its subsequent gobbling of the mouse, this being the ratio between enzymes and their substrates:

> ... Fortunately qualitative features do not change with the size of the protein, so that by studying the simpler proteins it is possible to understand the properties of proteins in general.
>
> A peptide chain with a molecular weight of only 25,000 daltons is still large compared with the molecular weight of most substrates, which are usually compounds in the molecular-weight range of 100 to 1,000 daltons. Occasionally enzymes act on very large molecules such as DNA (deoxyribonucleic acid), cellulose or other proteins, but when they do, they usually bind only a small portion of these large molecules, so that the effective substrate size is still only about 1,000 daltons or less. This difference in relative size means that only a small portion of the enzyme's surface is actually involved in catalysis. The rest of the surface is available for binding the molecules that are involved in regulation and for the association of subunits with one another.[16]

However, to reject all variants of the theory of archebiosis, of the gradual "complexification of matter", is not by the same token to adopt the obverse stand — that of a creation *ex nihilo*, whereby the greater and more complex causes or creates the smaller and less complex out of a void. Reality is anchored upon the mass of Existence intuited as a fact. The epistemological counterpart of existential facticity, consists of a refusal to consider any modality of nothingness — whether a Hegelian "pure nothingness" or the subterfuge called past-future, when the latter is given an ontological content. Faithful adherence to

16. Koshland, *op. cit.*, p. 56.

as-isness has paid-off by yielding a body of coherent insights into the nature of the Atom and of the cosmic mechanism in general. Under no circumstances must this progress be jeopardized. Thus, exactly as biogenetic and archebiotic ontogeny must be rejected, so must it be with the crude commonplace creationism which affirms that:

> we were produced from nothing by God; that He preserves us at every moment, by His positive act of conservation, from falling back into the original nothingness from which we came; ...[17]

I no more care or dare to mire God in nothingness, than I would myself. We Existential-Atom are — period. And since the relationship of each to each is of Cosmic-Presence to Cosmic-Presence, we are corresponsible for each other, each according to our power — a situation not at all demeaning for the Atom whose power is absolute. Applied to the present situation, the following scenario offers itself. Neither Lysozyme nor his substrate cause each other. *Both are.* Both reside and move in the Absolute and are corresponsible for each other's presence. More on this in the next and closing act.

In summary, any difference of opinion as to causality versus corresponsibility notwithstanding, the fact remains that by the standards of Materialism as well as of Scientific Existentialism, Lysozyme in particular, and enzymes in general constitute "material" entities endowed with "bodies". Insofar as Humanoid and Leucocyte are concerned, the outcome is obvious. In the time-space-matter-movement scenario, where Lysozyme resides a "hole" occurs in Leucocyte. The implications for Humanoid should gratify the masochistic tendencies of any Nihilist. Since Leucocyte already made a "hole" in Humanoid's "body", there is now a "double layer of holes, void or nothingness" — a situation tailor-made to tickle the funny-bone of Hegel and his disciples. The worst is to come. When and where Uranium and Iron enter the scene, triple layers of nothingness come to lay one upon the other — at which point, Sartre himself should fall into ecstasy.

---

17. Aelred GRAHAM, *The Love of God*, Image Books, Doubleday & Company, New York, ch. III p. 150.

12. The Outsiders of "Distant Cousins"

The role of the two remaining members of the cast is briefer but nonetheless important for each contributes new insights into the nature of "bodies" and of cosmic presentiality. In the case of Iron, briefness is possible because its basic relationship to Humanoid corresponds to that entertained by Leucocyte and Lysozyme, except for radical outsideness. A summary treatment of Uranium, also a radical Outsider, is justified on the ground that its relationship to Humanoid's "body" appears to be incidental and hostile — a status which unexpectedly makes its witness all the more unassailable. The relevance of the new characteristic which both share namely : radical outsideness, will be considered firstly to avoid duplication.

To refer to Uranium and Iron as radical Outsiders does not imply degrees of outsideness. Outsideness is an either-or-affair. An Outsider is an Outsider. Presently, attention is drawn to differing degree of coagentship. Whereas Leucocyte and Lysozyme can, to borrow from genealogy, be described as children of Humanoid, both Uranium and Iron are total strangers to him and demonstrate, more forcefully than the previous witnesses, the fact that the "bodies" of the "living" are not "owned", but are rather only foci of high intensity coagency. The reference to Leucocyte and Lysozyme as children of Humanoid is not a metaphor. Had he not been, neither would they. Man not only fathers his cells directly, but these bear his imprint quite as faithfully as do his human sons and daughters. This genetical relationship between warm blooded animals, (and possibly all Atoms), is confirmed by the rejection phenomenon which complicates most attempts at limb or organ transplants. The special relationship, in effect a type of double siring, which binds the animal or plant to its flesh, has always been a cause of confusion for the Bio-Philosophists. Here the term Bio-Philosophism is used to encompass generically any school of Becomingism (Aristotelian, Hegelian, Teilhardian, etc.), which seeks to stabilize its shifting ontology through the help of whatever hypothesis of evolution is in vogue at the time of their writing. The one characteristic which such strange bedfellows as Lorenz and Rensch, Haldane and Duhring, Bergson and Lamarck, Foucault and Lysenko not to mention the masters, all share is a lack of understanding of absoluteneity and outsideness. As a consequencc, when attempting to define and circumscribe the origin and/or locus of biological individuation and phenomena, all arbitrarily shunt the "source of life" from one cause or fount to another — the intricacies of modern biology providing them with a lode of new "scientific proof" for their minuets.

It was to eliminate such ambiguities, notably those prevalent on the subject of man's double sire relationship with certain species of organelles, that the status of Leucocyte and Lysozyme within Humanoid's "body" was analyzed in some detail. The same problem does not arise with Iron and Uranium. Both are genetically unrelated to Humanoid. Their relationship is that of foreigners or, at best, of distant cousins to each other and to whichever human they may jointly visit. Even the diehard Hylemorphist will hardly argue that an iron or uranium atom within a mammalian "body", is one ontologically with said "body". While the foreigness exhibited by either element is such that the mere fact of noting it, establishes further the "holeyness" of Humanoid's "body", the difference in the relationship which either entertains with man warrants a closer look.

13. **Uranium — The Dangerous Squatter**

The witness of Uranium X_1, need not detain us long. Statistical confirmation of its foreigness to the human "body" is evidenced by the fact, firstly, that they are found in somewhat the same proportion throughout the earth's crust ($4x10^{-16}$ g. per gram of rock) as in man (from $10^{-4}\%$ to $10^{-9}\%$ by weight), and secondly, that U^{238} and his relatives, do not, at least as far as ascertained to date, play a key role in any metabolic process. While the time of the imbedding of an uranium in a live "body" cannot as a rule be recorded precisely, its existence outside of and prior to the birth of the organism which it inhabits, plus its low metabolic relationship do establish a status of independent agent, i.e. it cannot be considered as under the genetical control of man. Rather, its status is akin to that of a dangerous squatter. Which brings up the characteristic peculiar to Uranium: its radioactivity or alternately its aggressivity. The following briefly sketched hypothetical event, involving an attack by our star against the "body" of Humanoid, can shed additional light upon the nature of "bodies" and of cosmic relationality in general.

The materials required are minimal: Humanoid and his "body", and a Ux_1 (a U^{234}) which has escaped into the atmosphere either through a leak in a reactor or its own wits, and subsequently invades Humanoid, during the latter's visit to said reactor. Given that set of circumstances, even the Hylemorphist will not affirm that immediately upon entering Humanoid's blood stream, Ux_1 loses its identity and becomes organically human. While the Outsider to Outsider relationship of Ux_1 to Humanoid is confirmed by its mode of entry into Humanoid's "body", the aggressive character of Ux_1 next provides ironclad evidence of outsideness. Not only are the two, Outsiders, but they are enemies.

It was noted in the opening paragraph that uraniums were more aggressive than most metalloids and could indeed be hostile — a trait which establishes a kinship of sorts, between them and man. Interestingly, they share further characteristics with humans. Birth and death, for instance. Uraniums die and sire other uraniums. The parallel in the latter case is so striking that physicists frequently speak of it in terms such as these:

> ... For some time it was regarded as a branch product, probably of uranium II, and it was also believed to be the parent of protactinium... Uranium Y is the daughter product of the emitting uranium isotope of mass number 235, the so-called actinouranium.[18]

The siring ability and death rate of uraniums being more directly related to entropy, the question is deferred to Part IV. Presently the point of interest is the emission of rays of electrons and other particles — for the three-way relationship, between Humanoid, Leucocyte and Ux_1, thereby established, throws considerable light upon cosmic corresponsibility.

Since our star is a Ux_1, its father was a natural uranium, most probably a U^{238}, whose life span is very long by human standards (a mean or half-life of 4.51×10^9 years) and much longer still by those of an Ux_1 whose life expectancy is a mere 24.1 days. Even rats do better. Upon its entry into Humanoid's

18. Ernest RUTHERFORD, *et al*, "Radioactivity, Natural", *Encyclopaedia Britannica*, vol. 18, Chicago, Benton, 1962, pp. 896E-896F.

"body", Ux_1, born from the emission of beta ray activity, may damage a considerable number of organelles, cilia and genes, and would do so until its death. However, the situation worsens when Ux_1 fathers his own offspring, called Ux_2s with a life expectancy of about 1.17 minute. The high energy rays emitted by Ux_2s are more damaging yet to the various families of organelles upon which man depends to maintain himself in decent health. Among the diseases which beta rays might trigger, is leukemia, to which Leucocyte and his tribe are prone — hence the possible multiplicand effect of a well-concerted uranific invasion. The two-fold relevance of Uranium to the investigation is, at this point, clearly established. Firstly, while the mass-weight of the uraniums in a human "body" adds up to a mere 4 milligrams, still trillions of individual uraniums are involved. Since each makes a "hole", Humanoid's "body" avers itself as an extremely fine-meshed sieve. That which applies to the human, applies equally to Leucocyte, Lysozyme and their relatives. In truth, the situation is tailor-made to induce wild-eyed ecstasy in Sartre — three solid layers of nothingness superimposed one upon the other! Secondly, the aggressivity of Ux_1 and his uranific relatives and offspring confirms the primacy of the Principle of Clash in the Now. Whereas Leucocyte, Lysozyme, and the fourth co-star, Iron, are friends and allies, residing within Humanoid's "body" fortress, the relationship of Ux_1 and his tribe to Humanoid approximates that of antimatter. Ux_1 not only bores a third hole in the two previous holes, but operates as a nihilating factor — as an agent of destruction and death.

14. **Iron, the Cooperative Outsider**

Iron, the last of the cast, belongs to one of the most useful of the metallic tribes known to man, for its coagency with man ranges over a much broader spectrum than that of the other players. With Ux_1 and other metals, it shares outsideness, and with Leucocyte and the organelles in general, metabolic integration with the life process of Humanoid. Such an all-inclusive spectrum of existential involvement gives added weight to Iron's testimony.

While the very presence of lysozymes, leucocytes and uranium in living organisms was ignored until recently, the therapeutic role of iron was long ago recognized. Its statistical presence and distribution within man has been determined with relative accuracy and many of its catalytic interactions are deciphered. Statistics-wise some 0.004% of Humanoid's "body" consists of iron — a paltry 3 centigrams, give or take a little. The several trillion atoms involved are divided into two main tribes, the ferrous and ferric. Our star belongs to the ferrous, whose function in the metabolism of mammals is important. While irons are widely disseminated, they are especially numerous in the blood — about 55% of the total body iron residing in the red cells alone, plus a smaller but nonetheless significant percentage in the leucocytes and the plasma. Of the balance, some 20% is stored in such organs as the liver and spleen, and in the bone marrow. Except for minute quantities in an unassociated state in erythrocytes, the remaining 20% is distributed somewhat evenly throughout the musculature, in the form of parenchyma iron.

It is a silent but glorious testimonial to the intellect of The Absolute, that a mere 3 to 4 centigrams of iron compounds could be disseminated in just the right proportions throughout 75 kilos of flesh and bone, and that each iron should know and play its individual role — some forming compounds with other elements, in particular with nitrogen and oxygen, others in compounds or independently interacting as substrates with thousands of species of enzymes.

The outsideness of Iron to Humanoid's "body" hardly requires demonstration. For instance, it is common medical practice to administer iron to combat dietetic and/or absorption deficiencies — in particular, hypochronic anemia. Clearly, prior to its ingestion, the iron involved was not man. Nor does it become human once incorporated. While a varying percentage of an iron compound administered to Humanoid would remain in his "body", under normal conditions a substantial portion is excreted shortly after ingestion. The excreted simply flow through the blood system and organs, much as fish float down a river — all the while retaining their identity. Further, should Humanoid die, Ferrous Iron could be recovered from the "body" ashes, unharmed. The above is common knowledge and no one will, in light of the recent developments of biochemistry, straight-facedly deny to irons the status of specific entities. As it was with uraniums, so with irons. Where irons reside, man is not —

neither space nor mass-wise. Stated otherwise, if the reader upon getting on a scale, sees it register 70 kilos, he must, if he whishes to be scientific and honest, deduct whatever amount of iron his "body" may contain. Thus the human sieve has, in standard materialistic terminology, sprung several million trillion additional "holes", and has, in the process, lost more weight. It is by now, "holeyer" than the best of Gruyère cheeses.

The self-evident character of Iron's outsideness to Humanoid's "body", is such that its mention undoubtedly added nothing to the knowledge of the situation. The same will apply where the technology of iron's metabolism is concerned, the latter's mechanism being common knowledge with anyone who has benefitted from a secondary education. It is when the time comes to evaluate its ontological implications that the unexpected and novel arise, and with these, controversy.

Presently, the consensus within the scientific community is that the Universe is composed of extended bits of "matter". These hypothetical particles have by now dwindled to infinitesimals. Nonetheless, as in the days of Democritus, the common belief has it that by playing games with such "nature", through an archegenetic process referred to as evolution, causes the more complex to be created out of nothing. In some instances, the dogmas of this quaint faith come all dressed-up in technical jargon *à la* Teilhard. At other times, poetry bolsters the faith of the believer — as witness the following:

> Since the first human eye saw a leaf in Devonian sandstone and a puzzled finger reached to touch it, sadness has lain over the heart of man. By this tenuous thread of living protoplasm, stretching backward into time, we are linked forever to lost beaches whose sands have long since hardened into stone. ... No one knows the secret of its beginning or its end. Its forms are phantoms. The thread alone is real; the thread is life... But the thread has run a tangled maze. There are strange turns in its history, loops and knots and constrictions. Today the dead beasts decorate the halls of our museums, and that nature of which men spoke so trustingly is known to have created a multitude of forms before the present, played with them, building armor and strange reptilian pleasures, only to let them pass like discarded toys on a playroom floor. Nevertheless, the thread of life ran onward, so that if you look closely you can see the

singing reptile in the bird, or some ancient amphibian fondness for the ooze where the child wades in the mud.[19]

The merit of Ferrous Iron is that over and above confirming the sieve-like nature of Humanoid's "body", it can, if its metabolic relationships are correctly assessed, contribute to a better understanding of the inner mechanism of the Atom, in particular, of coagentship and cosmic corresponsibility. Among the numerous instances of the man-iron exchanges, the reversibility of the ionization process which occurs through the agency of man — one could say under his supervision — is of special interest. This metabolism, briefly outlined by Edwin F. Orlemann (University of California, Berkeley), establishes the clear title of Iron and his relatives to a will, "body" and personality, as distinct as those of any "live" Atom. As an added benefit, it explains further the behavior of Leucocyte and Lysozyme, and simultaneously confirms cogenesis.

> ... Both ferrous and ferric iron form metalloporphyrins in which the iron atom is bound to the four nitrogen atoms in the centre of the flat porphyrin ring. The particular metalloporphyrin obtained from protoporphyrin and ferrous ion is heme, $C_{34}H_{33}N_{4}0_{4}$ FeOH. Heme combines with various proteins, presumably by the interaction of the iron atom in the heme with protein nitrogen atoms to establish the maximum co-ordination number of six for the iron. If the protein is globin the resultant molecule is hemoglobin, while other specific proteins give rise to such important enzymes as catalase, cytochrome, peroxidase and Warburg's respiratory enzyme. Hemoglobin, represented as Hb, reacts with oxygen to form oxyhemoglobin, HbO_2, in an amount that is proportional to the pressure of oxygen, until a maximum of about 1.36 c.c. of O_2 gram of Hb has reacted. This is an entirely reversible process and the oxygen taken up to form the equilibrium amount of HbO_2 at some particular pressure of oxygen will be given up by the HbO_2 if the oxygen pressure is reduced to its original value. It is by the use of this property that hemoglobin functions as an oxygen carrier in the body.[20]

The message is clear. Within the context of a humanoid-globin-iron-oxygen closed system, each player performs a well defined role. A discrete, embodied and free-willed agent, each responds

---

19. Loren Eiseley, *The Firmament of Time*, New York, Atheneum, 1960, pp. 56-57.
20. Edwin F. Orlemann, "Iron", *Encyclopaedia Britannica*, vol. 12, Chicago, Benton, 1962, pp. 648-649.

to outside aggression and blandishments in a personal and consistent way. Where the bodiness of Iron is concerned, if the same criteria of fluidity, flexibility and specificity are applied as to Humanoid and Lysozyme, then it also possesses a "body" — a "body" ironically quite as "holey" as those of the first three stars, for Iron pullulates with electrons, protons and muons, etc. The fact that Iron and the globins and oxygens with which it interplays are free-willed agents endowed with intellects, perhaps proves difficult to credit, especially by those who deny free-will even to man. Yet an objective assessment leaves no alternative. To reach out and grab with single-mindedness certain atoms only; to react to changes in ones environment; to reverse processes as the need arises, as do globins, irons and oxygens, testifies to an independence fully as specific as that of the reader when he chooses to read this page. Without doubt age-old thought patterns plus human pride, are mainly responsible for our unwillingness to grant other Existential-Atoms a full personality. As knowledge of microscopies develops, this bias will disappear. Indeed, there is a growing indication of such a shift, particularly among biochemists whose work constantly places before them evidence of a "vitalism" of sorts — hence, for whom the dividing line between animation and inanimation has been blurred. *The lives of a Cell* by Lewis Thomas, M. D., president of New York's Sloan-Kettering Cancer Center, is representative of the advanced trend in that direction. While Thomas allows his faith in the evolutionary hypothesis and a concomitant archegenesis, to vitiate his concept of a being, his observations of the As-is relationship of man to his cells and organelles have led him to conclusions which in many respects parallel my own, as witness:

> ... Man is embedded in nature... At the interior of our cells, driving them, providing the oxidative energy that sends us out for the improvement of each shining day, are the mitochondria, and in a strict sense they are not ours. They turn out to be separate little creatures, the colonial posterity of migrant prokaryocytes, probably primitive bacteria that swam into ancestral precursors of our eukaryotic cells and stayed there... I like to think that they work in my interest, that each breath they draw for me, but perhaps it is they who walk through the local park in the early morning, sensing my senses, listening to my music, thinking my thoughts.[21]

21. Lewis THOMAS, M.D. "Ideas: The Boswell of Organelles", *Newsweek*, June 24, 1974, p. 89.

15. Cogenesis rather than Biogenesis or Archegenesis

That the primary process of the Universe is one of cogenesis, rather than of biogenesis or archegenesis, was a corrollary of coevality. Once the relationship of Lysozyme to Humanoid is analyzed, cogenesis — the corresponsibility of all to all for their mutual beingness is further established on empirical grounds. Certainly, archegenesis (abiogenesis) which implies when transposed into the macroscopic realm, that the mouse creates the cat which eats it, is discredited. Facetiously the behavior of Iron towards globins and oxygens can be said to make the case for cogenesis ironclad. Since irons do not beget oxygens or electrons, the hypothesis of cosmic biogenesis must be abandoned, as must also be archegenesis. For, when next the reversibility of Iron's interplay with globins and oxygens is discovered, to see in Iron the offspring of oxygens, electrons or of a more primitive building block, such as the hypothetical quark encountered earlier, becomes specious.

Intellectual honesty leaves one avenue open to an understanding of the world and of ones relationship to the Outsiders. At the Real, cosmic presentiality is the norm. We men, oaks, oysters, and oxygens, are all Presences to each other. At the level of Now processes, cogenesis, the mutual generation of all by all, takes over.

In summary, Iron's contribution to ontology is considerable. By evidencing the power to commune in a reversible manner with recognized animates, with Humanoid for instance, and with the borderline animates such as Leucocyte, Iron and his multitudinous relatives provide a scientific answer to the question of origins. *In a universe where the Principle of Absolutes reigns, everyone is cogenetic; all are full brothers and correspondents — from the puniest to the strongest, from louse to God.*

16. Act Three: Orangutan, His Ux_1 and the Eternal Life of All Atoms

Now remember the second star, Orangutan, and his four co-stars, since except for their initial enumeration, all reference to them has been omitted. Orangutan has few additional insights to contribute on bodiness. Interest in him rather concerns his evidence as to the univocity of Existence and its implications, notably on the subject of coevality.

With respect to Orang's bodiness, it suffices to observe that since, clinically, the difference of metabolism between him and man is primarily quantitative, then, as with Humanoid, so with Orangutan alias *Pongo pygmaeus* alias the-man-of-the-forest (Malay). His phagocytic host bores a hole in his "body". In turn, his Lysozyme creates a hole in his Leucocyte and so a double layer of 'holeyness' in Orang — Orang becoming holeyer and holeyer with each step down the ladder of microscopies. In short, the man-of-the-forest no more owns his "body", than did *Homo sapiens*, the high-rise dweller. Their so-called "bodies" represent marvellously integrated dynamic fields, each of which, to paraphrase Gouiran's description of the particle, "in reality covers the entire universe, but the probability of finding it is almost entirely confined to a small space" — in this instance, to the microscopic area defined as Orang's anatomy. A summary treatment of Orangutan's bodiness in no way reduces his relevance, for he and his co-stars, particularly his Ux_1, contribute valuable insights into the coevality beyond time-space of all dinosaurs, angels, electrons and oaks — a state of full-fledged Cosmic-Presence. This evidence is of course empirical and circumstantial and can only buttress that drawn from the synacts, Reality, Truth and Existence, or alternately from the principle that: What-Is, Is, each of the former being universal in scope. The rationale is plain. Cosmic presentiality, a universal state, can only be confirmed by principles of the same order.

As indicated in section 2, chapter II, Part III, the main reason for including subjects as similar as *Homo sapiens* and *Pongo pygmaeus* in the last experiment, is to, on the one hand, deny the Materialists the opportunity to classify Dynamic Vision among the dichotomous philosophies, and on the other, to prevent the Thomists and their kin from equating their position in respect to souls, with the present. The intention is to make crystal clear that, in the democratic universe of Dynamic Vision, all Atoms share a common nature and it follows, a common fate. In the less convoluted terminology of Dynamic Vision, the same statement translates into the simple affirmation that *Beings are* — period.

To place the long-armed, redheaded man-of-the-forest on an equal footing with *Homo sapiens*, serves notice upon the Spiritualists that any distinction between souls is rejected. If one insists upon speaking of souls, and to this no objection since term-symbols are easily accommodated, provided only that there is agreement upon content, then all Atoms are endowed of souls, each, that of Orang and his Ux_1 inclusively, eternal. While the simian may not enjoy the beatific vision, it will nonetheless, to use their vocabulary, "enjoy eternity" — undoubtedly in a manner natural to a man-of-the-forest. Whereas they rely upon Revelation to salvage the human soul, while cavalierly concurring with the Materialists in the demise of the remainder of the souls, here it is upon the strength of the twin Principles of the Conservation of Energy and of What-Is, Is, that all souls, all Atoms are conserved.

Where Materialists are concerned, the duty of Orangutan is to stand shoulder to shoulder with Humanoid and, as proxy for the living remind them that honesty, common as well as scientific, demands that they account for the energies or powers generated by all living organisms. Whereas until recently, they and their correligionists in general could cling with a minimum of plausibility to the crude hypothesis prevalent throughout the 18th and 19th centuries, that life was an epiphenomenon resulting from the interplay of Democritan-like eternal molecules, today in the 1970's, this faith can be maintained only upon the basis of a reactionary sectarianism. Since it is scientific fact that the metabolism of metalloids such as irons or uraniums corresponds modality-wise, albeit not quality-wise, to that of the higher species, the enzymian or vertebrate for instance, then by their standards, the oxygens and uraniums, etc., are also mere epiphenomena. Ultimately the advocate of archegenesis who relies for the construction of his universe upon identical primary building blocks must embrace some more or less modernized version of the Leucippean scheme described as follows by Aristotle, in *On Democritus*:

> They (Leucippus, Democritus, Epicurus), said that the first principles were infinite in number, and thought they were indivisible atoms and impassible owing to their compactness, and without any void in them; divisibility comes about because of the void in compound bodies.

The bankruptcy of archegenesis is so transparent that a very influential school of Materialism rejects it vehemently, on other grounds and for different motives. These unexpected allies are none other than the Hegelo-Marxists. The following quote from H. Selsam's *A Marxist Introduction — What is Philosophy* — one of the rare Marxists works in which a genuine effort is made to develop an ontological theory consonant with Marxian "matter in movement" — makes the point aptly. To do so, Selsam avails himself of the support of no less an authority than Lenin:

> ... In recent years, one of the most popular arguments has been that matter has disappeared as a result of the advance of physical science and that the concept of matter is out of date. We no longer find any such thing as the early materialists believed in — hard, impenetrable particles. In their place science offers us the picture of the atom as a whirling system of forces, as composed of groups of infinitesimal electric charges moving at high velocities, with relatively vast spaces between them. This argument was answered by V. I. Lenin who, in his book Materialism and Empirio-Criticism, showed that this conclusion had arisen from the ignorance of scientists of any materialism other than the old mechanistic variety. He said that "dialectical materialism insists on the approximate, relative character of every scientific proposition concerning the structure of matter and its properties; on the absence of absolute boundaries in nature; on the transformation of moving matter from one state to another..." [22]

While Selsam and Lenin correctly observe that: "We no longer find any such thing as the early materialists believed in — "hard, impenetrable particles", one must apply to the Dialectical Materialists, the proverb: "They jump from the frying pan into the fire". If Selsam's statement made earlier in the same book that:

> the flow or movement of things in time is alone real, and things thought of as not being in time, as not beginning and ending, are but the shadows of things abstracted from their reality.[23]

is taken at face value, then he cannot rightly use a strict unit or absolute in his statements and equations. Otherwise, since a harmless numeral 2 constitutes an unmoving entity and as such, resides outside of dialectical movement, every time that the believer in the "matter in movement" theory uses, in his discourse, a series of absolutes as inoffensive as $2 \times 5 = 10$, a

22. Howard SELSAM, *What Is Philosophy? A Marxist Introduction*, New York, International Publishers, 1938, pp. 132-133.
23. *Ibid.*, p. 98.

miracle, more radical than the stopping of the sun by Joshua, must be performed — the cosmic process itself being arrested. The Marxist's only recourse is to argue that defined concepts, i.e. numerals and symbols are not "material". Immediately, however, the "matter-spirit" dichotomy, which Marx strove valiantly to eradicate resurfaces and the Marxist universe collapses. As indicated in section 8, chapter V, Part II, the need to account for a single stationary-point suffices to bring physically crashing down and to a standstill, the entire machinery of any "matter in movement" universe.

In summary, Orangutan and his Ux_1 establish the fact that neither "matter", in the one case, nor "matter" and the human "soul", in the other, is eternal, but rather that each Atom, individually, is eternal. The mechanics of the Universe predicate as much, and an unbiased reading of the latest discoveries of biochemistry, astronomy and subnuclear physics, when integrated into a coherent grid, leads to the same conclusion. Part IV will present a brief correlation of insights and factors drawn from the sciences enumerated, which seem to converge and foreshadow an identical fate for all Atoms: one of coexistence in peace and stability. The whole will be integrated into a cosmogonic theory referred to henceforth as the Theory of Cosmic Peace.

Since it is an understatement to note that such a theory may raise barriers of incomprehension, any development which draws undue attention to the subject will seem masochistic. If anything, it would be expected that, especially at the close, the question would be quietly shunted onto a side-track — in the hope that mercifully it might be forgotten — and that instead other features which offer insights of a practical nature, and upon which agreement is readily forthcoming would be emphasized. Such a course must be rejected. In the first instance, avoidance or even soft-pedalling of the issue would diminish the credibility of the whole, and would leave unanswered the one point upon which all comprehension of Reality hinges. In the second instance, there is no need to hedge. Its strangeness notwithstanding, cosmic peace is supported by evidence altogether as convincing as that upon which rests the alternative scenarios — most of which envision a universe dying from entropy, as witness these poignant paragraphs:

> ... Although it is true that the amount of matter in the universe is perpetually changing, the change appears to be mainly in one direction — toward dissolution... The sun is slowly but surely burning out, the stars are dying embers, and everywhere in the cosmos heat is turning to cold, matter is dissolving into radiation, and energy is being dissipated into empty space.
>
> The universe is thus progressing toward an ultimate "heat-death", or as it is technically defined, a condition of "maximum entropy". When the universe reaches this state some billions of years from now all the processes of nature will cease. All space will be at the same temperature. No energy can be used because all of it will be uniformly distributed through the cosmos. There will be no light, no life, no warmth — nothing but perpetual and irrevocable stagnation. Time itself will come to an end. For entropy points the direction of time.[24]

Barnett and the holders of related theories could be correct. The fate of the Universe and our own could be so dismal. Many reasons argue otherwise. One of these by itself — the need to conserve Energy or the Real — suffices to tip the scale in favor of cosmic presence and peace. Several other scientifically ascertainable phenomena also weigh on the same side.

---

24. Lincoln BARNETT, *The Universe and Dr. Einstein*, New York, Mentor, 1948, pp. 102-103.

Part IV

Death, Entropy and a Theory of Cosmic Peace

chapter I

The Universe of the Real, a Universe of Peace

"Another sun shines there! — another moon. Another light, not dusk, nor dawn nor noon. And they who once beholding come no more — They have attained My peace — life's utmost boon."

Bhagavad GITA, *Celestial Song*

And I heard a loud voice from the throne, saying, "Behold the dwelling of God with men... And he shall wipe away every tear from their eyes, and death shall be no more, neither shall mourning or wailing or pain be any more.

JOHN, THE APOSTLE, *Apocalypse* 21, 3–5

1. The Universe of the Real, a Universe of Hope and Cosmic Peace

THE physicist's dismal vision of entropic degeneration, absolute cold, death and dissolution, is undoubtedly worthy of the cannibalistic Aristotelian *degeneratio unius est generatio alterius* scenario; worthy also of the Becomingists' — that of the Santayanas, Marxes, and Russells — wherein a personified nothingness chases into the void a dissolving nothing, in an irrational, frenzied dance of movement exceeding that of the wildest whirling dervish. Our insistence upon imbedding aggression and its cruelties into the innermost fibre of the Atom is hardly more reassuring — Nietzsche himself seems outdone. To close on such a note would be to leave the task unfinished. Worse, it would paint a false picture.

Part IV is devoted to setting the record straight; to showing in particular, that the Universe is neither one of Sartrian absurdity nor of dissolution and Schopenhauerian despair. It is true. Aggression and its ghoulish cohorts, suffering and death, do occupy the center of the stage of the Now. So true that I dare affirm that:

> He who does not conquer does not live.

The Now, however, is not Reality, nor Truth, nor Existence, but rather only our perceived and *willed* contribution to Reality, Truth and Existence. Whereas the Now bathes in aggression and death, the Real subsists in beauty and peace, and for those who so will it, in love. Formulated in other terms, the real state of the Universe is one of *de-facto* cosmic peace, and the truthful canvas is not that painted by the subjectivating, misguided prophets of doom, but one which conforms closely to that of John, the Apostle of love:

> And I beheld a new heaven and a new earth; for the first heaven and the first earth were departed, and the sea is no more. And I saw the holy city, the new Jerusalem, coming down out of heaven from God.
>
> And he showed me a river of the water of life, bright as crystal, issuing forth from the throne of God and of the Lamb, in the midst of the street of the city.
>
> And there shall no more be aught accursed. And the throne of God and of the Lamb shall be in the city, and his servants shall minister before him, and they shall behold his face, and his name shall be on their foreheads, and night shall be no more, and they shall have no need of the light of a lamp or of the light of the sun, because the Lord God shall be their light; and they shall reign for ever and ever.[1]

That some modality of cosmic peace corresponds to Reality, was implicit in a correct reading of the mechanism of the Universe, in particular, of the phenomenon of maximization. An accurate interpretation of verifiable phenomena, in particular that of physical entropy, imposes upon the physicist and scientist in general, an identical vision — a vision of peace and "daylight around the clock".

2. The Theory Stated, or Orangutan, Ux_1 and Neutrino in Heaven

As noted above, the Theory of Cosmic Peace, a rational as well as physical imperative, merely explicits that which was implicit in coevality, mediumship, foundationship and maximization. It is presented not as a hypothesis, but as the final elaboration on the principle that: What Is, Is. As formulated, it integrates an hypothesis, based upon a revised interpretation of Clausius' Second Law of Thermodynamics. Whether or not this prevails, is irrelevant. Should the hypothesis have to be abandoned, the Theory would not be invalidated. Rather, only modalities pertaining to the Now would need re-evaluation. When drafted to include the said hypothesis, the Theory reads: *The Universe of the Now, having reached a critical-point of entropy, i.e., having experienced a climacteric level of deaths, will collapse instantaneously, into its true state; one of tensorial stability, or to use social and religious terminology, a state in which each Atom, residing*

---

1. JOHN, THE EVANGELIST, *The Apocalypse* 21, 1 and 2, 22, 1 and 2 and 23, 3, 4 and 5.

beyond time-space knows, in full communion, the presence of every other, each according to its nature. Since Cosmic Peace summarizes key premises established previously, only one point requires clarification, namely the phrase: "knows the presence of every other, each according to its nature".

As demonstrated in chapter VII, Part I, the senses and time-space are of the order of the qualitative, whereas the Atom operates at absolute-speed and, it follows, resides in a maximized As-is. Each Existent simply *is*, and sensations, whether of time, sex, greed or sequence, are the fruit of subjectification. We create speed, etc., tailoring them to fit our endowments. In-fact, our experiences, our immersion in Reality are of the order of the Absolute. While it is accurate to speak of every Atom as alive in tension and peace or still, as maximized, *tension and peace are not to be equated with a pleasurable gratification of the senses. One can maximize in a state of hate and hence of pain, if such is the overriding quality willed upon the Self. In a word, Orang's heaven can very well be a hell.*

While, apparently a theory of a wholesale cosmic tension and peace is novel, a state akin to it has been envisaged in various disciplines, as being that of certain Existents. A modality of cosmic peace, albeit restricted to privileged species, is implicit in the quotes from Plotinus and Guillemin used in the chapter I of Part III in reference to cosmic relationality. In these, Guillemin affirms:

> For neutrinos it is "daylight" around the clock; it might be said that for them the earth is like a sphere of clearest crystal.

while Plotinus states that:

> For them (beatified spirits) all things are transparent, and there is nothing dark or impenetrable, but everyone is manifest to everyone internally and all things are manifest. For everyone has all things in himself and sees all things in others.

Aside from their affirmation of a form of cosmic presence, the above offer a further point of interest, that of a common imagery. Both the third century Neoplatonist and the twentieth century physicist, when groping for words to portray the state of a neutrino and a beatified-spirit, have recourse to an identical image — one of bright crystal, perpetual daylight, absolute transparence — and in doing so, rejoin the Evangelist:

> And he showed me a river of the water of Life, bright as crystal, and night shall be no more, and they shall have no need of the light of a lamp or of the light of the sun, because the Lord God shall be their light; and they shall reign for ever and ever.[2]

While the concordance between John and Plotinus may be dismissed on the grounds that both are mystics, the same objection can hardly be raised against Guillemin and his neutrinos. Regardless of Guillemin's personal convictions or psychological bent, neutrinos, kaons, pions etc., are not subjects which normally trigger outbursts of mysticism. The plausible explanation for an imagery which rejoins Plotinus and the Evangelist can only be an attempt to describe effectively a relationship which technology seems to demonstrate is one of quasi absolute peace. Neutrinos rarely, if ever, clash with other particles, nor indeed with objects as huge as men.

A rapprochement can also be made between Cosmic Peace and the several mind-dependence theories now being debated, notably Eddington's as formulated in *Space, Time and Gravitation:*

> Events do not happen; they are just there, and we come across them. "The formality of taking place" is merely the indication that the observer has on his voyage of exploration passed into the absolute future of the event in question.[3]

While a chasm separates any mind-dependence theory which incorporates Becomingism and/or Idealism from Objectivism, views such as the above, coming from the other end of the philosophical spectrum, do have corroborative value. Further and affirmative witness in behalf of a cosmic peace is afforded by the concept of a hereafter — a heaven, happy hunting ground and/or hell — integral to a majority of the religious cosmogonies. The question is investigated briefly in chapter IV of this Part.

3. The Theory Should Be Assessed on Its Own Merits

The fact that the majority of mankind in times past as well as present should intuit and accept the eventuality of a peaceful universe, is one which the objective person may not lightly dismiss. Quasi universal appetites, when married to intuitions of equal

---

2. JOHN, THE EVANGELIST, *The Apocalypse* 22, 1 and 5.
3. Arthur Stanley EDDINGTON, *Space, Time and Gravitation*, London, 1920, p. 51.

scope, deserve a systematic analysis and evaluation. However, any parallel between other theories, as well as similarities between the concept of a heaven or nirvana and the Theory of Cosmic Peace, are fortuitous. The Theory is neither an outgrowth of another with which it might have some affinity, nor a corollary to a conventional heaven and hell. Rather, this convergence of intuitions is a happy chance. Regardless, many will find in it a source of satisfaction and to possibly as many it will prove objectionable. Actually, the proper approach to the Theory is one totally divorced from all preformed religious or ideological biases. It should be evaluated by the same criteria as are applied to other empirical cosmogonies — for instance, the Wipple, Lemaître or Gamow theories — because it rests not upon faith or revelation, but rather, upon arguments and evidence drawn from logic, physics, and the psychical sciences in general.

That logic should play a determining role in the development of a theory of cosmic peace, is a truism. To adhere honestly to the principle What-Is, Is leads inexorably to the coexistence beyond time-space of all Beings. Cosmic peace was embryonic in the first premise. The case became ironclad when, while investigating intensity, the real state of a Dynamic-Fact was discovered to be one of maximization, and the true speed of the Universe to be absolute. This established, only the spirit or modality of an existence beyond time-space remains in question; although even this is implicit in a state of maximum tension. The matter would normally have rested there, had not a body of circumstantial evidence accumulated, which pointed in the same direction. Some was imbedded in the structure of the Cosmos, as witness a universal appetite for stability. Some was phenomenal and equally cosmic in scope, as witness entropy and the puzzles which it presents to contemporary physics. The recently established birth and death in time of the metalloids was also a contributing factor. Finally, the evidence uncovered while delving into the Cosmic Laws — particularly those of Clash and Critical Point — played a key role. In summary, the structure, mechanism and jurisprudence of the Universe all tend in one direction, namely, stability, with as consequence that the actual state of the Atom becomes one of maximal tension and of peace.

4. General Outline of the Hypothesis and Its Key Premises

The setting of the hypothesis contained in the overall Theory is the Universe of the Now. A simple structure, the Now, a concept encompassing a fixed number of Atoms, bathes in aggression and death. It could also be described as the cosmic battlefield upon which, *at absolute-speed*, our private skirmishes and wars are ruthelessly waged. The hypothesis is that the conglomerate obeys the laws which regulate the relationships and fate of its components. In other words, the whole mirrors the behavior of the parts. The surmise is that, since aggression determines all Now relationships, the Universe of the Now, as a whole, is subject to the Law by which individual conflicts are adjudicated, namely, Critical Point, which is also the Law of Time and Death. Applied globally, Critical Point predicates that the Now Universe, upon reaching a given level of death or entropy, knows its true state: one of maximized tension and peace.

Such a view endorses the Clausius theory that entropy is not only a universal law, but also a law of the Universe as a whole. The divergence arises when the time comes to assess the impact of entropy. Whereas entropy is generally equated with the spread of disorganization (if mathematical), and to a loss of heat (if thermodynamic), here it constitutes a parameter of cosmic organization. While from the restricted point of view of a person situated in time-space, entropy is correctly defined as a measure of disorganization and loss of heat, within the context of the Real-Universe, it is a function of the latter's *de facto* state of maximization, and actually measures cosmic self-realization. Expanded upon, the above implies firstly, that entropy tabulates existential deaths, each triggered instantaneously by the breaching of a critical-point; and secondly, that entropy will not proceed to the last conflictive relationship in the Universe; rather that the Universe will experience a critical-point, a climax of death, at which the Atoms still in the conflict state — and this might include a substantial percentage of all Existents — simultaneously *know* peace.

The analysis of these two premises yields nine key factors, the first four of which have been dealt with:

1. The Universe consists of a fixed number, "X", of Dynamic-Facts or motors.
2. Each Dynamic-Fact, being an absolute, operates at absolute-speed.
3. Each, in its role of absolute, entertains but one contact or relationship with every other.
4. The mood of the Now is one of aggression.
5. The aggression content of the Universe is subject to erosion.
6. Erosion occurs through an event commonly described as death (existential).
7. An existential-death coincides with the breaching of a critical-point.
8. With each breaching, with each death the quantum of energy possessed by the deceased — whether carrot or neutrino — withdraws from the Now.
9. The cumulation of these departures accounts for the diminishing level of activity in the Now, i.e. for entropy.

Regrouped under three headings, in order of their decreasing universality and certainty, the above now can be verified and wedded into a synoptic whole. These headings are respectively,

A. *Universally Demonstrable Facts:*
   1. The Universe of the Real and of the Now consists of a fixed number of Atoms.
   2. Each, being an absolute, knows but one cosmic-contact or relationship and rests in a state of maximum tension.
   3. The state of the Real is one of maximization and peace.

B. *Universally Observable Phenomena:*
   1. Conflict, which pervades the Now.
   2. Critical-points and the Law which regulates these.

C. *Experimental Phenomena, Generally Observable:*
   1. Births and deaths.
   2. The growth of entropy.
   3. An universal appetite for security and stability.

5. **Relevance of a Set Number of Existential-Atoms and Their Maximization**

The two items listed under the heading of universally demonstrable require no elaboration. Both, a fixed number of Atoms and maximization are corollaries of the Principle, What-Is, Is established in previous chapters. Further, since both provide the base upon which the Theory itself rests, they will be automatically dealt with as they are incorporated within the body of the demonstration.

6. **Aggression: He Who Does Not Conquer, Does Not Live**

While the "B" or aggression items are universally observable, and as such rate as factors in a cosmic theory, they warrant some elucidation. This is especially the case where the Law of the Critical Point is concerned, since the term "critical-point" is given a different meaning by others, notably by Teilhard, and the Law itself, it seems, has not been formulated previously.

That conflict is a law of the land, need hardly be emphasized in the post-Darwin era. Yet some would not accept it as The Law of the land, because in certain circumstances, in a marriage for instance, cooperation and love is the law. In their view, even though clash is a very general phenomenon, it is neither universal nor a proper ground upon which to base a universal theory. The answer was given in sections 6 and 10 of chapter VII, Part I, when the role of aggression in thought was analyzed, for the same situation prevails in the broader context of inter-Atom relationships as that which applies to thought-quanta. To cover the present context it suffices to add these precisions. While cooperation, peace and love occur in every day life, a distinction has to be drawn between the localized cooperation, peace and love which flowers within a closed-system, and universal cooperation, peace and love. Only the former exists in the Now. Each closed-system when integrated into the universal-system, finds itself in conflict with other closed-systems. Such would be the case in a situation involving, on the one hand, Humanoid and Leucocyte and on the other an army of invading Tubercle bacilli. Humanoid and Leucocyte and the latter's relatives then constitute a closed-unit of cooperation in a state of war with the *Mycobacterium tuberculosis* tribe. The same condition prevails throughout the Now, with the consequence that the Prime Principle of the Now becomes that of Clash, and that not only the modality but the very purpose of life is conquest; a fact succinctly stated in the phrase:

He who does not conquer, does not live.

The observation is brutal. Yet, to face reality, it must be accepted.

Here a comment offers itself concerning the category of conflicts to be considered. Conflicts, conquests and defeats come under many guises, and afflict all types of units. As established in section 5, chapter VII and section 1, chapter VIII, Part I, even thoughts restricted to the internal circuit of a mind are quantized through measurement and decision — the passage from one thought to another involving a conflict resolved in favor of the more appealing. While all categories are relevant to the Theory and would require evaluation for the purpose of an in-depth study, the only one of interest, in a general exposition, is that of the ultimate defeat, commonly referred to as physical-death, because these alone increase existential entropy.

7. The Death of "Matter", a Hypothesis Within a Hypothesis

At this juncture a second hypothesis offers itself, namely that the beta decay process which assumedly produces neutrinos and possibly other unidentified particles corresponds at the submicroscopic level to the demise of the animates, carrot or parrot, and that for both classes the death event coincides with the state of Cosmic Peace as herein described.

The propositions which follow are made with the clear realization that they are presented by a layman and upon the basis of incomplete data. Furthermore, discussions with specialists in the field revealed that they also were very much in the dark and divided as to their interpretations of the events recorded. For instance, while the "existence" of neutrinos seemed to be accepted by everyone (as of 1975 at least), some qualified scientists nonetheless still doubt that any have actually been detected. In a word, the issue is controversial and, the mere hint that the impact of neutrinos upon their surroundings is not, as yet, an established fact, seems to arouse much the same heated reaction as does the questioning of the eternal status of souls in religious circles. I have in mind, here, a conversation at McGill University, Montreal, with a physicist of international renown. A straightforward question concerning a proper source of written information on the subject initially drew an unexpectedly defensive, not to say aggressive, outburst. Yet the "existence" of neutrinos, as such, had not in anyway been placed in doubt. Given the hypothetical nature of much of particle physics in general and of neutrino research in particular, our hypothesis does not rest upon the existence and fate of any one particle, but rather offers an explanation, firstly, of the more unequivocally established fact that much of the energy in the Universe has dissolved "into radiation, and (energy) is being dissipated into empty space", and secondly, that this wasted energy courses unimpeded through "empty space".

Philip Morrison, in the following, states the first point clearly:

> Beta-decay is much rarer, on the nuclear time scale, than death by meteorite bombardment among men. It is only the chance that some nuclei are immortal except for beta-decay that allows us to observe this event at all.
>
> Now this slowness of decay implies that the opposite process the capture of a passing neutrino by a nucleus, also is slow and rare. Gamma rays, which are notoriously unlikely to interact with nuclei, will travel on the average through eight or 10 feet of lead before they do so. But a neutrino, to interact with a nucleus, must travel on the average through about 50 light-years of solid lead! A shielding wall capable of thinning out a beam of neutrinos would have to be as thick as a hundred million stars. To all intents and purposes neutrinos simply do not see solid matter at all. Here is the nub of the difficulty. The neutrino is almost uncapturable.[4]

Some 15 years later the situation remains substantially unchanged, as witness this excerpt from *The Story of Quantum Physics*, which furthermore, has the merit of providing confirmation for the second premise upon which the hypothesis rests.

> After being created deep within the center of a star, neutrinos penetrate quickly to the surface and start on their journey through space, a journey which may truly be called eternal, for the chance of their being absorbed by matter is less than one in a trillion trillion (10^{24}) over a period of ten billion years, the estimated age of the universe. It has been conjectured that nearly all of the neutrinos born

4. Philip Morrison, *"The Neutrino"*, Scientific American, Jan., 1956, p. 61.

> since the dawn of creation are still coursing through space bearing most of the entire mass of the universe in the form of their energy.[5]

To our knowledge, the implications of the above have not been drawn. Yet they are obvious and troubling. If the energy lost through beta-decay is conserved in the neutrino state, and other energy, be it that of an uranium or human, nihilates, or, as is alternately held, constitutes a passing epiphenomenon, then the ultimate universe would have to consist entirely of neutrinos or like particles. An odd universe indeed. Such could be the case. However, if so, a great many awkward situations require explanation. To note but two, why should epiphenomena, human or quartzic, manifest themselves? Certainly a reference to the "action" of an abstract and gratuitous concept known as "nature and its forces" hardly satisfies. Secondly, why should the "product" of what is on the whole an insignificant decay event be privileged over every other? Also why should it avoid the transmutations to which other particles supposedly submit?

The theory that "matter" or more specifically the various elements i.e. radium, uranium and their components neutrons, protons, etc., die and pass into a state of peace, exactly as do the living, disposes of such enigmas and has the merit of providing for an honest accounting of all energy.

In answer to the objection that neutrinos are not in a "state of peace"; that some neutrinos do clash with the living and "matter" in general, the following suggests itself. If one takes into account the assumedly fantastic number of the neutrinos and the disconcertingly complex procedure resorted to, to try to seize a rare specimen, one can, in fairness, in the first instance, question the identity of the traced particle, and in the second instance, one must concede that, even should the captured prove to be a genuine neutrino, nonetheless the ratio of neutrino interaction with the living is incredibly inferior to the documented instances of contact between "living" and "dead" humans. P. Morrison, on the same page acknowledges the "A" proposition:

> But the capture of the neutrino is a rare event indeed, and when one looks for the highly improbable, he must be prepared to see many other events, probable and improbable, which are irrelevant to what

5. Victor GUILLEMIN, *The Story of Quantum Physics*, Charles Scribner's & Sons, New York, 1968, p. 143.

> he is looking for. The tons of scintillator liquid will flash many times — from traces of radioactive dirt within the liquid, from cosmic rays, from escaping particles other than neutrinos which may come from the reactor.[6]

As to the "B" proposition, this also receives support from the latest observations in the field of neutrino research. While the "existence" of this prolific hypothetical particle remains unquestioned, its contact with earth, some now theorize, "may even be essentially zero". In October 1974, Scientific American, (p. 50) in a condensed report of experiments by Raymond Davis, Jr., of Brookhaven National Laboratory, "to detect the solar neutrinos and to measure their flux", notes the following:

> Davis' experiment is heroic. His apparatus consists of a 100,000 gallon tank of tetrachloroethylene, a common dry-cleaning fluid, at the bottom of the Homestake Gold Mine in Lead, S.D. Twenty-two percent of the mass of tetrachloroethylene is chlorine 37. When a chlorine 37 nucleus interacts with a neutrino, it is transformed into a nucleus of the radioactive isotope argon 37. Such an interaction is extremely rare, however, since the neutrino has no detectable mass, no magnetic moment and no electrical charge... As of the summer of 1972 his results over the preceding five years indicated that only about a tenth of the number of neutrinos predicted by the theory of the sun's interior were actually reaching the earth. At a meeting of the International Astronomical Union held in Warsaw last fall, William A. Fowler of the California Institute of Technology summarized Davis' more recent results. The situation for the theory has grown even worse: it seems that the number of neutrinos reaching the earth may be as low as a thirtieth of the number predicted by the theory and may even be essentially zero.

The same difficulty, it seems, is experienced in detecting neutrinos originating from other sources.

Actually, the second point, that all Atoms die and pass into a state of peace, here advanced, far from attacking the premise upon which the "existence" of neutrinos rests, namely the need to account for the loss of mass due to beta-decay, gives it added validity. The present entropic scenario is predicated either upon the loss or the non-specificity of the energy or power of the animates, seeing in their "birth" an instance of archegenesis (see

---

6. Philip MORRISON, *ibid.*

sec. 15, chap. III, part III). A hypothesis of the death of "matter" occurring in an absolute-speed universe, corrects the flaw in the current interpretation of the theory of the Conservation of Energy. In such a context the universe's gradual winding down results, not only from the death of a select group of as yet unidentified primary particles, but from the death, at a given critical-point, of all entities, that of the stallion as well as of the uranium and willow, all of which certainly rate far higher on the energy-quality scale than a K-meson or charmed and flavored quark. To further answer the objection that some neutrinos have in-fact been detected, let it be noted that "existence" in a state of peace does not preclude contact between "the living and the dead", nor does it posit it. Rather, as in all similar situations, Dynamic Vision remains open-ended. The only condition which would have to be fulfilled would be that such contacts be peaceful. Peaceful here means merely that the "dead", being in a state of peace, is unimpeded by the type of resistance which we "living", Now Atoms, encounter in any intercourse which we entertain with each other. Certainly a neutrino which "must travel on the average through about 50 light-years of solid lead", before making contact, seems of a peaceful enough frame of mind. Interestingly, all reported "other world" apparitions or phenomena satisfy this same peaceable characteristic, as witness the Fatima event.[7]

---

7. The reference to contact between the "dead" and the "living", human or otherwise, does not address itself to occult and controversial cases such as "conversations" either through mediums with the ghost of ones relative at a séance or of an individual with apparitions, such as occurred to Bernadette Soubirou at Lourdes, where the event occurs privately, between individuals. In instances of the first type, it appears that in a majority of cases deception may be involved and in the second, hallucination is always a possibility, while confirmation remains impossible, there being no outside witnesses. On the other hand in either instance, the mere fact that "control" cannot be exercised does not justify an automatic dismissal. The proper scientific stance presupposes an ever open mind. As implied, the category of phenomena covered by the hypothesis should be limited to the class of preternatural events, much rarer, subject to normal scientific control. The phenomenon registered on October 13, 1917 at Fatima, Portugal would fall in such a category. To begin with the event had been forecasted several months earlier by the eldest of the three children, Lucia do Santos, a ten year old, who claimed to have seen and talked to Mary, the mother of Christ, on some six monthly prearranged occasions, the first on May 13th. A crowd, according to the most conservative estimates, in excess of 50,000, had congregated. Thousands of these witnesses were unfriendly, some being qualified scientists intent upon mocking the

believers. All, without exception whatsoever, agreed that an "unnatural" event had occurred. Among these unfriendly witnesses were reporters from two prominent and predominantly antireligious papers, "Daily News" (Diario de Noticias) and "The Century" (O Seculo). The latter reluctantly published a front page account on October 15th, entitled "Como O Sol Bailou Ao Meio Dia Em Fatima", How the Sun Danced at Midday at Fatima. This report describes a sequence of events, all or part of which were witnessed by everyone present: (1) The crowd looked, without the aid of dark glasses or other protection, upon a brilliance which they took to be the sun; (2) this dancing globe emitted rays of brilliant hues, which actually colored objects on the earth up to 15 miles away; (3) it fell toward the crowd inducing a great fright in the hearts of most; (4) within a few minutes the area (and the people), upon which it had rained all morning, was dry. Such a happening is relevant in that, *A.* it is documented. Many of those present still live; *B.* it has all the earmarks of an intervention by someone at peace with the world. Mary came and went, at will, without experiencing any resistance whatsoever, a behavior which duplicates that of the elusive neutrino. Also, the dancing, rotating globe which either was the sun or upstaged it, at once mocked the laws of "nature" and yet caused harm to no one.

chapter II

Third Cosmic Law, Law of the Critical Point and Death

All the phenomena of nature, visible and invisible, within the atom and in outer space, indicate that the substance and energy of the universe are inexorably diffusing like vapor through the insatiable void... The universe is thus progressing toward an ultimate "heat-death", or as it is technically defined, a condition of "maximum entropy".

Lincoln BARNETT,
The Universe and Dr. Einstein, p. 102

1. Critical-Points Defined and Described

SINCE a critical-point as herein defined and the Law which regulates its behavior are probably unfamiliar, and since both are pivotal to Cosmic Peace, both warrant a more detailed investigation than do other factors. Emphasis is further justified in that together they hold the key to two of the more intriguing mysteries which face mankind: the time-death pair and entropy; also they explain the linearity of perceived-time and the invariance of real or physical-time.

The phenomenon of critical-points as such, is familiar. Examples are the flash point in a bullet, the ignition in a car or still, a jugular vein. Actually critical-points represent a fact of life so basic that were dogs taught to read, the most uneducated mongrel would recognize Critical Point as a principle known to him since his youngest days: the throat of his enemy.

Operation-wise, a critical-point triggers at the precise point-in-time-space when and where an entity, human, vegetative or gaseous, or a combination of such, for instance an ant hill or the Aztec civilization, willingly ceases to or is forcibly prevented from exercising a minimum of any of its essential powers, as these *are* or *are defined.* Then, the entity if conceptual, dissolves or if existential vacates the Now. In every day language, either has lost the fight and dies. Every entity, conceptual or existential, harbors a multiplicity of such points and the breaching of a single one results in a death — the concept of a death herein extends to encompass Antropocities, meaning that nations and displays of jam in a supermarket when critically assaulted, die as did Charles I when his head rolled-off the block. The phenomenon, universal, partakes of the commonplace. However, when codified and used in conjunction with other Cosmic Laws to resolve issues pertaining to the Now, its heuristic yet mysterious character reveals itself nakedly.

2. Law of the Critical Point, Its Definition and Relevance

The Law of the Critical Point rates third place among the five which govern the Cosmos. As implied, the pseudonyms Law of the Jugular, of Time or still of Death, also describe it accurately. It reads:

Presence in the Now requires a minimum of efficiency at all critical-points.

For the present purpose, only two points require elaboration. One, it applies without exception to all entities. As behooves a law which aspires to cosmicity, Critical Point brooks no breach. Its dictatorship extends even to as indeterminate an entity as a truckload of logs — a fact which the experienced logger duly respects, lest he end-up buried in an avalanche of bone-crushing timber. Two, it is amoral. In common with Clash and Extremes, the Law of Critical Point ignores compassion, as well as all notion of right or wrong. Its only code of ethics, that of the ubiquitous Principle of Absolutes, asserts itself under the heading of finality. Inversely, it is through the agency of critical-points that Absolutes rules the Now. The same holds for the Principle of Clash, whose message is one of conflict and whose ultimate dictat is death! It also asserts its domination through critical-points. Such a similitude of modalities and the convergence of the two prime Cosmic Principles at the pivot of the cosmic mechanism, would seem to argue strongly in favor of the theory of a universe of adimensional Atoms.

3. Does the Universe of the Now Have a Critical-Point?

Next to be determined is the critical-point, if any, of the universe of the Now, for the characteristics of the critical-points of different entities, witness an automobile, a horse and a nation, will not be the same. The answer is contained in Similitudes, fourth Cosmic Law, whose message is:

The modality of all processes is similar.

Similitudes dictates that each critical-point should evidence the characteristic of the entity concerned; that an entity's critical-points be compatible with its nature, if existential, or with its definition, when, as in the present case, the entity is a concept. For instance, critical-points which place in jeopardy the life of a flesh and blood Atom must be biological, viz. a spinal cord severed by a hangman's noose. In a mechanical entity, a climacteric point which reduces the efficiency of the machine, let us say a 1975 Chevrolet, to zero and removes it from the ranks of real machines, will be involved, viz. the ignition key. Emphasis upon the term "real machine", implies that a non-operating auto is a non-auto, and becomes one only through the addition of the missing factor — its owner's will-power to start it, for example. Until its automotive duty, i.e. to move someone or something somewhere is being fulfilled, an auto is but a mass of parts.

The above applied to the universe of the Now, predicates that, as any conceptual-conglomerate, the Now must stand or fall by a single criterion, namely, that which defines and makes it operative. This criterion, already established, is aggressivity — the Now being a battle-field upon which an X-number of minor battles rage, each reaching its dénouement independently. The question therefore becomes one of aggression ratios. The Now can be expected to reach its critical-point and "die", when its ratio of aggression to entropy falls below a certain level.

Before proceeding to search for physical evidence that the Cosmos indeed undergoes a process of cumulating deaths apt to culminate in a cataclysm, it seems advisable, due to the controversy over the meaning of death, to investigate it and birth, in more detail.

4. **Births and Deaths Are Subjective Percepts**

The issue of death, as every phenomenon or event, is subject to individual interpretation, colored by ideological considerations. For instance, the Liberal and Marxist place upon it a value radically different from that of a Moslem or Christian. In turn, the Hindu sees death in a light again unlike that of the other four. In all five instances (as in any other), the parameter is not one of intelligence, rather of norms, the accuracy of a master theory and of its variants, being a function of its conformability to Truth.

Since the complexity of the problem precludes an in-depth analysis, the reflections which follow will concentrate upon establishing that the metals ("matter"), are born and die in time-space, exactly as do the animates. This will serve a dual purpose. Firstly, it will document the axiom that "there is no such thing as life", or inversely, that "all Atoms are alive" (see sec. 11, ch. I, Pt. III) and will establish on an experimental basis, that neither birth nor death involves an ontological accretion to or excision from the cosmic mass. Secondly, it will demonstrate that:

A. births are subjective percepts;

B. deaths, also subjective percepts, merely witness the exhaustion of a given Atom's quota of conflictive relationships, and

C. the cumulation of deaths, with its concomitant increase in entropy, will trigger a climacteric event coincident with a state of cosmic peace.

5. Irons, Neutrons and Neutrinos Are Born and Die

Until recently the thesis that birth and death affect the inanimates exactly as they do the animates, would have been rejected out of hand. Only animals, it was held, are born and die. Everyone agreed that the inanimate realm constituted an ill-defined, primordial and self-regenerating magma, from which, through some occult process, the life-force oozed. After a more or less prolonged "time interval", this latter just as mysteriously as it oozed from the void, evaporated, soap bubble-like, into an assumedly different void, and the opening and terminal phases of these specialized epiphenomena were defined as birth and death.

The fundamental principles which demonstrate the error in the notion that animation or life and life's terminals, birth and death, are characteristics of some but not all Atoms, were established in sections 11, 13 and 15 of the previous chapter, when the univocity of Existence and the similitude of all processes were investigated. The case was then made through a comparative evaluation of the metabolism of Lysozyme and Ux_1 on the one hand, and of Humanoid and recognized animates, on the other. It will now be observed that the latest findings in the field of radioactivity and astrophysics confirm those of cosmontology and biophysics.

Since the "birth in time" phenomenon is but indirectly related to a cosmic critical-point, it will be sufficient to restate the earlier observation that a birth of any type can never be situated accurately in time. The reason is simple. Perceived-time is a conceptualization, or, as the Scholasticists would have it, *numerus motus secundum prius et posterius* (the numbering of movement according to the before and after). Since befores and afters are subject to unending minutization, evidently while one can, time-wise, satisfy the criteria of the local office of the Bureau of Vital Statistics as to the birth of ones child, scientific accuracy is never achieved (the term scientific accuracy here refers to ontological truth i.e. absolute accuracy).[1] To say: "my son was born on such a date, at 12:01 Greenwich time", merely publicizes the fact that one became conscious of a son's yelping presence within a mutually agreed frame of reference. The same applies to the time at which his parents cooperated to breed. This event will suffer from a greater indeterminacy — confirmation depending upon pregnancy tests, etc. While anyone who gives the problem more than perfunctory consideration realizes the above, the fiction qua dogma that the animates are born at a precise point-in-time, is nonetheless blindly endorsed by an overwhelming majority, and its antithesis, the no-birth-no-animation-no-death status of the metalloids and so-called inorganics, is as staunchly upheld.

Prior to the 1940's, faith in these musty Aristotelian dogmas was understandable. They did square with common sense, with Reality as perceived, and further, did gratify the human ego — setting man up as the imperial master of a rather exclusive, albeit ephemeral, aristocracy, that of the living. Since then their validity has to be questioned. When the conditions are propitious, man can observe being born, the transuranium elements, the first two, among some thirty now identified, being neptunium and plutonium, the 93rd and 94th elements respectively on the periodic

1. The temptation to deny physical significance to durations shorter than 10^{-22} of a second is understandable. 10^{-22} of a second, for instance, bears somewhat the relationship to a millionth of a second as a millionth of a second bears to 10,000 million years (some 3,000 millions years more than the currently hypothesized age of the Universe). However, to yield to this temptation, is a sin against Truth and science. From either point of view, no event, even of the order of 10^{-60} millionth of an erg, can be ignored without thereby vitiating the entire Cosmic Equation.

table. As of now these elements are described as mechanical creations of man and listed in the category of phenomena. Such a view, while narrowly anthropocentric could of course be accurate. Interestingly, however, the birth of a mendelevium (101) or rutherfordium (104) follows a process identical with that utilized to create a man — a "Rutherford son".[2] In either case, a bombardment; which is to say, aggression, is ressorted to — cyclotrons, etc., and millions of subatomic particles in the case of a rutherfordium or k-meson, and a penis and hundreds of thousands to several million spermatozoa in that of the humanoid, both being aimed at a susceptible target. Result? In some instances, sterility — the hoped for event does not manifest itself in either locus. In others, fecundity — the k-meson of ones desires and the ardently sought for son make their appearance in the cyclotron and the womb respectively, a parallel, be it noted, in accord with Similitudes, the fourth Cosmic Law.

The Phenomenologist can be expected to object that when a rutherfordium is detected, it is not the birth of a prime particle of "matter" (Existential-Atom) which the physicist witnesses, but rather an epiphenomenon of the order of an automobile, the Woodstock Rock Festival or still, a tree.[3] He will contend that the genuine constituents of the Universe, the natural elements such as oxygens, heliums and irons originated simultaneously. Or somewhat more coherently, he may argue that the "natural elements" themselves are epiphenomena issued from a synaptic process involving an as yet unidentified counterpart of the Democritan atom or conventional primary particle.[4] The flaws in

2. In the U.S.S.R., rutherfordiums are known as kurchatoviums, after Igor Vasilievich Kurchatov, who led the Soviet team which developed the U.S.S.R.'s atomic bomb.

3. The epiphemenological interpretation may well be correct in a specific event, especially one involving exotic subparticles. Thus it is understood that while occasionally a subparticle may be referred to as an Existential-Atom, in such cases, judgement is reserved as to whether or not the entity under consideration, is existentially discrete. Errors of classification do not wound the objectivity of the Real. The "X" in the Universal Equation, while an indeterminacy factor, remains a set number, unaffected by the miscalculations or misinterpretations of man.

4. Faith in the Democritan hypothesis is still strongly entrenched, as evidence, this closing paragraph from "Quarks with Color and Flavor":

> Finally, even if a completely consistent and verifiable quark model could be devised, many fundamental questions would remain. One such

either thesis, are numerous, and having been exposed, need not be taken up. Instead, confirmation of the data obtained through an analysis of the Cosmic Equation can be derived from an evaluation of several recent developments in astrophysics and chemistry. Among these, two in particular discredit entirely any Leucippean or Democritan phenomenalism, whether of the *regressio ad infinitum* or of the "big Bang" species. These are the birth on an ongoing basis of elements which until recently were assumed primordial, and the death of the radioactive elements. While the first remains open to questioning, the second is established statistically and experimentally. Indeed the atomic energy industry is founded upon a commercial exploitation of the fact that the radioactives (radiums, thoriums, uraniums, etc.), die exactly as do men and trees, and that their death is paced at what is described as a half-life tempo. The term half-life, introduced by Rutherford in 1904, constitutes a stylized formula which describes the randomness of the death event in an average metalloidal colony. Isaac Asimov outlines the sequence succinctly.

> ... For instance, let us say that experiment shows that, in a given sample of an atom we shall call X, the atoms are breaking down at the rate of one out of two per year. At the end of a year, 500 of every 1,000 original X atoms in the sample would be left as X atoms; at the end of two years, 250; at the end of three years, 125; and so on. The time it takes for half of the original atoms to break down is called that particular atom's "half-life"... consequently, the half-life of atom X

> perplexity is implicit in the quark-lepton symmetry that led to the charm hypothesis. Both the quarks and the leptons, all of them apparently elementary, can be divided into two subgroups. In one group are the *u* and *d* quarks and the electron and electron neutrino. These four particles are the only ones needed to construct the world; they are sufficient to build all atoms and molecules, and even to keep the sun and other stars shining. The other subgroup consists of the strange and charmed quarks and the muon and muon neutrino. Some of them are seen occasionally in cosmic rays, but mainly they are made in high-energy particle accelerators. It would appear that nature could have made do with half as many fundamental things. Surely the second group was not created simply for the entertainment or edification of physicists, but what is the purpose of this grand doubling? At this point we have no answer.

(Sheldon Lee Glashow, "Quarks With Color And Flavor", *Scientific American*, Oct. 1975, p. 50.)

One can only marvel at the intellectual masochism of those who seek so desperately to deny man and an iron — both clearly endowed with flavor, charm and quality — all title to genuine facticity, and to instead vest facticity and Reality in entities as poor and naked as quarks and leptons.

> is one year. Every radioactive nuclide has its own characteristic half-life, which never changes under ordinary conditions. (The only kind of outside influence that can change it is bombardment of the nucleus with a particle or the extremely high temperature in the interior of a star — in other words, a violent event capable of attacking the nucleus per se.)...
>
> Although the isotopes of an element are practically identical chemically, they may differ greatly in their nuclear properties. Uranium 235, for instance, breaks down six times as fast as uranium 238 ; its half-life is only 710 million years. It can be reasoned, therefore, that in eons gone by, uranium was much richer in uranium 235 than it is today. Six billion years ago, for instance, uranium 235 would have made up about 70 per cent of natural uranium...
>
> Clearly any nuclide with a half-life of less than 100 million years would have declined to the vanishing point in the long life-time of the universe. This explains why we cannot find more than traces of plutonium today. The longest-lived plutonium isotope, plutonium 244, has a half-life of only 70 million years.[5]

The similitude of the death pattern of the animates and inanimates is complete. In each order, different species have different life spans, and within each species, some specimens live longer than others — some die as babies, others as centenarians. Finally, and most relevant to the Theory of Cosmic Peace, entire colonies or cities, in either order, are exterminated by unusually intense and concentrated aggression. Two examples of such a cataclysm striking humanoids, are the systematic and wholesale extermination of the population of Herat (circa 1222) by Jenghiz Khan and that of Hiroshima by the first atomic bomb.[6]

---

5. Isaac ASIMOV, *Asimov's Guide to Science*, New York, Basic Books 1960, p. 454.
6. An estimated 1,600,000 persons were massacred during a week of systematic executions. The sadism was pushed to the point of lining up the hapless victims, in close formations, in an open plain, where, awaiting their turn to be beheaded, they were forced to scrape and polish the skulls of their predecessors. The sculls were then built into a pyramid at the entrance of the razed city — a warning to other cities which might dream of revolt. Stochastically the death rate of the residents of Herat, is comparable, at once, with that of the citizens of Hiroshima and the uraniums in the bomb which levelled the city. The latter event is doubly revealing, in that the death-destruction of the humanoids, was achieved by the simultaneous death-destruction of an uranoid community, subjected to the type of "violent event capable of attacking the nucleus per se", mentioned by Asimov as occurring in stars. (ASIMOV, *op. cit.*)

The implications of these twin discoveries — that metals die and die randomly — upon any theory related to the origin or age of the Universe seem to have initially escaped most astrophysicists and philosophers. However, these are gradually being drawn and accepted in scientific circles, and as a consequence several key tenets of physics and ontology are being revised. David N. Schramm deals with the issue in from "The Age of the Elements". After noting that:

> ... There are several ways in which the age of the universe can be determined, ...

he then states that:

> The use of radioactive nuclei to estimate the age of the universe is such a technique...
>
> In order to make these calculations it is not necessary to know the actual abundance of the elements today or at any time in the past. One need only know the ratio in which a suitable pair of elements is found today (the "abundance ratio") and the ratio in which they were found when first formed (the "production ratio")...
>
> A simple way to see how these ratios can be used to determine the age of the elements is to assume that all the elements were made in one event. This assumption is known to be wrong, but it provides an idealized model of the nuclear dating processes. ...
>
> For example, with the chronometer pair Th-232 and U-238 it can be shown by experiment that the abundance ratio today is about 4.0. The calculated production ratio is 1.9; one can determine from the half-lives of the substances that the period required for such a change in ratio is seven billion years. That is the age of the hypothetical single event according to this chronometer pair.
>
> More than a decade ago William A. Fowler and Fred Hoyle used Th-232, U-235 and U-238 to determine the time scale of nucleo-synthesis. With only those chronometers it was not possible to definitely rule out the single-event model. In the past few years, however, techniques have been devised for the use of two new nucleochronometers. They are iodine 129 and plutonium 244, and their observed presence in the solar system cannot be made consistent with a single nucleosynthetic event.
>
> Measurements of the abundance of I-129 and Pu-244 require some subtlety. The half-lives of both substances are much less than the age of the solar system; whatever amount was present at that time, therefore, must by now have been reduced by radioactive decay to virtually zero. (The present abundance would not be zero, although it

> approaches zero asymptotically and may well be unmeasureable. Investigators at the Los Alamos Scientific Laboratory and the General Electric Company have recently detected traces of Pu-244 in nature.)[7]

The author's thesis is based upon a series of highly complex experiments and calculations, of which the above relates but the core. His verdict, founded upon the weight of his own findings and bolstered by the identical opinion of numerous other researchers, is that:

> The one-event hypothesis is obviously implausible because it is most unlikely that all the supernovas of the past billions of years exploded at a single moment. The hypothesis is demonstrably wrong because the several nucleochronometer pairs each give a different date for the single event. Indeed, those chronometers with relatively short half-lives would have all but vanished if the only production event had occurred billions of years before the solar system formed. More complicated models are needed. ... For example any valid model must include some nucleosynthesis within a few hundred million years of the formation of the solar system or it could not explain the presence of U-129 and Pu-244 decay products. This condition alone precludes a single-event model in which the elements were formed seven billion years ago.[8]

In summary, the inanimates are born and die in time on exactly the same basis as radishes and cobras.

---

7. David N. SCHRAMM, "The Age of the Elements", *Scientific American*, January, 1974, pp. 72–74.
8. *Ibid.*, p. 76.

chapter III

Real or Physical-Time as a Measure of Death-Units

> There are several ways in which the age of the universe can be determined... The use of radioactive nuclei to estimate the age of the universe is such a technique... In order to make these calculations... One need only know the ratio in which a suitable pair of elements is found today (the "abundance ratio") and the ratio in which they were found when first formed...
> A simple way... is to assume that all the elements were made in one event. This assumption is known to be wrong, but it provides an idealized model...
>
> David H. Schramm,
> "The Age of the Elements"

1. "If You Knew Time as Well as I Do, Said the Mad-Hatter"...

THE moment of Truth, the critical-point of science is at hand. If, as cosmogenetics indicate, all species of Atoms are born randomly in time, the conventional cosmogonic scenarios collapse. The objectivity, presently assumed to underpin the exact sciences, evaporates. Literally, our common destination becomes the Realm of the Absurd, into which the Sartres and Kafkas have for decades been beckoning us. Stating the predicament differently, one must conclude that if all births and deaths (whether viewed as existential or epiphenomenal is irrelevant), are random events, then the link between temporal causality and origins is severed. The Universe becomes irrational. Energy cannot be conserved, let alone accounted for. The edifice of science crumbles into a haystack of arbitrary mind-constructs, to which applies with full force, the Everett-Wheeler interpretations of quantum physics — the Multiple Reality Theory, according to which, at every "instant" the Universe "splits" into "alternative branches" each the "possible outcome" of a situation involving quantum effects. Then also, the Heisenberg Uncertainty Principle, spreading its domination beyond the realm of particle physics comes to reign, supreme. This dilemma, concerning the complex of cause-origin related issues, has haunted philosophical man from the beginning of speculative thinking. So has its key, known, since Zeno and before, to revolve around the question of time, that pliable, accommodating character of whom Lewis Carroll's Mad-Hatter so aptly affirmed:

> ... If you knew Time as well as I do, you wouldn't talk about wasting it. Its him. Now if you only kept on good terms with him, he'd do almost anything you liked with the clock.

In a word, until the nature of time is deciphered, every effort to make sense out of existence is doomed.

The chameleon-like character of time and the consequent difficulty of coming to grips with it, are immediately revealed when one makes an inventory of its several species, genuine and spurious. A list of the more commonplace would include the absolute and relative, the geometrical and relational, the epistemological, the solar, the durational (Bergson's durée), the perceived and the physical or real-time, plus all of the subspecies characteristic of the branch theories. While, no doubt each of the above has relevance within a given context, such a proliferation of views upon a key issue is suspicious. Close scrutiny reveals that the problem is the same as that noted in respect to atomism versus monism, namely a failure to distinguish between Reality-Truth and perception-knowledge. Effectively there are but two species of time, the real or physical and the epistemological or relative. Here the thesis is that real or physical-time numerates deaths and that all other varieties are the fruit of a subjective intellectual exercise, in the nature of a real-illusion, quantized according to arbitrary norms, to wit, solar time.

Since only physical-time, which roots into Reality, can add to a knowledge of the physical universe, comments upon epistemological-time can be restricted to a summary reiteration of the point made earlier, namely that it is compounded from elements of Leibnizian and Kantian time, superimposed upon the scholastic notion of a numbering of motion. This statement of C. D. Broad describes it well:

> There is not something called Time which could exist even though there had been no events; Time just consists of the relation of before and after among events.

As demonstrated in the case of atomism versus monism, no epistemological exercise, no matter how strenuous and exquisite, can penetrate the Real. To deal with time as a step-child of epistemology, is to grasp at a shadow. A summary survey of two of the more legitimate avenues being explored, can serve as illustration. These are the theory of a chronon and that of a geometrical time, as defined by H. Minkowski. Effectively the chronon is a time interval consonant with quantum mechanics and it follows, with the Uncertainty Principle. Such a Universe, it is thought, might operate with Plank's constant (the chronon) as its time unit.[1] The solution, an ingenious one, does not cure the disease. It only introduces to the time question, the Leibnizian notion of "a point smaller than which one cannot imagine". By Heisenberg's own admission, Einstein, among others, steadfastly refused to accept the relativisation of the Real and of time implicit in any attempt to conciliate Truth with quantum mechanics. Here is, in Heisenberg's own words, Einstein's gut reaction to the proposition:

> The discussion usually started at breakfast, with Einstein serving us up with yet another imaginary experiment by which he thought he had definitely refuted the uncertainty principle. ... Later in life, also, when quantum theory had long since become an integral part of modern physics. Einstein was unable to change his attitude — at best, he was prepared to accept the existence of quantum theory as a temporary expedient. "God does not throw dice" was his unshakeable principle, one that he would not allow anybody to challenge. To which Bohr could only counter with: "Nor is it our business to prescribe to God how he should run the world."[2]

If the chronon or Heisenberg time interval (it is not often recognized as such), is unacceptable upon rational and physical grounds, it at least has the merit of attempting to reduce time to an ultimate or primary physical unit. As the Leibnizian stratagem, a pragmatist's solution, it can be used to good purpose to solve engineering problems, since in such situations approximations suffice. The same cannot be said of the many species of geometrical time conjured from multidimensional universes and infinite curvatures, etc. Sheer conceptual embroidery, all such remind one of the mental calisthenics of the Scholasticists of the late period as these strove valiantly to bury the fundamental Becomingist error of Aristotelism under a mountain of words. The following quotes from H. Minkowski's celebrated essay *Space and Time* state the basics of one of the more coherent attempts to explain time within the parameters of contemporary physics.

---

1. The chronon, a speculative entity, held by some to represent the duration of the briefest possible natural event, is obtained by dividing the diameter of a proton (10^{-22} cm), by the speed of light. This yields an interval of approximately 10^{-24} seconds.
2. Werner HEISENBERG, *Physics and Beyond: Encounters and Conversations*, (Ed. by Ruth Nanda Arshen, trans. by Arnold J. Pomerans), New York, Harper and Row, 1971, pp. 80-81.

> The views of space and time which I wish to lay before you have sprung from the soil of experimental physics, and therein lies their strength. They are radical. Henceforth space by itself, and time by itself, are doomed to fade away into mere shadows, and only a kind of union of the two will preserve in independent reality.
>
> First of all I should like to show how it might be possible, setting out from the accepted mechanics of the present day, along a purely mathematical line of thought, to arrive at changed ideas of space and time.

The objective and methodology being clearly stated, the nature and dimensions of the project are then established:

> Not to leave a yawning void anywhere, we will imagine that everywhere and everywhen there is something perceptible. To avoid saying "matter" or "electricity" I will use for this something the word "substance". We fix our attention on the substantial point which is at the world-point $x, y, z, t,$ and imagine that we are able to recognize this substantial point at any other time. Let the variations dx, dy, dz of the space co-ordinates of this substantial point correspond to a time element dt. Then we obtain, as an image, so to speak, of the everlasting career of the substantial point, a curve in the world, a world-line, the points of which can be referred unequivocally to the parameter t from — *oo to* + *oo*. The whole universe is seen to resolve itself into similar world-lines, and I would fain anticipate myself by saying that in my opinion physical laws might find their most perfect expression as reciprocal relations between these world-lines.

It hardly needs mentioning that in a construct of indeterminate "substantial points", there is no room for flesh and blood, qualitative Existents. Even though the author performs one of those intellectual *tour de force* which succeeds, as is often the case in research, in bringing him tantalizing close to a major breakthrough; when, shortly thereafter, he adds:

> We will now introduce this fundamental axiom:
>
> The substance at any world-point may always, with the appropriate determination of space and time, be looked upon as at rest.
>
> The axiom signifies, that at any world-point the expression
>
> $$c^2dt^2 - dx^2 - dy^2 - dz^2$$
>
> always has a positive value, or, what comes to the same thing, that any velocity v always proves less than c.

the relevance of that particular equation and of this overall scheme is destroyed, for "*c*" was previously defined as follows:

> I will state at once what is the value of c with which we shall finally be dealing. It is the velocity of the propagation of light in empty space. To avoid speaking either of space or of emptiness, we may define this magnitude in another way, as the ratio of the electro-magnetic to the electrostatic unit of electricity.[3]

Since the speed of light is only *relatively* greater than that of a turtle, Minkowski finds himself firmly embraced by the strait jacket of relativity, and must lapse into mind-dependence. Yet, the Minkowskian Theory is among the less objectionable. At least in it, all events spread out on a single and effectively timeless, four dimensional branch which bears some relationship to Reality. As much cannot be said of the schemes involving "Multiple Reality or Probability Theories" developed by Cantor, Weyl, etc., and which lack the "relative simplicity of conception" of Minkowski's. Most sprout more branches and assumedly more "time-leaves" than any full grown oak and would, by their subtleties, awe and delight a medieval scholar.

2. Real or Physical-Time: A Measure of Death

To seek an understanding of physical-time in calculus, in probability theorems or in model "Branching Universes" is, to state the case facetiously, to bark up the wrong tree and branch. Such enterprises are doomed on two counts. To begin with, intellectualizations never transcend into the physical. One will never shoot a real partridge with a hypothetical 22 caliber rifle. While the sin of intellectualization by itself, thwarts any Minkowskian or similar scheme, the difficulty is compounded when the researcher lacks the concept, let alone an understanding of the nature of the ontological unit. For physical-time happens to physical entities, and, to our knowledge, no recognized theory of time deals with it as a function of the interplay of discrete Dynamic-Facts. Yet, as emphasized, basic logic indicates that the

---

3. H. MINKOWSKI, "Space and Time" (A translation of an address delivered at the 80th Assembly of German Natural Scientists and Physicians, at Cologne, September 21, 1908), in *Principles of Relativity*, Dover, pp. 75, 76, 79 and 80.

precondition to an understanding of a phenomenon, is the discernment of the entities to which the phenomenon occurs. The question of real or physical time, when approached thus, reveals itself relatively simple. Its formula can be stated succinctly:

real or physical-time is a measure of the death.

In this context the death and a death are not metaphors. A death means that of someone's father, of any nondescript U^{238} and of the reader himself. The spring of the clock of the Now, powered by aggression, ticks not in chronons, seconds or eons, but in critical-points or deaths. The connection between birth, death, time, entropy, aggression, critical-points and cosmic peace must now be manifest. The entire complex of issues is amenable to a simple mathematical computation — the basic subtraction operation of arithmetic, situated in the Absolute and performed at absolute-speed.

Using the Universe's Prime Principle as a first point of reference, we discover the relevant feature of Absolutes listed under the heading, "universally demonstrable premises", namely that the number of existential and conceptual-entities in the Universe is fixed. The implications are clear. In the Now, which consists of a set number of conflicting entities, each subject to a critical-point or death, the end of the line, at-some-point-in-time, is reached. The same can be expressed by noting that at-some-point-in-time, the number of conflictive relationships must become exhausted. The term "conflictive relationships in", analogical, serves to emphasize the terminate aspect of any series composed of a set number, as for instance the number of dimes in a piggy bank. Once allowance is made for the container analogy, the parallel between the coins and the number of critical-points and deaths holds, for, as established in section 1, chapter VII, Part I, thought also is quantized. *With the breaching of each critical-point, with each death, the conflict level of the Now falls inexorably, and it is only a matter of subtraction before the universe of the clashing Atoms know the maximization and peace which the analysis of the tensorial character of Energy revealed to be the* de facto *state of the Real.*

The above is as ineluctable as 2 minus 2 equals 0. Mind-boggling as it may appear, Reality and within this, each of we Atoms, do rest in the plentitude of the As-is, or as Eddington would have it, "events do not happen; they are just there". A rigorous analysis of the mechanism of the Real had confirmed as much. The triadic Law of the Critical Point, of Time and of Death, now adds a mathematical confirmation.

3. Entropy, a Function of Death, Speaks of Cosmic Peace

The test for an existential theory is that its formulae be verifiable experimentally and that it should explain related phenomena more coherently than any other. A Theory of Cosmic Peace unambiguously satisfies this criterion, for it provides the rational and mathematical framework through which entropy can be accounted for, and thereby resolves the several paradoxes which growing physical entropy presents, when evaluated according to current criteria.

The above is not a challenge to the principle formulated by Clausius. Rather, it proposes a new explanation of the latter's mechanics and involves mainly the substitution of an aggression-death factor for the heat factor. Since heat is a function of friction, such an alteration leaves the Clausius Equation intact, for what is friction but a generic term used to describe indeterminate aggression? A second innovation is the substitution of quanta of energy, for the vague concept of heat. This merely broadens the Second Law of Thermodynamics to make it embrace all cosmic phenomena in their specificity. From a vague observation, dynamic entropy achieves the status of a mathematical formula.

While all modalities of entropy, the thermic, statistical, epistemological and relational, etc., are related and relevant, the analysis, for the two following reasons, is limited to the thermic. Firstly, only the thermodynamic is inherently existential, and Existence-Power is our exclusive subject. Secondly, the interest in entropy is restricted to its relationship to the Theory of Cosmic Peace and the statistical and other modalities offer no direct evidence in this area. The one innovation consists in introducing a relational dimension to entropy — hence the inclusion of relational éntropy in the list. The process itself of thermic entropy need not be analyzed in detail. Its long-term impact upon the Cosmos was graphically depicted in the Barnett quote which closed the previous chapter. It suffices to indicate that its theory was formulated during the 19th century as an outgrowth of a study of heat, and that its key postulate affirms that an irreversible change occurs when heat passes of its own accord from one part of a system to another where the temperature is lower. The fact that it rests upon two of the few pillars of classic physics still standing, the First and Second Laws of Thermodynamics, seems to confirm its validity.

Where the First is concerned no departure is proposed. Since Carnot's Law merely restates the Principle of the Conservation of Energy and this latter is the physicists' formulation of the premise: What-Is, Is any tampering with it would be ill-advised. From the Second Law also: that "Heat cannot of itself pass from a colder to a hotter body" (R. Clausius 1822–88), no divergence is contemplated; rather, only a reassessment of its implications and a concomitant substitution of factors. The bearing of the proposed reinterpretation is however considerable. By substituting a physical explanation for the primarily epistemological theses of Boltzman *et al.*, it solves the paradox rightly denounced by Loschmidt, concerning the incompatibility of the invariance of the laws of dynamics with the irreversibility of molecular entropy. The suggestion is that the Second Law as formulated is valid, but meaningless beyond the restricted field of thermodynamics. Satisfactory from the perspective of its author whose primary interest was heat, it is inadequate ontologically, since the relevance of dynamic entropy reaches far beyond the boundaries of mechanistic heat theories. Key to an in-depth understanding of the Now relationships, dynamic entropy being a function of aggression and a blueprint of time, hinges the Order of the Now to that of the Real.

4. The Entropic Equation Is Not One of Quality Into Quantity

While it is rarely appreciated, the current theory of dynamic entropy predicates a disappearance of quality from the Cosmos. Of course no one speaks of quality, rather of a loss of heat and a concomitant reduction in the work potential of the system under observation. As a superficial description, the assessment is correct, as is the conclusion drawn; namely, that the cosmic machinery undergoes a slow death by cold. Its heuristic value however is nil. Worse, it induces into error. Ontologically such an accounting of entropy turns poor Hegel on his head a second time. Marx, by insisting in transmuting "idea into matter", performed a first radical inversion; the conventional view of entropy now implies a second permutation, that of quality into quantity. Unhappily, the turning of faulty ideas inside out is as futile as the turning inside out of a worn jacket. In either case, the holes in the sleeves and the errors remain as gaping after as before.

The nature of quality and the error referred to having been analysed in chapter VII, Part II, one needs only reiterate that quality is integral to Reality and specifically to Energy. Indeed, quality, when grounded in Power, is of the very "substance" of the Atom, or, to speak "physicalese", of the particle. While, for the rough calculations of the nuclear physicist, the qualitative can be ignored with impunity, the same inaccuracy cannot be condoned at the cosmic level. To write-off as a mirage, dream or otherworldly intellectualization, any quality — be this the sex appeal of a woman, the poetry of Keats or the light of a photon — is to evidence a lack of realism and a poor sense of accounting. Reality is of one piece and its manifestations rate equal consideration. The spell of a dichotomous hellenic world of unmiscible spheres of "matter and spirit", is hard to break. Yet, broken it must be, if scientific accuracy and honesty are to prevail. On this issue the Marx-Engels hypothesis, of a one level universe, its errors notwithstanding, does have merit.

To proclaim, when one observes increasing entropy, that death by cold sets in, is meaningless. The reference to death is accurate, but to rest the case upon a facile reference to a decreased work potential smacks of intellectual dilettantism. *While entropy can be rightly considered from afar as a general phenomenon, it results from the cumulation of individual deaths, each of which, if due scientific process is respected, must be taken into account.* The proper interpretation is that the minutiae of dynamic entropy consists in a multitude of deaths, some as insignificant as that of a mosquito or a neutrino. The process accrues from the cumulation of these piece-meal deaths and a subsequent withdrawal from the conflict-laden Now, of the power quota of each dead — their power not being lost, but rather being in a state of peace. Such a reading in no way contradicts Clausius. On the contrary, closer scrutiny reveals that the two main substitutions suggested are fully compatible with his thought, and together raise his Principle from its present status of a generic observation to that of a precision tool.

The substitution of the specific notion of quantized aggression for that of heat as the operative factor in entropy respects scientific procedure. Heat, a generic term, merely describes one of the effects of sustained aggression — as witness the heat of a meteor entering the atmosphere or the fire lit, Boy Scout fashion, or still the heat engendered by quarrelling minds. To proceed beyond the observation of an indeterminate or generic phenomenon to that of individual facts such as those of a death, fulfills one of the objectives of research. The above, conjugated with the critical-point mechanism which regulates aggression and the death rate, provides a deeper insight into the process of cosmic degeneration. Within such a context, a theory of Cosmic-Peace imposes itself as a corollary firstly, of the fact that death does not involve a transfer of Energy, from Atom to Atom and secondly, of the conservation of all Energy. Both imperatives can be satisfied only if, upon death, the dead and its energy-quota — the two being synactive — vacate a conflict-prone Now to enter a tensorial Real. An adequate description of such a state is that of peace. In mechanical terms, one could speak of a state of experienced or lived maximization, or still of tensorial stability.

In summary, a reinterpretation of entropy along the lines suggested, offers the following advantages. By accounting for each Atom individually, it corrects the error concerning the wastage of quality which vitiates the current view. Simultaneously, the Carnot-Clausius theory, can thereafter be incorporated in an overall cosmic scheme resting upon sound actuarial principle. Most importantly, only thus is the sum of the Energy in the Universe accounted for and the Principle of the Conservation of Energy safeguarded.

chapter IV

Aggression and Conflict a Function of Peace in the Now

Comrades — workers, soldiers, peasants and all toilers!... hand over to the revolutionary courts all who dare to injure the people's cause, we shall go forward firmly and unswervingly to the victory of socialism — a victory that will... bring the people lasting peace...

V. I. LENIN, Pravda,

Lord, let thy hand be exalted, and let them (the wicked) not see: let the envious people see, and be confounded: and let the fire devour thy enemies. Lord, thou wilt give us peace: for thou hast wrought all our works for us.

ISAIAH 26–11, 12

1. A Universal Thirst For Security and Stability Substantiates a Theory of Cosmic Peace

A last phenomenon will provide evidence of a circumstantial nature. Some would call it an argument based upon antecedent probability. Yet, its universality makes it one of the more powerful adducible in behalf of a theory of Cosmic Peace. Indeed, even though it involves a measure of faith, nonetheless, humanity unanimously endorses it — which makes it one of the rare, possibly the only issue upon which Hindu, Marxist, Liberal and Christian, etc., agree. The phenomenon in question is that all Atoms and all Antropocities, individually as well as collectively, consciously as well as subconsciously, tend toward a state of equilibrium; a state, when sought and achieved by intelligent Atoms, defined as peace.

By way of illustration, one can consider these instances, each representative of a different order of fact-phenomenon. A first example, from the realm of microscopies could be propane heating gas under high pressure in a tank. Instinctively, each molecule seeks escape, that it may diffuse in the equalizing expanses of space. Waters manifest an identical tendency. Roiled waters, once the roiling agent relaxes, waste no time in returning to calm. Before even the lonely loon, taking-off for parts unknown, is out of sight, the northern lake reverts to the soothing, cool placidity of an early dawn. Antropocities behave similarly. Rocks tumbling down a mountainside have but one goal — a spot whereat to rest in stability and peace.

The members of the vegetable realm are no exception. The graceful weeping willow troubled by the passing squall, immediately as quiet returns, resumes its normal posture — every branch tending toward that ubiquitous, mysterious peace, the peace imposed by gravity. The behavior throughout the animal kingdom is identical. All animals, while aggressive, seem to view their aggression as but a mean. The starved cow, which savagely decapitates helpless cabbages and timothies, does so with the obvious objective of lying in some shady nook, to there placidly, in peace, chew its cud. The cat, whether leopard in the wild or siamese in a back-yard, no doubt kills not only for food, but for pleasure also. Yet, its sadism, like that of its counterpart, the human hunter, is subordinate to a more basic urge — the comfort of a warm undisturbed siesta.

Nor is man an exception. Whether *petit bourgeois* or visionary, security and peace are his prime objectives. The former, in his millions, yearns for nothing more than the security of a good job and the quiet enjoyment of his own home and family. Yet, Hitler who shrieked revenge, war and blood, in the name of the Fatherland, and Lenin who kept the firing squads busy in the name of the proletariat and class warfare, both gave a similar justification for their violence: Peace. The peace of the 1,000 year Reich and the peace of the Red Paradise. A striking example of this dualism in which violence in the Now is equated with peace in a future, is provided by these excerpts from Lenin's 1917 Pravda article: No. 182, Nov. 20 (7).

> Comrades — workers, soldiers, peasants and all toilers!
>
> The worker-peasant revolution has definitely triumphed in Petrograd, ... It is perfectly understandable that the landlords and capitalists, and the *top layers* of civil servants... react to the new revolution with hostility, resist its victory... The majority of the people are with us. ... Our cause is a just one. Our victory is assured. The resistance of the capitalists and the high-ranking officials will be smashed. ... Arrest and hand over to the revolutionary courts all who dare to injure the people's cause, ... we shall go forward firmly and unswervingly to the victory of socialism — a victory that will be sealed by the advanced workers of the most civilized countries, bring the people lasting peace and...[1]

1. V. I. Lenin, *To the Population, On Democracy and Dictatorship, What Is Soviet Power?*, Moscow, Foreign Languages Publishing House, 1955, pp. 7–10.

One must not see in the ambivalence of the above and similar pseudo-political sentiments of a peace to be acquired through violence, an ideological perversion peculiar to our era. The earliest records of human history speak the same language. Twenty-six centuries ago the political prophet, Isaiah, harangued God himself in identical terms:

> Lord, let thy hand be exalted, and let them (the wicked) not see: let the envious people see, and be confounded: and let the fire devour thy enemies. Lord, thou wilt give us peace: for thou hast wrought all our works for us. (Isaiah 26-11, 12)

If anything, the ancient Bhagavad-Gita is harsher, for in it Krishna positively equates aggression with cosmic peace, with Brahman, as witness this dialogue between Krishna and his pupil Arjuna:

> *Arjuna:*
>
> "As I look, O Krishna, upon these kinsfolk meeting for battle, my limbs fail and my face withers. Trembling comes upon my body and the upstanding of hair. ... Ah me! a heavy sin have we resolved to do, that we strive to slay our kin from lust after the sweets of kingship. Better it were for me if these folk with armed hand should slay me unresisting in the fight." So spake Arjuna and sat down on the seat of the chariot and he let fall his bow and arrows, for his heart was heavy with sorrow.
>
> *Krishna:*
>
> O Arjuna the truly wise mourn neither for the living nor for the dead. ... That Reality which pervades the universe is indestructible. No one has power to change the Changeless. Bodies are said to die, but That which possesses the body is eternal. It cannot be limited, or destroyed. Therefore you must fight. ...
>
> *A relieved Arjuna:*
>
> "Yea, by your grace, O Lord, my delusions have been dispelled. My mind stands firm. Its doubts are ended. I will do your bidding. 'OM! Peace! Peace! Peace!- "[2]

The aggression-peace equation is more unequivocal in this next passage, where Krishna actually defines Brahman as a state of peace:

2. L. Adams Beck, *The Story of Oriental Philosophy*, Philadelphia, Blakiston, 1928, p. 111-12.

> The man who casts off all desires with no thought of *mine* or *me* enters the peace. This is the state of abiding in Brahman, O son of Pritha. He that has entered it is not confounded. If even at his last hour he enters, he passes to absorption in Brahm.[3]

A believer in the Absurd can be expected to find in the above an argument against rather than for cosmic peace. Clearly also the Materialist and/or Positivist, is entitled to discount such evidence on the ground of antecedent improbability, or to take refuge in a legitimate agnosticism.

To the Absurdist, the answer is that his reaction would seem rooted more in pessimism and a disgruntled ego than in reason. For their part, the Materialist and Positivist may note that while it is their privilege to discount hypotheses involving probability, this implies poor scientific posture, especially when, as in the case under consideration, each Atom and Antropocity strains its every fibre towards achieving some modality of peace; when astoundingly, an overwhelming majority of mankind is of one mind on the subject; namely, that peace is conquered through aggression. Furthermore, the probability factor is incidental. The issue hinges upon the Principle of Non-Frivolity. While we Now residents cannot encompass the Cosmos visually to ascertain whether or not peace prevails, there exists in the Now a parallel situation, observable on a smaller scale and whose outcome corresponds to that postulated to be cosmic. The reference is to the fact that in the Now, appetites and propensities are always satisfied to a degree, and that in every case aggression is needed — as witness the examples cited, in particular those of waters and a hungry cow. This uniformity of processes (a corollary of the Law of Similitudes), is such that upon its strength it is proper to posit that in the Now, all urges are to a degree satisfiable. If next the criteria pertinent to critical-points and maximization (see sections 1 to 3 of chapter II of this Part) are applied, the outcome translates into a state of cosmic peace — the whole being subject to the parts.

3. *Ibid.*, p. 113.

2. What Does a State of Cosmic Peace Involve?

One aspect remains to be considered: the nature of a state of cosmic peace. Or to put the question in intimate terms, What does it mean for man, for each of us to know cosmic peace?

Since cosmic peace immediately brings to mind an after-life, some may equate it with a nirvana, happy hunting ground or a heaven of sorts. Such a conclusion would be inaccurate. Between a state of cosmic peace and any known version of a heaven, the chasm is unbridgeable. None of the latter are genuinely cosmic. None embraces the fullness of Reality. To all intents and purposes all are private clubs — and at that highly discriminatory. Invariably membership is restricted to humans who, in some instances, share it with angelic or "superior" species. Worse, membership is further restricted to a select group: that of the believers. Finally, even these need the password — as a rule, a minimal quota of good deeds and reputable behavior. With all this I am not quarrelling — neither commending nor condemning — for while all have cosmogonic undertones none are nor claim to be cosmontologies. In effect, the difference is one of disciplines. *The religions are concerned primarily with the science of human behavior and destiny, Dynamic Vision is the science of the Real and its unit, the Existential-Atom. While heavenly scenarios have merit and often provide valuable insights into Reality — here in particular the Christian and Hindu views come to mind — their similarity is limited and in some instances marginal. Generally, the correspondence between a given heaven and cosmic peace will vary in direct ratio with the percentage of the Atoms (Energy) seen as being conserved in the heaven (most would no doubt speak in terms of "being saved"). The lesser the percentage, the lesser the correspondence.* From a physicist's point of view, the difference is of the same order as was that between Dynamic Vision and the becomingist philosophies, namely a question of Existence and Truth or of the Conservation of Energy versus processes. In summary, whereas the heavens are private clubs, cosmic peace, shunning the slightest element of discrimination, welcomes all in the most democratic spirit.

Effectively, the above covers a major aspect of the issue. If in the state of cosmic peace all Atoms without exception are conserved, the primary characteristic of each Atom's relationship is defined. A relationship of total coevality, it unites Nero and the mosquito which last bit him together with Beethoven and his mosquito, and sets all four in full physical communion with every Silurian dinosaur and crinoid lily which "once upon a time" graced the earth. This brings us to the secondary characteristics of a unitary and coeval relationship, or, to state the case colloquially, one must next find out how it feels to be present in peace, in and before all Atoms.

The question can only be dealt with in a general manner, for any description which would profess to picture the minutiae of such relationships must prove fanciful. On the other hand, analysis, if restricted to basics, yields an accurate representation. The reason is clear. We are not presently embroidering upon ones status and pleasure in a heaven arbitrarily defined upon the basis of the dogmas of one fideic religion or another. Rather, the investigation centers upon the positive aspects of the Real as revealed by research, and involves pure physics. Paradoxically therefore, if the proper scientific safeguards are maintained, ones findings will be more realistic than those intermittently derived from the study of temporo-spatial phenomena, all of which are subject to the distortions which the subjectivity of each individual psyche inexorably imposes. Such a statement may knock the breath out of the old-fashioned Materialist — a whiff of good faith mixed with realism should revive him.

Visualizing the feeling or mood of a state of cosmic peace, as this applies to man, is also feasible, since as noted, even in the Now, an imperfect version is experienced. The Now being a pale copy of Reality, the problem reduces itself to one of absolutization and extrapolation. For purpose of an analysis, peace, a unitary state has two key characteristics, one, unimpeded passage, a modality corresponding to a blend of mediumship and foundationship, and two, mutual enjoyment, closely related to coagentship.

A classic Now example of unimpeded passage would be that of 100 infantrymen walking in formation toward a receding objective which never resists. The example of soldiers marching into an ever welcoming Universe constitutes gross oversimplification, and as all analogies, involves misrepresentation. This is however attenuated by substituting for the erroneous notion of the soldiers being coextensive to their bodies, that of their being dimensionless motors and, thus physically immanent in and present to every Atom in the Universe. Allowing for the distortion element, one can draw from such a situation clear indications of the type of sensation which the platoon would experience in a locale 100% conflict-free. As long as they remain in the aggression-laden atmosphere of the Now, resistance looms from a multitude of sources. The air, other soldiers, rivers, mountains, bacteria — a series of enemies without end — dog them. Time-space determines their every move. On the other hand, the moment that peace is made with the Outside an entirely new sensation fills them. Catapulted beyond time-space, like Gouiran's element of matter, they fill the Universe. Encountering enmity nowhere, they lose all sense of moving. The Universe bursts. As far as the hundred are concerned, unimpeded passage presentializes them before and in every Atom. For practical purposes, they *are*, period. The same privilege extended to all of the Existential-Atoms in U=X(E : A), provides a clearer picture still. One of openness of each to all, but of an openness which does not go beyond applied or operative as-isness. By this it is meant that if there are unsentient Atoms, for such cosmic peace implies mere as-isness. These offer themselves at once as willing foundations and mediums — to be repaid in kind. The unsentient would also evidently coagentize, but from their point of view coagency has little meaning. They *are*, in the most naked sense of *to-be*. A second approximation involving a richer, more intimate relationship, that of mutual gratification, would be the peace of a newly wed couple. Deeply in love, jealous even, both anxiously gratify each other to the utmost; each is, to the other, the center of the world. Between them no obstacle resists. Should the husband leave his Montreal home, his young wife physically travels with him. At dinner in Paris, he is more conscious of her in Montreal than of the young woman, possibly more lush and gifted, sitting at the next table. In the case of lovers, the factor added to the adimensionality resulting from unimpeded passage, can be described as a conscious, reciprocal gift of Self. With the reciprocity of Selves, we touch upon the nexus of Reality and are at the source of wisdom, a wisdom distilled in the saying: flesh of the flesh of the Universe. In a sense this book is an analysis of this intuition, with the remaining pages being devoted to its meaning and implications for man.

Mutual enjoyment and gratification is, in our subjectivating world, appraised according to a multitude of norms, each emphasizing a personality trait and reflecting the preferences, loves, dislikes and values of their proponents. Some equate it with immanence, with a form of communion, others with cooperation, others still with aggression and also simultaneously with love. The two most accurate terms, it seems, are corresponsibility and love, because each in its way encompasses the fulness of relationality. From a human point of view, the concept of love, due to its high intuitive content, is the more effective. For general scientific purposes, that of corresponsibility which lends itself to analysis and tabulation, has greater heuristic value at both Orders. For instance, the corresponsibility criterion applied to lovers, reveals that their reciprocal gift of the Self, when situated within the Now, is tantamount to a making of the one by the other. M. Buber has a passage written in respect to the mystery of humility, but which nonetheless describes beautifully this simultaneous giving and making:

> There is a light over every man, and when two souls meet, their lights come together, and a single light emerges from them. And this is termed to generate.[4]

As with unimpeded passage, an insight into the mutual enjoyment aspect of cosmic peace is gained by absolutizing, by setting the husband-wife love relationship in a medium of absolute-speed. It then becomes evident that their corresponsibility for mutual self-fulfilment, for their Buber-like generation of each other, differs from their relationship with any other Atom only in respect to quality and intensity — all Atoms being univocal and adimensional. That which applies to them, applies universally. Once their mutual relationship and simultaneously their relationships with the Universe become peaceful, the corresponsibility of each to all takes on a character identical to those of husband and wife. Each makes every other physically, and reaps as recompense an increase in his own enjoyment, proportional to the fulness of the peace-love relationship established with the Outside. Unhappily the same logic has it that an individual's true or tensorial state could also be one of hatred or envy, etc., with all the pain which accompanies such conditions.

4. Martin Buber, Jewish Mysticism and the Legends of Baalshem, in Victor Gollancz, *A Year of Grace*, London, Camelot, 1950, p. 352.

3. Summary

That the Universe is headed for a state of peace is not open to debate. Growing physical entropy and the Second Law of Thermodynamics provide incontrovertible physical evidence of a slow creeping toward a peace of sorts. The cosmic rationale, as embodied in the Cosmic Code, further confirms this. Speculation on the subject must be restricted to modalities; to the type of peace which one may anticipate. In final analysis, two options offer themselves: The peace of the dead and darkness or that of the living and of Truth.

Option one is dramatically described in this passage, parts of which were quoted previously, of Lincoln Barnett's *The Universe and Dr. Einstein*:

> ... All the phenomena of nature, visible and invisible, within the atom and in outer space, indicate that the substance and energy of the universe are inexorably diffusing like vapor through the insatiable void. The sun is slowly but surely burning out, the stars are dying embers, and everywhere in the cosmos heat is turning cold, ... The universe is thus progressing toward an ultimate "heat-death", or as it is technically defined, a condition of "maximum entropy". When the universe reaches this state some billions of years from now all the processes of nature will cease. All space will be at the same temperature. No energy can be used because all of it will be uniformly distributed through the cosmos. There will be no light, no life, no warmth — nothing but perpetual and irrevocable stagnation. Time itself will come to an end.[5]

The peace of the dead indeed!

Option two, the peace of the living, briefly investigated in this chapter, recognizes all the principles of physics which underlay the conventional entropic scenario, with one difference only. In it, death is interpreted not as a nihilating event, but rather as one in which due to the breaching of a critical-point, the dead's total relationship with the universal commonwealth of the Atoms is perceived. Death, in other words, coincides with a state of perceived-maximization and peace, but not necessarily a state of happiness. Two key factors militate in favor of option two. One, it alone provides for the Conservation of Energy. Two, human

---

5. Lincoln Barnett, *The Universe and Dr. Einstein*, New York, Mentor, 1957, pp. 102-103.

tradition, bolstered by evidence that the entire inanimate realm, even in the Now, strains its every fibre to achieve some modality or other of stability. For example, one reads in the "Celestial Song" of the *Bhagavad Gita* the following description of Brahman, in which Conservation of the Real, but in a state of peace, is succinctly affirmed:

Another sun shines there! — another moon.
Another light, not dusk, nor dawn nor noon.
And they who once beholding come no more —
They have attained My peace — life's utmost boon.[6]

While the Theory of Cosmic Peace as advanced owes nothing to a fideic scheme, Brahmanic, Christian or other, but rather, child of cold research, represents the inescapable conclusion which intellectual integrity imposes, there is no gainsaying that its optimism coincides with and even exceeds that of the conventional heavens. This was inevitable, for, as we next discover, to be present before all in peace, to be one in all and all in one calls forth the ultimate boon, the fulness of love: cosmic love. Thus, there is no more apt a way in which to summarize, than to borrow these words from John, the Apostle of Love:

> And I heard a loud voice from the throne, saying, "Behold the dwelling of God with men, and he shall dwell with them; they shall be his peoples, and God himself shall be with them. And he shall wipe away every tear from their eyes, and death shall be no more, neither shall mourning or wailing or pain be any more, because the first things are passed away."
>
> And he who sitteth upon the throne said, "Behold, I make all things new". (Apocalypse 21-3, 4, 5)

6. L. ADAMS BECK, *The Story of Oriental Philosophy*, Philadelphia, Blakiston, 1928, p. 119.

Part V

Love and the Splendor of Cosmic-Man

chapter I

You Are a Cosmic-Presence

The paradox of consciousness and personality is that each of us is situated precisely at the centre of this world. Each is at the centre of infinity.

J. Maritain,
Existence and the Existent, p. 75.

There are no clear edges and every particle in reality covers the entire universe, ...

R. Gouiran,
Particles and Accelerators, p. 11.

1. Where Theory and Practice Are Joined

THIS last and briefest of five parts is at once a summary and an introduction — which makes it an unusual summary. Its unusual feature is that, as its title indicates, it introduces a new element to the discussion : the human psyche or Id. Effectively, these closing pages answer the questions foremost in anyones mind : What am I ? What is my role in life ? What is the meaning of life ?

The opening paragraphs in which the discovery of the primary particle of "matter" and the affirmation that each Atom, that each of us is flesh of the flesh of the Universe, were juxtaposed, may have left both the technician and the layman perplexed. The former, perhaps found it difficult to link the physicist's primary particle with a human or feline atom. Vice versa the layman — poet or businessman — would have deemed the question of particle research irrelevant to his intimate problems, to the nitty-gritty of daily life. The correspondance between muon and man does seem remote. The analyses and experiments which followed have possibly, to a greater or lesser extent, disposed of such reservations. Yet it is doubtful that, even at this point, all impression of esoterism is eliminated. Cosmic presentiality, the fact that both the reader and Nero's pet mosquito, together with the reader's as yet unborn great-great-grandchild are Presences *before* and *in* me, does seem "a bit too much". At this stage nothing of substance can be added to the technical demonstration as such. On the other hand, by considering the human personality in the summary, it is possible to demonstrate at once the validity and the practical value of the insights and principles developed. In other words, as the title of this section implies, theory and practice can now be joined. This will be achieved by presenting a cameo of *Homo-cosmicus* — the man whose behavior conforms to the Cosmic Code. The advantages of such an approach are two-fold. By enabling the reader to relate personally to the data accumulated, it should provide an in-depth understanding of the relevance of the work as a whole. Also it should erase all trace of the arcane, of the esoteric which may persist. The profile of the man whose broadly etched psychological portrait will emerge is, in the full sense of the phrase, that of a citizen of the Universe. Yet one in which each can readily recognize himself.

Just as the physical world of Dynamic Vision differs more radically from the present composed of Copernican time-space, than the latter did from the geocentric Ptolemean, so will *Homo-cosmicus* differ radically from *Homo-sapiens*, the myopic, space-bound creature. This is not to say that Cosmic-Man is a mutant. *Rather it is a question of power and dimensions — the power of thought, freed to occupy the Absolute, beyond which nothing resides*. In that sense Cosmic-Man having conquered the ultimate frontier, is the ultimate man. To the Absolute there is no beyond. In the Absolute no one becomes. All *are*. When man uses thought-power to conquer the ultimate dimension of the Absolute, his person remains unchanged. Rather his vision of the world, and of his Self transforms. Two key factors account for this progression. The impact of living in the Absolute versus life in time-space, and a heightening of the basic character traits of the Atom. The first will be very summarily described on the basis of two personal experiences and the second by drawing a five facet psychological portrait. The experiences referred to can be defined respectively, as a possession-of-the-Self which results from a feeling of achieved transcendence; and lived presentiality, which is to say the feeling of being a Cosmic-Presence; of being flesh of the Universe. The five character traits, whose intensification will be briefly explained and described, are those of self-assertion, dedication to truth, a will to conquer, breadth of vision and love.

2. **The Psychology of Man and Muon: Identical**

"Love and the Splendor of Cosmic-Man", the title of this last Part seemingly implies, a break with cosmontology and a consequent failure to respect the framework initially laid out. Such an assumption would be correct within the context of the conventional split-level universe of "matter and spirit". It is not so in the one-dimension universe of the univocal Existential-Atom. What follows does concern human psychology but, given the nature of the data available, no mixing of disciplines need result. Firstly, an inquiry into the broad lines of the psychology of the Atom is legimate, for psychological attitudes and responses *in se* involve relationality, and fall under the province of relationy. Secondly, due to existential univocity, or to state the case colloquially, to the fact that all Atoms are made of the same stuff and differ only as to their quality-power, the choice of a subject for general psychological investigation is optional. Where univocity reigns and two cosmic principles govern all relationships any findings in respect to basic stimuli and reactions apply *mutatis mutandis* to all species or genera. For example, presently, we will discover that a prime characteristic of the new man is an efficiency-oriented aggressivity, a will to conquer. In the real life of our Now universe whose first principle is that of Clash, an aggressive personality can hardly be considered an exclusively human trait. Lions and leopards are as aggressive as man. But so are uraniums and trees — the latter ruthlessly competing for *Lebensraum* in their forests. Conquest is the universal modality of Now relationships and to center upon man's response to aggression involves no undue partiality. For all, success is a function of the efficiency of a struggle for survival. If the short-tail bush weasel, itself a ferocious adversary, does not want to die in the embrace of a steel trap, it must outwit the trapper; it must ignore his convenient bait. In a word, to aggress and oppress for financial gain or as would a cat for the pleasure of tormenting a mouse, is to aggress. Any distinction is strictly of quality. What applies to aggression applies equally to other behavioral traits. To give but one further example, the love appetite draws together calcite atoms exactly as it does human atoms, inducing either to form more or less extensive "national" communities.

In summary and in accord with the Fourth Cosmic Law, of Similitudes, the basic psychological traits of all Atoms are similar and differences of behavior are only of an indiviqualitative order. Such a view in a society which lives according to the anthropomorphic criteria of Aristotelism may prove hard to swallow.

But so it is ; and if realism is to prevail, man must someday resign himself to existential democracy — to an Assisian respect for brother wolf and sister uranium. The rationale must now be obvious. If, when the time comes to study the Atom's basic behavior patterns, the specimen chosen is human, it is for pragmatic considerations. Technically, the same results could be achieved with a cobra or muon, the psychology of man and muon being identical.

3. From Homo-Sapiens to Homo-Cosmicus

All the pages which precede can be summarized, and those which follow are embryonic in the statement that *the Universe is a true sum of qualitative, adimensional motors (Dynamic-Facts) bathed in a medium of absoluteneity*. When the above is used to take the measure of *Homo-cosmicus*, three words: those of qualitative, motors and absoluteneity are central.

As noted, in an univocal world, the structure and characteristics of all Atoms are identical, and any differentiation is, firstly qualitative and, secondly subject to intensification, intensification being synonymous with motricity and maximization or alternately with facticity. To see in man a motor of sorts, capable of more or less intense activity, is to affirm the commonplace. Everyone from Aristotle to Pascal, Fromm and Skinner would acquiesce. So would any tenth-grader. However the situation changes the moment absolute-speed or absoluteneity invests the scenario. All dimensions as presently understood, to state the case facetiously, are altered absolutely. The universe of the person, who by and by learns to live in the Absolute, is eons away from that of a 20th century time-space man. Then, the observation by William James that: "The greatest revolution of our generation is the discovery that human beings, by changing the inner attitudes of their minds, can change the outer aspects of their lives," takes on its full meaning. The man himself is not mutated. His vision is recast. He sees his Self and the Other is a new light. Most importantly, his attitude towards the key facets of his personality, namely selfness, sense of truth, aggression, vision and love is transformed. Each of the five, when situated in a context of absoluteness acquires a new dimension.

In view of the novelty of the twin notions of the facticity of each individual and of absolute-speed, before sketching our cameo portrait, it is advisable to consider both in a human context. The next three sections are therefore devoted to the following. In the first, the two personal experiences of lived cosmic presentiality mentioned earlier are narrated in capsule form. The second, by comparing life to a one card poker game played at absolute-speed, situates man in a medium of absoluteneity. The third consists of an outline of and a few reflexions upon the Cosmic Code. The rationale for the latter is that the code provides the framework within which the five psychological characteristics can be coherently correlated.

4. **Cosmic-Man, Self and Flesh — A New Outlook on Life**

Someone to whom the gist of Cosmic-Presence was being outlined, remarked : That's alright for a philosopher or physicist, but I can't for the love of me, imagine of what practical use it can be.

He had missed the point entirely. Granted, research into particle structure or the fine points of epistemology offers little of interest to the average person. Yet, without a doubt, basic or seminal ideas are food for the whole man. We all know of cases where positive thinking, for instance, revolutionized an individual's behavior, turning a life of failure into a success story. On a broader scale, the progress or stagnation of races and societies can also be gauged according to their ideology or social attitudes. Each religion or philosophy of life yields different norms and standards of living. In a word, ideas are power. Ideas mold men and nations. And to this phenomenon there is one constant. In every case, individual as well as collective growth or lack of growth can be traced to a key insight from which all flows and to which all returns. In Dynamic Vision this critical factor is a deeply felt sense of being unique, of being One, of being a dimensionless Cosmic-Fact, as opposed to the traditional view of man as a passing, evolutionary phenomenon, a fermentation, a cheap evanescent process — here today, gone tomorrow.

If variations of a strictly ethical character, upon a common theme, which is all that separates ideologies such as Liberalism, Hinduism, Marxism, Christianism or Islam, can affect human behavior as radically as they presently do, how much more profound must eventually be the impact of the discovery of a new Universe. For the universe of Dynamic Vision, whose sole dimension is the Fact-of-to-be, is indeed a new universe, whose every province is subject to conquest by the power of thought. The development of modern technology, particularly as this allows man to master the quasi instantaneous phenomenon of electricity, and of its offspring, the computer industry, has prepared a fertile ground for such a conquest. One can say that such technologies have liberated the mind for the ultimate conquest. These liberated energies, married with a new understanding of the cosmic structure: one of Dynamic-Fact to Dynamic-Fact operating in the Absolute, will now allow man to discover the real meaning of life, its purpose and goal. For such, indeed, is the might of intellect-power. In final analysis, it alone explores, conquers and shapes our lives. John Dewey makes this same point clearly in *How We Think*.

> We may not need to do any thinking now when some event occurs, but if we have thought about it before, the outcome of that thinking is funded as a directly added and deepened meaning of the event. The great reward of exercising the power of thinking is that there are no limits to the possibility of carrying over into the objects and events of life, meanings originally acquired by thoughtful examination, and hence no limit to the continual growth of meaning in human life. A child today may see meanings in things that were hidden from Ptolemy and Copernicus because of the results of reflective investigations that have occurred in the meantime.[1]

A universe, wherein Reality rests, unscathed, in the As-is, and time and space are demoted to the status of subjective percepts, eliminates any "limit to the continual growth of the meaning in human life", all barriers being torn down. The key to this ultimate liberation is, in the first instance, a more accurate understanding of the nature of selfhood and in the second, the experience, albeit fleeting, of being, in the full physical sense of the term, a Cosmic-Presence. Hence the title of this section "Cosmic-Man, Self and Flesh".

In way of demonstration, I will have recourse to what may appear as an unusual procedure, namely the relating of two

1. John DEWEY, *How We Think*, Boston, D. C. Heath & Company, 1933, p. 21.

personal experiences, one could even talk of happenings. There is of course nothing unusual in the narration of personal experiences. That they should be embodied in a work on particle physics may, however, be deemed inappropriate by some. Such a view, while warranted in a split-level universe of "matter and spirit", loses all validity in a universe of univocal Existential-Atoms. Even from a strictly empirical point of view, in a one-decision universe, research into the human-atom yields many fruitful insights. Furthermore, it offers the added advantage that every reader can serve as his own control specimen. Their inclusion, furthermore, is indicated, in that they provide a preview into the psychological impact of a Parmenidean outlook on the Real and Lived. Anyone familiar with behavior patterns and norms, I dare suggest, will be of the opinion that the wilful, self-assured responses to life's challenges which a dynamic view promotes, must prove healthful and in many cases will have a healing effect upon common neuroses and possibly even in cases of paranoia.

These two happenings, which can be triggered by a profound understanding of the Self as a radical Oneness bathed in a timeless medium are, respectively, a "Taking-Possession-of-the Self" and a "Feeling-of-being-flesh of the Universe", of Lived-Presentiality. The first could be defined as an exercise in applied transcendence, while the second speaks of achieved immanence. Both, described upon the basis of personal experience, (which others have also lived), are merely sketched, the purpose being, on the one hand, restricted to giving a technical insight into the ultimate universe, and on the other, to introduce the reader to the basics of these happenings, should he wish to investigate them further.

A *Taking-Possession of the Self*

The Taking-Possession experience took place for the first time many years prior to that of Lived-Presentiality. As noted, in footnote 19 of chapter VII, Part I, detailed data on the subject is available in a polygraphed work entitled: *Taking Possession of the Self.* For the present the following suffices. The experience can aptly be described as the supreme act of identity or of humaness. It results from a deliberate, utterly internal and intense, act of the intellect and will operating in unison, intended to provide the subject, the I, with a flash-like knowledge-mastery of himself as Outsider.

As the term indicates, Taking-Possession presupposes the outright investing by the Self of his Self. As long as any other person, thing or any extraneous force whatsoever continues to impinge, even to the slightest degree upon ones consciousness, Taking-Possession has not occurred. Now, it is not an easy feat to radically exclude all the Outsiders from ones world — for each Self is indeed a private world, or at least should become one. The first requisite is a clear understanding of the nature of genuine outsideness: the second, a desire and will to achieve Possession and the third, a proper frame of mind and locale.

The following incident can illustrate the importance to mental health of achieving such a deep consciousness of ones full identity. Recently, while I was expounding upon the nature of the Existential-Atom before a university audience, someone interjected that he could easily grasp the Other as a something or object but that when he sought to seize or even know his own Self he felt only a "néant", a void, a painful nothingness. The gentleman, it turned out, was an adept of phenomenalism, which he applied rigorously to his person. An intelligent man, which he was, in the grip of such a theory, cannot escape the anxiety of self-doubt. Literally, he becomes flotsam upon the sea of Absurdity. Anyone in such a frame of mind, obviously, does not nor cannot possess himself. *To escape from the foggy swamp of Becoming he must seek a deliberate awareness of the fact that his person is whole, unique and self-motored; that he is not a composite, but rather a free Self, able to dwell in and upon its Self, to the utter exclusion of all Outsiders.*

Granted, all men instinctively feel and act as discrete individuals. However, such an intuition does not suffice. The fullness of Self-Possession requires that this intuition be bolstered by a conscious effort to perceive and grasp oneself as a dimensionless motor; literally as a Dynamic-Fact. Indeed, the awareness now being protrayed predicates first and foremost the exclusion, from the mind, of all Outsiders.

Briefly, the conditions to be fulfilled, to achieve Possession are a knowledge and desire, the prerequisites of any undertaking. Beyond this, the state of mind, locale and timing, all optional, may be tailored to the personality and interests of the individual. However, regardless of the where and the when, success depends upon achieving a sense of identity — of being a lone agent — so intense that gradually all Outsiders, cast out in the cold Outside, are excluded from ones consciousness. Here, Outsiders refers not only to a brother, wife or chair, but specifically to the body and all of its inhabitants, such as enzymes, irons, lymphocytes, etc. The strait jacket of "matter", no matter under what guise it invests one, must be rent, the Self or Ego becoming the sole point of focus. One could speak of Possession as the ultimate act of introspection. Possession itself is bound to be fleeting, so difficult it is to grasp ones identity, as independent of all dimensioned entities, of all "matter". If achieved it will come as a flash ; as a fleeting, but peaceful and sensuous instant when the ego, in solitude, communicates itself to itself. Words fail to describe the feeling which then fills the soul. In an attempt at providing a more apt portrayal one might add that the Self, at that "instant", shorn naked, transcends. Thereafter a new light floods the world. Aloneness becomes a lived state. The will, strengthened, welcomes challenges. Finally, Possession, while short-lived can be repeated, each experience achieved more easily, each more complete, more intense and fruitful.

The instinctive, gut reaction to the above description of an utterly self-possessed individual may be negative. Quite generally, aloneness, mistakenly equated with loneliness, frightens. For that matter, an acute sense of Self, unless accompanied by a proper understanding of the structure of the Universe can indeed prove dangerous. It is therefore important to keep in mind that Possession marks but the first step in a serene integration to the Whole. Before one can face the Others, one must be full master of the Self. Possession, far from alienating from the Outside, from the body or loved one or associate, etc., situates the universe of ones relationships in its proper perspective : a marvellous universe all the more clearly seized and loved, in that the feeling of belonging intensifies in direct ratio with that of independence. One might add that Possession offers the best antidote to the alienation syndrome, so prevalent throughout our schizoid "Western" civilization. The Self-Possessed ignores the very meaning of alienation. He knows that he is a loner. However, being a realist, guided by the principle that : What-Is, Is, he accepts the fact. Loneliness, which can easily degenerate into a semi-pathological condition, he realizes, is of ones own making and with it he deals accordingly. No one is immune from loneliness, but its dread vanishes with the knowledge that, while in a strife ruled world it can never be fully overcome, yet is does not kill and indeed can at times be savored. The essential is that the distinction be drawn between the knowledge of an infrangible selfhood and the legitimate, but unfulfillable and hence painful yearning which any normal person experiences, as well during the day's bustle, as in the dark solitude of the night.

Once the distinction between aloneness and loneliness is understood, the subject, far from being frightened, fills with a new sense of power and of pride in his newly found inviolability. A sense of calm ensues. Not instantly. Rather this grows upon one, slowly but surely, as the months pass and the true vision of the Self reinforces. Yet extremes are to be avoided. Possession is no cure-all for emotional troubles. Nothing could be farther from the facts. It does not guarantee protection from enemies, nor sanctity. Rather it dispels illusions; reduces dependence upon others, pulls the rug from under persecution complexes and generally makes for a better understanding of the great dignity of the individual.

Summing up, Taking Possession means exactly what the term implies. It does not change the individual's nature, nor the world about him and his relationships to it. It gives him at once a better perspective on life and a better grip on himself. While the hurts and heartbreaks inflicted by both friend and foe hit with the same intensity, these become easier to bear, for instead of looking upon himself as the helpless victim of a cruel universe, the individual who is aware of his personal independence and responsibility tends to respond more positively. The advantages are considerable. Not only will many occasions for bitterness and even at times despair be eliminated, but also, by reacting aggressively to challenges, no matter what these may be, the Self-Possessed will, nine times out of ten, come out of the conflict, if not the winner, at least in much better shape than he would have, had he or she meekly and fatalistically submitted to the enemy's onslaught. In a nutshell, to Take-Possesion of the Self is to transcend, to become ones own man. That is the beginning.

B. *Flesh of the Universe or Lived-Presentiality*

To trip, one of the "in" colloquialisms of North American culture, offers an insight far more profound into Reality than is usually appreciated; an insight laden with philosophical implications and which does credit to the "common man's" fund of raw intelligence. While the term assumes a different meaning from one circle of initiates to the other and indeed carries, in the mind of many, a pejorative connotation, nonetheless it testifies, in every instance, to an identical basic intuition. The idea of "tripping", of "a trip", infers a bursting out of ones bodily bonds; out of "matter", to enter an unknown, mysterious dimension. Hence the staid burgher's raised eyebrows. One must after all, keep both feet firmly stuck to the ground.

Within the cultural mold of a "matter-spirit" universe, the mere hint of a "trip" or psychic adventure, regardless of how induced, witnesses to an unusual degree of daring on the part of the "tripper", since to transcend, in any manner, places the norms of a material universe into question. For, whereas the Dewey thesis of an intellectually expanded "meaning of life", namely:

> that there are no limits to the possibility of carrying over into the objects and events of life, meanings originally acquired by thoughtful examination, and hence no limit to the continual growth of meaning in human life.

fits comfortably within the traditional view of "man, the thinking animal", any theory or affirmation which implies a transgression beyond a "material" body and its narrowly defined universe, challenges all of the latter's values. Yet, as long as the subject continues to consider itself confined to time and space, an experience of transcendence has no radical consequences, because its impact must prove marginal and ephemeral. This would apply with special force to any mental state triggered exclusively by chemical agents.

The above brief remarks serve a dual objective. Firstly they are intended to emphasize the fact that the psychic, derided in some circles, plays an integral and useful role at all levels of daily life. Psychic, here, encompasses not only the strictly occult phenomena, indeed these are marginal, but any operation or function of the senses which results in a heightened perception, allowing the individual to delve into usually hidden depths. At the extreme end of the spectrum, within that context, one must include charisma and hypnosis. The second objective is to make it abundantly clear that, while Lived-Presentiality, i.e. the feeling of being flesh of the Universe can be considered a psychic experience, when psychic is defined broadly, as above, on the other hand it is not even vaguely related to the category of conventional occult phenomena, such as radiaesthesia (divining), mystical intercourse with ghosts and spirits in general, and telekinesis, clairvoyance, etc., in particular. Actually, it is a much simpler and perfectly "natural" phenomenon. To awaken to the fact that one is a Cosmic-Presence and eventually to live as such, merely implies the discovery and occupation of a territory in which one has, of all time, dwelled. The adventure belongs to the same order as that undertaken by the 16th century Europeans when these set out, in earnest, to discover and occupy the Americas. These latter had been there all along and as much had been surmised by the more learned and open-minded, for centuries already. Lived-Presentiality shares yet an other characteristic with voyages of exploration. It endures, meaning that the newly discovered universe becomes a permanent home. In this respect the difference between it and phenomena such as drug induced "trips" or occult happenings, is radical. The latter, episodic, leave little or no lasting traces. The former alters the individual's geographic perspectives, as well as his social norms and values. Once it is achieved in-depth, a new world unfolds. "Things that were hidden from Ptolemy and Copernicus", and to 20th century man, are revealed. Effectively, one enters the one-dimension cosmos of Dynamic Vision : that of the Fact-of-to be, each Fact residing beyond traditional time-space, in full cosmic communion, each with every other.

In such a universe, two "poles", two realities, only subsist, that of the Self, free and master absolute, and that of the Outside, flesh of the Self. And from this ultimate universe, there is no return.

The long range implications of such an event are not immediately obvious. Before they can sink in, the awesome weight of a perceived time-space and of an imaginary past and future have to be gradually and painfully shucked. The bedeviling notion of infinity, curved, elliptical or otherwise, fearfully poised at the edge of the insatiable void, must be exorcised. In a word, all of the thought patterns of an era and civilization require revamping. One must learn to look at the world with new eyes. However, the reward is worth whatever toil it may demand, for he who transcends the Self, even for a fleeting instant, thereafter learns to commune with a timeless, spaceless All, knows and loves a new world: the world of his flesh.

This bipolar issue, that of Self and Flesh, warrants emphasis because it is at once the nexus of this book and the passport to a most profitable adventure. Any extra effort, devoted to grasping it fully, will be amply rewarded. It constitutes a nexus in that every major tenet previously established such as, for instance, the physicality of thought-power, the adimensionality of the Existential-Atom and the Principle of Absolutes, etc., all find, at this juncture, a common application. The adventure to which it holds the key is the discovery of the Ultimate-Universe promised in the first chapter. As then noted, every discovery in any field is, in the final analysis, a mind discovery, achieved with a mindscope. The knowledge of the Self as Existential-Atom, as true Outsider, adimensional and dynamic, served to set the mindscope in focus. To now burst out physically, one could say feelingly or emotionally, into the Absolute and to there learn to bask in the Outside, as in ones flesh, corresponds at the existential or physical level, to the mental compassing, by the 20th century physicist, of the Lorenz-Einsteinian, four-dimension universe.

Stated otherwise, the objective at this point is to portray the difference between the somewhat detached state of the scholar who contemplates dispassionately any of the three following, namely, a four dimension Lorenz universe, a mind-dependence Eddingtonesque universe or Dynamic Vision's universe, adimensional and bathed in the Absolute and the lived experience of cosmic presentiality. The former three, each addressed to a specific facet of Reality, share common features and together prepare the stage for ones entry into the universe of Lived-Presentiality: the universe of the Cosmic-Presence. The term "Lived", in particular, deserves consideration. It draws attention to the chasm between a strictly bookish understanding of adimentionality, etc., and the warms feeling of cosmic fleshhood in which every emotional fibre participates, a feeling which words fail miserably to convey.

Undoubtedly, many, even without the aid of book learning, achieve a measure of the state now being described. Closely related to love and natural, our feeling of our presence to the Universe succeeds, now and then, feebly, in breaking through the artificial walls which the concept of "matter" erects around us. As long, however, as one remains beholden to the theory of time-space dimensions, one never truly escapes. At best, one peers longingly, through cracks, here and there. The merit of the experience of Lived-Presentiality is that it irremediably shatters these walls.

As is the case with the Taking-Possession of the Self, Lived-Presentiality, the feeling of a timeless communion with the All, may strike at a privileged moment, as lightning. Yet, if genuine, its impact, even in such instances, will endure. Literally, one enters ones ultimate dwelling, to never again leave it.

Insofar as the physical requisites of timing and locale are concerned, somewhat the same standards apply as to the Taking-Possession. The key is a sense of solitude, be this in a crowded forest or bar. Here, crowded solitude means that the crowd of Outsiders, trees or men, be not permitted to invade the Self. Yet they are present, to be subsumed — in love. Implicit in the above is the need to have previously achieved a sense of ones radical identity or ego. Finally, this feeling of cosmic communion must be deliberately sought. It does not "just happen". Rather it comes as a maturation, as a fulfillment. The psychological atmosphere being proper, the Self explodes, to embrace intuitively, which is to say, at a speed which exceeds computation, an awesome, pregnant Reality. Whereas Possession presupposed concentration upon a naked Self, Lived-Presentiality calls for a diffusion of a Self which ignores itself, that it may fleshify the Outside; that it may intensely, embrace all in all. If Possession can be defined as the ultimate act of introspection, Lived-Presentiality constitutes the ultimate in extroversion.

The reference to a maturation seems justified by the fact that, in our case at least, the fulness of Lived-Presentiality was achieved only long after all the usual ontological problems had been sorted out and solved. While a cold dissection of the dynamics of the Universe had, several years earlier, caused me to write down the phrase : Flesh of the flesh of the Universe, its full meaning became clear only gradually. Initially, the words remained naked, as symbols in a chemist's equation. The code was deciphered, but I did not feel. Slowly, however, it acquired an intimate content, it became a something lived, an added dimension to my Self. My personal universe was being transformed. Imperceptibly, at first, the world opened up. Space and soon after time, lost their power to constrain. The Others were not so alien anymore. Barriers fell. The world was becoming one; one and many.

Then one night, the conditions being all propitious, late, in a loud disco, I knew, I saw, I felt the universe of the flesh, in all its drama, its splendor and warmth. The fulness of the cosmic feeling climaxed. Of a sudden, as I watched, in-truth, I was flesh — not only of that gyrating, pulsating dance floor, but the living flesh of a Universe, present, before and in me, beyond the ages, past and to come: a cosmic feeling of love.

Since then, I can affirm, in all sincerity, (as do others who have experienced the same state) that the past is nevermore a real past, nor the future a real future. All is present, albeit in a diffuse sort of way. And the Others, they are full Strangers, no more. We are flesh of each other. How can one not love this Universe of ours?

5. **Absolutes: Or Life As a One-Card Poker Game**

The key to understanding what life is all about and specifically to the "how" of being a Cosmic-Presence is the Principle of Absolutes. Absolutes crashes the barrier beyond which the nature of existence has, as in a fog, lain hidden: the time barrier. It reveals life to be a one shot affair, an exercise in cosmic presentation, performed in the Absolute — all sense of time and space, of beginnings and endings being subjective percepts, tailored to suit each individual. Its answer to the double interrogation of the "what" and "how" of being a man can be summed up in the cryptic statement: "life is a one-card, many faceted poker game, played at absolute speed".

To grant to man a measure of eternity, does not of itself constitute an innovation. In millennia past the *Bhagavad Gita* spoke of the "Changeless and Boundless Ones". In the West, so did Plotinus. The Thomistic notion of *sub specie aeternitatis* as it applies to man, can be interpreted in the same vein. More recently, Leibniz and Spinoza advanced an identical concept; as have Whitehead, many of the mind-dependence theorists and the physicists in general — the latter seeing all primary entities as "reaching out to infinity". However, the notion of a Cosmic-Presence, situated in the Absolute, goes far beyond any of the above — to the point of turning the traditional universe inside out. Its repercussions upon the sciences, especially ethology and epistemology prove more radical than Galileo's insights upon the cosmology of his times. This is nowhere more evident than in Absolutes' answer to the mundane question under consideration; namely: What am I? If Absolutes were made to speak as did the Greek deities of old; its answer would no doubt be:

> Oh human! if your wish to know yourself is sincere, you must learn to transcend the lie of time-space. You must enter my Realm, the Realm of Absoluteneity, wherein only reside Reality and Truth. Then self-knowledge is yours. Then, freed of all bondage — a free-willed Self — you conquer. You establish your presence in the midst of all Presences. And the Universe is richer for your conquests. Oh human! yours is the presence, the power and the will unbound.

Since the concept of our operating in-fact beyond time-space scandalizes, a recapitulation of its rationale is in order, especially when self-knowledge is being debated. For, an understanding of the mechanism of absoluteneity is essential to a clear image of the Self and of the nature of the will and freedom — the ultimate determinants of action and success in life. The rationale from which absoluteneity flows is straightforward. Each Atom being an absolute, each can only relate absolutely. The above, once determined, the empirical demonstration of absoluteneity becomes a simple operation.

That space and the sensation of moving in it are qualitative and phenomenal and partake of subjectivity and relativity, is a consequence of being an adimensional motor. An adimensional motor can entertain only a single physical contact with another adimensional entity. It follows that no one actually moves. Rather, each is a Presence to every other, cosmically — a situation which confirms the first postulate of the Special Principle of Relativity.

The grip of time upon man's imagination offers a more serious challenge. Yet time, as difficult as it may be to transcend, also turns out to be a paper tiger which Absolutes in a masterful blow shreds to bits. Of the many factors responsible for our greater subservience to its wiles, one stands out; its two-facedness, and an appreciation of this can do much to help view it in a correct perspective. Two-facedness means that there are two species of time, the real or physical, measured with deaths and responsible for entropy, and the inneal or perceived-time, a qualitative by-product of thought. As established in the last chapter of Part IV, the two are unrelated. Physical-time, the measure of the aggression content of the Now, is objective and terminative. Its ticks are deaths and/or absolutes (percepts). Hence its irreversibility. Hence also, its fixed duration and ending, because the number of "die-ables" being a true number, must at some point exhaust. It follows that the relevance of physical-time to any Now aspect of the question: What am I? is marginal. When it strikes — when we die — we are beyond its grip. We are in cosmic peace. Perceived-time also is physical or dynamic, but in a different way. Its physicality is inneal and qualitative; inneal in that it operates entirely within its owner, and is a function of free-will and aggression; qualitative in that it is a creature of a mind which perceives sequentially. In that sense it is more real than physical-time for whereas the latter is objective and external, perceived-time operates as a real-illusion. Indeed, our difficulty in transcending time-related perceptions results from the latter's high content of subjectivity — a fact exquisitely satirized in Lewis Carroll's famous *sortie*: "If you knew time as well as I do, said the mad-hatter... he'd do almost anything you liked with the clock».

At this point, the one-card poker game character of life comes to light. *Physical-time, the death-clock, contributes to Reality only one essential factor: invariance or irreversibility. It guillotines our aggression-prone relationships — putting an end to them. One could say that it encircles them, but that its circle or limit is neither temporal nor spatial, but rather has as dimension an absolute: ones global relationship with the clash-prone Outsiders, which perceived-time cuts up into subsidiary absolutes.* A mechanical counterpart would be the frames in a motion picture, except that instead of moving at 16 or 20 frames per second, each percept occurs at absolute-speed, but is perceived as a sequence. This relativity or subjectivity is further confirmed by the fact that, to different beholders, each event seems to occur in different time and space frames.

In a word, the Bergsons, Marxes, Haldanes and Teilhards read the time script upside down. *Time, whether real or perceived, does not make man. Man creates time.* We contribute to real-time by our death. As to perceived-time, each mindfactures his personal brand, as we dart at absolute-speed all over the card called "our life", in a febrile effort to assert our presence evermore forcefully before the universe of the Outsiders. The next concern is obvious. All games, even those played at absolute-speed, have rules. What then are the rules of the cosmic game called life? Or to state the case technically, what is the code of behavior of neutrinos, sharks and men?

chapter II

A Code of Cosmic Jurisprudence

The law is good, if a man uses it lawfully.

St. Paul, 1 Timothy 1–8

If a future theory is to unify atomic knowledge, it must contain all established theories as particular cases, and the path towards its more general principles must lie through the discarding of redundant restrictions. ... Thus the major advances of theoretical physics, once it has reached the stage of a comprehensive system, must arise from the rendering conscious and the elimination of unnecessary unconscious features which have either crept into, or always been present in, traditional thought.

Lancelot Law Whyte,
Essay on Atomism, p. 9.

A Code of Cosmic Jurisprudence

TECHNICALLY the Cosmic Code, being the subject of the second volume, does not belong within these covers. However, two reasons suggest that its basics, at least, should be presented. Firstly, to ignore it would do injustice to Dynamic Vision because to the latter, as to any global theory, this comment of Einstein in respect to the General Theory of Relativity applies:

> The chief attraction of the theory lies in its logical completeness. If a single one of the conclusions drawn from it proves to be wrong, it must be given up; to modify it without destroying the whole structure seems to be impossible...

Since the Code — in a sense the fruit of the tree — demonstrates the coherence and practicality of the whole, an introduction to it is proper. Secondly, a summary expatiation upon its key principles and their psychological implications is essential to an understanding of the mechanism or "how" of life.

In accord with the Principle of the Proportionality of Extremes, the Cosmic Code is simplicity itself. It consists of the two Prime Principles and five Laws. These, the Principles of Absolutes and of Clash, and the Laws of Clash, Extremes, Critical Point, Similitudes and Oneness, read as follows:

Principles

1. *Absolutes*: The modality of the Universe and of its processes is one of absolute to absolute.
2. *Clash:* The modality of all processes, at the Order of the Now, is one of aggression.

Laws

1. *Clash*: When clashing the stronger conquers the weaker.
2. *Extremes*: All motors operate between two extremes of efficiency, namely 0% and 100%.
3. *Critical Points*: Presence in the Now requires a minimum of efficiency at all critical-points.
4. *Similitudes*: The modality of all processes is similar.
5. *Oneness*: The efficiency of the part and of the whole is a function of that of the part.

While the Code as Code has not been discussed, its components except for the Fourth Law, Similitudes, and the Fifth, Oneness, were the subject of some analysis. Moreover, since the bearing of all seven items is basic and consequently readily deduced, the following will suffice. One, a brief investigation of the one critical feature common to all seven components; two, general comments intended to demonstrate its validity and relevance to science, and three, its impact upon the subject at hand: the "how" of being a Cosmic-Presence, man or wolf.

Item one is the Code's universality. Each Principle and Law binds all Atoms and all Antropocities, with no exception whatsoever. It follows that a characteristic of a universal code is commonplacedness. Indeed each component, with the possible exception of the Principle of Absolutes and the Law of Similitudes may initially seem tautological. Tautological the Code is not, but catholic it is — to the point that in the case of Critical Point, even puppy dogs are familiar with it. Instinctively, in a fight, these go for the throat — a prime critical-point. If anything, Clash's message that "the stronger conquers the weaker", rates less questioning. The weaker and the stronger once defined, the defeat of the weaker follows. Equally unchallengeable are Extremes and Oneness. Only Similitudes, a corollary of the univocity of the Atom, may initially be queried — mainly because it flies in the face of the theory of a dichotomous universe of "matter-spirit". Nonetheless, in its case also, a systematic survey of its application to real-life situations confirms its universality.

Actually, the Code's commonplacedness constitutes the best warranty of its validity and usefulness. If its several ordinances bind inexorably, even at the level of the trivial, then since the universe is composed of a raw material univocally shared by all

Atoms, its jurisdiction extends to the Cosmos. It is worth noting that this same quasi tautological quality characterizes the only other statute which can lay claim to infallibility, the mathematical. The latter, in effect a special case of the Cosmic, consists of three laws, addition, subtraction and division — each intuitively applied even by those who lack a formal education. Yet its simplicity notwithstanding, without basic mathematics civilization would grind to a standstill. If the impact of a mere epistemological tool is so pervasive, that of a code used to solve ideological equations must eventually revolutionize social mores.

While the Code contributes to epistemological techniques through a mathematization of social problems, only its impact upon the behavioral disciplines is of interest presently, for these alone deal with the "how" of living, of being a Cosmic-Presence. To this day, the bane of the human sciences is their reliance upon systems of fideic dogmas, as witness the Christian, Marxist or Moslem codes, or worse upon an incoherent maze of empirical value-judgements, as in the case of Nazism and Liberalism (Humanism), to name but the more outstanding. Anyone familiar with religious and political issues, is painfully aware of this confusion. The Code puts order in humanity's sloven ideological and ethical household.

The above is not to be viewed as the blueprint of a new religion or ideology, the two being synonymous. Granted, the theory that all Existents inhabit each other beyond time-space may be classified, by those who subordinate the rational sense to the visual and tactile, as an article of faith and hence the basis of yet another creed. That is their privilege. The vistas of reason are as unreal to the closed-minded as are the vistas of the Rocky Mountains to the blind. The Code as such is not a matter of faith. Each of its Principles and Laws belongs to the domain of household knowledge. Daily, we all apply it to isolated situations. It innovates only by recognizing the oneness of the world and by codifying all relationships. Thus, it fulfills one of the undertakings made initially, namely that the Existential-Atom would eliminate the "matter-spirit" dichotomy and simultaneously would lay the groundwork for a unified world view. In a general and technical manner, this was achieved once the Cosmic Equation was formulated. Universal Law now puts the seal of workability upon the whole. With it one of mankind's most fundamental quests, the common ground for a unified world view, ends. Initially, the Atom, univocal and the open-ended matrix of qualitivity, had eliminated the physical dichotomy, the Whiteheadian "bifurcation" which plagues contemporary science by providing the uniform raw material from which each discipline can draw, each according to its needs. Now the Code establishes the legislative link between the disciplines. Through it the crossfertilization of ideas which Niels Bohr, in the following paragraph, describes as essential to the continued advancement of science becomes a reality.

> The importance of physical science for the development of general philosophical thinking rests not only on its contributions to our steadily increasing knowledge of that nature of which we ourselves are part, but also on the opportunities which time and again it has offered for examination and refinement of our conceptual tools. In our century, the study of the atomic constitution of matter has revealed an unsuspected limitation of the scope of classical physical ideas and has thrown new light on the demands on scientific explanation incorporated in traditional philosophy. The revision of the foundation for the unambiguous application of our elementary concepts, necessary for comprehension of atomic phenomena, therefore has a bearing far beyond the special domain of physical science.[1]

Of necessity the Code's edicts and spirit will coincide more closely with those of a given ideology or religion, than with those of every other. However, this correspondence is a function of the said ideology's concordance with Reality.

In summary, the Code differs from the value systems of ideologies such as Bahai, Marxism, Islam or Hinduism, in that it contains no article of faith. It merely presents the basic principles which govern both the inner mechanism of each Atom, and the relationships between Atoms, whether vegetable, electrical or animal, etc., in a scientific manner. Since this book's objective is limited to the discovery of the prime particle and to an analysis of its workings, the observations which follow will be restricted to the impact of the Code upon the behavior of the human atom. Effectively this will imply a correlation of the Principles and

---

1. Niels BOHR, *Essays 1958–1962 on Atomic Physics and Human Knowledge*, New York, Random House, 1963, (preface) pp. V-VI.

Laws with the basic features of all Atoms, as revealed in the X-ray picture or graph provided in section 8, of chapter VI, Part II.

The coherence of the whole is established when one discovers that the five key character traits of *Homo-cosmicus* correspond, on the one hand to those of the ideal personality and on the other to those which appeared on the X-ray screen. These are, as noted, a high sense of selfhood, dedication to truth, a will to conquer, breadth of vision and love. Only the fifth, love, did not appear on the screen, the reason being that love operates the synthesis of the whole. In a universe wherein each is flesh of the other, each, naturally, should embrace every other as a brother.

Chapter III

Selfhood, Truth, Conquest, Vision and Love

The more I enter into the whole of an activity with the whole of myself, the less legitimate is it to say that I am autonomous... In the scale of sanctity and of artistic creation, where freedom glows with its fullest light, it is never autonomy. For the saint and artist alike, autocentricity and the self are entirely swallowed up in love.

Gabriel Marcel, *Being and Having*

1. Selfhood

Why must Cosmic-Man stand out in a crowd of Selfs ? Why must one of his key character traits be a keen sense of selfhood, of identity and autonomy ? Because of his feeling for the Absolute ; of his living in the Absolute. The person who knows itself as fact, immune to outside interference ; as a Cosmic-Presence whose norm of action is maximum efficiency in every field, cannot help but to become self-assured. Knowledge inexorably translates into act. To know oneself as a true Outsider, is to know a total person, alive in an eternal present.

Each Atom, each person, as demonstrated, owns its quota of Energy, with as consequence, that each is an adimensional motor, powered by its specific blend of fuel. In man's case the prime carburant is mind or thought-power — by far the most potent of all types of energy. Through its effective use, the individual can at once master his inner urges and, within reasonable limits, his surroundings, including other men. Only the cataclysmic forces of nature, such as major earthquakes, cyclones, etc., which strike unannounced, on a gargantuan scale, escape its control. And even these are slowly being brought to heel, as forecasting techniques improve. When harnessed by ideological movements, the might of the mind is more glaring still, as a casual glance at the globe shows. Clearly the efficiency of civilizations, measured upon an absolute scale, is a function of their ideology. Its compassing and profound impact is confirmed further by the fact that each world view molds the psychology of its adherents, stamping the individual so indelibly as to inhibit meaningful social intercourse between the members of the various schools. The phenomenon of ideological suasion and/or imperialism creates an intellect or mind-field, whose isolating and binding properties parallel in every respect those of the better known electrical or magnetic fields. In the case of "fanatical", usually minor movements, the tension can build up to the point where collective self-destruction or martyrdom is preferred to enforced comingling, as witness the Masada tragedy or the Christians' reaction to the edicts of Diocletian and other Roman emperors.[1] In our day, anyone involved in ideological debate has encountered the same attitudes, even between the

1. The following excerpts from the official "act" of conviction (July 17, 180) of Christians from Scillium (North Africa) illustrates stunningly the power of ideas. Here we find men and women which, the text seems to imply, were "normal, well-behaved citizens", explicitly affirming that they "do not recognize the empire of this world", and who choose beheading with eagerness. Such evidence is all the more telling in that it is founded on official reports, with very little added by the editor. It is no exaggeration to note that even before their execution these people, in-fact, lived in another universe.

> In the consulship of Praesens, then consul for the second time, and Claudian, on the seventeenth of July, Speratus, Nartzalus and Cittinus, Donata, Secunda, Vestia were brought to trial at Carthage in the council-chamber. The proconsul Saturninus said to them: "You may merit the indulgence of our Lord the Emperor, if you return to a right Mind".
>
> Speratus said: "We have never done harm to any, we have never lent ourselves to wickedness; we have never spoken ill of any, but have given thanks when ill-treated, because we hold our own Emperor, in honour."
>
> The proconsul Saturninus said: "We also are religious people, and our religion is simple, and we swear by the genius of our Lord the Emperor, and pray for his safety, as you also ought to do."...
>
> Speratus said: "I do not recognize the empire of this world; but rather I serve that God whom no man has seen nor can see. I have not stolen, but if I buy anything, I pay the tax, because I recognize my Lord, the King of Kings and Emperor of all peoples."
>
> The proconsul Saturninus said to the rest: "Cease to be of this persuasion."...
>
> Donata said: "Give honour to Caesar as unto Caesar, but fear to God."
>
> Vestia said: "I am a Christian."...
>
> Speratus said: "I am a Christian." And all consented thereto.
>
> The proconsul Saturninus said: "Do you desire any space for consideration?"
>
> Speratus said: "When the right is so clear, there is nothing to consider."...
>
> The proconsul Saturninus read out the sentence from his notebook: "Whereas Speratus, ... and the rest have confessed that they live in accordance with the religious rites of the Christians, and, ... persevered in their obstinacy, it is our pleasure that they should suffer by the sword."...
>
> Nartzalus said: "Today we are martyrs in heaven: thanks be to God!"

Believers of the major religions. The dedicated Moslem and Marxist, Christian and Liberal, each live in a world of their own making, with only the more gifted and knowledgeable appreciating the culture and aspirations of the enemy — but not for all that accepting these. In each instance, the resulting psychological apartheid is a function of the breadth of the given world view — the more narrow and erroneous breeding the more closed-minded and dangerous Believers, the more truthful and universal breeding men of broader understanding and openness. To quote E. Fromm:

> Man's nature, his passions, and anxieties are a cultural product; as a matter of fact, man himself is the most important creation and achievement of the continuous human effort, the record of which we call history... But man is not only made by history — history is made by man. The solution to this seeming contradiction constitutes the field of social psychology.[2]

Which brings us back to absoluteneity and the Absolute.

If, to give but one example, the mere laying of emphasis upon a minor theological issue, such as that which distinguishes the Lutheran from the Calvinist creed, could foster two quite distinct mentalities, the one given to a somewhat romantic, not to say visionary view of life, and the other, more pragmatic and devoted to the work ethic, certainly a quantum jump into the Absolute should transmute the individual and the society which comes to live by its criteria. As noted, the five Cosmic Laws, as such, introduce no new psychological factor. They merely provide a universal setting for principles which are of the common patrimony of mankind. Yet, even as limited a development as this codifying of Universal Law must eventually have repercussions,

---

The proconsul Saturninus commanded that proclamation be made by the herald: "I have commanded that Speratus, Nartzalus, Cittinus, Veturius, Felix, Aquilinus, Laetantius, Januaria, Generosa, Vestia, Donata, Secunda be led forth to execution."

They all said: "Thanks be to God!"

And so all are crowned with martyrdom together, and reign with the Father and Son and Holy Spirit for ever and ever. Amen.

2. Erich FROMM, *Escape from Freedom*, as in *From Medicine Man to Freud*, Jan Ehrenwald, New York, Dell Publishing, 1956, p. 363. It may be noted, in passing, that the "seeming contradiction" referred to by Fromm is resolved when absoluteneity takes over.

if for no other reason than the fact that all secondary codes are thereby unified and a common link binds the disciplines.

The impact of the Principle of Absolutes upon personal and social behavior patterns is, however, of another order altogether. Absolutes shatters all conventional norms, even ethics being profoundly influenced. To use the mechanic's terminology, the notion of absoluteneity beneficiates thought-power to a maximum. Not only is time transcended, but perfection becomes the sole acceptable goal. Every facet of the perception of the Self is affected. Life assumes a new meaning. Man becomes an absolute and it follows, his concept of the Self's role in society radicalizes. Teilhard would possibly speak of a "break in the phyllum". Between the concept of the person as "the last bubble in a long process of fermentation" or still as B. Russell's "series of experiences connected by memory and by certain similarities of the sort we call habit", and that of the person as a conquering Dynamic-Fact, resident of the Absolute, the distinction is not of degree but of order.

Thus, while other factors in the Code will foster selfness and independence — in particular the Principle and Law of Clash — nonetheless the absoluteneity feeling, above all, will strengthen Cosmic-Man's sense of identity and make him stand-out in any crowd of Selfs. The realization that he is a Fact, possessor in fee simple and in perpetuity of his quota of the cosmic energy; that he is a free agent, will imbue him with the ultimate personality. Nothing is more conducive to a sense of calm and well-being, even in adversity, than the conviction that, regardless of any aggressor's threats, the aggressor cannot penetrate the Self; that, in final analysis, each is master of his destiny and indestructible. Such is the intuition which underlays the theory of Individual Psychology of Alfred Adler, as witness the following:

> ... It is here that individual psychology breaks through the theory of determinism. No experience is a cause of success or failure. We do not suffer from the shock of our experiences — the so-called trauma — but we make out of them just what suits our purposes. We are self-determined by the meaning we give to our experiences; and there is probably something of a mistake always involved when we take particular experiences as the basis for our future life. Meanings

are not determined by situations, but we determine ourselves by the meanings we give to situations.[3]

If this innate sense of Self, which not only man, but even the kitten manifests when attempting, with his puny growl, to ward off the dog out to steal "his" milk, is powerful enough to withstand the corrosive assaults of philosophy's sulphuric acid, Becomingism; if the raw sense of identity can thrive even in an atmosphere of Skinnerian-like reductionism, how much better should it not prosper in the person who discovers, through a scientific dissection of Reality, that he owns his parcel of the Universe before and against all comers; that he is not "in-act" but is a Dynamic-Fact.

To know the Self as a true and permanent entity, is to enter a new world — the person being maximized to its nth degree. Presently man is drawn between two cultural poles, the Christian and the Libero-Marxist. The strength of christian-oriented societies can be, in great part, traced to their commitment to the promotion and protection of the individual as individual — his rights and worth being valued above all else. The spread of the Humanist or Liberal and Marxist religions, whose central dogma makes of man a cheap on-going project of so slight value in the cosmic balance sheet that he is to be written-off at death, quite as casually as a useless symbol off a blackboard, is slowly but inexorably undermining the sense an authentic eternal Self or soul which centuries of Christian civilization nurtured. This dissolution of selfhood, and the neuroses which it breeds have proceeded to the point where a trade-mark of the hybrid 20th century "Western" civilization becomes a lack of purpose, social and personal, compounded with cynicism and a morbid preoccupation with alienation. Nor could it be otherwise. Convince the rational man that he is "a nothing issued from nothingness", slimeingly oozing into a Santayanan or Marxian void, and anguish and despair must haunt his days and his nights, making a hell, especially of the night of his life.

A doctrine of genuine selfhood, not only reverses the debilitating Libero-Marxist trend, it actually betters the Christian inspired "sense of a person". Out-Gestalting the most radical of Gestalts, the Cosmic-Self, having lost ownership of the prison of

3. Alfred ADLER, *What Life Should Mean to You, ibid.*, p. 348.

his "body", gains an inalienable title to his portion of the Universe. No matter how frail, sickly or poor, he is real. He is permanent. Ontologically free, he stands proud before the cosmic community. And not for a mere lifetime. He is not "born in time" to thereafter, according to traditional Christian terminology "exist for a time without end". A Cosmic-Presence, he is what he is, and that for him suffices. And he conquers. The above is enough to promote realism, inner calm and a joy of living. That is the foundation.

Consider next the self-confidence — glorious because warranted — of the Self whose mind's eye, as his life adventure develops, opens upon the realization that he is needed; that he is an essential factor in the Universe; that without him the entire cosmic scenario has to be written anew. His calling is of maker of the Universe, and his code one of self-expression. A true Outsider, in fear of no intruder, immune from foreign graspings, from God even, the Cosmic-Presence dwells in serenity and peace of mind. In and through him, the paradox of the *I* and *Thou* is resolved. While aware of his outsideness, of his transcendence, he is equally conscious of his cosmicity, of his immanence, of his being flesh of the flesh of the Universe. Alive to the dependence of each upon the other for mutual self-fulfilment, he seeks fulfilment in corresponsibility — beyond time and space. Exceeding the noble yet subjective vision of Maritain, for whom:

> ... The paradox of consciousness and personality is that each of us is situated precisely at the centre of this world. Each is at the centre of infinity...[4]

the Cosmic-Self welcomes lovingly the Outsiders which are in him, that together they may make the world a better place. Such is the glory of the authentic Self.

2. **Truth**

Upon the subject of Cosmic-Man as man of Truth we need not dwell, for our concern is not the general theory of truth but rather the individual's psychological response to the universally accepted notion of *a Truth.*

---

4. Jacques MARITAIN, *Existence and the Existent* (trans. Lewis Galantiere and Gerald B. Phelan), Garden City, New York, Doubleday, 1956, pp. 75-76.

As with selfness, man's yearning for truth is so visceral that all ideologies and religions aggressively declare allegiance to The Truth. A similar preoccupation haunts the academic community, as witness the obsession of the students of formal logic with the truth of propositions and the exquisitely chiseled reams of equational tapestry which they weave in a hopeless quest for the ultimate "logical" demonstration. Such unanimity, while outwardly surprising, is readily accounted for when one recalls that Truth synacts with Reality and Existence, and that Truth as Truth constitutes the epistemological expression of selfness. Alternately, it represents the conceptual counterpart of the principle that What-Is, Is, of which, as noted, even Bertrand Russell, observed: "it could not be doubted". Indeed, it may be that this obsession with the logic and the epistemology of Truth — a trade-mark of 20th century philosophy — arises from a subconscious urge to compensate for the loss of existential truth which attends phenomenology and all theories of Becomingism.

Be this as it may, in matters of Truth, Cosmic-Man's position excells on both theoretical and pragmatic grounds. Whereas the Phenomenologist or Becomingist is left to wrestle with some more or less sophisticated version of the nonsensical affirmation, "it is a truth or dogma that there is no dogma, all is phenomenal; all is bathed in perpetual movement and change", his case rests upon the bedrock of physical truth, for he alone unhesitatingly obeys the admonition of the Prophet of Truth:

> ... Meet it is that thou shouldst learn all things, as well the unshaken heart of well-rounded truth, as the opinions of mortals in which is no true belief at all. ... (fr. 1) ... the only ways of enquiry that exist for thinking: the one way, that it is and cannot not-be, is the path of Persuasion, for it attends upon Truth; the other, that it is-not and needs must not-be, that I tell thee is a path altogether unthinkable. (fr. 2) [5]

For him, as for Parmenides, the beginning and ending of scientific inquiry are contained in an objective "What-Is, Is" and a concomitant refusal to entertain even the thought of an ontological negative. His is the Positivism *par excellence*.

5. PARMENIDES, *Greek Philosophy, Thales to Aristotle*, (trans. Reginald E. Allen), Toronto, Ontario, Collier-Macmillan, 1967, p. 45.

Let us now consider the fortunate consequences. *Homo-cosmicus'* entire universe, his Self inclusively, rests immutable in the facticity of the Absolute, in as-isness. For him, *The Truth* is objective. However, being the proud possessor of his parcel of Reality, he can afford the humility to admit that *The Truth*, which is to say all of Reality, is not his to dispense of or even to compass. Given the influence of ideas upon behavior, one can readily deduce the two seminal traits which, in respect to truth, characterize *Homo-cosmicus*: positivity and humility — each in turn being responsible for secondary characteristics which cover the behavior spectrum.

A first benefit of Positive Realism is a serene objectivity in scientific endeavors, those of justice inclusively. For example, presently, the Heisenberg Principle of Uncertainty engenders considerable confusion and anxiety throughout the scientific world. Technical accuracy, it would seem, is unattainable. Indeterminacy reigns. Cosmic-Man, having at his disposal an intellectual tool kit whose precision surpasses that of the conventional by the same factor as the astronaut's navigational instruments exceed that of Columbus and his crew, remains unperturbed. To tackle this challenge, acute enough to trouble Einstein, he simply turns to three key instruments, the Principle of Absolutes, the Existential-Atom and the Antropocity. The three, together, by reducing uncertainty to the status of a particular case within the compass of Absolutes and by revealing incertitude to be a function of the limitations of the human mind, dispell any Heisenbergian threat. Existential truth, since it partakes of the Obscure-Absolute whose trivia remain forever beyond the grasp of man's non-absolute intellect — only the fact of its presence being grasped in-truth — rests secure in the As-is. Heisenberg, it turns out, merely came to deflate the prideful ego of the applied scientist, who offers no truths, only his puny man-made thought-quanta, the strictly relativistic produce of the carnal senses and of the latter's mechanical slaves such a caliper or telescope or x-ray crystallograph.

Cosmic-Man, conscious simultaneously of the objectivity of Truth, as it resides in the Absolute, and of the subjectivity of sense percepts, as he mindfactures these into Antropocities, loses faith neither in applied science nor Truth. Rather, he dismisses

Humian skepticism as well as the assumed Heisenberg uncertainty as the fruit of superficiality wrapped up in pride.

Objectivity serves him well in yet another field, one of greater import to the welfare of mankind, that of justice. Justice here encompasses the entire spectrum of social relationships. Even a cursory analysis into the nature of responses to social challenges reveals the privileged position of the person for whom Truth is objective as compared to that of the social relativists — Deweyean, Skinnerian or other. When one looks upon all realities, human or uranific, as transitory phenomena whose truth resides in the perceiver, then the respect, let alone the defense, of the rights of others must eventually be assessed according to personal interests. Truth, reduced to a subjective percept, inexorably becomes the plaything of individual fancy and passion. Classic cases of this perversion were those of Stalin and Hitler. These however differ from the pretty tyrants in ones home or office in scale only. Nor are the evils of situation-truth perpetrated exclusively by psychopaths, famous or non-famous. Even a man of goodwill can with utmost difficulty escape equating his interests with The Truth, with justice, if he views the Real as shifting Humian sense-data.

In this respect, *Homo-cosmicus*, for whom Truth rests "unshakeable and well-rounded" upon the Absolute is, fortunate. Granted. His innate hunger for Truth is no greater than that of the relativist. He remains subject to the frailties of the human nature. For reasons of ambition, shame or fear he, as other men, may lie and deceive. Nonetheless, when doing so he knows that he is wrong. Where others feel free to lean upon the will of the majority or changing social mores to justify their behavior, he must stand upon principle, accepting, when the case calls for it, his share of guilt.

Some, far from being favorably impressed with steadfastness on questions of principle, may view it with suspicion and be tempted to speak of narrow-mindedness, of dogmatism or even fanaticism. Blind fanaticism and calm dedication to principles are most different attitudes, the former being as ugly and dangerous as the latter is desirable. Closer analysis of the psychology embryonic in Dynamic Vision reveals it to be nowhere as superior as upon this point, for it provides the individual with a universal rationale for his uncompromising respect of Truth, while impressing upon him a duty to approach all human relationships with humility, understanding and compassion.

Where others must place their faith, either in revealed codes or upon a subjective assessment of their appetites and ambitions, Cosmic-Man has available the Code, securely anchored in the physical structure of the Universe. *Where the truth of facts is concerned he neither believes nor subjectivates. He knows. Phenomena and relationships, however, he only senses.* And the senses are poor, often false witnesses. His sight does not see very far nor very clearly. His hearing is of yet shorter range and quite as unreliable. In a shouting crowd he cannot tell friend from enemy. As to his mind's eye, it serves him most poorly of all. His understanding of the motives and feelings of ally and foe, of his loved ones even, remains forever primitive, as each hides, unfathomable, in the obscurity of its Self. Thus, he who transcends the wisdom of *Homo-sapiens* to that of *Homo-cosmicus*, and for whom the Universe is present, albeit obscurely, does not compromise upon principle — the Truth of the Universe being at stake. Yet he judges not neighbor or stranger or lover, but extends to all within the limitations of his poor means, compassion and love.

3. **Cosmic-Man, a Man of Conquest**

He who has not conquered, has not lived! Such is the message of Dynamic Vision. *Conquest!* This is the motto of Cosmic-Man. Nor is there in our strife-ruled Now any other road open to the rational one. But his conquests are not just ordinary conquests. They are the conquests of the efficient one — the first-born of a will to perfection — systematic and constructive, without rancor or bitterness.

That Cosmic-Man should aver himself a man of conquest may surprise and frighten. Indeed, the very thought of a breed of uncompromizing, conquest-minded Selfs will send scurrying, like so many scared mice, the world's weaklings and the not so weak but more gentle souls who, being conditioned by our soft, pleasure seeking societies, equate weakness with virtue, compromise with statesmanship. In a general way, a fear of and withdrawal from situations calling for an aggressive response of any type, is perfectly natural. Struggle and conflict are demanding, nearly always painful and, at least on the surface, destructive. Yet a refusal, instinctive or rationalized in the name of pacifism, to stand up to challenge is unmanly and a danger. Pacifism under any guise, at its mildest a sign of immaturity, when extreme or worse when ideological, is evil and a sign of degeneracy. Those who promote the peace at all cost, the "better Red than dead" mentality, so prevalent throughout the "Western" world, are guilty of the basest of crimes. By undermining the stamina, the will-to-be of the masses, they contribute to the current and frightening rapid disintegration of our social fabric and, ultimately must share in the blame for the suicide of the most promising civilizations ever developed by man.[6]

---

6. The reference is to the assumption that since cosmic presentiality implies a rejection of ontological change and evolution, the individual who lives accordingly must be static-minded, a social conservative, a "stick in the mud" type. Such a surmise is dispelled when the psychological impact of as-isness and its corollary, absolute-speed, is assessed in its true light. Exactly as a refusal to compromise Truth comes from the realization that neither past nor future are real, and that actually life, a one card poker game, is a timeless bursting of the Self into cosmic peace, so is a dynamic and aggressive attitude, a consequence of absoluteneity. Anyone familiar with responses to stimuli appreciates that the individual who lives his cosmic presentiality, must prove anything but passive, especially since for him the Law of the Now is that of Clash. If anything, the problem would seem to lie in the opposite direction, that of uncontrolled agitation. The instinctive reaction to the discovery that self-realization depends upon a massive outpouring of energy, would normally be the straining of ones every fibre to achieve maximal presentialization — before it is too late. Indeed, being under compulsion to transcend time and space, the cosmically oriented is saddened by the fact that to whatever extent he composes with either, his Self diminishes proportionately. Hence the danger of a wanton activism.

Such would be the outcome were it not that Dynamic Vision provides an inhibitor, which acts not as a tranquilizer — an ideological Valium — but whose impact rather parallels that of heavy water or carbon used to slow the neutron emission in an atomic pile, namely the law of efficiency, viewed in its cosmic setting. A by-product of the Law of Extremes, the notion of maximal efficiency, as a norm of action, is the ideal antidote for the complacent, "no excess" type of behavior which the hellenic, *in medio stat virtus* philosophy of life, promotes. He who paces his activities according to a deliberate extremism, one could even speak of a sensible fanaticism, is on the one hand encouraged to avoid mediocrity as well as excesses, and on the other sees his natural aggression urge compounded by a will to absolute efficiency. Effectively *Homo-cosmicus* is put on notice that he, the adimensional motor,

While such outright degeneracy usually afflicts a minority only, nonetheless for a majority, in particular those of goodwill and the kind of heart, the presence of strife in the world, its inevitability and random cruelties are a constant source of unending anguish and scandal. For Cosmic-Man, the anguish and compassion remain. But there is no scandal; only a quiet, if sorrowful, determination to conquer — conquest and life being for him one and the same thing.

The complexity of the question of aggression, with its dilemmas, injustices, pain and often death, precludes any in-depth analysis. These brief pages, rather, seek two objectives: to present the basics of a healthy response to life's challenges, and simultaneously show that an unnatural, morbid fear and avoidance of struggle results from a misreading, one might even hazard a perversion of Universal Law.

We have seen that a spirit of selfness and positivity can be traced directly to the no-nonsense realism embryonic in the premise: What-Is, Is. This same cool realism plays an equally major role in promoting a wholesome attitude towards aggression. Stark realism is dangerous, degenerating easily into fatalism. Or worse, associated with pride, it breeds in the aggressive one the bully's callous indifference to the suffering of the weak; even the cold contempt of a Nietzsche for whom:

> Compassion works on a man of insight almost to make him laugh — like tender hands laid on a Cyclops.[7]

Fortunately there are other factors responsible for a willingness to embrace challenge. There is law, science and love. Such an assertion calls for an explanation because law, science and love are the last things normally connected with the promotion of

---

operates between "two extremes of efficiency: between 0% and 100%", and that the ideal 100% is always "ahead". Life's motto becomes *excelsior* — forever onward. In a self-willed world, his goal is to be top man in his field. Ignoring fatalism, under any disguise, he strives towards perfection unto his last breath. The social implications are clear.

The "better red than dead" syndrome, is characteristic of the Libero-Christian for whom pluralism and appeasement at all costs are a gospel. The explicit statement referred to, was, to the outrage of most Canadians, uttered by their Prime Minister, Lester B. Pearson, circa 1963.

7. F. NIETZSCHE, *Beyond Good and Evil*, (trans. by Marianne Cowan), Chicago, Henry Regnery Company, 1955, p. 88.

aggressivity — all three being rather thought of as conducive to effeteness or meekness. The answer to this paradox is simple. It lies in the Cosmic Code, wherein the Real and Now unite into a rational whole.

The first application of the Code to a practical issue, the central one of everyday life, comes to justify the claim made earlier that its key characteristics : simplicity and universality, make it a useful scientific tool. Not only does it rule with an iron hand over the Cosmos, but its dictates, susceptible to fine tuning, can also promote noble sentiments and ideals — in particular an unrequited appetite for learning and a profound compassion for the weak and ones enemy. A brief analysis of the manner in which a simple, yet universally binding code can influence behavior favorably, suffices to explain this surprising proposition. That the Cosmic Code is uncomplicated relative to other behavioral statutes requires no demonstration. Its inexorability is equally unchallengeable. Its edicts allow for no exception, for the very basic reason that its seven components, each drawn from physics, are valid as well between two electrons as between man and electron. Whereas other codes draw their authority from *de fide* revelations or from subjective, hence narrow and contestable value systems, the Cosmic owes nothing to man's idiosyncracies or perversions, cultural or otherwise. In a majestic sweep, it takes in as particular cases all man-contrived ordinances, and voids any intrinsically unjust law of society. Its strength and cohesion is compounded by the fact that its austerity reduces the distortion factor to the lowest feasible level. It is difficult, if not impossible, to lose sight of a problem when its parameters fall under three headings only : conquest, efficiency and oneness. One could say, that the Code, as the guillotine, is the ultimate leveler, with the difference that its services are as constructive as those of the guillotine are destructive. Before its five Laws all problems are equal. In short, it is genuinely cosmic. Exceeding the rigid and often petty formalism, the "Thou shall not do so and so" spirit characteristic of ethical laws, it provides at once the absolute ideal : the will-to-be one in all and all in one, and the detailed programming needed to make this ideal live.

The harmonizing of conquest with law, science and love offers a choice opportunity to vindicate the above claim. If to this day, law, science and love seem incompatible with aggression, the fault is due to the tunnel-like perception which results from the pulverization of Universal Law into a multiplicity of narrow statutes — each held to be binding within the parameters of presumably independent disciplines. The Code, whose grid consists of four value-norms only : absoluteneity, clash, efficiency and oneness, begins by eliminating these interdisciplinary dichotomies. Having through Similitudes unified Reality, it provides the researcher with basic theorems applicable to any secondary issue. In a nutshell, it forces one to situate all problems in a cosmic setting and to assess them accordingly. Where aggression is concerned the message then becomes clear. While Absolutes and its mode of absoluteneity reign supreme throughout the Cosmos, in the Now, the Prime Principle and Law are those of Clash ; which read respectively :

> *"The modality of all processes is one of aggression", and "when clashing the stronger conquers the weaker".*

Thus, the compatibility of law with aggression, far from being open to question, is so complete that aggression and law are one and the same. *In the Now, aggression is The Law.* Every act assaults, even one apparently as neutral and/or inoffensive as sitting down in a chair or drawing air into the lungs. All of men's edicts, taboos and ordinances, most emphatically the Law of the Survival of the Fittest, merely embroider upon the master law : *Aggress.* The profound wisdom of the Vedanta here comes to light. To all intents and purposes, the Principle and Law of Clash jointly reiterate Krishna's command to Arjuna : "Therefore fight". Cosmic-Man, by adopting a conqueror's view of life, merely conforms to the nature of the Now. It is the Pacifist, whatever his motive, who sins against Reality.

This brings up the next point : the conciliation of science with aggression. What possible connection can there be between science and aggression ? More specifically, why must the realist who willingly faces up to the fact that his every move aggresses, simultaneously be science-minded ? The answer lies in Principle Absolutes. Was the Code's message restricted to a command of conquest, it would hardly rate mention, certainly not a favorable mention. Firstly, naked aggressivity destroys wantonly. Secondly, aggression as a philosophy of life is not in the least exclusive. The human tribe pullulates with conquistadors who scorn all decency, all justice. The Code however is universal. Its foundation is not the Principle of Clash but of Absolutes, a corollary of existential facticity. From the first pages, the relevance of facticity to a proper outlook on life was stressed. The present considerations confirm this.

As we have seen, the Evolutionist, whether of the radical Marxist or the mitigated Aristotelian species, must, if coherent and intellectually honest, make his Santayana's vivid but barbaric statement that:

> A soul is but the last bubble of a long fermentation in the world.[8]

And with a bubble, why be concerned? So it is that the realist, the pragmatist — and their kind rules — knowing but one Law: that of the Jungle, tramples underfoot the weak and the old, the non-conformist and the enemy in general. Oh, for sure it is all rationalized. The human bubble is after all an intelligent bubble. But to the victim, what difference does it really make? To be liquidated in the name of the dictatorship of the Proletariat or to starve in that of economic laissez-faire, what difference does it make? Certainly, Cosmic-Man also conquers. However, his outlook is literally from another world. Aggression and struggle are to him but applied realism, a mode of behavior and a prelude. Since in the Now conquest is the game, conquer he will. He has no alternative. To survive he must perpetrate a continuous flow of cruelties. To keep the "body" functioning, he must gasp the oxygens in the atmosphere and devour meek chicken and helpless lettuces. To defend justice he must shed the enemy's blood upon the battlefield. But for him this conflict-ruled Now is not imbedded in the Real. The Now is only his own narrow, dimly perceived reserve. Reality, he knows, is cosmic. Flesh of the flesh of the Universe, his faintest yearning leaves an indelible imprint upon the face of his neighbors — those flitting about in Cleopatra's court, and those who some day inhabit Mars. With everyone he is corresponsible for a mutual self-realization. While resigned to Clash, he takes note also of Extremes, the law of efficiency and perfection. Then does science come to join law in an aggression-filled world.

For, what is science but a quest for knowledge, a will to overcome intellectual barriers, a chase after perfection, all of

8. G. SANTAYANA, *Reason in Religion*, New York, Collier Books, 1962, p. 125.

which merely elaborates upon Extremes which declares that: "All motors operate between two extremes of efficiency". This compatibility of a scientific bent with aggressivity is self-evident and any protracted demonstration would be an insult to the intelligence. A single commentary suffices, namely that the definition of science predicates efficiency and a concomitant respect for the Laws of Extremes and Clash, as witness, from Webster:

> 2. Knowledge, amassed, severely tested, coordinated, and systematized, specially regarding those wide generalizations called the laws of nature.

That a scholarly approach to life should come naturally to the cosmically-oriented whose motto is: "Conquest", follows. Amassed knowledge, tested and systematic, equals an efficient victory; an exercise in thought-power, aimed at maximizing the Self, through an intimate knowledge of the Other. So it is that Cosmic-Man, at peace with himself and the world, having learned the lesson of Extremes which bids him to strain his every muscle toward 100% efficiency, and maximization, sets about his task, scientifically and with steadfastness.

At this point, it may be countered that even though theoretically a cosmic perspective could promote a legal and scientific will-to-power, it remains inconceivable that the conquering could simultaneously be loving and compassionate. Is not a calculated ruthlessness the trade-mark of the master? Have not the conquistadors, the Cortez, the Lenins and Hitlers, through the ages, invariably contempted the weak and the meek? Did not Nietzsche, the prophet of the super man, place these words in the mouth of his hero:

> 265: At the risk of displeasing innocent ears, I propose the following: Egoism belongs to the nature of a distinguished soul. I mean that immovable faith that other beings are by nature subordinate to a being such as "we are"; that they should sacrifice themselves to us. The distinguished soul accepts this fact of its egoism without any question mark, and also without any feeling that it is hard or oppressive or arbitrary: rather as something which may be founded in the basic law of all things. If it were to look for a name for its feeling, it would say. "This is justice itself".[9]

9. F. NIETZCHE, *op. cit.*, p. 216.

That is true. But only for as far as it goes. Only for the asocial ones; for those who inhabit a one dimension "material" universe, wherein man, imprisoned in the strait jacket of time-space, is born and dies isolated, a radical Outsider and the enemy of every other. In such an evolutionary world, the Nietzsche-Lenin thesis of ruthless conquest is logical. He who is a world unto himself, is a fool if he does not stamp the enemy into the ground — all the more so if he has been convinced that, bubble-like, he is a fleeting phenomenon, soon to vaporize.

Dynamic Vision, by revealing to man his immanence to-and-in all Atoms beyond time-space, and his corresponsibility, denies him the right to entertain the Nietzschean thesis, or of ever uttering the pitiable welpings of a prideful, despairing Sartre, for whom "l'enfer, c'est les autres" (hell, is the others); for whom "le conflit est le sens original de l'être-pour-autrui", which is to say, the purpose of conquest is the enslaving of the other to avoid being enslaved. Equally abhorrent is the Liberal's economic egoism, born from a subjective interpretation of Darwin and immortalized in this text from Herbert Spencer's, *Social Studies*:

> That state of universal warfare maintained throughout the lower creation, to the great perplexity of many worthy people, is at bottom the most merciful provision which the circumstances admit of. ... The poverty of the incapable, the distresses that come upon the imprudent, the starvation of the idle, and those shoulderings aside of the weak by the strong, which leave so many "in shallows and in miseries", are the decrees of a large, far-seeing benevolence. It seems hard that widows and orphans should be left to struggle for life or death. Nevertheless, when regarded not separately, but in connection with the interests of universal humanity, these harsh fatalities are seen to be full of the highest beneficence — the same beneficence which brings to early graves the children of diseased parents, and singles out the low-spirited, the intemperate, and the debilitated as the victims of an epidemic. ...[10]

A man of mastery, Cosmic-Man is a whole man, obedient to the plenitude of the Law. As Arjuna bowing before Krishna's command chose to fight, so is he, in sorrow, reconciled to conquest. However, he does not stop there, for he knows that Clash is one of five Laws, strictly modal and computative, whereas Oneness and Extremes are normative and paramount.

---

10. Herbert SPENCER, *Social Statics* (London 1851), pp. 322-323.

Oneness in particular reveals socialization as the basis of life. This socialization norm is further strengthened by Extremes which makes of excellence, the norm of the Now. If he wishes to keep his feet realistically planted on the ground, Cosmic-Man must conquer. However, where other men are concerned, his aggression subordinates to cooperation, to oneness, for therein lie increased efficiency and mutual maximization. Rejecting the haughty scorn of a Sartre, for the "salauds", literally for the "filthy Outsiders", rejecting the naked cynicism of a Spencer, refusing to wrap himself up in the cold storage of a Nietzschean Super-Ego, he offers his brother his hand, that together they may:

> be fruitful, and multiply, and replenish the earth, and *subdue it*; and *have dominion* over the fish of the sea... (Genesis 1–28)

Then, aggression losing its sting, becomes the catalyst needed to make of conquest a factor of maximum efficiency. Ennobled, transcending cooperation, it blooms into an act of love whereby each is made whole. Then, the language of Cosmic-Man rejoins that of G. Marcel:

> In the scale of sanctity and of artistic creation, where freedom glows with its fullest light, it is never autonomy. For the saint and artist alike, autocentricity and the self are entirely swallowed up in love.[11]

Conscious of his status of Cosmic-Presence, in communion with the Universe, he goes forward in a cosmic project of self-realization.

4. The Vision

Self-possessed and conquering, Cosmic-Man is also a man of vision — the awed and joyously humble vision of he whose home is the Universe.

The affirmation that Scientific Existentialism opens upon an optimistic, loving universe, may seem contradictory; pessimism and gloom rather than joy being the trade-mark of most Existentialisms. The harsh psychological portrait — of selfness and conquest — just etched, has done little to alter such an impression, if it has not reinforced it. Actually, upon fusing this composite picture into a harmonious whole, one discovers that

---

11. G. Marcel, *Être et Avoir*, (trans. by Katherine Farrer), Dacre Press.

the inaccuracy arises from understatement; that indeed any commonplace optimism is far removed from the spirit of he who lives the splendor of cosmic presentiality.

Through the centuries floods of ink have flowed over the question of Idealism versus Realism, and in particular over the nature of ideas and their relationship to "matter". And the debate rages unabated. Among the more radical, but in its way more effective solutions, is that of Marx-Engels. Their doctrines eradicate the conventional "matter-spirit" dichotomy. Unhappily the cost is outrageous. The Self must be nihilated, to be, irony of all ironies, replaced by an idea, the "historical category". Recent developments in subnuclear physics, far from cooling tempers, have added fuel to the fire — the Uncertainty Principle, in particular, having in the mind of many shattered Truth and vindicated Hume's direst intuitions.

Throughout, it was emphasized that the issue was wrongly tackled. Reality, parcelled-out among a universe of Dynamic-Facts, is one, meaning that thought-power differs from fist or magnetic-power in quality only. Thought-quanta (ideas) are *in*, are integral to the thinker, each requiring an expenditure of his energy-quota. The thinker does not through thought set himself outside of the physical world in a haughty Cartesian seclusion. On the contrary, *thought-power, the most physical, the most potent of existential bonds, cements knower and known. To think is to impregnate the Universe.* One does not feel and touch and then think. Nor does one think and then proceed to touch and see, etc. The modality of the Universe being one of absolute to absolute, thought and senses, object and objectifier, operate and are grasped inneally and absolutely. *We are each other's flesh.* And it is thought's privilege to make us aware of this marvel and mystery, allowing us to savor it, to delect and wallow in it. Thus must one interpret the statement that he who lives the magnificence of his being a Cosmic-Presence, is a man awed, a man of vision, joyous, humble yet triumphant.

It is common knowledge that thought, concentrated upon the emptiness of numerals whose contribution to existential involvement is quasi nil, leaves the thinker coldly dispassionate. Equally of common knowledge is the fact that the dwelling of the mind upon a passion — love or hatred — automatically engenders psychical turmoil. Then the innermost chords of the Self tremble, in revolt or yearning. How much more overpowering and ennobling must be the state of he who, by and by, feels with increasing sensuality, his being a Presence *before and in* the Universe — the universe of the dead, the living and the nascent!

The reaction which I describe is not to be confused with an aloof, clinical "intellectual prehension" which haughtily surveys the Outside — each individual an "object", each stowed away on the shelves of the cranial library for possible "future" reference. No! I speak of a feeling of involvement brought about by a dawning upon the Self that its every nerve, every fleshy fibre communes with the flesh of each Atom — throughout the "infinite eons". I speak of the brotherhood which binds one to the swan gliding upon the pliocene sea, "long, long ago"; to ones progeny "in remote epochs" and to The Absolute Presence, the Great Spirit of the Sioux, the Yahweh of the Hebrew, *He who* simply *Is*, which is to say, whose consciousness of Himself, swan, reader and grandchild is absolute. In summary, I witness to the searing emotional experience which comes from a sensuous consciousness of our being, each makers and flesh of each other.

The statement "flesh of each other's flesh", may be interpreted as a literary prop, intended for effect. Not so. The phrase describes exactly our mutual relationship. As demonstrated in the third experiment, "bodies" are mind-constructs which differ from Antropocities such as a chair, only in that the latter describe nonspecifically attributable knots of relationships, whereas "bodies" identify the prime focus of relationships (dynamic-field) which an Atom entertains with the universe of its brother Atoms — the spatialization, the dimensions of a "body" being a function of prehended intensity. *Flesh is not something which we possess, but is rather in the nature of a condominium.* One could talk of an inneal or immanental interfaciality. This explains health and pleasure — the immanence is peaceful and loving; and disease and pain — the relationship assumes the character of a refusal to commune with the Other or Others, due to incompatibility or possibly even hatred.

Viewed thus life, its shallows and miseries, its defeats and triumphs, death also, assumes a new and wondrous meaning. Having broken all bonds of space, time and "matter"; citizen now of the cosmic commonwealth wherein he knows that in-fact each resides in all and all reside in peace, Cosmic-Man fears life no more. Nay, he welcomes its challenges, whether an army of cancer cells or the hordes of an ideological enemy. His motto is: conquest. Keenly aware that the enemy can harass and oppress him in the petty realm of the factory and the office, in the hell also of the *Goulag*, he remains for all that an optimist, for theirs is not the dominion and power — save only if he surrenders. His fight is not that of the congenital bully or the sadist. It is the conquest of the reluctant, loving enemy — supremely realistic, progressive and humbly optimistic. While agreeing with Arjuna that:

> More blest would it be to eat the food of beggary without the slaughter of noble masters,[12]

his first instinct being one of peace, reluctantly he bows before Reality's dictat that the mode of his Now is one of conflict. Saddened, he nonetheless obeys the Lord Krishna's ancient command, for the language of Krishna is his language:

> But know that THAT which pervades the Universe is imperishable. None can destroy that Changeless One. It is the bodies of the Everlasting, Incomprehensible Body-Dweller which (only) have an end. Therefore fight![13]

And he fights. He fights without rancor — with love. He fights on all fronts; first and foremost, the home front of self-improvement. Fully aware that the splendor and intoxication of cosmic citizenship are not to be grasped and lived on the cheap, but rather that the Now currency is discipline and knowledge painstakingly acquired by will undaunted, Cosmic-Man, a man of science, of progress, greets the unknown — the unknown of the Self and of the Outsider.

For him that episode which our civilizations call life, having neither beginning nor ending, becomes a venture, in awareness and efficiency — a bursting of the Self upon the cosmic stage. Evermore penetratingly he probes the secrets of the innerself, that his bodily health and intellect be maximized and his presence to himself should achieve fulness. For identical motives his mind

12. L. Adams Beck, *The Story of Oriental Philosophy*, Philadelphia, Blakiston, 1928, p. 111.
13. *Ibid.*, p. 112.

devours the Outside. For knowledge is communion in the flesh of the Other. Knowledge is power. *Knowledge is* de facto *presentiality.*

And with knowledge comes a loving awe and adoration. Throughout the ages, in all civilizations, the grandiose torments of the human soul and the wild raging seas, the mysteries of the mighty atom and a baby's smile, the haunting, azure depths of the boundless heavens have drawn from poet and scientist, from thinking men and women, testimonials of wonderment. Thus a Walt Whitman, with the poet's true sense of proportion, would cry:

> I believe a leaf of grass is no less than the journey-work of the stars...
> And the running blackberry would adorn the parlors of Heaven...
> And a mouse is miracle enough to stagger sextillions of infidels.

Thus also speaks Einstein in tones of admiration, of mysticism to which one need not attempt to add:

> The most beautiful and most profound emotion we can experience is the sensation of the mystical. It is the sower of all true science. He to whom this emotion is a stranger, who can no longer wonder and stand rapt in awe, is as good as dead. To know that what is impenetrable to us really exists, manifesting itself as the highest wisdom and the most radiant beauty which our dull faculties can comprehend only in their most primitive forms — this knowledge, this feeling is at the center of true religiousness. ... My religion, consists of a humble admiration of the illimitable superior spirit who reveals himself in the slight details we are able to perceive with our frail and feeble minds. That deeply emotional conviction of the presence of a superior reasoning power, which is revealed in the incomprehensible universe, forms my idea of God.[14]

To Cosmic-Man at rest in the Universe, such sentiments are natural. Having transcended the narrow immediacies of time-space, he knows the Other not as an object nor as an Outsider, but as kin, cosmic, flesh of his flesh, everyone aquiver in the plenitude of an existential communion. In truth his world is a

14. Albert EINSTEIN, as quoted by Lincoln Barnett in *The Universe and Dr. Einstein*, New York, Mentor, 1957, pp. 109-110.

new world, more different from our Copernican world, than the latter is from that of Ptolemean man.

And so a vision fills him, a dynamic vision of conquest, bathed in the Absolute; a vision of awe and adoration.

epilogue

And Then There Is Love

THESE last pages have perhaps perplexed some, their tenor being seemingly so out of context with the cold, systematic dissection of Reality and the Atom which over so many chapters has occupied us. Let them be reassured. The continuity is total. No exaggeration is involved. On the contrary, the unexpected lyricism conveys but a pale shadow of the ecstasy of he whose vision achieves its full physical dimension; of he who combines a knowledge of his being a Cosmic-Presence with an unrestrained outpouring of the Self, with a cosmic embrace, with love.

Beyond the groping effort of scientific analyses, beyond philosophy and the mechanics of existence, beyond and in spite of the grim, cruel atmosphere of an aggression-laden Now, beyond self-knowledge and self-possession, beyond awe and adoration even, there lies the true dimension of the Universe, which he who has invested himself with the fullness of cosmic presentiality discovers: love.

Without a doubt, in all of us love, as an ember, lies hidden, dormant.

To some it is given freely as a birthright to fan this ember. They are those who know love as an intuition, naturally, and who enjoy and give it in a gratuitous outpouring. They are the lucky ones.

For others the road is different, often rocky. Thus, in many the ember dies. These it seems never love. And that is their business. And each being an Obscure-Absolute, mysterious before every other, their condition is for no one to judge.

Different yet is the lot of a last group: those in whom love is in great part the fruit of knowledge. To them Dynamic Vision and its message of cosmic presentiality has much to offer.

As noted, love is a gift, natural not only to man but to the universal kingdom. To the partridge, for instance, which feigning a broken wing decoys the hunter, tempting death that its young should live, Christ's saying rightly applies:

> Greater love than this no one hath, than that he lay down his life for his friends. (John 15 - 13).

When therefore I speak of cosmic presentiality as the key to love, I have something more in mind than the natural love of which all Beings are capable, and which most do enjoy and give. I am referring to the ultimate frontier — to the land of cosmic love which by and by the Cosmic-Presence comes to inhabit.

It is my humble suggestion based to a degree upon experience, that lived cosmic presentiality can operate a transformation of the soul or Self for which any term short of conversion must prove inadequate. This applies with special force to the third group, that of the "rational ones", in whom love is a function of acquired knowledge.

Consciously achieved and lived cosmic presentiality — a state born of the union of the sense of awe and adoration so beautifully depicted by Einstein with ones sense of communion with The-All, with the great and the small, with the strong and the weak, with the dying butterfly and the "superior intelligence" — is a wondrous state indeed.

With the blossoming of a deep emotional sense of cosmicity, that prideful sense of being a genuine Self in inalienable possession of ones own parcel of the Universe — cornerstone of Knowledge and Truth — grows exponentially.

His mind's eye awed, surveys in wonder the marvel and mystery which is outsideness. The Others can reach him no more:

> Tremendously rich, but alone
> Alone, but master abolute

the conscious Cosmic-Presence has achieved possession-of-the-Self. The conscious Cosmic-Presence has transcended — beyond the beyond...

Yet the conscious Cosmic-Presence knows that he is one in all and all are him; each being himself in truth, and in truth all being flesh of each others flesh, in the timeless, spaceless medium of the Supreme Existentialist — He who advised an inquiring Moses:

> I Am Who Am... Thus shalt thou say to the Children of Israel. (EXODUS 3 - 13)

And so the Cosmic-Self in all sincerity and with truth, makes his the words of Juan Yepes:

> On a dark night, Kindled in love with yearnings — oh, happy chance! — I went forth without being observed, My house being now at rest.[15]

And, in the serenity of his aloofness, he loves. For how can he not love? Is he not the timeless brother of the dying rabbit and the fading rose? Is not the slightest quiver of the flesh of his dearest enemy, a quiver of his own flesh?

---

15. Juan YEPES, (better known as St. John of the Cross), Opening Stanza of the Canticle of the soul, as found in *Dark Night of the Soul*, (trans. and ed. by E. Allison Peers), Garden City, New York, Doubleday, 1959, p. 33.

Bibliography

ADLER, Alfred. *What life should mean to you*, 1931, As in *From Medicine Man to Freud*, Jan Ehrenwald M.D., New York, Dell Publishing, 1956.

AQUINAS, Thomas. *De Ente et Essentia*, trans. George G. Leckie, New York, Appleton-Century-Crofts, Inc., 1937.

ASIMOV, Isaac. *Guide to Science*, New York, Basic Books, Inc., 1960.

BARNETT, Lincoln. *The Universe and Dr. Einstein*, New York, Mentor Books, 1957.

BECK, L. Adams. *The Story of Oriental Philosophy*, Philadelphia, Blakiston, 1928.

BERGSON, Henri. *Creative Evolution*, (authorized trans. Arthur Mitchell, Ph. D.), London, MacMillan & Co., 1913.

BOHR, Niels. *Essays 1958–1962 on Atomic Physics and Human Knowledge*, New York, Random House, 1963.

BRIGHT, Lawrence, O.P. *Whitehead's Philosophy of Physics*, New York, Sheed and Ward, 1958.

BUBER, Martin. *Jewish Mysticism and the Legends of Baalshem*, in Victor Gollancz, *A Year of Grace*, London, Camelot, 1950.

DEWEY, John. *How we think*, Boston, D.C. Heath and Company, 1933.

EDDINGTON, Arthur Stanley. *Space, Time & Gravitation*, London, 1920.

EDDINGTON, Arthur Stanley. *The Expanding Universe*, Cambridge University Press, 1933.

EISELEY, Loren. *The Firmament of time*, New York, Atheneum, 1960

FEINBERG, Gerald. "Particles that go faster than light", in *Scientific American*, February 1970.

DE FINANCE, Joseph. *Connaissance de l'Être*, Paris, Bruges, Desclée de Brouwer, 1966.

FROMM, Erich. *Escape from Freedom*, 1941, as in *From Medicine Man to Freud*, Jan Ehrenwald M.D., New York, Dell publishing, 1956.

GLASHOW, Sheldon Lee. "Quarks with Color and Flavor" in *Scientific American*, October 1975.

GOLLANCZ, Victor. *Plotinus, Fifth Ennead*, in *A year of Grace*, London, the Camelot Press. 1950.

GOODAVAGE, Joseph F. "Have Scientifists Found the Electronic Key to Man's Soul?" New York, in *Saga*, June 1974.

GOUIRAN, R. *Particles and Accelerators*, New York, McGraw Hill Co., 1967.

GRAHAM, Aeldred. *The Love of God*, "Image Books", New York, Double day & Company.

GRENET, P.B. *Ontologie*, Paris, Beauchesne et ses Fils, 1939.

GUILLEMIN, Victor. *The Story of Quantum Mechanics*, New York, Charles Schriner's & Sons, 1968.

HEISENBERG, Werner. *Physics and Beyond*, (trans. Arnold J. Pomerans), New York, Harper & Row, 1971.

HUXLEY, Julian. *Evolution in Action*, New York, Mentor Books, 1957.

JEANS, Sir James. *Some problems of Philosophy*, in *The World's Great Thinkers, Man and the Universe: The Philosophers of Science*, New York, Saxe Commins and Robert N. Linscott, Random House, 1947.

JOHN, the Evangelist. *The Apocalypse*, New York, Hawthorn Books, 1958.

JOSEPHUS, Flavius. *The Great Roman-Jewish War*: A.D. 66–70 (De Bello Judaico), (trans. William Whiston), New York, Harper & Brothers, 1960.

KANT, Immanuel. *The Critique of Pure Reason*, BK IX, (trans. Kemp Smith), London, Macmillan, 1953.

KANT, Immanuel. *The Critique of Pure Reason*, (trans. F.M.D. Meiklejohn), London, J.M. Dent & Sons Ltd, 1934.

KIERKEGAARD, Soren. *Concluding Unscientific Postscript*, Book two, New York, Bantam Books, 1971.

KINDERLEHRER, Jane. "Natural is Beautiful and Better", in *Prevention*, Pennsylvania, Rodale Press, January 1974.

KOSHSLAND, Daniel E. Jr. "Protein Shape and Biological Control" in *Scientific American*, October, 1973.

LANGDON, Davies John. *On the Nature of Man*, New York, Mentor Books, 1960.

LENIN, Vladimir Ilyich. *To the Population, on Democracy and Dictatorship, What is Soviet-Power?* Moscow, Foreign Languages Publishing House, 1955.

LESSING, Lawrence. "The Life Saving Promise of Enzymes", in *Fortune*, March 1969.

LUCRETIUS. *The Nature of the Universe*, (trans. R.E. Latham), Penguin Books, 1951.

LUCRETIUS. *De Rerum Natura*, ed. Smith and Leonard, Wisconsin 1942, in Alan D. Winspear *Lucretius and Scientific Thought*, Montréal, Harvest House, 1963.

MARCEL, Gabriel. *Être et Avoir*, (trans. by K. Farrer), Dacre Press, cf. Paris, Aubier-Montaigne, 1968.

MARITAIN, Jacques. *Existence and the Existent*, (trans. Lewis Galantière and Gerald B. Phelan), New York, Doubleday & company, 1956.

MILLS, C. Wright. *The Power Elite*, New York, Oxford University Press, 1959.

MINKOWSKI, H. *Space and Time*, in *Principles of Relativity*, Cologne, Dover Press, 1908.

MORRISON, Philip. "The Neutrino", in *Scientific American*, January 1956.

NIETZSCHE, F. *Beyond Good and Evil*, (trans. by Marianne Cowan), Chicago, Henry Regnery Company, 1955.

ORLEMANN, Edwin F. "Iron", in *Encyclopedia Britannica*, vol. 12, Chicago, Benton, 1962.

OSTRANDER, Sheila and SCHRODER, Lynn. *Psychic Discoveries Behind the Iron Curtain*, New Jersey, Prentice-Hall, 1970.

PARMENIDES. "The Way Of Truth", (trans. Reginald E. Allen), in *Greek Philosophy, Thales to Aristotle*, London, Collier-Macmillan, 1966.

PASSMORE, John. *A Hundred Years of Philosophy*, Harmondsworth, Middlesex, England, Penguin Books, 1976.

PLATO. *Sophist*, in Jowett's translation.

ROSENBLUETH, A. and WIENER, N. *Purposeful and non-purposeful behavior*, in *Philosophy of Science*, vol. 17, no 4, 1950.

RUSSELL, Bertrand. *Why I am not a Christian*, New York, Simon and Schuster, 1957.

RUTHERFORD, Ernest et Al. "Radioactivity Natural", in *Encyclopedia Britannica*, vol. 18, Chicago, Benton, 1962.

SANTAYANA, George. *Reason in Religion*, New York, Collier Books, 1962.

SANTAYANA, George. *Winds of Doctrine*, New York, 1913, in Will Durant *The Story of Philosophy*, New York, Washington Square Press, 1970.

SARTRE, Jean-Paul. *La Nausée*, Paris, Gallimard, 1937.

SCHRAMM, David N. "The Age of the Elements", in *Scientific American*, January 1974.

SELSAM, Howard. *What is Philosophy? A Marxist Introduction*, New York, International Publishers, 1938.

SPENCER, Herbert. *Social Statics*, London, 1851.

TEILHARD DE CHARDIN, Pierre. *Phenomenon of Man*, London, W.M. Collins Co., 1959.

TILLICH, Paul. "The Problems of Theological Method" in *The Journal of Religion*, vol. XXVIII, no 1, January 1947.

THOMAS, Lewis, M.D. "Ideas: The Boswell of Organnelles", in *Newsweek*, June 24, 1974.

VENNESLAND, Birgit. "Enzymes" in *Encyclopedia Britannica*, vol. 8, Chicago, Benton, 1962.

WEYL, H. *Philosophy of Mathematics and Natural Science*, Princeton, 1949.

WHITEHEAD, Alfred North. *Process and Reality*, New York, The Free Press, 1969.

WHEELER, John A. and TILSON, Seymour. "Dynamics of Space-Time", in *Science and Technology*, December, 1963.

WITTGENSTEIN, P., *Philosophical Investigation*.

WHYTE, Lancelot Law. *Essay on Atomism: From Democritus to 1960*, New York, Harper and Row, 1963.

YEPES, Juan (St. John of the Cross). *Dark Night of the Soul*, (trans. and ed. by E. Allison Peers), New York, Garden City, 1959.

5466